THE SENATE NOBODY KNOWS

Also by Bernard Asbell:

WHEN F.D.R. DIED
THE NEW IMPROVED AMERICAN
THE F.D.R. MEMOIRS

The Senate Nobody Knows

BERNARD ASBELL

DOUBLEDAY & COMPANY, INC., GARDEN CITY, NEW YORK
1978

Grateful acknowledgment is made for permission to use an excerpt from:

"Ford Asks 5-Year Freeze on Auto Emission Curbs," by E. W. Kenworthy (June 28, 1975) © 1975 by The New York Times Company. Reprinted by permission.

Library of Congress Cataloging in Publication Data

Asbell, Bernard.
  The Senate nobody knows.

  Includes index.
  1. United States. Congress Senate. 2. Muskie,
Edmund S., 1914–   I. Title.
JK1161.A9   328.73′07′1
ISBN: 0-385-04215-9
Library of Congress Catalog Card Number 77–77646

To Larry and Chris,
camera one and camera two,
who watched me watching

THE PRINCIPAL CHARACTERS

Senators, Ninety-fourth Congress (1975–76):

EDMUND S. MUSKIE	Democrat of Maine
JAMES B. ALLEN	Democrat of Alabama
HOWARD H. BAKER, JR.	Republican of Tennessee; ranking Republican, Public Works Committee
BILL BROCK	Republican of Tennessee; member, Intergovernmental Relations Subcommittee
JAMES L. BUCKLEY	Republican of New York; ranking Republican, Environmental Pollution Subcommittee
ROBERT C. BYRD	Democrat of West Virginia, Majority Whip
PETE V. DOMENICI	Republican of New Mexico; member, Environmental Pollution Subcommittee
GARY W. HART	Democrat of Colorado; member, Environmental Pollution Subcommittee
PHILIP A. HART	Democrat of Michigan
WILLIAM D. HATHAWAY	Democrat of Maine
HUBERT H. HUMPHREY	Democrat of Minnesota
EDWARD M. KENNEDY	Democrat of Massachusetts

JAMES A. McCLURE   Republican of Idaho; member, Environmental Pollution Subcommittee

GEORGE McGOVERN   Democrat of South Dakota; Chairman, Select Committee on Nutrition and Human Needs

MIKE MANSFIELD   Democrat of Montana, Majority Leader

JOSEPH M. MONTOYA   Democrat of New Mexico; Chairman, Economic Development Subcommittee of Public Works Committee; also member, Environmental Pollution Subcommittee

JENNINGS RANDOLPH   Democrat of West Virginia; Chairman, Public Works Committee

ABRAHAM A. RIBICOFF   Democrat of Connecticut; Chairman, Government Operations Committee

ROBERT T. STAFFORD   Republican of Vermont; member, Environmental Pollution Subcommittee

JOHN C. STENNIS   Democrat of Mississippi; Chairman, Armed Services Committee

Representatives, Ninety-fourth Congress

WILLIAM S. COHEN   Republican of Maine

PAUL G. ROGERS   Democrat of Florida; Chairman, Subcommittee on Health and the Environment of the Interstate and Foreign Commerce Committee

HARLEY O. STAGGERS   Democrat of West Virginia; Chairman, Interstate and Foreign Commerce Committee

Some members of Senator Muskie's personal staff:

MAYNARD TOLL   Administrative Assistant (to October 1, 1975)

CHARLES MICOLEAU   Executive Assistant; Toll's successor as Administrative Assistant

DOLORES STOVER   The Senator's personal secretary

GAYLE CORY   Assistant for Travel and Scheduling

FRANCES MILLER   Office Manager

JIM CASE   Legislative Counsel

RICK BAYARD   Legislative Assistant

BOB ROSE   Press Secretary

SUSIE NICHOLAS   Secretary to Charlie Micoleau

CLYDE MacDONALD   Field Representative, Bangor office

JOHN DELEHANTY   Field Representative, Waterville office

Principal members of Senator Muskie's committee staffs:

ENVIRONMENTAL POLLUTION SUBCOMMITTEE

LEON G. BILLINGS   Chief Staff Professional

KARL R. BRAITHWAITE   Staff Professional

HAROLD H. BRAYMAN   Staff Professional for the Republican Minority

INTERGOVERNMENTAL RELATIONS SUBCOMMITTEE (IGR)

ALVIN FROM   Staff Director

BUDGET COMMITTEE

DOUGLAS J. BENNET,   Staff Director
  JR.
JOHN T. McEVOY   Chief Counsel

THE THREE CHAIRMANSHIPS OF SENATOR MUSKIE

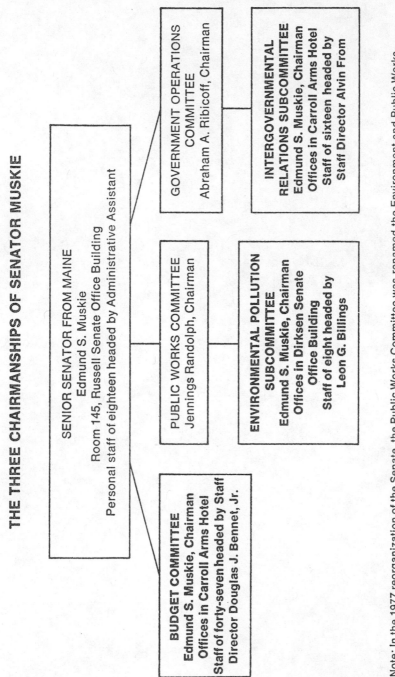

SENIOR SENATOR FROM MAINE
Edmund S. Muskie
Room 145, Russell Senate Office Building
Personal staff of eighteen headed by Administrative Assistant

GOVERNMENT OPERATIONS
COMMITTEE
Abraham A. Ribicoff, Chairman

INTERGOVERNMENTAL
RELATIONS SUBCOMMITTEE
Edmund S. Muskie, Chairman
Offices in Carroll Arms Hotel
Staff of sixteen headed by
Staff Director Alvin From

PUBLIC WORKS COMMITTEE
Jennings Randolph, Chairman

ENVIRONMENTAL POLLUTION
SUBCOMMITTEE
Edmund S. Muskie, Chairman
Offices in Dirksen Senate
Office Building
Staff of eight headed by
Leon G. Billings

BUDGET COMMITTEE
Edmund S. Muskie, Chairman
Offices in Carroll Arms Hotel
Staff of forty-seven headed by Staff
Director Douglas J. Bennet, Jr.

Note: In the 1977 reorganization of the Senate, the Public Works Committee was renamed the Environment and Public Works Committee, and Government Operations became the Government Affairs Committee.

"Congress is designed to be slow and inefficient because it represents the total diversity in this country. Yet people are accustomed to instant gratification, and when they don't get it, they have instant disappointment and instant cynicism. I don't know if we will ever be able to measure up to public expectations."

Representative William Cohen
Republican of Maine
Quoted in Time, *June 9, 1975*

Wednesday, May 7

Senator Edmund S. Muskie of Maine slips a key into a secret, unmarked door and leads me down a short, dim, melancholy corridor. Instead of meeting at his office in the Russell Senate Office Building, known better as the Old S.O.B. (the Dirksen being the New S.O.B.), we are to have lunch in Senator Muskie's "hideaway" in the Capitol. At the end of the dark corridor he selects another key and unlocks a second door.

Suddenly, sunlight and splendor. Crystal chandelier, two big, puffy, brown leather chairs and matching sofa, color television, a balcony vista of the long reflecting pools of Constitution Mall, the Monument and, barely discernible out near infinity, the Lincoln Memorial. Pleased that the view catches his guest's eye, the Senator draws aside the white curtain.

He is imposingly tall but, despite what reporters say about the somber and lonely lean to his gait, he doesn't exude the aura of Abe Lincoln. Too broad. From long legs and high, flat hips his frame fans out evenly, powerfully, to immense shoulders, the structure climaxing in a big, tough, intimidating jaw.

A staff assistant, Gayle Cory, in a yellow turtleneck and green pants suit, has arrived in advance of us from the Senator's office. She is Muskie's conduit to the out-of-Washington world, especially Maine, evaluating requests for speeches, for meetings with constituents, constructing travel schedules and unruffling feathers when requests are turned down. When the Senator and I sink into the sighing brown leather Mrs. Cory, standing cheerfully and wordlessly at relaxed attention, pours us sherry. A waiter soon arrives from the

Senate Dining Room kitchen with a huge tray. Mrs. Cory checks our luncheon table and quietly departs.

"Yes, a very nice room," Muskie allows, boyish pride seeping through. "Until last year it was Sam Ervin's. These walls know a lot about the strategies of the Watergate Committee. Did you notice that door on your right down the little hall? That's the john where the radicals blew off their bomb a few years ago."

Does every Senator have a Capitol hideaway?

"Lord, no. You wait, as you do for everything around here." In a sardonic drone he adds, "It comes with *seniority.*"

Are the great old characters like Sam Ervin missed?

"Once they're gone, they're never missed."

After a silence Muskie abruptly asks, "Just what's your book to be about?"

"The Senate. How this place works."

I have already discussed this in some detail with two of his staff members, and I'm sure they've discussed it with him before he agreed to meet me today, but he asks questions and we go over it again.

There's been a great deal of writing about this place as an institution, a process, a club, as the "greatest deliberative body in the world." But virtually none of that writing, including the memoirs of many Senators, has descended from the altitude of aerial photography and moved close enough to focus on the skin pores of its subject. The true way to learn about this place is the same as learning about any other place: watching its people—Senators and their staffs —do their work and live their lives day by day. Which means, of course, access to where the work is done, where and when decisions are made.

He nods.

"Is that really practical?" I ask. "Because if it's not, there's no point in starting. Would your visitors—would other Senators—permit an outsider, a writer, to sit in on your private meetings with them, to walk along a corridor when you're working out an understanding with them? Will your acceptance of me put them at ease?"

Muskie shrugs. The other fellow, he says, would always have to know why you're there. In most cases, it wouldn't make any difference. People around here are far less guarded than outsiders think. In some cases, they may object. But there's very little you can't find out once you know it's taken place.

At times he may feel his own privacy invaded, I suggest. (He chuckles ruefully that he gave up expecting privacy long ago.) I want to pierce as deeply into one Senator's life as he will permit, on the theory that that will shed more light on the meaning of life in this place than a broad skim of the lives of one hundred men. I'd rather take the measure of other Senators through the experience of one member, through his trusts and distrusts, affections and abrasions, than to observe them "impartially" and detached, as a gallery watcher.

So the book, I conclude, will chiefly follow one Senator, Ed Muskie, around. But its intention is to reveal the Senate.

The forthcoming year in the life of Edmund Muskie promises to shed as broad a light on this Society of One Hundred as that of any other senior member. . . .

. . . This is an election year. An election year? Nineteen seventy-five? Yes, it is, a head start in Muskie's drive for re-election to the Senate in 1976. Before year's end he will have spent one hundred days—virtually every weekend and recess day—in Maine, trampling out the impression that his heart and mind are too much in Washington on national affairs and too little on his home folk. That impression destroyed Maine's indestructible Margaret Chase Smith in 1972, and there are signs it is now hurting Muskie.

. . . This year the Clean Air Act of 1970 expires. For Muskie, as the Senate's Mr. Environment, and for the Subcommittee on Environmental Pollution, of which he is chairman, merely to recommend renewal of the act won't do. Something has gone terribly wrong with that law, and nobody knows just what to do about it. Theoretically, automobiles are belching eighty per cent less pollution in 1975 than in 1970. Factory and power-plant smokestacks in urban areas are putting out fifty per cent less sulphur dioxide than in 1970. (Both were supposed to have been reduced ninety per cent by 1975, according to the law's targets.) Despite those dramatic reductions, people are still choking and dying from poisons in the ambient air. The National Academy of Sciences attributes 15,000 deaths a year and four million man-days of illness to air pollution. Failure to achieve the ninety per cent cleanup as mandated by the law is only part of the tragedy. If car manufacturers, for example, knew how to comply fully with ultimate requirements of the Clean Air Act—and they claim they don't—twenty-three major cities will still be laden in 1985 with levels of hydrocarbons called unsafe by law, and nine out of ten cities now breathing excessive nitrogen oxides will still be doing so. What are Muskie and his committee and the Congress to do? Get tougher and turn the technological screws tighter? Auto makers and smokestack emitters have been on their knees demanding mercy. The auto industry claims flat out that the law is madness, that the technology for meeting its standards *does not exist*. Another head splitter: while the law and human health demand less pollution, the government—and the market place—are demanding more fuel economy. Those two goals, says the auto industry, are mutually exclusive. As a direct result of the 1974 gasoline drought and public fear that it may return, car sales have collapsed and hundreds of thousands of auto workers are out in the street, jobless. Give us more time, the industry pleads. We cannot meet the new emission standards the law requires for 1978 models. Even if we could, those standards will cost heavily in fuel consumption. Please, please, give us a five-year delay. Muskie and his committee must decide in the next few months: Whose pleas against strangulation and death shall be heeded? Those of victims of emphysema and heart disease? Or of the auto industry, which is indeed the economic lifeblood of millions?

. . . Muskie is chairman of the newest and potentially most powerful standing committee of the Senate. This year the Senate Budget Committee, together with its House counterpart, begins a mammoth yet delicate attempt at what no congressional committee has ever reached out to do, although every responsible householder has. It is charged with helping Congress determine *in advance* how much the government ought to spend—and what it ought to spend it for. The awesome subject material of this committee is not essentially dollars but the pitting of public health against the building of battleships, of subsidies for food stamps against subsidies for schools—what is the relative budget importance to the American people of each? Congress has never forced itself to face our most fundamental public questions in that direct way. If the new system succeeds in its revolutionary goal (as of this date, virtually ignored—and, I suspect, insufficiently understood—by Capitol Hill journalists), Congress may open a new era in management of the economy and selection of public priorities. If it fails, Congress' evasive habit of surrendering budget management to the White House may be reinforced for another quarter century.

As we conclude our lunch I comment that I'd like to rely now and then on having time alone with him to talk things over, to check observations, interpretations, to ask for his version of what really happened behind the stage sets. Also, besides keeping up with what happens inside the "process," I'd like to keep up with what happens inside *him*. Another assenting nod, and a surprising sentence from this somber-faced man:

"It might be fun." Then he adds, heightening my optimism for the project, "It might be a chance to unburden."

The tourists file into the Senate gallery, hushed and expectant. Senator James Allen of Alabama, with the dreariest voice and stoniest gray eyes this side of death, is drawling, droning, pacing, occasionally flailing an arm. The visitors' awe turns to wonder and puzzlement: Where are all the Senators? Why is he talking if no more than two or three are here to listen? A guide explains they are off doing important work. In committees.

Then buzzers sound for a vote and, through swinging doors, out of the four walls of the sunken chamber, stream the Senators, calling "Aye" or "No." If they haven't heard the speeches, how do they know how to vote? It's all cut and dried, intimates one tourist to a companion. Whispers another: See the fellow at the big roll-top desk by the door? That used to be Bobby Baker's desk. That fellow tells them what the party wants.

Feeling superior, having just lunched with a Senator, I think of the Senate's better hours. You've got to catch the hour right, which takes luck. I've seen it on better days. Maybe the Senate has seen better days. Maybe it's no longer the great exhibition it used to be. . . .

As a schoolboy, the way other boys memorized batting averages and faces on baseball cards, I studied voting records of my favorite (heroic as well as villainous) Senators. After class hours I'd go to the library and read the Congressional Record. Can't explain why. I knew the names, the states, the parties of all the Senators (then ninety-six).

Then came an opportunity for a boyhood trip to Washington and a visit to the gallery—this gallery. Senator Bilbo of Mississippi was holding the floor in a filibuster to kill the—which was it, the anti-poll-tax bill or the anti-lynching bill? In that day killing a filibuster through a vote of cloture—limiting debate in this house of unlimited debate—required a vote of two thirds of the Senators, virtually unobtainable. A vote for cloture was about to take place, accounting for the unusual attendance of a body and face behind almost every desk. And Senator Bilbo, savoring his full audience, was telling about Nigras, about the high esteem in which Nigras are held in Mississippi. The Senators, drawn into the enchantment of the performance, the mesmerizing musical cadence of it, waited for the cadenza and the snapper, and Bilbo said especially Nigra deppety sheriffs, and that no Mississippi sheriff would think of not having a Nigra deppety sheriff, and when there's trouble in Nigratown, we don't send down some white sheriff, who might just have a tetch of *prejudice* in his heart, which, mind you, few of us have. No, we do the right and fair and Christian thing, we send our *Nigra* deppety sheriff down there to take care of that Nigra trouble. And that's sure to put an end to the trouble. Do the distinguished Senators know why? Do they know *why?* (An eye-glinty pause and slow gaze around the transfixed chamber.) Because if there's one thing a Nigra can do better'n anybody else, it's to beat up other Nigras.

A ripple of tense laughter, exchanges of amused glances, tolerance, understanding, and traces here and there of professional admiration.

The memory, that quintessential Senate moment, lingers like a dangling film clip. Nobody in today's Senate talks like that. But certain elements remain, essentially unchanged: acceptance, admiration for doing skillfully and artfully what a Senator is there to do. He may say or do anything, no matter how outrageous to the eyes and ears of anyone else, as long as, first, he does not violate the rules and customs of the Senate or personally disparage any Senator, and, second, as long as the people of his state can be expected to approve of what he says or does. Or at least not punish him. A Senator is sent by his state and accountable only to his state. His rights as a Senator are equal to any other Senator's rights. He is accepted and respected simply because he is there.

This lovely aura of senatorial ethics, which rises like a fragrance to the gallery, oozing through the florid prose of the Congressional Record, is the stuff of great staging, a set motif for the world's grandest and longest-running political show.

But what goes on in the dressing rooms? What goes on in the "other important work" that keeps Senators too busy to show up behind their semicircle arrangement of desks to listen to their brethren debate, as tourists believe God intended them to do? What is it like to live behind the swinging doors of that sanctified sunken chamber?

As a youngster, I wondered, longed and ached to know. The career and travels of a writer on political and other affairs have dampened and drowned many another romantic curiosity. But this one has just hung on.

Sunday, June 15

"Russell Baker knows your secret," says my wife, thrashing through the Sunday New York *Times,* which is not made for reading in vibrating bucket seats on the New Jersey Turnpike.

"What secret?" I inquire, grateful for being aroused out of the stupor of treadmill miles and auto fumes along the deadly southbound passage to Washington.

"Your big insight, your theory, your—"

"Why don't you just read me what he says."

She reads: "'After six months away from Washington, the place seemed only slightly less remote than Zambia. Little that happened there seemed to have much to do with the daily trials of American life. . . . While Washington labored, the world I inhabited seemed unaffected. Goods continued to become more expensive. More people lost jobs. Education continued to collapse, crime to increase. The trains were breaking down. . . . Large corporations engaged in bribery of the rich and larceny against the unrich. . . .

" 'Washington's influence on all this, and most other matters of daily human consequence, seemed negligible. . . . Was there still a Cabinet? Perhaps. Did it matter? Surely not. And the Congress. One read constantly about the Congress, its turmoil, its ferocity, its proud new assertion of power, and yet oil prices still went higher, cities still rotted, and trains still broke down.

" '. . . Seen from a distance, it is Washington that seems isolated, small, not terribly consequential, casting little weight in the scales of daily American life, but combing its hair for the ball in the East Room, confident that everyone will come from miles around to press noses against the White House fence. . . .' "

After a while I say, "Want to turn around?"

After a while she says, "We've paid the rent on the sublet."

After a while I reply, "What's the sense of spending months and months on a book that nobody cares about?"

After a while she replies, "He's not saying a book doesn't matter. He's saying Washington doesn't matter. We're just going down to press our noses."

Tuesday morning, June 17

Mere minutes into the first brass-tacks meeting of the Environmental Pollution Subcommittee of the Senate Public Works Committee devoted to what may be a labor of several weeks to reappraise and rewrite the national law on air pollution, a member scratches at the most inflamed surface of the issue. Automobile emission control gadgets, according to a horrifying recent discovery, are exhaling sulphates, which may be more dangerous to human life than the pollutants the gadgets get rid of.

"Mr. Chairman," says Senator Pete V. Domenici, a sandy-haired, forty-three-year-old Republican from New Mexico, with resolute jaw and uncertain eyes that quiver behind thick glasses, "what are we going to do about sulphates?"

Chairman Muskie responds not with an answer but with more questions:

"We're concerned with two other things. One, what is the level of research activity in this field? Secondly, how effective is our monitoring effort around the country? What are we learning about sulphates, about fine particles, and so on? Do we need to know more? Is that the problem or part of the problem? Do we know all these answers?"

Half a dozen Senators are sitting around three sides of a rectangular arrangement of tables. Behind them, unoccupied, curves the raised, ornate dais from which Senators grill witnesses at an open hearing. This is not a hearing, however, not a public show. It is a "markup," as working, legislation-writing committee meetings are traditionally called.

This year, for the first time in history, most markups are open to public view. Newspeople have virtually ignored reporting this innovation, as though it were a mere detail, a doodad of window dressing in the cause of open government. The fact is that the traditional public privilege of attending open hearings and watching the full Senate from the gallery is the doodad, the window dressing. The most prevalent myth about the houses of Congress, spread by the Capitol guides and guidebooks, taught in schools, and fed daily by news bulletins which scarcely ever mention legislation until it comes to a floor vote, is the myth that the Senate floor (or the House floor) is the main arena of significant action.

The markup, first in subcommittee, then in full committee, takes place after public hearings close and before a finished bill is sent to the floor. The subcommittee markup is not merely a step in the legislative process. For most bills the markup *is* the legislative process. Later approval by the full committee and by the full Senate is, for most bills, a formality. There may be debate and opposition, but the final outcome of a bill arriving at the floor is, most often, foregone.

At this markup an audience of about fifty occupies chairs at one end of the two-story-high courtlike hearing room of the Public Works Committee. Clearly they are not the star-seeking tourists and sightseers who drop in to a Foreign Relations Committee hearing to watch George McGovern grill Henry Kissinger. Who are these people, leaning forward to catch the subdued conversational voices of the Senators, scribbling notes on long yellow pads? The Senators, for a change not on stage, appear oblivious to them.

The answers to Domenici's specific question and Muskie's rhetorical ones come from the fourth side of the rectangle of tables. Facing the Senators, their backs to the small audience, are five alert, tense men who all seem to be in their thirties. Before each is a busy assortment of papers, hearing records, technical reports, in contrast to the neat spaces in front of the Senators, who deal, in the main, only with one sheet of agenda and a cup of coffee. Behind these five young men is a library cart stacked with more papers, reports, and folders. The five are the key members of the subcommittee staff. In this case, three are advisers to the majority, which in reality means they are the chairman's men. The remaining two advise the minority. The man in the center, slumped into a round heap with the feigned nonchalance of a cat poised for trouble, has hair as close to orange as nature dares bring it. The silken mop, tailored in a Prince Valiant, drapes around the pink innocence of a dimple-chinned, blue-eyed Cub Scout face. Only the Senators, who face him, discern that those blue eyes are computerized scanners, squeezed into half-closed, wary focus. This is the subcommittee's staff chief, Leon Billings, at thirty-seven a nine-year veteran at fielding questions, yielding information, and shielding his chairman's legislative designs against unexpected attacks. Billings' words come fast in a voice of low volume and fuzzy sibilants that forces Senators to concentrate on him with eye as well as ear:

"We have a certain amount of information. . . . EPA [the Environmental Protection Agency] does have an ongoing roadside monitoring test in Southern California. . . . For instance, there is some question as to the extent their monitoring equipment could make a distinction between what kind of sulphates there are in the ambient air, whether they're lead sulphates or any number of other sulphates."

"Or whether they're derived from smokestacks as against cars and trucks," Muskie suggests.

"Yes. This is still a bit of witchcraft."

Muskie nods, and suggests that Billings name the next issue. They are running down an agenda that will occupy the subcommittee for the coming weeks, perhaps months.

"Next, do current air quality standards adequately protect public health and welfare?" says Billings. "There's significant dispute as to whether the standards are too high or too low."

"I was on an airplane yesterday," says Senator James McClure, a Republican from Idaho with an outstandingly consistent voting record of superconservatism, a man who, when sitting silent, has a most forgettable face, made all the less prepossessing by its one distinguishing feature, a finely carved, shiny nose that seems too small beneath his wire-rimmed spectacles. But when he speaks, a friendly brightness lighting his eyes helps one envision him wading through a crowd reaching for hands. "One of the passengers was an emphysema patient. They had too many smokers aboard the plane, so they started to expand the smoking section. The emphysema patient objected. Suppose he had a very critical emphysema case. Could they have said there would be no smoking allowed anywhere in the airplane? The question is, how far can the requirements of one member of society inhibit the actions of all other members of society?"

Chairman Muskie responds dryly: "The right to smoke would be more important than the right to live, I suppose."

McClure picks up the tone: "I suppose whether you are the smoker or the emphysema patient would have to be considered."

"It also depends," Domenici joins in, "on where you are going and whether you have good reason for being in the airplane."

"He's right," says Muskie brightly. "He might be there for frivolous reasons."

"And the smoker," adds McClure, "for very important reasons."

Senator James Buckley of New York, surprisingly slight of build and prissy of walk, arrived tardy and has been listening, eyes aflutter with scholarly attention. Although a Senate first-termer, he is senior Republican on the subcommittee, seated next to Chairman Muskie, at whom he occasionally gazes with unabashed admiration. The banter spent, Buckley plunges the conversation into the dark heart of a problem that confounds clean-air true believers. You can't have perfectly clean air, and there's no point at which one can objectively claim that air is acceptably clean. In environmentalist terms, there is no "threshold" above which the concentration level of certain pollutants is dangerous to health and beneath which it is not.

"Wasn't that one of the things that came out in the testimony," Buckley asks Billings, "that with respect to some pollutants there is no threshold?"

"That is correct."

"I think that has to be one of the most troublesome problems we have had." McClure re-enters teaming up with his conservative colleague, feeding an assumption that these two, McClure and Buckley, see eye to eye on environmental issues. "The difficulty when you try to set limits is that there's no limit to sensitivity. Dr. Feingold has demonstrated in the laboratory that certain cells in the body are affected by concentrations as low as one molecule, which would obviously push us to a point where it's impossible to regulate. So somewhere there has to be an arbitrary threshold established either by law or by regulation, whether we like it or not."

McClure is even-voiced, conversational, undramatic, as he assaults the central defense of tough environmental laws: the defense that these laws are based on a "health standard," as distinct from an economic or any other standard. McClure argues that, no matter what the standard, it is arbitrarily chosen, therefore, no less or more defensible than any other:

"The example has been used many, many times that we know that slowing automobiles saves lives. We passed a fifty-five-mile-an-hour national speed limit—not to save lives but to save gasoline. The right to gasoline is more important than the right to live, one could conclude. We could keep pushing that speed limit down, but apparently we have decided that beyond this chosen point it isn't worth it. Society isn't going to tolerate it. Therefore, x number of people are going to die because we would rather drive fast.

"We get into that same argument here. Somewhere, obviously, there is a limit to how far we go. And I don't know if we know enough or are capable of defining that."

Muskie, inventor and defender of the "health standard," will now strike back. But no. Muskie comments:

"I would agree with you, Jim, that whatever we do has the effect of imposing thresholds. No question about that. Very difficult to quantify and fix with precision. I couldn't agree with you more."

As the two Senators throw rhetorical arms around one another, each in a covert attempt to pull the other away from a well-planted stance, Senator Lloyd Bentsen, Texas Democrat, has strolled in, exuding solemnity, shaving lotion, and the self-awareness of a man actively campaigning for—and envisioning himself as—President. Bentsen never forgets for a moment that he is a self-made millionaire, a fact which freed him from the influence of family millions into which he was born. A young man, seated behind Bentsen's chair since the meeting opened, whispers to the Senator. Behind the chair of each Senator, whether the principal is present or absent, is an extremely attentive young man (rarely, a young woman) taking notes. He is a legislative assistant on the Senator's personal staff. Just as a Senator on this subcommittee specializes in pollution matters for the whole Senate, so this aide specializes in pollution matters for the Senator. He is—or rapidly becomes—a technical specialist. He is also political eyes and ears. When a Senator arrives at the markup tardy, which he usually does, the aide leans into the Senator's ear and catches him up. Frequently during the subcommittee discussion the aide leans in to interpret or suggest comments or questions. He appears to be an important fellow in the making of national law; his actual importance and influence will be something to assess in the coming months.

"I have another facet that bothers me considerably, and that is the cost," says Bentsen solemnly, presidentially. "I think we ought to be developing more of a cost-benefit analysis in this, not as the ultimate decision, but that it be factored in to be one of the very major considerations in setting up a time frame and in what it might mean in the way of loss of jobs in this country. So I'm going to be coming up with language which I would ask the committee to consider."

Responds Muskie, "Of course."

At noon Muskie halts the markup until 10 A.M. tomorrow. Members start making their way to the alien territory of the House of Representatives side of the Capitol. A joint session is to convene at twelve-thirty to hear a speech by the President of Germany.

The Senators leave through a mirrored door behind the dais, a short cut to a private men's room and elevators marked "Senators Only." At the opposite end of the high-ceilinged room, audience members mill and buzz, chatting with staff aides and among themselves.

"Hi," says a big fellow with wavy brown hair and a salesman's teeth, extending a welcoming hand to me. The warm gesture conveys that the other people know one another and that I stand out as a stranger. "I'm John Adams." He's a lawyer and lobbies for a group of power companies. Obligingly, he points out other lobbyists, keeps pointing them out until almost the entire audience is accounted for.

The few not pointed out turn out to be reporters for industry and environmental news publications. That fellow's from General Motors, those two from Ford, that one American Motors. There's the American Petroleum Institute, the Chamber of Commerce. Those young women, I think they report for law firms, don't know which, might represent all sorts of interests, or they might be from trade associations. That group there—Adams points to a youngish, raffish cluster —are the environmentalists, there's Nader's man, there's Friends of the Earth, the Sierra Club, the National Clean Air Coalition.

I strike up a conversation with the Friends of the Earth man, Rafe Pomerance, tall, bushy-haired, deep morose eyes, the air of a 1960s political radical, but his conversation is restrained, dispassionate, given to cautious understatement. He's fascinated by what he's now permitted to see and hear in markups which, during his previous years of lobbying, were sealed off from public attendance by big locked oaken doors.

"The whole operation is much more subtle than I thought. One of the surprises is that the orchestration of deals is not apparent, at least to me. What goes on is the working out of compromise. I mean, they can quietly gut a provision and you'd never know it. It's all done very quietly. I imagined, when they were behind closed doors, that the decisions would be much faster. You know, the chairman names the issue, everybody's already made up his mind or made his trades, and they vote. But it's not like that. There's a real *process*."

"Toward compromise, accommodation?"

"Yes, definitely. I have nothing against compromise—sometimes. It's understandable that you don't want to bring a bill to the floor with three or four committee members in opposition, or who won't represent you effectively, because then you're in trouble. On the other hand, you have to hope sometimes for *some* confrontation. You can't just compromise everything away without a fight.

"The best thing about markups, the reason I go to them religiously, is that you can pick up the nuances of each member's thinking. You don't get that from their public statements and public postures. You get to see who's articulate, who's respected, who isn't, how the dynamics work. When you know how they really think, it's much easier to affect their thinking. We used to operate blind."

I voice my earlier thought that it's surprising that the press, champions of full access to government, enemies of secrecy, have scarcely mentioned this revolution of letting people witness the real process, the markup meeting.

"Reporters aren't that happy that they opened the markups."

The comment is from a companion of Pomerance, a short, round-faced man with a timid air, who, lest one should fail to identify him as an eccentric or, worse still, not notice him at all, wears a denim railroad cap—keeps wearing it all through the meeting. He is Richard Lahn, formerly a Sierra Club lobbyist who, with Pomerance, formed a lobbying federation called the National Clean Air Coalition.

Lahn goes on to explain that, when markups were closed, all a reporter needed for a hot story was a friend in court, either a Congressman or staff member, who would "leak" the substance of what took place. The reporter could develop a neat package of "inside" news through a single conversation. Under the new rule of open markups, if the subject of the meeting is important enough the reporter has to sit through several hours of what may be tedious quibbling and bargaining. More likely, he doesn't cover the markups. There are just too many to cover, and nobody knows in advance which will produce printable news. So, staying away, he's always nervous that some other reporter has made a contrary decision—and will beat him to a story.

So, while approving the principle, reporters are bothered by open markups for their sheer inconvenience.

Tuesday afternoon, June 17

Sprinting through the June steam bath of First Street between the New and Old Senate Office Buildings is no way, especially in summer, to get from the Public Works Committee hearing room (in the New Building) to Senator Muskie's first-floor office (in the Old).

If the stunning blast of humidity isn't bad enough, there's the brief-case inspection upon re-entering Senate territory. A bored guard fingers your Washington *Post,* to make sure it contains nothing but news, and indifferently inspects your tape recorder like a shopper squeezing a grapefruit he knows he's not going to buy.

The better way is not to get off the New Building push-button elevator at the street level but to continue down to the basement, meanwhile having an extra moment to ponder the most naked featherbedding operation in all of the American labor market. About two thirds of the time a bright-eyed, clean-cut, fastidiously dressed college-age man or woman, whom you first assume to be a Senator's staff aide, asks, "Floor, please?" Elevator operators are patronage appointees of Senators, usually for several months or a year, at a generous wage of up to a thousand dollars a month. It's heart-warming that Senators care enough to provide this means for youngsters to earn their way through school—those attending school—although it cools the heart to learn, in informal survey, that some Senators (Muskie not among them) award these jobs to "needy" sons and daughters of campaign contributors, campaign vice-chairmen, and corporate clients of the Senators' law partners. About one third of the time the elevator has no operator because of mid-term exams or whatever, meaning that the carriage can accommodate one more passenger, and the passengers, pushing their own buttons, lo, get up and down just as happily and swiftly. Some Senator, some year or other, suggested as an obvious economy move cutting out this adornment on the public payroll, but no one can quite recall who it was or when it was, since the suggestion was unthinkable. The ride to the basement corridor ends with stepping into a catacomb which one may follow seemingly for miles beneath the office buildings, under Capitol Park to the Capitol itself, and continuing beneath the far end of Capitol Park to the vast office quarters of the House of Representatives.

The basement is a basement—stony, dim, a tunnel of echoes—yet a busy, merry, uplifting place of purposeful footsteps, overheard fragments of office and political gossip and name-dropping sorely in want of context. Near the elevator is the door to an immense cafeteria with two long lines of Senate aides, all chatty, almost all young. Any male over, say, thirty-eight, draws double takes. By that age most aides—many of them lawyers—have departed to cash in the chips of their glamorous experience. If you walk the long length of the line, then down a corridor alongside the kitchen, you discover the cafeteria's immense twin—with two more long lines. For employees too impatient or too busy with the people's business, or not interested in the cafeteria's specialty of steamboat round of beef, a short walk down the catacomb lies a smaller, quicker cafeteria dubbed disparagingly but fondly the "plastic palace." On the way there is a cigar stand, a beauty parlor, a barbershop with sign, "Senators and Senate Employees Get Priority by Order of the Rules Committee," and a large stationery store where you must display your Senate I.D. card to buy leather wallets and chrome-rimmed briefcases at forty-five per cent off, big cigar-sized ashtrays with the seal of the United States Senate, flags (for gifts to constituents) that are supposed to have been run up and down the Capitol flagpole (although the letter accompanying the gift never quite says *which* Capitol flagpole or how long it flew there), pencils imprinted "United States Senate" for twenty-eight cents a dozen, and all manner of other goodies for office-supply freaks. This Senate shop will not sell even to employees of the House; nor can Senate folk buy at the House stationery store which, they admit ruefully, has a wider choice of good stuff. It's hard to get an opinion comparing the House and Senate Office Building barbershops, but there's general agreement that the barbershop in the Capitol building—House side, not the one on the Senate side—is the best on the hill.

In the basement barbershop the bootblack, a sixty-two-year-old bald man from South Carolina, shrugs off an invitation to reminisce about the greats who must have sat for his artistry over the years. "Sometimes they come, sometimes they send down their shoes." Then in a deeply felt non sequitur: "Tell you one man I was sorry to see leave, that's Senator Ervin. Just before he left, his doctor told him he had to wear a different kind of shoes, so he came down and give me four pairs. They're mighty good shoes and they fit me 'cause I got big feet just like Senator Ervin." Proudly he shows me two pairs, lovingly shined. He has already sold one pair for twenty-five dollars. The other brought sixty dollars, the man tells me, creasing his face in respect for how good Senator Ervin was to his feet.

This basement commercial community also has a credit union, numerous storerooms (one piled high with unopened cartons of IBM electric typewriters at about six hundred dollars a box), and behind a door marked "Elevator Department" a shabby room decorated with a George Wallace poster. (This building is as broad-minded as it is consummately political. Upstairs, beneath a desk loaned to me in Senator Muskie's office, is a wastepaper basket with a Bentsen for President sticker.) And there's an enormous card- and poster-covered community bulletin board: Potomac cruises and parties by Senate employee clubs and dozens of offerings of used Volkswagens, stereos, and the likes of "Senate employee, male, 20's, seeking same to share basement apt. Capitol Hill." What if a House employee applied, or a male, 20's, from the Department of Agriculture, or, perish forbid, a teller of a privately owned bank? Would such a heathen be permitted beyond the moat?

And, finally, a post office, where employees are selected not by the Postmaster General but by Senators—as patronage. Senator Muskie has been favored with one of these jobs to fill, and he awarded it to Craig Rancourt, son of a Maine labor leader, who is working his way through Howard University Law School. I drop into the post office to buy a stamp and chat with Craig about my subterranean sightseeing. He is a chunky young man, sandy mustache, glasses, a mischievous hunch to his posture, and lively eyes that are afraid they might miss something. Still fresh with his own discovery of the place, he says, "There's quite a life down here. It's sort of complete. Just last night I was in a poker game with some of these building men, the electricians and plumbers from those rooms down the hall. They play every week. They're surprisingly intelligent, nice guys, and they really like their jobs. One of them comes from the Maryland shore and he goes there weekends. Each guy chips in five bucks before he goes and he brings back a big load of Maryland crab, precooked, including the extras. And in one of those little rooms they have a stove and what not for recooking it, and they fix themselves a bigger crab dinner than they can eat. Every week. These guys don't need anything else. Once you get into this Senate life, the rest of the world just sort of doesn't exist. You get removed from it. Nobody has to reach to the outside."

All afternoon Senator Muskie has been inaccessible behind the closed doors of his private office, conferring intensely with his two key staff members of the Budget Committee, Doug Bennet, the staff director, and John McEvoy, committee counsel. Muskie seldom confers that long with anybody, I'm told, particularly with staff people. This would be a fine time to test my privilege of access, except for one thing. It's too soon to get immersed in the complexities of the Budget Committee: I must get a sure grasp on the issues of air pollution first, a full enough plate for the time being. So it's a good time to become more at home in the mini-world of Room 145, office of Mr. Muskie of Maine, really a row of six equal-sized rooms off the great marble corridor of the street level of the Old Building. Across the hall is Mr. Tower of Texas, and next door is Mr. Jackson of Washington.

The door with the name plate and the seal of Maine opens on an unstuffy reception room made warm and lively by Jenny Wood, a long-tressed, dark-eyed girl in her early twenties, who has the unmistakable air of "good family," and a talent for welcoming not visitors but persons.

From this oasis of calm, the "working" offices lie to the left, the power to the right. The first room to the left should be called "the Maine room," because all matters directly related to the interests of Maine—economic, political, and helping constituents get better service out of government agencies—are handled by six people crowded into it. But no one dares call it the Maine room, partly because it sounds like the "main room," which it is not, and partly because everything done in any of the six rooms ostensibly is for Maine. So it's simply called "Charlie's room," for Charles Micoleau, who heads it with the title of executive assistant but is more intimately known as Muskie's "political man." In his early thirties, Charlie, with a master's degree in international relations, a young family, and a schedule of long working days, fills his nights cramming for law courses at George Washington University. A law degree, he says, will provide "my ticket back to Maine someday." One suspects he's interested in a round trip, as are many young staff people on the Hill: first, a "ticket" home for settling down long enough to establish a "base," then a run for the House and, in the wildest of dreams, for the Senate.

Near Charlie's window alcove there's a corner desk generally invisible behind a cloud cover of cigarette smoke buried under a catastrophe of scribbled notes and call-back messages, and unapproachable through an endless wall of telephone conversation on one of the office's two WATS lines—toll free—to Maine. The desk is occupied by Gayle Cory, Muskie's out-of-town scheduler, who is also charged with managing the official obligations of the Senator's wife Jane, and the limits of what is "official" have a way in Washington of becoming fuzzy.

Next are Jim Case, a young lawyer, and Estelle Lavoie, his co-worker, who handle "projects and cases." Projects and cases are, respectively, big things and little things that people in Maine want their Senator to get done for them. A big thing might be a defense contract involving hundreds of jobs and the economy of a county. A little thing might be finding out why the Veterans' Administration hasn't straightened out a requested change in an ex-soldier's life insurance. (Such requests are so common, and considered so important to the good standing with his constituency of a member of Congress, that there's a Veterans' Administration outpost office located in the basement tunnel near the credit union.)

Beyond Charlie's room is the "legislative room," an appellation only partly correct. Equally jammed, this room houses Rick Bayard, Muskie's chief legislative assistant, who keeps track of every bill worming through committee on its way to the Senate floor. Rick is the lookout for bills that do *not* pass through the three committees of which Muskie is a member. Thus he is the advance scout and adviser on votes that Muskie must cast most often—votes on the floor—yet those about which he is sometimes least informed. This could be the most interesting job in the shop. I must get to know more about him and it.

The legislative section also includes Anita Holst-Jensen, a legislative assistant, Patty Webster, called a research assistant, and a secretary, all of whose working days are made long and hard because so many Americans believe in the importance of "writing to my Congressman." All day they answer letters. Some extremely bright, well informed, worthy of serious response. Some as unimpressive as they are sincere. Some stupid. Some mass-produced, some uproarious. And all are answered. Either by individual letter composed by Anita or Patty, or by machine, Muskie's standard response on an issue, punched out at Anita's or Patty's command by a computerized typewriter in another building.

Across the aisle of the legislative-room-which-is-not-all-legislative sits the two-person press section, Bob Rose and Alyce Bouchard, both under thirty, both formerly of Maine newspapers. They comb and sift every tape, every transcript of a Muskie utterance for news releases that may be mimeographed and rushed to the Senate Press Gallery or phoned on the WATS line to newsrooms and wire services in Maine. They write newsletters to constituents and tape-record Muskie in short (less than a minute) comments on lively issues, furnishing them by phone to Maine radio stations for inclusion in news broadcasts. All this promotion activity, duplicated in every congressional office, often on a far more ambitious scale, is for the "information" of taxpayers and is never, ever to be construed as a form of year-round campaigning for votes at the expense of voters.

The quietest room in the suite, at the end of the row, is a tribute to the mechanization of the political man. True, it's occupied by two warm humans, Margie Buckland and Diana Vigue, mail clerks, but they are outnumbered by machines. There's a telecopier that stares at a piece of paper in Washington and duplicates it through transmission over ordinary telephone wires in one of Muskie's five offices in Maine, and vice versa. There's a huge and busy Xerox copier. Least attractive and most interesting of all are two metallic monstrosities side by side under the window. On being presented with a letter or any other document, the machine, asking no questions, signs "Edmund S. Muskie." Its twin machine, reserved for intimate friends and special campaign contributors, tosses off a friendly "Ed." No rubber-stamp phoniness about those signatures. Absolutely convincing. Even to a bank. Muskie's personal checks are signed by machine.

If a visitor is directed from the reception room not leftward to the "working" offices but rightward—toward the power—he enters a crowded room that houses, with no partitions separating them, Maynard Toll, Muskie's administrative assistant; Dolores Stover, the Senator's personal secretary; Fran Miller, chestnut-haired, unquenchably cheerful office manager; and Leslie Finn, part-time executive assistant chiefly in charge of keeping the books on the Senator's sizable and complicated allowance for office and travel. (Part time does not mean junior. In her early thirties, Mrs. Finn is a Capitol Hill elder, having previously worked for other Senators. In the high turnover of Senate offices, experience that can reach back a decade or more is valued, its possessor enjoying a certain status not unlike the reverence a Senator earns solely through the inertial force of his endurance.) Those lucky enough to pass through this command-post room enter the sanctum of the Senator. The whole layout is less than a hundred feet long, but it stretches, in a sense, to Siberia. The farther from the Senator's office, the darker and older the furniture, the freer fly four-letter oaths, the higher the heaps of unfiled and unattended papers culminating in a frenzy of pulp in the press section and, ultimately, the cold steel of machinery. In fact the importance of everything is measured inversely by its distance, one way or another, from the Senator. Status in the office is measured not by title or salary (salaries are published in a government book, and they are surprisingly unrelated to status) but by access to the man whose election gives them all a *raison d'être*.

Two people—Maynard Toll, the administrative assistant, and Dolores Stover, private secretary—walk through the Senator's door at will. Four others—Gayle Cory, Charlie Micoleau, Rick Bayard, and Bob Rose—may see the Senator "at will," but there's a ritual to perform: "Is he in?" Even if the door is open and Himself is plainly there, the ritual calls for a subtle exchange of eye flicks, Maynard or Dolores nodding assent to go in. Anyone else comes as a supplicant. In fact some privates of the eighteen-person army virtually never come into firsthand contact with the man around whom their working lives, to a great extent their personal identities, revolve.

And so the people up front, in headquarters, think and feel differently from the troops, especially toward those in positions of responsibility and power.

"We had two factions, no kidding, the morning Nixon gave that farewell speech in the East Room," says Dolores Stover, whose self-assured demeanor and good tailoring make her the perfect barrier and gracious no-sayer to outsiders who would impose on the Senator's time. One needs to know Dolores for at least ten minutes to discover that her tough New York Irish heart is a pincushion of soft spots. "We had two television sets brought in, one in here and one in the legislative room. At one point Nixon said something about 'I don't care if you're a plumber or an electrician'—and at the word 'plumber' the other room burst out in uproarious laughter. But not here. In this room we were all crying. I swear, Fran and Leslie and I were crying, even Maynard was very quiet. At what? At just the sadness of the whole thing that was happening to the government and to—well, someone from the other faction came here laughing and asked what in the world we were crying about, and we had to ask, 'Don't you have any feelings for the family?' I know it sounds crazy. Right now I'm reading Teddy White's book about Watergate, and I don't even like it because it's too soft on Nixon. I've hated Nixon ever since Helen Gahagan Douglas, just detested him, I *abhor* him. But the tragedy of that day, of the government coming into such disgrace, and the disgrace for the family, I—we just couldn't help but feel it."

As Dolores rounds out her reminiscence, Charlie Micoleau peers inquiringly into the room for about the fourth time in an hour. For the fourth time Dolores' eyes signal no. The Senator is still locked up with the Budget Boys. As his head disappears, Dolores sympathetically explains to me, "Charlie's *got* to see him." It seems he has just received from Pat Caddell, the young Cambridge political pollster made famous by his 1972 success with George McGovern, the eagerly awaited results of a "deep" poll of Maine measuring the state's moods and intentions regarding Muskie's re-election to the Senate in 1976. Caddell is flying down late tomorrow afternoon to interpret and discuss the findings with Muskie. Tonight, Muskie is committed to a social engagement (he rarely accepts one), a dinner for ex-governors living and working in Washington given by Vice-President Rockefeller at his place on fancy Foxhall Road. And at five o'clock sharp, by unanimous prearranged consent of the Senate, there's to be an important vote. Charlie is in agony.

At four forty-five the room is stabbed by an electrifying buzz. Then another. Nobody except me is electrified. Maynard Toll remains fastened to a memo, Dolores continues to peck out tomorrow's appointment schedule for the Senator. The sounds emanate from a wall clock, where with each buzz a light on the dial face flicks on. Two buzzes, two lights, the signal for a quorum call, a signal to be ignored. A Senator on the floor "suggests the absence of a quorum" when debate for any number of reasons needs a stall. Two antagonists may be negotiating compromise language. Perhaps a Senator who promised a bill's author that he'd rise to make a point in its support is suddenly not to be found, not in the cloakroom, not in the dining room. So "the absence of a quorum" is suggested, and the clerk begins to drone "Mister A b o u r e z k. . . . Mister A l-l e n. . . ." with in-between pauses so long that the gallery leans forward to see if the clerk has defected. Usually, before the roll reaches even to "Mister B u m p e r s" the absence-suggester withdraws his quorum call. Also, a quorum call is likely to be called, as in this case, some minutes before the time of a prearranged roll call, to keep the Senate "alive" after both sides have wrapped up their debate.

Gayle Cory, whose words race nervously in big-city tempo, but with vowels as Maine as a lobster pot, bounces in, inquiring, "Anybody know how the Senatuh's going to vote?"

Maynard Toll, most likely to know, has run off somewhere.

"What's the vote on?" asks Fran Miller, the office manager.

"The Weicker resolution," says Dolores.

"A motion to table," amends Gayle.

For days the Senate has been paralyzed by debate over an election dispute in New Hampshire, unsettled since last November, more than seven months. John Durkin, the Democratic candidate for Senator, came out ahead of Louis Wyman, the Republican, by two votes in the first official count. In a recount (supervised by a commission of politicians appointed by a Republican governor) Wyman won by ten votes. The Senate, controlled by Democrats and empowered by the Constitution to determine the qualifications of its own members, refused to certify Wyman's election, turning the matter over to its Rules Committee. The Rules Committee, finding the ballots and records in something of a mess, came to a tie vote, dumping the matter back on the Senate.

Senator Lowell Weicker, the Connecticut Republican, submitted a resolution to send the matter back to New Hampshire for a new election. Weicker is not on the Rules Committee, and therefore normally would not be expected to lead his party's position on a matter which, by Senate custom, is scarcely his business. But Weicker's strong disposition to "let the people decide" was welcomed by his party colleagues, who undoubtedly would rather decide the issue themselves if only they had the votes to decide it in their own favor. So a good fallback is Weicker's righteous stance, especially since Weicker earned his buttons as Mr. Righteous during last year's Watergate hearings, for which he is still trying to redeem himself with his party. The Democrats, led by Rules Committee Chairman Howard Cannon of Nevada, wanting the disputed New Hampshire seat, have constructed an equally principled and righteous position. The Constitution doesn't say the Senate shall pass the buck; it says the Senate shall *determine*. To send the matter back to New Hampshire, unresolved, is to set a terrible precedent that would weaken the Constitution; furthermore, it would weaken the credibility of the Senate in the eyes of the people. (The latter argument presumes that "the people" out there are watching with bated breath, when the fact is that newspapers are virtually devoid of mention of Durkin and Wyman, and possibly not one in ten Americans could identify who they are and what the facts of the dispute are.)

"I think he'll vote no—with the party," says Dolores.

"That means voting yes. The motion's to table," says Gayle.

"Why table?" I ask.

"So they can kill it without exactly going on record against it," explains Gayle, a shrug saying, You figure it out, I can't.

"I heard," says Dolores, "that the Senator was quoted in the papers in Maine over the weekend, saying that it should go back to New Hampshire."

"No," says Gayle authoritatively. "What he said was he doesn't know how it's going to turn out in the Senate and that it *could* go back to New Hampshire."

Dolores and Fran agree that that's different.

"I wouldn't be surprised," says Dolores knowingly, swiveling back to her desk, "if he hasn't made up his mind yet." For my benefit: "You'd be surprised how often he makes up his mind on the way to the floor."

The stab again, this time one long buzz. The vote. Still Muskie remains locked with his Budget staff. Is he going to miss the vote? After a very long time, like ten minutes, by which time one might assume the vote is all over, the buzzer buzzes again, a series of five— and five lights on the clock. Out of the office burst Doug Bennet, John McEvoy and, finally, Muskie, still wrapping up their conference. The five beeps mean last call—about five minutes—before the roll call ends. I hear Muskie's long stride echo down the marble hall toward the subway car to the Capitol. In a minute or two, gallery watchers will see that familiar but not widely understood mad rush of Senators suddenly bursting through the swinging doors of the Senate chamber like schoolboys released from class.

Soon Rick Bayard strolls into the administration room, picks up a phone, dials, says nothing, listens, hangs up, says blandly, "Weicker resolution to table, defeated 55–43." A straight party-line vote, except for three Southerners going with the Republicans.

"I didn't hear you ask anybody anything," I say. "How do you know?"

"It's on tape. Democratic cloakroom. You dial in any time, you find out the floor situation, what's happened and what'll be happening next—if they know, and they don't always know. If I really have to know, I might dial the Republican cloakroom. Sometimes their tape has better information."

"Who's they?"

"One of Charlie Ferris' boys keeps updating the tape. Charlie's the top staff man for the majority."

I jot down that handy number: 4-8541. Rick adds, "Try it from outside sometime, 224-8541. Even long distance. A lot of Senators call in before they shave in the morning. The tape runs all night."

By now, Charlie Micoleau is in the hall waiting for Muskie's reappearance. Soon Muskie, fastidious about time as well as grooming, will be down to his underwear in his closed office, shaving for the Rockefeller affair. But Charlie's *got* to get with him about that Caddell poll. At last the boss appears, and both men move as one into the sanctum.

Dolores never leaves before the Senator does. Fran feels guilt about leaving before Dolores. And Gayle doesn't like to leave when the others are still there. Some decision might come up that touches on her bailiwick, and since the boundaries of her bailiwick are blurred, she stays a lot. One definite area of Gayle's charge is Jane, which is to say Mrs. Muskie, which is to say all matters relating to the family. But the family is now at Kennebunk Beach, Maine, for the summer, which slightly thickens the haze around Gayle's jurisdiction.

"Pat Caddell is flying in tomorrow night," Dolores reminds Gayle. "He's on the schedule for dinner. Should they have it here?"

"Here?" Gayle is puzzled.

"I thought," says Dolores, glowing maternally, "maybe we could have a little dinner catered in the office from some nice restaurant. This poll is so sensitive—you know, Maynard doesn't even want me to look at it—they'll be afraid to talk about it in a restaurant."

"Who's seen it?"

"Nobody but Maynard and Charlie, and the Senator told me to send a copy to Clark Clifford. By hand."

"I have an idea," says Gayle. "Why not get some steaks out to the house, and the Senator and Charlie and Caddell can do them on the outdoor grill?"

"Does he like to do that?"

The Senator's likes and dislikes are generally Dolores' department, but once the setting is "out at the house," in suburban Bethesda, Maryland, the authority shifts delicately to Gayle. Gayle says, "I'm sure he would."

Nobody suggests asking *him*. Clearly he doesn't expect to be consulted.

Gayle has another idea: "They could have the dinner brought in at the Capitol hideaway. Be cozier than here."

"I've got it. If tomorrow's anything like today, he just might want to eat alone, shower, then sit down with Caddell. Why don't we have Charlie take Caddell out to dinner while the Senator goes home to eat? Then Charlie can bring Caddell there. That way, if the Senator decides to have dinner with Charlie and Pat, it's easy to change the plan."

Like the Durkin-Wyman New Hampshire dispute, this issue is left unsettled.

Wednesday morning, June 18

At ten o'clock, when Ed Muskie leaves his office, he has been thinking about environmental pollution, about strategies for this morning's markup, for five hours. Last night—as he does every night before a major meeting—Muskie took home a black loose-leaf briefing book. It contains summaries of the main factual information brought out in hearings and studies, and Leon Billings' advisory memos synthesizing the issues. Muskie often hits his briefing book before breakfast; in fact, before dawn.

As I huff and puff to keep up with his long, rapid stride, I mention that I was surprised yesterday at the involvement of committee members in the difficult technical challenges of writing a clean air law, and at how they seem to check their partisan competitiveness at the door. "They're a well-educated committee, much better than most," Muskie replies. That's what he has tried to encourage over the years, he adds, not trying to shove something down their throats as some chairmen are reputed to do.

At ten-eighteen Muskie gavels the ten o'clock meeting to order. Diagonal shafts of sunlight from the high windows light a larger audience than yesterday. Only Senators Buckley and Domenici and Mike Gravel, the Alaska Democrat, are present. Gravel, with a large head and long face over a short body, has black hair pin-striped with silver and cut modishly full, and wears good suits, also dark and pin-striped. He is the man who dramatically attempted one night to legitimize the publication of the Pentagon Papers by reading them into the record of a one-man subcommittee meeting (thus making the papers legally quotable), finally breaking down in exhaustion and tears. The display did not enhance his standing in the Senate and, oddly, did not make him a notable hero of the anti-war movement. For all the pin stripes, head to toe, Gravel comes off resembling a night club silent partner more than a mortgage banker.

"What do you envision as a windup for taking the bill to full committee?" asks Domenici.

"Well, I would like to get to the floor by mid-July," Muskie replies, "so that we could have a chance to clear the Senate before the August recess."

At ten-twenty, in strolls the television-familiar face of Senator Howard Baker, the Tennessee Republican of Watergate fame, jiggling a wax-loosening pinkie in his ear. Baker, the ranking Republican on the full Public Works Committee, walks with a barrel-like roll. He looks just as amiable as, but somewhat stockier and more rumpled than, the Baker who in delighted disbelief during Watergate asked Tony Ulasewicz, the White House's comical straight man of an ex-cop, *"Who thought you up?"* He is handed a message and disappears.

At ten forty-five Baker reappears with the chairman of the full

Public Works Committee, Jennings Randolph of West Virginia, the roundest and courtliest man in the Senate. A deference, an expectancy, greets him as Randolph stands behind his chair, making no move to sit. Randolph and Baker are only ex officio on the subcommittee, not obliged to attend sessions. Randolph apologizes for having to go to the floor to manage debate on a bill, then mentions that he knows the subcommittee is to discuss pollution aspects of coal. (He does not mention—need not mention—that as a West Virginian he has some interest in coal, indeed as Arabs have some interest in oil.) Randolph remarks with a feather touch: "You know whether it would be convenient to have that discussion at a later time."

Muskie responds unhesitatingly, "Why, we'll put it at the end of the list, Jennings. If you can't be here, we'll take it up when you can be."

Randolph and Baker leave for the Senate chamber. At eleven Senator McClure joins the meeting. Like all new arrivals, he is offered coffee by a tall young man with Mediterranean skin, high black pompadour, a pin-striped suit with vest, and a haughty cool. McClure nods acceptance, and the young man strolls slowly and aloofly to fetch it from an urn in a side conference room. The young man, son of an intimate political friend of Chairman Randolph, is employed as a "clerical assistant" at $11,008.98 a year.

Leon Billings, continuing from yesterday, is still enumerating issues to be discussed and comes to a Ford Administration proposal that civil penalties for polluters be added to criminal penalties not included in the law. Law enforcers, he explains, seem to be reluctant to charge polluters with crimes. Besides, there's a school of environmentalists who believe that the threat of heavy civil penalties—cash fines—would provide a strong economic incentive to industries to clean up and meet deadlines. Senator Buckley is one who leans toward that approach.

Gravel says, "Let me indicate I would champion this."

Senator Gary Hart has arrived. His, too, is a face not unfamiliar to TV viewers. He was often interviewed as campaign manager for presidential candidate George McGovern, and in fact helped turn prospects away from his candidate, some feel, by talking presidential politics in open shirt and dangling hair, thus accenting the campaign's counterculture tone. As Senator from Colorado, he is suddenly a dandy, in knife-creased Edwardian suits, tooled boots, and elbows crooked close to his waist in a self-conscious walk. He is whisper-briefed by an aide with thinning blond hair and immense forehead, then says: "Coming in on the middle of the discussion, I, also, would like to suggest a great interest on my part in this concept. I have been interested in it for a number of years. . . ."

Gary Hart and Jim Buckley, ultra-liberal Democrat and ultra-conservative Republican—seeing eye to eye! Not on some nonphilosophical issue of administrative technique, or some regional self-interest that often brings political adversaries together. No, on a fundamental issue of economic and social motivation: how to coerce profiteers into doing social good. The environment as a political issue has a way of doing that—of splitting familiar old camps, rejuggling their members into new alliances that do not yet suggest clear lines of common ideology. Energy seems to be another such issue. Still another is abortion. Perhaps an enormous revolution is sweeping over us and nobody's announcing the news. Perhaps we're shifting from the politics of man's abuse of man into the politics of man's self-abuse through misuse of his physical environment and technology. From the politics of social change to the politics of technosocial change. And the political players come out with different numbers on their backs, often on different teams.

"The next item," says Leon Billings, "is page 89, statutory standards . . . for hydrocarbons and carbon monoxide and oxides of nitrogen[1]. . . . The material backing up those issues is so complicated that it belies explanation."

Belies [sic] explanation! For twelve years this subcommittee has been collecting, sifting, evaluating facts, scientific studies, legal approaches, legislative concepts to justify statutory standards for auto emissions, starting with the original air quality law of 1963. The existing tough law of 1970, now being re-evaluated and amended, was passed by the Senate *unanimously,* yet no one in 1963 or 1970 was—or in 1975 is—sure of what the facts are.

At least two small groups have sounded perfectly sure of the facts. Auto manufacturers then and now have insisted that the law—both its standards and its deadline—set a technologically impossible goal.

[1] These poisonous emissions are described in most subcommittee conversation by their chemical shorthand, which will hereafter be used freely. Hydrocarbon is HC. Carbon monoxide, CO. Oxides of nitrogen are NOx (pronounced "knocks").

Environmental purists, confident that only greed stands in the way of overnight technological accomplishment, see the issue just as clearly: "Set a date, grind the bastards down, and clean the air the same way we made it to the moon."

To summarize oversimply what does appear to be known, automotive emissions are the biggest source of air pollution in America, accounting for about forty per cent of air poisons, and, in certain ways, are hardest to control. In large metropolitan centers the auto's share becomes overwhelming.

Smokestacks of factories and power companies are expensive and difficult to depollute, true. But if you properly control all the smokestacks in a region, you still must reckon with those damnable cars. Cars won't sit still like smokestacks. Clean a car in Illinois today, but tomorrow into Illinois sputters a car that yesterday was polluting Nebraska. Except for, say, New York taxicabs, cars can't be treated as a local problem. You must clean them up nationally or forget it.

As a result of the 1965 amendments to the original Clean Air Act a fifty per cent reduction in air pollution was ordered by 1970. In 1970 the Clean Air Act amendments required that the remaining thirty per cent be reduced by ninety per cent no later than January 1, 1975, for HC and CO. The deadline for reducing NOx was extended a year, to 1976.

That's what the law demanded. It's nothing short of a miracle that the Congress demanded it—by any majority, let alone unanimously —since the transcript of the debate shows clearly that the Congress knew it was doing something utterly radical, without precedent. The Congress, composed of lawyers more than any other occupation and of scarcely any engineers, dictated to the auto giants of Detroit that they must engineer a car so as to produce a specified result—drastically cleaner air. It didn't say how. In fact, the Congress knew perfectly well—the debate clearly reflects it—that in 1970, when it passed the law, the technology for accomplishing the goal did not exist. Strictly speaking, some experts said the technology existed, but only in the laboratory; indeed, some of it only in theory. But as to whether these mockups would actually work on the road, whether they could be mass-produced consistently, how long they would last —on these questions, knowledge and experience were absolute zero. Yet Congress mandated that result.

To make matters more dramatic, Congress mandated that result for a target date—the appearance of 1975 models. That date, in auto manufacturing terms, was nigh onto immediately. Detroit claims that forty-three months must go by between the introduction of a new piece of technology and its appearance on the road. Under tough questioning, they allow it might be done in three years. So if the deadline was five years, and setting up a production pipeline required three years, Detroit had less than two years to invent a technology. Detroit was already loudly denouncing that goal as foolish, insane, impossible—scarcely the recommended attitude for accomplishing the admittedly difficult.

Even President Richard Nixon planted his feet in the middle of clean air. In a 1970 New Year's Day address he identified air and water pollution as America's number one problem. In the opening days of the 1970 session he sent Congress a special message on pollution, urging that Congress indeed set standards for clean air and standards for auto emissions—severe ones. He, too, proposed a war to eliminate ninety per cent of auto pollution. But a *slow* war. Instead of five years, give 'em ten years. By no coincidence, that was exactly the span of time the auto companies themselves had said was soon enough.

Ten years does not mean ten years. It means twenty. If, as Nixon and Detroit proposed in 1970, the 1980 model car were to be the first required to be drastically cleaner, the 1979 car would remain excused. All cars made before 1979 would be similarly excused. Cars last an average of ten years. Therefore, in any given year there are ten "used" cars—those a year old or more—cluttering the road for every current model car. So by mandating 1980 as the *clean car* year, the *clean air* year would have been put off to 1990. Twenty more years of choking, headaches, dizziness, hastened heart attacks, creeping brain damage, and deaths.

What's so difficult technologically about making a clean air car?

Engineers can get rid of ninety per cent of deadly hydrocarbons and carbon monoxide without too much difficulty. The big trouble is NOx. In fact, getting rid of NOx isn't too hard either, *unless* you want to get rid of HC and CO at the same time. In the chemistry of the internal combustion engine, reduction of HC and CO fumes causes an increase in NOx fumes. Passing a law won't change that.

The plot thickens. The two main elements of life-giving air itself, oxygen and nitrogen, combine into molecules of noxious NOx at about 2,300° F. The hotter an engine runs, the more NOx. The cooler it runs, the less NOx. Efficiency—better gas mileage—works the other way around. The hotter the engine, the more efficiently it runs. The cooler the engine, the more fuel it consumes. So reduction of NOx and improved fuel economy are directly opposed. As Detroit likes to put it: *irrevocably* opposed.

In a major sense, the tough clean air standards of 1970 were creatures of the political mood of 1970 and could now become victims of the political mood of 1975.

In 1970—suddenly and dramatically—preservation of the natural environment became an overpowering national concern. Rachel Carson's *Silent Spring* helped seed it, scientific studies and frightening statistics helped nourish it, and Earth Day made it bloom. The new environmental movement, fed by science, was led by the young. And their parents were grateful beyond bounds, which may have had less to do with the threatened loss of green forests and clean air than with other fears. For it was also a time among many of the young of proliferating drugs, and of justification of violence in the name of love and peace, of hatred of almost anything traditional and established, including government, a complex of alienations brought to a boil by the Vietnam war.

The war was a curse upon the Congress, whose majority saw no choice but to keep dragging us through the tunnel in uncertain pursuit of the light at the end. And now came this bill out of committee —this fresh, clean bill for fresh, clean air—that would give the crazed kids and their distraught parents something they wanted for a change, that would cast the Congress in the role of good guys, on the side of life and health—a moral substitute for peace. Was Congress to quibble about technical obstacles?

This is not to imply that Congress did not seriously scrutinize every implication of the clean air legislation of 1970. The subcommittee that produced it, headed by Senator Muskie, agonized over it, tore themselves apart, put themselves together trying to harmonize every difference. To understand why and how an eager but uncertain Senate passed it on September 22, 1970, after only two afternoons of debate, requires understanding of a fundamental truth about the Senate, without which that institution would collapse in paralysis and uselessness.

On most legislation, even most major and controversial legislation, a Senator must trust the subcommittee that produces a bill. If not the whole subcommittee, at least those members of it with whom a Senator feels generally in tune. He must do that or his job becomes impossible. An individual Senator cannot spend on every major bill the seven years, the hundreds upon hundreds of hours of reading, of hearings, of debate, of haggling, of compromising and resolving that members of the Muskie committee spent on clean air. Each Senator is a member of three major standing committees and of subcommittees under each. On the bills coming before his subcommittees he must become expert, spend the grueling hours, the outstretched years. And other Senators must trust *him*.

In that sense, a law is not the "work of Congress." That idea is a romantic myth—an impractical delusion. A law is the work of a few men, perhaps three or four or five active participants. It may be the work of only one, whose enthusiasm and insight and will are employed as a driving lash over an ambitious staff. That zealous individual's colleagues on a subcommittee are often carried along by the sheer force of his commitment.

So, on any single issue, almost all Senators and Congressmen are followers, are the less than well informed "men in the street." They are eager to be, need to be, instructed as to what to do. On his own bill, however, or on his subcommittee's bill, a Senator is eager to lead, to instruct.

In 1970, the United States Senate, yearning for an embrace from an estranged constituency, could scarcely be more eager to believe, to trust, when a responsible subcommittee and its respected chairman in effect assured them: "This clean air bill is all right. We have thought it through carefully. Trust us." Although twenty-five Senators absented themselves from the chamber, and two obvious opponents, including Robert Griffin, Republican of Michigan, the Senate's most reliable spokesman for the auto interests, declined to vote, not a single Senator voted against the clean air amendments of 1970.

But the climate of 1975 is different. The buzz words of this year are not "Vietnam" and "ecology." They are "energy" and "recession."

Befuddled "experts" still have not adequately explained 1975's unprecedented combination of inflation and unemployment. We have been teetering all this year at the edge of a major depression, the most terrifying economic threat in thirty-five years, and don't yet understand it. We know the world is faced with a long-range shortage of energy, but we don't know who brought on last year's shortage of oil, or how or why. We know that the gasoline scarcity and high prices have dried up auto sales, but we don't know whether automobile plant shutdowns (due to the oil shortage) were the chief cause of the general recession. We know that the internal combustion engine uses more gasoline if it's to exhale less NOx, but we don't know how modifications—or another kind of engine—might ultimately correct that problem.

So energy, unemployment, and pollution control are all inextricably tangled. In the uncertain, tender political condition of 1975, the mention to a member of Congress of clean air legislation reflexively sounds the buzz words, "energy," "recession." Passed in the most favorable of years, 1970, the Clean Air Act now must be reviewed in the least favorable of years.

This year the auto companies, for the first time, have a powerful ally, a voice capable of reaching a major section of the Congress that the auto companies could never get near enough to woo. Leonard Woodcock, president of the United Auto Workers, is to many liberal Congressmen their favorite labor lobbyist, owing as much to his intelligence and appealing restraint as to the size of his constituency. In 1970 the UAW lobbied hard to clean the air, on the ground that auto workers not only make cars but breathe as well, and so do their kids. A month ago, however, on May 15, in testimony before this same Environmental Pollution Subcommittee, Woodcock, accompanied by David Ragone, the University of Michigan dean of engineering, was a changed and distraught witness:

"There is a big difference now. I represent 170,000 people, indefinitely laid off, who are becoming increasingly desperate. They see foreign cars, because of the fuel economy problem, taking more and more of this market. . . . I'm not in the hip pocket of industry as some people in this Congress are now saying on the liberal side of the Democratic Party. I am representing desperate men and women and their children."

Senator John Culver, a freshman Democrat from Iowa, tried to untangle pollution controls from high oil prices and unemployment, but Woodcock persisted in retangling them.

"President Woodcock, do you have any figures to indicate how the 1977 emission standards might affect the unemployment rate of the automobile industry?"

"No, I don't. All I'm trying to say, Senator, is that if we had no fuel economy problem the UAW would not be here today arguing for a pause. . . . I want to apologize to this committee for being so emotional, but I hope you understand I am in constant, increasing daily pressure and I have no answers for people."

Woodcock guessed—he said he had no figures—that a car equipped to meet the 1978 emission standards would have to sell for a substantially higher price, and that the higher price would further impede sales and prolong the industry shutdown. This led Senator Domenici to prod:

"How can you give us some kind of evidence that this will occur?"

"I can't."

"I have seen no evidence that stricter clean air standards will have an impact on whether the consumer buys more American cars. I think that is basic to your premise. It is basic to the automobile manufacturers' premise. We have to know that it is going to have that kind of consumer impact. If it isn't, why not go with the higher standards and clean up the ambient air at a more rapid pace? That is the heart of the whole issue."

Impeccably reasoned or not, Woodcock's testimony left a powerful impression, not only with Woodcock's friends among the subcommittee Democrats but with liberal members throughout the Senate and House. The shaky reasoning was less important than Woodcock's obvious and sincere stress. In fact he closed his testimony, putting a hand on the shoulder of Dr. Ragone, his technical adviser, saying:

"Thank you, Mr. Chairman. May I apologize to the committee for an Englishman being emotional. That is why I have an Italian with me being so calm."

It is important to understand here what the Muskie subcommittee is considering—and why it's considering it. It is not considering passage of a new Clean Air Act, or amendments to tighten the screws on the old one. The law exists. Emission standards for 1975—postponed for two years by the EPA and Congress to 1977—are set. What the committee *is* considering is a crescendo of demand by auto interests as well as other industries and power companies to delay and loosen those standards. Muskie is vigilant for flaws that might justify non-compliance or even major losses in the act's political support. The law, to use a highly charged word in the Muskie lexicon, must have *credibility*.

As the law now stands, with a mandated ninety per cent reduction of emissions, 1977 model cars must conform to the following emission standards:

Hydrocarbons (HC)	.41 grams per mile
Carbon monoxide (CO)	3.4 grams per mile
Nitrogen oxide (NOx)	.4 grams per mile

Of those goals, the toughest is .4 NOx, bobbing up repeatedly in the conversation of members and committee staff, pronounced "point four knocks."

And so that brings us back to where we were, Leon Billings telling the committee that the mounting scientific uncertainty behind the statutory standards "is so complicated that it belies explanation." Suddenly Muskie says to Billings:

"You have not mentioned sulphates."

"No, sir, I have not."

"Why not?"

"I do not understand the sulphate problem." Senators laugh, as much in relief as amusement. "I think the staff has read virtually everything that has been said about sulphate. We can come to these conclusions: number one, nobody knows exactly how to establish any kind of standards for sulphate because you have no testing. We do know that . . . sulphur dioxide oxidized into sulphur trioxide and, mixing with water, mixes to H_2SO_4, which is chemistry, which I know nothing about, as you know."

More laughter.

"Sulphate is a highly reactive molecule, I am told," Billings continues, "and it very likely changes to a lead sulphate or ammonium sulphate, a less toxic sulphate, but nobody knows what is happening to it out there. In my opinion, there is not enough information on sulphates to dictate an auto emissions policy."

McClure, a lawyer, enters with a flourish of chemistry one-upmanship:

"The sulphate question was predictable. . . . I had only one year of chemistry. I can speak with as much authority on this as other people with no chemistry authority. The basic chemistry of catalysts *required* the production of sulphuric acid. It was just absolutely predictable. What other things ought we be predicting?"

Muskie asks Billings:

"What other things are other people predicting?"

"The rare earth questions. EPA scientists have been able to show that, because of weight loss in the catalyst, obviously something is disappearing and obviously it is going somewhere."

"It is going to show up," says McClure, suddenly the environmentalist, "in the lungs of some little child in some city somewhere."

"Or some seal in Alaska," mutters Muskie.

"Like the disappearance of asbestos off tires," contributes Billings, "the elements are going into the engine or the exhaust pipe. They disappear and nobody knows where they go."

Muskie reaches for a positive note to end the morning. Gazing at a chart on the wall listing the 1977 statutory standards—.41 for HC, 3.4 for CO and .4 for NOx—he inquires:

"Could I ask, what were the numbers for each of these before we put in emission controls?"

"Well," Billings replies, "8.0 for hydrocarbons, carbon monoxide was 87, and oxides of nitrogen 3.5"

Those numbers, although meaningless to me, to most any layman, suddenly sound startlingly high. The gunk we once breathed! But McClure gets in the last satisfied word. The dramatic reduction, an inspiration to press onward, can also be a laurel to rest on:

"I think we've made tremendous progress. I think that is worth pointing out."

It is twelve-twenty. The head-numbing talk has droned for more than two hours. Muskie recesses the meeting until next Tuesday morning.

Striding through the catacombs, returning to the office, Muskie is more intent on getting there than on sociability. In a jab of small talk, I ask, "How did the Rockefeller dinner go last night?" He grumps: "It was all former governors. The Republicans were in the majority."

In his office Muskie slips off his jacket, drapes it on a hanger with elaborate care—he's a tailor's son—sinks into his favorite big leather armchair near a couch, and feels better. The office is subdued, lit gently by a chandelier of candlelike bulbs, a personal possession of Muskie's which has moved with him as he and his staff over the years have moved about the Old Senate Office Building. Except for his desk, set diagonally in a corner, the office is more like a formal but comfortable sitting room: the couch, two stuffed chairs, a couple of side chairs with arms, a couple without, all dispersed widely around a coffee table. The chairs, unfailingly, are self-selected marks of rank among visitors: visiting principals and Senators move naturally to the couch and stuffed chairs. When those seats are taken, assisting lawyers, assisting lobbyists, and senatorial staff assort themselves in the side chairs, armed and armless respectively, according to status. Opposite the desk a wall of walnut shelves is laden with mementos and trophies of politics and travel, their overflow dispersed on a mantel and end tables around the room.

On the wide leather arm on his chair I place my miniature tape recorder. Its presence makes him not the slightest bit apprehensive. And so we begin the first of our talks. I am as curious to observe the evolution of their form and tone as their content.

A CONVERSATION WITH SENATOR MUSKIE

Would you amplify your comment of early this morning that the subcommittee is "well educated"?

—It's really very simple. I assumed from the beginning that if any man on the committee, whatever his politics, were given a meaningful role, a meaningful input into the legislative process, he'd be glad to become part of it. You have to remember that in my days in the Maine legislature, my first experience in office, the Democrats were in a very small minority. We were just sort of tolerated. It was recognized that the two-party system had to be there, but you weren't really invited to participate. We weren't asked to offer our ideas or be part of the creative legislative process. When I first came here seventeen years ago the minority on the Public Works Committee was just sort of tolerated. It was recognized that they could advance their proposals. Then there'd be an automatic party-line vote. The majority would work its will. The final product was usually shaped around the chairman's ideas. But constantly there was this air of confrontation. Which was the old politics.

—When I got a subcommittee of my own, it just seemed to me that it would be better to invite the others to get involved, to accept their ideas as though they were members of a committee. So that's been the style of this subcommittee ever since it was created. And it has worked.

Buckley and McClure are as conservative on other issues as one can be. Do you run into problems of wrestling with ideology?

—You have as much potential of conservative-liberal division on this issue as on others, in that you're regulating business. And Republicans are described as the party of big business. So that Senators who are so disposed could easily divide along ideological lines. I suppose that Buckley in particular is often a free enterprise type, but on this issue he seems very strong.

No inhibitions about government control?

—Not in this field.

McClure seems interested in the economic angle, always balancing the economic costs against the pollution factors.

—Well, he's more inclined to—I don't know if I'd say he thinks it's more important than the environmental, but he thinks there needs to be a balance, that we have to be concerned about costs, about the cost-effectiveness of the marginal gains.

—I think everybody on the committee is in the process of shaping his position, including myself. So this is the way it typically works. We bounce our ideas off each other. In a few sessions it will begin to crystallize. A lot of people introduce legislation and they want it to come out, you know, as Public Law Blankety-Blank, exactly in the form they introduced it. When I introduce legislation it's simply to— to provoke the dialogue, to begin the dialogue. Committee hearings are supposed to make a contribution, in my judgment. You try to shape the hearings so that there is dialogue, debate. Questions are raised so the committee understands the underlying complexities.

So if you come out with eighty-five, even seventy-five per cent of what you want, at least you know you've got Buckley and McClure with you when the bill comes to the floor.

—That's right. Or if they're not with me, I've probably blunted their opposition. But to the extent that you can get the partisan or the liberal-conservative element out of this, you can have meaningful intellectual exchange, get people to focus on the issue. I'm not averse, just because he's a conservative, to having Jim Buckley influence my judgment on pieces of legislation. He's going to have good ideas on this issue. Even on other issues, I'll listen. When he makes a point it usually has intellectual integrity, so if I don't accept his point of view—my previous view may be eliminated by what he has to say—I might alter my point of view to meet the objections he's raised. Why should I lose the benefit of that? If he's found a weak point and attacks it, and his attack is credible intellectually, then I'm challenged to grapple with it. And I think you just come out with sounder legislation.

—So I don't come before them with a *fait accompli*. I don't begin markups saying, "Now, this is what I think we need to do." I let the thing evolve. But I make proposals as we go along, as I will next Tuesday. I'll lay out issues, one at a time, as something I think has merit, that I'm willing to discuss and debate, and listen to their reactions. So I will take initiatives. But I don't try to put a full plate in front of them and say, "Now you eat all of this, or reject it."

Wednesday afternoon, June 18

Muskie has had lunch alone at his desk, on a cafeteria tray brought up by Dolores, his secretary. He is now protected in his office by a closed door.

That works two ways. The administrative room is also protected from him. His immediate lieutenants live at three levels of tension. They're most relaxed, of course, when the Senator—or just plain He —is out. Then Maynard stretches out in his swivel chair as he chats quietly on the phone. Dolores downs allergy pills and relates the details of an office crisis to Leslie Finn. Fran, usually a non-stop work machine, chuckles at the caustic repartee that flits lightly among Dolores, Maynard, and Leslie.

The second level is when the Senator is in but the door is closed. The banter is about the same, but eyes dart constantly, apprehensively toward the door, faces ready to straighten and go solemn in a flick. The tensest time, of course, is when He's there and the door is open. Maynard sits relatively upright. On the phone or face to face, Dolores is only half in touch with whomever she talks to. She eyes that door, poised to spring even before he thinks of summoning her.

Susie Nicholas, Charlie Micoleau's olive-skinned secretary, makes a grand entrance, a faint put-on of the undulating glide of Miss America. Her slim forearms are loaded down with letters, surely more than a hundred, and she announces demurely, "He's got to sign these personally. And when Big Ed sees this, he's going to—" Her eyes roll.

No staff member is known to have ever tried the "Big Ed" to his face, but Gayle, needing an immediate decision, once pouted, "Oh, where the hell is Big Eddie?" And a deep voice from behind her—he'd just walked in—responded, "He's right here." Even Leon Billings, after nine intimate years as possibly his most trusted aide, has never called his boss anything but Senator.

The letters that trouble Susie are a stack of personal thank-you notes for financial contributions to Muskie's 1976 re-election campaign in Maine. Many are to old supporters and close friends. A policy decision has been made (presumably by Charlie: Muskie is victim of a lot of policy decisions) that they must not be signed by machine. True, Muskie (and every Senator) has been accused of machine-signing letters that were signed by hand at least as often as constituents have been thrilled by the personal autograph on a machine-signed letter. But you can't take a chance—is Charlie's position—that one of these contributors might already have a machine-signed letter, or for that matter a hand-signed one. The point is, the two have *got* to be slightly different.

Ensues a big discussion among Dolores, Fran, and Susie as to whether he'll sign them. He has a severe distaste for the necessity of seeing, knowing about, taking part in anything to do with campaign finances. He likes to have someone else make the decision and report it to him so he can approve it by grunt, and at the same time pretend he didn't even hear it. The women finger the material of possibilities:

"Suppose he just lets them lie there."

"How many are from friends?"

"Depends on what you call a friend."

"Could we just take out the twenty closest friends and let the machine do the rest?"

"It'll be that twenty-first that hits the fan."

"We've *got* to get them out, or we can't face these people with the next mailing."

"He's going to have to face some of these people in Maine next weekend."

"I tell you, he's just going to let them lie there."

Dolores' phone rings, she says, "All right," and goes out to the reception room. Returning with a worried look, she tiptoes to his door, opens it, steals in, and eventually reappears. Rolling her eyes with relief, she says, "I was afraid he was taking a nap. He was reading." She explains:

"There are two ladies from Maine out there, drop-ins. One is the sister of the man who used to own the Augusta House, a great old hotel in Maine that's no longer standing. They asked Jenny could they see the Senator. Well, we've been talking about that, Maynard and Charlie and Gayle and I. So I went in and said, 'Senator, there's a new policy around here.' And he looked at me over his reading glasses, you know his way, and said"—Dolores' voice deepens to basso—"and said, 'Nobody tells *me* about pawlicy.' Well, I just kept on, I said, 'The new policy is that when people from Maine come by and if you're in the office, this is until the election only, we'll try to give them a quick walk-in.' "

"What did he say?" I ask.

"Oh, he said"—Dolores lofts her hand grandiloquently—" 'Oh, you *know,* Dolores, I would just be de*light*ed.' "

"Did he?" I ask naïvely.

She repeats the burlesque exactly. "Just de*light*ed."

I've been had.

I dart into the Senator's office just ahead of the visitors. Muskie, looking oppressed, is slipping his jacket on, smoothing out imagined rumples. As Dolores, the gracious escort, shows the women in, Muskie's face, from out of nowhere, has acquired a glow, sincerely expectant and pleased. One of the guests effuses, "What a *lovely* office." He replies, "Yes, and we just had a nice new rug put in yesterday. Doesn't it remind you of Maine sand?" And she says, "This is such an honor and a privilege, you can't imagine." He reaches his arm appreciatively around her shoulder and she all but sinks to the floor. She asks about the family, and he tells her, and as she reluctantly leads her friend toward the door, she says, "This is the greatest moment of my life."

For several minutes after their departure the administrative office is abubble with the visitors' excitement. "See, it just takes a minute," Dolores comments with satisfaction, "and tomorrow everybody in Livermore Falls will hear about this." Leslie adds, "And everywhere else."

The buzzer summons Muskie to the Senate floor. There will be several votes during the rest of the afternoon on amendments, motions to table, possible motions to limit debate on the New Hampshire business, which is starting to anger the Senate. Many times the Senate has been paralyzed by a single Senator, but this is the first time within memory that it's been bound hand and foot, the national business brought to a halt, by a single empty chair, the non-elected, non-existent junior Senator from New Hampshire. Each side is accusing the other of filibustering. Each side, with innocent astonishment, denies the charge, declaring it's ready to end the debate this moment—or just as soon as the Senate accepts *its* position, which, after all, is where justice resides. Senator Robert Byrd, the Majority Whip, has passed word that the Senate will stay in session until six-thirty tonight. He has also started and is keeping afloat a rumor, but will not confirm it, that the Senate will convene on Friday and Saturday, extremely unusual for the hot months, to force this New Hampshire business to conclusion. Gayle Cory is distraught over that rumor. Muskie is scheduled to fly out of National Airport at 4:50 P.M. on Friday for Maine. On Saturday he is to address the American Legion state convention, an obligation not to be missed in an election year.

Dolores' chief worry—now—is that the Senator's 3 P.M. appointment is waiting in the reception room. Well, not exactly an appointment, and that's the problem. He is not on the daily typed schedule, but at the urging of Jim Case, the projects aide, Dolores, seeing that the afternoon's program seemed relatively clear, told the man to come in. He is a vice-president of the Maremont Corporation. I assume at first that the visit has to do with the Clean Air Act, since Maremont is a manufacturer of auto mufflers. But no. It turns out that the company has diversified into gun parts. Specifically, it has a plant in Maine that makes parts for the M-16 automatic rifle, which Secretary of Defense James Schlesinger said last week would hereafter be purchased from Belgium, apparently a trade-off for a Belgian choice of American aircraft over European competition. Maine doesn't give much of a damn where Belgium buys her planes, but Maine has several hundred jobs at stake at Maremont, and they by God want that gun contract renewed.

Dolores explains to the Maremont visitor about the sudden vote, about the New Hampshire thing, about the possibility of several votes, about that's the way the Senate is some days, and she's sure the Senator will be back soon. Two hours later the reassurances are growing limp. Finally she calls the cloakroom, asks for Spiros Droggitis, a young Senate doorkeeper who is a Muskie patronage appointee. The Senator, Spiros reports, is in the President's Room, a reception lounge just outside the chamber, being interviewed by several reporters. Eventually Muskie calls back, keeps saying "Who? Who?" over Dolores' reminder that a few days ago he'd approved seeing the man, and finally Muskie acquiesces. "Okay, send him over." Dolores summons Jim Case, instructing him to take the case pleader to S-199.[1] She calls after him in a full-voice whisper, "I don't know when the Senator'll get there. Pour the guy a sherry or mix him a drink. He'll like that."

During the welcome lull, Maynard Toll suggests that this is a good time—Lord knows when there'll be another—to have a talk we've wanted but have delayed. We take over the comfortable couch in the Senator's quiet office. Maynard is thirty-three, scholarly and

[1] Muskie's hideaway in the Capitol. Actually, I have changed the room number. To reveal the correct number would be an unforgivable breach of Muskie's trust, indeed of Senate tradition. Hideaway numbers are not published anywhere. The phone extension number is so secret that Dolores Stover will not permit it to be written down anywhere in the Senator's office. If an aide ought to know it, he or she memorizes it. The fact is that even Senators do not necessarily know which other Senators have hideaways and where they are. When a Senator "comes of age," the sergeant at arms, on behalf of the Rules Committee, slips him a key.

witty, son of a prestigious California lawyer, schooled in international relations. He started as a legislative assistant assigned to Muskie's work on the Foreign Relations Committee; Muskie later vacated his seat upon formation of the Budget Committee.

A CONVERSATION WITH MAYNARD TOLL

What is the administrative assistant's main reason for being?

—The administrative assistant wears many hats, but the key job is management of the Senator's time. He's the guy responsible for trying to put some rhyme and reason into the Senator's schedule in a way that maximizes the Senator's effectiveness but doesn't drive him to distraction. In some offices this work is delegated to the personal secretary. A few offices have a position of appointments secretary.

—Now, here. Here is his calendar from June 8 to July 5. It doesn't look very crowded, just these few out-of-town commitments, a few evening social commitments which are rarely social in a strict sense, and a few important office appointments that are made well ahead. Nothing is scheduled in the morning except committee work. In the afternoons the advance appointments are sparse, well separated, so we can juggle to allow plenty of room for floor votes, and meetings and briefings with his committee staff people. The way I do that is I get the staff people down here—Doug Bennet and John McEvoy from Budget, Leon Billings from Public Works, and Al From from Government Operations, that's the Intergovernmental Relations Subcommittee, or IGR, and we talk about what they see coming up that the Senator has to do. For example, the Budget Committee must complete its work—bring its annual budget resolution to the floor—in May, and a sort of midyear review of the budget in September. That's in the law. So we know that May and September are going to be busy. We know that Leon has to try to get this clean air thing out of the way before the August recess, so we hold a good number of mornings through the summer for that.

—My function is not to be taking requests on the phone for appointments. Press requests will go to Bob Rose, the press secretary. Out-of-town events to Gayle Cory. In-town events, including committee notices and that sort of thing, to Dolores. But I'm the person who has to say yes or no to the actual commitment on these things. I have to be the last gatekeeper. Some he has to personally approve himself. Press appointments, for example. Bob screens them, but the Senator wants to approve them. Some others, I have to make a judgment as to whether to approve them on my own. If I think he's going to have some question—"Why is this thing on my goddam schedule today?"—I may take the precaution of getting his approval. He still reserves the right to complain when the time comes, "Yes, I agreed to see him, but why did you have to put him in the middle of such and such?"

—The real problem is that you're confronted with a lot of reasonable requests, good things to do, but you have to tell people no. For example, I had a request the other day from a former governor of Arizona, a friend of the Senator's. He wanted the Senator to speak for just a few minutes right across the street in the Dirksen Building. It seems the United Way is training a bunch of volunteers in urban services or something, and they'd all be here. It's to be one-thirty in the afternoon, not too bad a time, a nice thing to do, a good group, didn't cost anything, and the speech was to be on revenue sharing, and the Senator's an expert on revenue sharing. But I said no—automatically. I had to ask myself, What benefit is there in it? What good does it do Ed Muskie? Sure, the organization is good, but there are a lot of good organizations. I used as an excuse the Clean Air Act, that the markups are going to be intensive right about then. Well, they put a lot of heat on me. People called up, and Governor Goddard told me he wanted the Senator personally to know of his request. Well, I thought, this guy is a friend, so in good faith I ran it by the Senator. The Senator said he didn't want to say no to a friend, but he didn't say yes either, so I walked out and called back Mr. Goddard and said, "No, I'm sorry, we just can't do it, I hope you understand." The next thing I know, there's a letter from Mo Udall saying that Goddard got in touch with him, and how important this meeting is. Well, that did it. The Senator said, "If Mo really wants me to do it, I'll do it." So I had to go back to these guys and blow my credibility, saying, yes, now it's possible, even though I'd already given them an overwhelming case against it.

—Having done that, there are two ways to get a plus out of it. I can say that the Congressman made a personal appeal, which is nice for Udall, and someday we may ask him to do something nice for us. Otherwise, I can say the Senator thought this over and, although it's going to be terribly difficult, et cetera—you know, like we're making a really big sacrifice, which makes the Senator look good.

—You wait. If you're here on the day this thing happens, he'll say, "Why the hell am I doing this goddamned thing?" I should say, incidentally, that I think I'm very good at this business, but the Senator thinks I'm just miserable. He thinks that all the people who have anything to do with his scheduling are just totally out of their minds.

Then in your appointments function you have a constant adversary relationship with Muskie.

—I once described it to the Senator: "Look, Senator, you have an unavoidable adversary relationship with your staff." It really, well, it hurt his feelings. He said, "I don't see why I need to have an adversary relationship with my staff." I tried to explain it, but he said, "I've got an overactivated staff." Well, of course. Because everyone thinks his own thing is most important. Leon thinks his environmental stuff is most important. Al From thinks revenue sharing is most important. And the Budget Committee thinks the Budget Committee is most important. And Muskie thinks these guys are all overactivated. He's got a lot of funny images he uses: "I feel like I'm a monkey at the end of a stick." "I'm just a body that you guys just shove from this appointment to that appointment."

—This is one of the more frustrating—possibly *the* most frustrating aspect of being a Senator. In order to be effective you have to give yourself up to your staff. He can't do everything himself. The Senator's unhappy because he doesn't have enough time for reflection. Well, there are a lot of Senators around here who are reflective-type Senators, but you never hear about them. They might have an impact in at most one particular area. Maybe a case might be made that that's how you ought to organize the job: take one committee assignment and really do that in depth, not go crazy being run around from committee to committee.

—Really, if we're to maximize this guy's impact, especially now that we have to use all free time, all weekend time, all recess time for Maine campaigning, it's true, he doesn't have time to think. He really has to be a body shoved around from event to event. But he's good. He *does* have time to think. He doesn't *think* he has time to think. After all, thinking is cumulative. Over the course of these markups on the Clean Air Act, which he's been doing for twelve years, he's become one of the country's experts on this whole business. He sits two hours in a morning at a hearing or a markup. That's thinking time. He's absorbing a lot of stuff.

(*Toll's face becomes absorbed. Instead of jogging him with another question, I let him form the observation he's obviously forming.*)

—He's a very private person. For a politician, he's not an instinctive backslapper. He is reflective. He's private. If you want to write about him personally, you might look back into his childhood. There are some aspects of it—he grew up extremely shy, as I'm learning a lot of politicians do. The profession is sort of a denial of your instincts. And frankly, he gets resentful that his freedom is taken away from him by this job. And it is. I've concluded that I would not want his job because I would not want to be managed. I would have the same resentments he has. And yet, in a reflective moment, he'll admit—grudgingly—that he knows it's in the nature of the job, and that he appreciates the staff work that's done for him. It seems to make him feel better to complain all the time. You're going to hear a lot of complaining. There have been times when I've had to say to him, "Yell at me in private, but don't complain to me in front of other people. It makes you look churlish and ungrateful."

—He's had a couple of incidents in Maine recently, that problem of being churlish, one of which I witnessed. It was up in Presque Isle, way up in Aroostook County where there are a bunch of potato farms. We'd called the meeting so a group of people could let him know what was on their minds and so he could talk about economic problems as seen in Washington. It was a good group. He bedazzles these people. But every once in a while you get someone who's very hostile. Most of the time he handles it very well, but sometimes that kind of person gets under his skin. This particular person asked some political question and pressed for a yes-or-no answer. And the Senator didn't want to give a yes-or-no answer. It was a complex issue and he wanted to answer in his own way, but this guy just interrupted and shouted, "Look, don't give me all that, just tell me yes or no!" Finally the Senator blew—really angry—and he just lost everyone. A few special friends said, "I'm glad you told that guy off." But it frosted almost everyone else. I heard someone say, "A United States Senator, one of the great men of the country, shouldn't get pulled down to the level of that asshole and lose his temper."

—In Maine it's all right to cut someone down by being somewhat acid, a little dry. But the Senator's got a volatile quality to him. For one thing, he can talk very loud, and one of his great attributes in an argument is that his voice gets loud and you feel sort of overwhelmed. Here's this great big guy and his voice sounds like God speaking to Moses, and he uses it. He uses it with staff. You'll see him using it when a staff guy is trying to get him to do something, and the staff guy won't back down with the Senator's first objection. The Senator's voice will get louder and louder and louder, and you'll wonder, Why does the staff guy persist, it's obvious the Senator isn't going to accept this thing? But the Senator is testing. He's testing which will stand up better, the suggestion or his objection to it. If the staffer doesn't cave in, the Senator might say, "Okay, all right, I'll do it." Then afterward you'll say to him, "You shouldn't have blown your temper at that guy." And he'll look ever so surprised and say, "I didn't blow my temper."

—A lot of people feel intimidated by the Senator, and it's only people who have been around him for a while who learn to stand up under that. You know, in the small towns of Maine, if he blows up even slightly, it's the biggest thing that ever happened there and word gets passed around. He hates to give anything away in an argument. In a way, it's kind of a nice trait. He's not giving saccharine answers just to play politics. Last time I went to Maine with him he said, "You know, I never used to have a reputation for a temper. But you guys program me around, it's no wonder I get temperamental."

How does his day begin?

—He usually gets in between nine-fifteen and nine-thirty. He's an early riser and has worked at home, both the night before and early in the morning. We send a lot of stuff home with him. That's another of his constant complaints: "You guys just fill me up with paper." But the thing is he'll read it. He's very good. Every night, a briefing book on the issue of his hearing or markup the next morning. Last Friday for his weekend reading we gave him one—a very good one prepared by Rick—on the information then available on the Durkin-Wyman controversy over the New Hampshire election, how the debate was going to be structured, who was taking what position and on what ground, sort of a basic intelligence report on the issues. When he comes in, he likes to be left alone. Often, driving in, he'll have five or six ideas, things he wants to get done, quick phone calls, a letter to dictate. He doesn't want staff people pouring in and hitting him the minute he walks in. You get him a cup of coffee. Maybe by about nine-fifty he'll be ready for a staff person, but that's usually for a last-minute briefing on the meeting he's going to. Increasingly we don't need that because of the paper he's read overnight or he's been briefed the afternoon before. I don't schedule him for office meetings between twelve-thirty and two. That gives him options. He can have lunch with somebody at the Capitol hideaway, or sometimes just eat in the Senators' dining room, especially if he's over there for votes. The third alternative is we'll tell him what they're serving down in the cafeteria and one of the girls will run down and bring it up on a tray and he'll eat alone here. He prefers to have lunch with people, but part of the problem—you ought to look into the financial burdens of being a Senator—is that he winds up paying for most of those lunches personally and that can get to be very expensive. He doesn't have any independent wealth. He's got kids in college, homes both in Maine and Washington, and all the rest. So if a staff guy's having lunch with him—well, I've instructed all staff people, "Whether he offers or not, you pay for your own lunch." There's no question it might be desirable to schedule a lunch every day with a different person, but it's no exaggeration to say it would wind up being an unbearable expense for him. Some mornings, though, he'll suddenly say, "Call up Senator Stevenson" or "Call up Senator Hart" —Adlai Stevenson and Phil Hart are his two closest friends in the Senate—"and see if he's available for lunch." But that's rare.

It's now past four o'clock and Dolores is in her accustomed late afternoon state of suppressed panic. Majority Whip Byrd is, as threatened, holding the Senate in session until six-thirty, and Pat Caddell will arrive within the hour from Boston. What will she do with him?

It is the story of Dolores' life that the more painstakingly and elaborately she arranges something the more likely its collapse due to the uncontrollable. She's put tender care into tonight's Muskie-Caddell dinner. It won't be in the office, the hideaway, or on Muskie's Bethesda patio after all, but at Muskie's favorite Chinese restaurant, the Moon Palace, on Wisconsin Avenue out beyond Massachusetts. Since it's so unlike Muskie to participate in a business-talk dinner, Dolores, sensing the importance of this one to him, has wanted to make it especially relaxed and pleasant. She has invited Muskie's Bethesda neighbors and favorite relaxers, John Charles Daly, the former newscaster and "What's My Line?" host, and his wife Virginia, daughter of late Chief Justice Earl Warren. When Muskie and Caddell appear ready to talk business—the findings of that super-secret Maine poll—Charlie will harumph and the Dalys will suddenly develop an acute case of a commitment elsewhere. All that beautiful planning, and now . . .

This new crisis reminds me of today's old one. I ask Dolores how the issue of the fund-raising letters was resolved.

"Oh, he signed them," she replies blithely. "Every one. Not a whimper."

Cool and lovable Rick Bayard shuffles in with news that may shatter Dolores' already fragile hold on events. Rick, in brown Brooks Brothers pants that have never been pressed and once black cordovan shoes scuffed to gray, transmits news, good or bad, with the detachment and security of a DuPont, which, by blood connection, he is.

"Just had a call," he tells Dolores, "from Caddell's secretary. He may have missed his plane."

Dolores' eyes enlarge in disbelief. "*May* have missed?"

"Well, yes." Rick's thermostat is impossible to dislodge from low. "She said that Pat left a little late and gave her instructions to make a backup reservation. She doesn't see how he could have made it, but she hasn't heard from him yet either."

Dolores' stare remains frozen as she nods and Rick ambles out. Suddenly her face reshapes with hope. "That means the Senator will have time to look at the poll before Pat gets here."

Rick soon returns. Caddell *has* missed it and the backup arrives at National Airport at ten minutes to seven.

"He'll be here at seven-thirty," Dolores calculates. "Just right. I'll call the Dalys."

After the Chinese waiters remove the dishes, after Charlie's harumph, and after the Dalys' departure, Muskie and Caddell, swarthy, slightly overfed and rumpled, turn to the Senator's prospects for re-election in 1976. For the first time since his surprise election twenty-one years ago as a Democratic governor in unshakably Republican Maine Muskie has some serious obstacles to worry about.

First of all, in Maine, having nothing to worry about is always something to worry about. Maine's Republican Party, virtually unchallenged since the Civil War, certainly had nothing to worry about in 1954 when Muskie, a minority state legislator and not very prosperous lawyer from Waterville, talked about "reviving" the Democratic Party by selecting a candidate who would be willing to go through the motions of campaigning. When they couldn't find such a volunteer for slaughter, Muskie offered his own neck. Muskie conducted a rigorous and penniless crusade to unearth and persuade potential friends in remote towns that literally had never seen the looks or likes of a major Democratic office seeker, and the people of Maine, turned off by Republican carelessness and complacency, produced an ornery surprise. Two years later Muskie was re-elected governor with a solid fifty-nine per cent vote, and in 1958 he beat an incumbent Republican Senator who had nothing to worry about by a 61–39 landslide.

Senator Margaret Chase Smith, a Republican securely in her seat since 1948, had nothing to worry about in 1972. She rarely traveled to Maine and found it unnecessary to maintain an office in the state. Her complacency appeared fully justified when a Republican businessman, Robert Monks, challenged her in a primary, spent $200,000 against Mrs. Smith's refusal to spend a penny on advertising, yet all that money failed him. She paid scant attention to a Democratic challenge by Congressman William Hathaway from Maine's Second District (the larger, northern district of the state's two), who visited every one of the state's 495 cities, towns, and plantations. It was like the crashing of a great pine when Margaret Chase Smith went down.

And 1974 was the year that Democrats had nothing to worry about. In that year of the Nixon resignation, of revulsion against Watergate and a Democratic landslide, both of Maine's House seats went to Republicans. The Democrats' candidate for governor, Muskie's great fan and good friend George Mitchell, felt he had nothing to worry about from his Republican opponent—and he didn't. Mitchell ran well ahead of James Erwin, but both were beaten by an upstart independent, efficiency-minded businessman James Longley.

So Muskie's general obstacle for 1976 is, as Muskie well knows, that voters of Maine can be taken least for granted when they're taken most for granted. Muskie's vulnerability is that in Maine he appears—on the surface—to have become invincible.

His more specific obstacle is a thirty-five-year-old, blue-eyed, earnest, glamorous Congressman from Bangor—Hathaway's successor from the Second District—named William S. Cohen, who has not yet announced his candidacy for the Senate as a Republican but is "assessing" his prospects with disquieting fervor. Everywhere you look, there's Cohen—especially around the First District where voters don't yet know him. Or do they?

The trouble is, they *do* know Billy Cohen. He became a major state hero while becoming a minor national one. As a member of the House Judiciary Committee, this handsome freshman, struck by the lightning of the Nixon impeachment proceedings, was brilliantly illumined in a nationally televised portrait of virtue. Right before the camera Cohen grappled with his conscience, pure blue eyes pleading genuine stress, as he bolted loose from his party, compelled to vote for impeachment, even knowing, he said, that many of his constituents would not forgive him and that this might end his political career. With Nixon's resignation and public disgrace, Cohen's courageous position soon emerged, even among Republicans, as one better to have taken too early than too late.

Caddell has sent ahead two red-covered copies of the 146-page poll report, which Charlie immediately locked in a safe. No staff member other than Maynard and himself was to see it. Now Muskie and Charlie open the copies. Caddell has brought his own.

What a newspaper reporter would like to get his hands on is a trio of numbers that appears on page 8. It asserts that if the election were held today, Muskie versus Cohen, the results would be:

Muskie	48%
Cohen	40%
Undecided	12%

A perturbing departure from the 67 per cent and 62 per cent with which Muskie swept the state in 1964 and 1970, respectively. If somehow Cohen can be tantalized, coerced, or otherwise persuaded out of the race, how much prettier the picture becomes. Facing Bob

Monks, whose 1972 primary challenge scarcely chinked Margaret Chase Smith, Muskie would roll up 68 per cent to Monks's 16 per cent, with 16 per cent undecided. Head to head against Governor Longley, Muskie would roll up 60 per cent to Longley's 30 per cent, only 10 per cent undecided. In a three-way race involving Cohen and Longley, however, Muskie would be most threatened: Muskie 42 per cent, Cohen 37 per cent, Longley 16 per cent, undecided 6 per cent.

Watching the Senator, his "political man," and his pollster thumb and analyze their way through the scores of pages and dizzying statistics is to experience the difference between politics as a spectator entertainment and as a profession. They scarcely spend a moment on the foregoing summary of who's ahead and who's behind. Those figures are for the fans and reporters. They do little to inform the experienced coach of what to *do,* where the other team's weaknesses are, which plays will exploit those weaknesses, which plays to avoid; in short, how to turn peril into victory.

To the state-of-Mainer whose doorbell has been rung by one of Pat Caddell's pollsters, the questionnaire was simple enough, though perhaps it seemed a little lengthy: If the Senate race pits Muskie against Cohen, for whom will you vote? If Muskie-Cohen-Longley, for whom? The pollster shows a card marked something like this:

Cohen   1 2 3 4 5 6 7   Muskie

If "1" represents feeling strongly for Cohen and "7" represents feeling strongly for Muskie, what number would you circle to position your own feeling? (A subjective, vague question. But when the poll is computerized, answers to this question become the critical ingredient to designing the campaign.)

More questions. What do you like most about Ed Muskie? ("He's honest," "He's for Maine," "He's experienced," "He's for the poor," "He's for the two-hundred-mile fishing limit.") What do you dislike most about Ed Muskie? What is Muskie's best accomplishment as Senator? What's been his biggest mistake? How old do you think Ed Muskie is? And more questions and still more, virtually none about Muskie's actions or votes on specific issues, virtually all on how people perceive him, *feel* about him. It's almost as though people were asked to plumb their emotional reactions to a piece of art, the design of a new model car, or a movie star.

Then a parallel, almost identical questionnaire about William Cohen.

Of course, every polled voter is also recorded by party affiliation, age, income, sex, religion, length of residence in Maine, education, ethnic group, occupation, voting district, whether or not the family breadwinner is a union member, and how he or she voted in 1972 and 1974.

Pages and pages of statistical matches and cross-matches now examined by Muskie and Charlie Micoleau boil down to this:

> In a head-to-head match, Muskie does best with voters under 35, low-income voters, Catholics, French, Germans and Italians, and less-educated voters. On the other hand, Cohen's best groups are voters aged 46–65, upper-income voters, Protestants, English, the better-educated, and residents of the Second Congressional District. The highest number of undecideds are voters aged 18–25 and residents of central Maine.
>
> . . . Muskie voters overwhelmingly give experience and job performance as their major reason [for liking him], while Cohen voters [like their man for his] youth and honesty.
>
> . . . Cohen's job performance was not mentioned often in the list of likes; there is also a bit of uncertainty about how much Cohen is actually doing. . . . In summary, Cohen is an exceptionally popular candidate and has almost no negative image. Voters perceive him as honest, sincere, and energetic; they are more familiar with his personality than specific accomplishments.

The poll report next draws direct comparisons between Muskie and Cohen. Voters have been read a list of words and phrases, then asked whether each applies more to Muskie or more to Cohen: words and phrases like "honest," "vigorous," "too ambitious," "decisive," "part of the establishment." Caddell concludes from their answers:

"Muskie wins most of the comparisons—*both good and bad*—and wins most decisively on 'qualified,' 'knowledgeable,' 'best deals with complex national problems,' and 'part of the establishment.' *Cohen wins 'vigorous' by a large margin.*" (Italics in this and subsequent Caddell quotes are mine.)

Now comes that all-important rating of Cohen and Muskie on a scale of 1 to 7. The results come out like this:

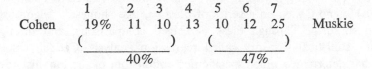

	1	2	3	4	5	6	7	
Cohen	19%	11	10	13	10	12	25	Muskie

40% 47%

Muskie's hard-core support ("7") outnumbers Cohen's ("1"), 25 per cent to 19 per cent. When you add those who only lean toward Muskie, they outpoll Cohen's lovers and leaners 47 per cent to 40 per cent. But that is not what's important. Caddell gives that finding the back of his hand:

"We will spend much time in this report analyzing the attitudes of the *soft* Cohen supporters ("3's"), undecideds ("4's"), and *soft* Muskie supporters ("5's") on this scale. Those are people *whose votes are most movable* and it will be crucial for the Muskie campaign to *focus on this third* of the electorate."

The nasty, harsh, unmentionable truth that every experienced political pro understands is that his most ardent and reliable supporters —and his opponent's most ardent supporters—can be virtually ignored in a campaign. Of course he throws them a gesture of affection now and then—a blood-warming slogan, some vigorous restatement of the issues that originally bound them to him. But the people who count in an election are those whom the superloyalist regards as a kind of trash: the undecided, the uncaring, the uninformed, and perhaps the most despised yet most desirable of all, the unfaithful. Some candidates don't fully understand this. They play constantly to their own flock, recycling old love. They're called losers.

How does a winner reach out for the "soft" voter? In the middle ages of politics—say, a decade ago, before the computer bounced in, led on a leash by bright young Harvard-type analysts like Caddell—a candidate's adviser would say, "Talk about prosperity," "Hit the peace issue," "Hit the old reliable, a job for everyone, with the government as employer of last resort."

Today, with television, media specialists, image magicians, high-cost campaigning, and the miracles of higher mathematics, politics has gone beyond that. The adviser now advises as to what change of image will produce exactly what percentage of change in votes, and thus which change will best produce the most ballots for the buck.

Caddell reminds Muskie and Charlie that voters have compared Muskie and Cohen on a series of phrases, like "honest," "vigorous," and so forth. Through these perceived comparisons, and through some statistical wizardry called regression analysis, Caddell asserts he has determined which specific perceptions out of the long list have the highest impact on the voters' choice between Muskie and Cohen. Furthermore, he has estimated *how much the vote between Muskie and Cohen will change by changing each perception a single percentage point.*

The six perceptions most strongly associated with whether a person intends to vote for Muskie or for Cohen involve the words or phrases "honest," "vigorous," "close to me personally on the issues," "too partisan" (a negative perception, associated with opposition to the candidate), "he understands my problems," and "he best deals with complex national problems." Of these, the three highest-impact distinctions, mathematically speaking, are on "vigorous" (which Cohen wins), "partisan" (which, being a negative, Muskie loses), and "complex national problems" (Muskie wins). Out of three high-impact comparisons, Muskie loses two. That means big trouble.

No, Caddell doesn't see it that way at all. After pages of mathematical calisthenics, he concludes:

> Thus the perception of Muskie's dealing with complex national problems contributes almost half his total lead. The perception on "partisan" and "vigorous" together *detract* between 4 per cent and 5 per cent from Muskie's potential lead. In other words, if Muskie could erase the distinctions made on "vigorous" and "partisan," he would lead by 12 per cent instead of 8 per cent. . . . It is clear that Muskie gains, on an average, twice as much by convincing a voter he is better on the issues than by convincing him that he, Muskie, is vigorous. However, the voters presently see a bigger gap on vigorous.
>
> These results . . . present the Muskie campaign with a choice. The campaign can try to change perceptions which currently hurt Muskie; they can try to open new distinctions that help him. . . . The campaign may wish to try to change

Muskie's issues with one group [of voters] and his vigor with another.

Caddell's report summarizes with these observations:

> Senator Muskie is personally popular—as well liked or better liked than most incumbent Senators. . . . On the whole he has few negatives. . . . Cohen is extremely popular. . . . He is seen as just a little too ambitious and perhaps lacking in substance. . . . A race between Muskie and Congressman Cohen would be a close one. While Muskie leads, victory would not be assured.
>
> . . . A few disturbing trends: First of all, Muskie's support among younger people . . . not students or youth, but young families . . . was very "soft." . . . They are somewhat more concerned than the rest of Maine about economic problems, particularly unemployment.
>
> A second area that disturbs us are the so-called "growth" areas . . . a set of towns in the southwestern part of the state which have experienced a rapid influx of population in the last decade. . . . These areas in Maine seem inclined toward Cohen. . . . [They are] more concerned about and more in favor of environmental controls, land-use planning and similar measures. . . . The Muskie campaign will have to take special steps in these areas to convince them that Muskie, not Cohen, represents them best.
>
> Maine voters, like those everywhere, are concerned about the economy. They want more jobs; they also fear inflation. Furthermore, they are afraid of the federal deficit. They just got done electing Jim Longley to cut the budget. *Muskie's own soft voters are more inclined to be afraid of deficit spending than other groups of voters.*
>
> . . . The best Republican ploy against Muskie would be to use his position [as chairman of the Budget Committee] to make him responsible for the deficit, and thus for whatever inflation is going on in 1976. . . . We therefore think that Muskie ought to take some steps to differentiate himself from the other Democrats, and thus from the deficit. This might involve a call to eliminate some program, or area of spending. It might be as simple as arguing that problems can't all be solved by throwing money at them. In any event, we strongly suggest that Muskie

adopt a somewhat conservative fiscal tone when talking to
Maine.

A large number of simple "image" things might be done as
well. Obviously, stress should be laid on Muskie's vigor and energy. Perhaps a "day in the life" piece would show Muskie
working sixteen hours a day, or whatever. Other Muskie efforts
with the press might try to subtly reinforce this idea.

Out of this longest of long days, the dominant theme of life in and
around the United States Senate unmistakably asserts itself: the constant changing of subjects. A day has taken Muskie through pollution control to an interview on the education of committee members,
to the constitutional issues of the New Hampshire election dispute, to
an impromptu President's Room news interview on his presidential
prospects, to snatching a military contract away from Belgium and
restoring it to Maine, to the mood of the voters in Maine and
whether Ed Muskie gets his contract renewed for the next six years.
And he's never permitted to say, "I don't give a damn" or "How the
hell would I know?" or "Go away, you bother me"—or "I'm
bushed."

Does he yearn for that six-year renewal? No question about it.

Does he enjoy being here? I don't have the slightest idea.

Thursday morning, June 19

This morning the subject changes again.

Al From, the staff chief of the Intergovernmental Relations Subcommittee, waiting for Muskie to emerge from his office, tells me the
morning may be interesting. At nine fifty-five Muskie appears and we
leave for a markup. Muskie psychs up for these morning meetings
like an actor for a role. In the theater, that last-minute delicate rear-

rangement of himself into the character he wants to be, an actor calls an "adjustment." I don't know what Muskie calls it, or if he calls it anything, but he does not stroll into a meeting casually. He goes in with a mental set, a goal in mind, options if that goal eludes him, and a headful of facts and persuasive phrases.

Plunging through the basement corridors and riding up to that ever so familiar fourth floor of the other Senate building, to the chambers of Public Works, he's just a shade grimmer than usual. Al, every fourth step or so, has to double-skip to keep up. Muskie, about six feet four, staffs himself with short men. Maynard Toll, someone observed to me the other day, is his first administrative assistant of average height or more. Of all of Muskie's short men, Al From is shortest, about five feet four, owing mostly to a compressed, thick neck over a chunky, compact body. His round face, hinting a premature double chin, is often absorbed in something beyond the person he's talking to. And you soon find out what: Al is always calculating three steps beyond what the other fellow thinks is the subject at hand.

The reason Muskie doesn't stroll into meetings casually is simply that he rarely goes to a committee meeting of which he is not chairman. This morning's is one of those rare exceptions. Furthermore, it's the wrong committee, in the strict parliamentary sense, for the bill he is determined to put over. Worse still, he suspects he's about to suffer a defeat. But that defeat, Al has convinced him, may be the shortest route to a victory. Muskie apparently agrees—he's going along—but is nervous about it.

What begins this morning has all the makings of a marvelous side show in the black art, the now-you-see-it-now-you-don't, of parliamentary maneuver. That potential fascination is concealed in a bill known as S. 1359, the Intergovernmental Countercyclical Assistance Act. I first heard of this bill on May 7, at a hearing where I whiled away a couple of morning hours waiting for my scheduled first lunch with Senator Muskie. Governor Hugh Carey of New York was thumping away in support of the bill before the Intergovernmental Relations Subcommittee. But nobody from the subcommittee was interested enough to be there—except the bill's sponsor, Chairman Muskie.

As the bill began to shine through its murky and forbidding title, I found it clear, relatively simple, novel, and grabby, with two central ideas, a major and a minor. It's a bill to help combat economic recession, and its major idea corrects what has been wrong with most anti-recession programs. The bill would provide economic stimulation (1) quickly, before human suffering becomes too widespread and the tide is too strong to reverse readily; (2) only where the stimulation is needed most; and, (3) perhaps most important, with a built-in, automatic device for shutting itself off as soon as the urgent need has been satisfied. The latter feature is a response to longstanding justified criticism by conservatives of liberal social programs.

More specifically: when national unemployment rises to six per cent or more and stays there for three consecutive months, automatically two billion dollars in federal funds would become available to needy state and local governments. For every additional percentage point of unemployment that lasts three consecutive months, an additional billion would become available. Thus, at seven per cent unemployment, three billion; at eight per cent, four billion. Unlike most federal aid programs that spread funds widely to insure that every congressional district gets its bit in return for its vote, this bill would give aid only to states and municipalities with their own local six per cent unemployment rate. So in the current recession the city of Dallas, for example, which has maintained a continuing healthy job picture, would not get a dime. And the *pièce de résistance* of the bill is that when the national unemployment rate subsides below six per cent the whole machine shuts down.

That's the major idea. The minor one is that its target is relatively narrow, making the bill somewhat experimental. Instead of trying to be a grand-scale, put-America-back-to-work operation, the bill simply tries to prevent city and state governments from having to throw their own employees—policemen, firemen, garbagemen, teachers—out of work. When recession hits, the impact on governments is swift and cruel. Tax collections sink almost overnight and cities, sometimes states, can't meet payrolls without borrowing at high rates of interest, thus cramming their debt into the future. Quick assistance to these local governments kills several birds with one stone. It preserves jobs. It maintains *some* normal flow of purchasing power into the economy. It maintains the delivery of vital local services of protection, sanitation, education. And aside from all that, this Muskie bill would provide a practical test of the novel "trigger" mechanism

—the automatic turn-on and shut-off at the six per cent unemployment signal. If it proved effective in the limited realm of protecting local payrolls, it might also work as a broader anti-recession trigger.

Simple, understandable. No new bureaucracy; no social services to dispense by professionals newly hired, who later become impossible to get rid of; just a computer print-out and the mailing of federal checks to cities and states to replace taxes that are temporarily uncollectable and to support existing payrolls. Unlike public works projects as recession medicine, this would not require choosing of sites, selection of construction projects, drawing up of architectural and engineering plans which have plagued recessions of the past; with public works, by the time the medicine is ready, the patient often is either cured or so much sicker, the medicine won't help. And there's that other curse of public works: when we find ourselves lifted out of recession, the countryside is dotted with half-built dams, half-built roads, half-built hospitals. So the expense goes on to build the other halves, like taking penicillin after the disease is cured because the nature of the medicine requires finishing the dose to the bitter end.

All is simple and clear about this morning's markup, except one thing: if I first heard testimony on this bill before the Government Operations Committee, why are we huffing and puffing our way to the Public Works hearing rooms? Why is Al From of the Intergovernmental Relations Subcommittee (of Government Ops) "staffing" Muskie for this morning's meeting of the Economic Development Subcommittee (of Public Works)? The pegs seem to be in the wrong holes.

Enter the hocus-pocus.

While Muskie has been concentrating on clean air, Al From peered down the legislative tunnel to be traveled by the countercyclical bill. What he saw was not light but a stone wall. In the Government Operations Committee he anticipated two strong supporters of the bill and no do-or-die opponents. Muskie's supporters would be John Glenn of Ohio, the Democrat and pioneer astronaut, the most junior member of the committee, and, far more significantly, Bill Brock, the Tennessee Republican, the committee's most thoughtful, articulate, and respected conservative. The bill would make it through the committee. Following that, with two prestigious yet contrasting figures such as Muskie and Brock piloting it, the bill should successfully navigate the full Senate.

But Senate passage alone doth not a statute make.

Al also peered across Capitol Park and did not like what he saw. In fact, what he saw was nothing. When the bill, passed by the Senate, is sent across to the Other Body, as each chamber haughtily calls its counterpart, it will surely be referred by the parliamentarian to the House Government Operations Committee, and thence to *its* Intergovernmental Relations Subcommittee. Not all committees have such direct parallels in the Other Body, but since this one does, the journey of the bill is entirely predictable. Too predictable.

The chairman of the House IGR Subcommittee is ten-term Representative L. H. Fountain of Tarboro, North Carolina, a summertime devotee of white linen suits, who is regarded in the House as a one-issue man. Granted, an important issue. He has made himself the nemesis of the Food and Drug Administration, dedicating his career to crusading against that agency's alleged complacency in licensing potentially dangerous drugs for the market place. His subcommittee is otherwise virtually inactive. Newfangled schemes for federal-state and federal-city relations, as exemplified by the countercyclical bill, are simply not Fountain's dish. The full Government Operations Committee is chaired by Jack Brooks of Texas, who represents the oil-rich and high-employment cities of Galveston, Texas City, Beaumont, and Port Arthur, which would not benefit from the bill's needy-only formula.

How is a thirty-two-year-old staff operative of a Senate committee to cope with such a blockage in our bicameral system of creating national law? A smart, experienced staffer doesn't bother his Senator with such trivia. He thinks, confers with other staff employees who in turn do not bother their Senators, thinks some more, then hatches a plot. In this instance, From arranged a meeting with Dick Wegman, staff director of the Senate Government Operations Committee (Chairman Ribicoff's man) and Barry Meyer, chief counsel of the Public Works Committee (Chairman Randolph's man), and Meyer's assistant counsel, Phil Cummings. Meyer has any number of reasons to have an appetite for the countercyclical bill. Recession is almost a permanent way of life in Jennings Randolph's West Virginia. Secondly, although a considerable stretch of the imagination is required to regard this countercyclical bill as public works—it calls for no dams, no bridges, no construction of anything—committee chairmen dearly love to stretch their imaginations in the cause of expanding their influence. If this year's countercyclical assistance bill can somehow be engineered through the Public Works Committee, where it does not properly belong, perhaps in future years its successor bills may *learn* to belong there. This year's experimental two billion may one day ripen into—who knows?—ten billion. It is the nature of chairmen to sponsor the spending of funds or to oppose the spending of funds, but not to be indifferent about expanding the reaches of their influence.

Al From's scheme was to reroute the countercyclical bill around his own Government Operations Committee and have it ride piggyback—as an amendment—on a multibillion-dollar public works bill, also inspired by the recession. That would route it through the Public Works Committee. President Ford had recently vetoed a public works bill to create emergency jobs, but there was growing doubt that he could afford to do so again. The Senate version of a new public works bill would undoubtedly bear a different dollar authorization than the House version. That difference would have to be resolved in a House-Senate conference committee, at which all *other* differences would also have to be resolved—including the Senate's piggyback rider. Al knows that the House's strong support of a public works bill is the weakness through which the Senate can shove the countercyclical assistance bill. In the conference committee Senate participants need only stand firm for their countercyclical amendment, trading off other differences, and the House must accept the Senate amendment or junk the entire public works bill, which it would not do. Thus countercyclical assistance would "pass" the House without ever going through committee or debate on the House floor, an ingenious end run around L. H. Fountain.

It's the kind of delicate and perilous maneuver that you admire extravagantly if performed in behalf of a bill that you like. But if it's done by the other side it's one of those things that proves the American political system is autocratic, corrupt, and "unresponsive to the needs of the people."

From's exploratory meeting with the Government Ops and Public

Works staff chiefs was inconclusive but promising. The day before
yesterday Al dictated a memo for Muskie's overnight reading:

MEMORANDUM
June 17, 1975

TO: Senator Muskie
FROM: Al From
SUBJECT: *Possible Merger of Countercyclical and Public Works
           Bills*

After meeting yesterday with Barry Meyer, Phil Cummings
and Dick Wegman, I think there are very good prospects for
merging our anti-recession assistance bill with a Public Works
bill and then going to conference with the House on the Public
Works bill.

At our meeting, we all agreed that it would be in both our interests to try to bring about that merger, and that we should do it
in a way that would make it most difficult for the House to
reject any notion of countercyclical assistance in conference.

From our point of view, the plain fact of the matter is that the
House is not about to move on our bill. So that any hope we
have of getting any countercyclical assistance enacted will have
to come by attaching our bill to another vehicle.

On the other hand, Barry is realistic about the difficulty the Public Works Committee would have in enacting a Public Works
bill over a Presidential veto. . . .

Markup on the Public Works bill will begin Thursday morning
in the Economic Development Subcommittee. . . . At Thursday's markup, I think you might want to suggest the possibility
of combining the two bills, but only after Senator Montoya presents his Public Works proposal and other subcommittee
members have a chance to respond to it. There is likely to be
considerable Republican opposition, at least, to the Public
Works bill.

If you decide to suggest the idea of a compromise on Thursday,
I think it would be advisable for you to forewarn Senator Montoya of your intention. It is the view of Phil and Barry that of
the four principals that would have to be involved in a compromise—you, Ribicoff, Randolph, and Montoya—Senator Montoya would likely be the most reluctant to go along.

Cummings and I will begin exploring—hopefully tomorrow— how we can best combine the two bills. But it is unlikely that we will have any specific proposals for a compromise by Thursday's meeting.

Room 4110, a smallish committee room in the Public Works group of chambers, is jammed, mostly by about twenty staff people around the walls ready to whisper catch-up briefings to their Senators as they arrive, or to carry back detailed notes to the no-shows. The Economic Development Subcommittee is strange territory for Muskie. And that fact is itself strange—because the cast of characters is so familiar. Those present are a musical chairs reshuffling of Muskie's Environmental Pollution Subcommittee of Public Works: Domenici and McClure, Stafford of Vermont, and Morgan of North Carolina, augmented by Quentin Burdick of North Dakota, and the full committee's ranking Republican, Howard Baker of Tennessee. There's one other new face, that of the subcommittee chairman, Joseph Montoya, the New Mexico Democrat. Neither Muskie nor Montoya attends one another's subcommittee meetings without compelling reason, possible explanations for which I'm about to discover.

To the list of TV stars that the Watergate hearings produced— Senators Ervin, Baker, Weicker, and Inouye—one must add Senator Montoya. His face became imprinted on the national consciousness as a symbol of undistractable persistence. Every day he had his list of prepared questions, composed overnight by a devoted and sleepless staff, and Montoya read them. If the question had been asked of a witness before, its answer chewed and rechewed, no matter; it was there on that list, and Montoya read it. If a response suggested a startling new area of inquiry, no matter; instead of a follow-up question, Montoya read the next question on his list. He is a determined man. The Washington columnist, Vic Gold, has related in print an exquisite example of Montoya's determined capacity to read on, no matter what.

The Senator was welcoming the National Legislative Conference, meeting in Albuquerque, New Mexico, in mid-August 1974. The same devoted staff that prepared those Watergate questions prepared a speech. The staff also observed the usual Senate practice of preparing a news story for distribution to the press, containing highlights of the prepared speech. The aide "staffing" him that day, however,

slipped up. Instead of handing Montoya the text of the speech, he
handed him the news release. According to Vic Gold, Montoya
began to address the assemblage:

"For immediate release!" He read onward: "Senator Joseph Montoya, Democrat of New Mexico, last night told the National Legislative Conference meeting at Albuquerque that . . ."

Despite a rising buzz of befuddlement in the audience, Montoya
read on relentlessly, through six pages of press release, through the
non sequiturs of selected highlights and journalistic transitions, right
down through the reportorial conclusion:

"During the course of his remarks Montoya was repeatedly interrupted by applause."

Montoya, gaveling to order the members of the Economic Development Subcommittee, explains at some length his public works proposal for appropriating slightly more than two billion dollars for the
emergency stimulation of jobs. Muskie sits silently, biding his time
before presenting his "amendment," the unrelated countercyclical
bill.

When an earlier public works bill of five billion dollars was passed
and sent to the President, says Montoya, the President vetoed it
(Montoya pronounces that word with strong emphasis on each syllable, "vee toed"), and the Congress was unable to override that vee
toe. "That will continue," he says, "unless this committee finds some
way to turn the Administration around." The way to do it, Montoya
asserts sagely, is to pass a bill of a *smaller* amount that the President
may *not* vee toe.

When Montoya springs an explosively bright idea, his face snaps
into a beseeching smile, teeth flashing like a movie marquee, eyes
twinkling, fluttering, eagerly inquiring, "Do you get it?" As that smile
now searches the room, Montoya discovers that Baker, Domenici,
McClure, Stafford, Burdick, and Morgan, one by one, have departed.
Montoya says:

"Senator Muskie, any questions? You're the only one here."

Muskie has none. Domenici strolls back in: he has none either.
Satisfied that he has sold his bill beyond question, Montoya invites
Muskie to discuss his amendment.

Muskie touches on the high points of his bill, dwelling on a careful
explanation of the innovative approach of countercyclical assistance.

"It sounds like revenue sharing," says Montoya.

"It is not revenue sharing," says Muskie, who is often called the father of revenue sharing because of the intense going over that concept received at the hands of his IGR Subcommittee. The fundamental idea of revenue sharing, Muskie explains, is the transfer to states of federal funds, with no instruction as to how the money is to be used. Its whole idea is local discretion according to locally perceived need. This countercyclical assistance money is strictly categorical—to be used only to insure payment of salaries to local civil servants in times when recession reduces local tax revenues.

Montoya is disturbed, confused, but eager to ingratiate. It is not public works, he protests, flashing a smile. It does not create jobs in physical construction. Muskie responds that it accomplishes the aim of emergency public works, only better. It pumps money into the economy in the fastest, easiest possible way, through existing payrolls. Montoya protests that it adds a great "burden" on the public works bill, an additional potential of more than two billion dollars, which may insure a presidential vee toe. Beseeching smile. It may not, Muskie replies stubbornly. The White House may like the countercyclical idea better than the public works idea. Several Republicans do. Senator Brock does. How do we know the President would veto it before we try it on him? His defenses under siege, Montoya demands in unconcealed annoyance:

"What does countercyclical mean? Where did it come from?"

Muskie replies with dauntless patience, clearly ignoring the first part of the question with which he has already dealt at length: "Charlie Schultze[1] invented it. He first discussed it with me about four years ago. I've been partial to the idea ever since. It takes effect as the economy deteriorates and backs off as the economy improves."

"Except for that part, it's revenue sharing," says Montoya.

Muskie's big hand slams down on the table. He roars, "It is *not* revenue sharing." Eyes gleaming in gun-metal gray, lips tightened in suppressed irritation, Muskie explains it again. With each descent of Muskie's palm to the table top, each volley of devastating phrases from his huge arsenal, Montoya appears to hunch his head for protection in his shoulders, turning on the beseeching smile, pleading for surcease.

[1] Assistant director and director, U. S. Bureau of the Budget, under Presidents Kennedy and Johnson, now Brookings Institution economist, and soon to become President Jimmy Carter's chairman of the Council of Economic Advisers.

I see why these two men try to avoid one another's meetings. Montoya can make Muskie lose his constant effort to control his temper. That makes Muskie feel not only a loss of control but guilty. Montoya, on the other hand, feels in Muskie's presence the vulnerability of a man standing under a giant compacter. These two men do not communicate well.

Montoya resolves the disagreement by evading it altogether. Since a quorum of the subcommittee is no longer present, he points out, the subcommittee can't vote on the amendment. So why not just send both bills up to the whole committee and let *it* decide whether to approve Muskie's bill as an amendment to Montoya's bill? Muskie stretches his arms, palms up, a disarming gesture signifying that Montoya has come up with a Solomon-like solution. The "solution" is exactly what Muskie anticipated and wanted: Subcommittee Chairman Montoya tossing the matter into the higher lap of Committee Chairman Randolph, where Muskie, through his man From, and through Randolph's man Meyer, already knows he will find a warmer reception.

Rising from his place at the table, Muskie surreptitiously wiggles his eyebrows at me, whispering sidemouth, "The labor pains were rather intensive today."

Thursday afternoon, June 19

Today I am discovering another facet of Edmund Muskie, totally new, but not surprising.

One can only guess, and probably poorly, at the sources of the profound shyness or fear or suspicion that compels the guarded distance he keeps between himself and other adults—*all* other adults, so far as I can see. But today I'm finding he is not at all shy with youngsters.

This morning when Muskie appeared so relieved that the labor pains were at last over, he was weary, irritated. A doubt crossed my mind about his wanting company—even silent company—back to the office. At that moment the worst happened, or so I thought. A group of five teen-age boys who had slipped into the door of the markup during its closing moments approached the Senator. Dolores must have directed them there.

"Hi," said their leader, extending his hand. "We're from Maine, the 4-H Clubs."

Muskie's face immediately lightened, brightened. "You are? What brings you here?"

"Just a 4-H trip."

One by one, the Senator asked the name and home town of each. If I had the slightest doubt of the genuineness of Muskie's welcome, it vanished when he showed them into the elevator marked "Senators Only," kept chatting with them animatedly through the subterranean corridors, mostly about the potatoes of Aroostook County, and led them past the wide-eyed gazes of Dolores and Maynard into his office. As with the visiting ladies yesterday, he toured them through his shelves of mementos, this time remarking, "When you're in politics you collect a lot of junk." Then he singled out a few non-junk items: a temple rubbing he'd brought back from Pnom Penh in 1965; a carving of the head of Christ he'd bought in the Philippines; a hand-carved bear brought from Russia and given to him by a former governor of Maine. I had not previously seen him so relaxed or in less of a hurry to end a conversation.

Early this afternoon Dolores is called to the front desk. More teen-agers have turned up, this time seven Maine delegates to the National Teenage Republican Convention. It happens the Senator is in, but Dolores has doubts about applying her election-year drop-in "policy." Does it extend to *Republicans?* She tiptoes into Muskie's office to ask, emerges glowing, and shows the visitors in.

Unawed, the kids plunk themselves onto his couch and chairs, and he asks airily, "How's the convention going?"

"They've been drilling us," a girl states solemnly, "in how disorganized Congress is."

"Disorganized?" he repeats, dismayed, as though he's never heard of such a thing.

They chat for fully twenty minutes about the difficulties of getting a majority of 535 members—from different regions, different economic interests, different ethnic mixes—to agree on anything. Clearly,

Muskie enjoys the encounter. And the youngsters enjoy being taken seriously by a man with a forceful and meticulous mind, even though from the *other* party.

When the clean air markups resume next Tuesday, again Muskie and McClure will spar, testing each other's positions for combat, and no doubt the cast will expand as the fight shapes up. The central character, in a sense, is not a Senator, however, but the staff spokesman. Leon Billings, with his helpers, is the store of information, and information is the weaponry, the ammunition of legislative battle. Before the doors of markups were thrown open, few outsiders clearly comprehended the position of hirelings in the lawmaking process. Yes, on television we saw Samuel Dash as the Perry Mason of the Watergaters, Bobby Kennedy for the McClellan investigators of labor rackets, the unforgettable team of Roy Cohn and David Schine for Joe McCarthy. Such "investigations" are something special, however, a departure from the day-to-day lawmaking work of the Congress.

Who are the Leon Billingses? How do they get here? What gives them their special power over Senators, even while deferring as servants? Is it academic mastery of specialized knowledge or just plain political skill? How do they perceive themselves, their jobs, their place in the Senate? How do they regard Senators, and how do they perceive Senators as regarding them? These are more questions than I can hope to satisfy in a single conversation, but perhaps the answers will come in time. To begin, I stroll across First Street to the Dirksen Building and a chat with Muskie's man in the office of the Environmental Pollution Subcommittee.

A CONVERSATION WITH LEON BILLINGS

—I was born and raised in Helena, Montana. My dad and mom, from 1946 to 1969, edited the only liberal newspaper in the state of Montana, called *The People's Voice*. It was a small weekly newspaper put together by a bunch of young radicals, like Lee Metcalf[1]

---

[1] Since 1961, Montana's junior Senator. He served in the House of Representatives from 1953 to 1961, following a period as a justice of the state supreme court.

and others. Back in those days, all the papers except one were owned by a subsidiary of Anaconda Copper, and they wouldn't cover political news. I come from a very long line of journalists. Our house was the mecca for liberal intellectuals in the state. When they came to Helena they ate and drank in our house.

—My dad and Mike Mansfield[2] had a falling out in 1954, and I don't know if they've ever spoken to each other since. Mike speaks to me about once a year—he says hello. Actually, he's been very nice to me in the last year or so. He's gotten used to the fact that I'm around.

—I worked toward a master's in history, then took a job with a liberal farm organization in California, organizing, writing, covering meetings. That was 1961, so I was twenty-three. A year and a half later I met a guy from the American Public Power Association, the association of municipally owned electric utilities. He asked me if I wanted to go to Washington and be their lobbyist. Well, I wanted to get married, and that California job just didn't lend itself to marriage, so I came east in January of 1963. Today, the environment issue has united all power companies, private and public, into one bloc, but in those days it was "them" and "us."

—One of my first involvements was a movement for a hydroelectric project in northern Maine requiring an act of Congress and federal funds, the Dickey-Lincoln School project, and on a couple of occasions I met Muskie. He created the project, basically. Along the way I got to know a guy named Ron Linton, who was chief clerk of the Senate Public Works Committee under [then Chairman] Pat McNamara of Michigan. Early in 1966 Ron asked, "How would you like to work here?" I had become bored with what I was doing. I said, "I don't know." He said, "I've got a problem here. Pat McNamara's dying of cancer and Jennings Randolph is going to become chairman." They had formed what was then called the Special Subcommittee on Air and Water Pollution. Ron said, "It's not likely that Muskie's interests are going to be consistent with Randolph's interests, especially in environmental stuff. I need someone to protect Muskie's flanks." I thought about it, and called Linton and said, "If McNamara's dying and Randolph's taking over and if I'm to work for Muskie—I know enough about this town—I want to be hired by Muskie or I won't last three months. I want a letter from

[2] Montana's senior Senator and Senate Majority Leader.

Muskie saying he talked it over with Randolph, that Randolph agreed, but that Muskie's hiring me. And what's the salary?" Ron got back to say that Muskie would sign the letter and the salary's $16,700[3] a year. I was then making $10,000. I said, "When do you want me to start—yesterday?" So I came here as a professional staff member of Public Works to handle air and water pollution, and didn't know anything about pollution, but nobody else knew anything about it either.

—How the subcommittee got set up is an interesting story. When Muskie first came to the Senate and on Public Works, he wanted to be chairman of the Rivers and Harbors Subcommittee, because it would help him get dams built in Maine and so on. Well, Randolph wanted the same subcommittee. McNamara settled it by making the entire committee the Rivers and Harbors Subcommittee, which automatically made him chairman of the subcommittee. He gave Randolph the Subcommittee on Roads, which pleased him because Randolph was formerly the treasurer of the American Road Builders Association. Then McNamara tossed Muskie a bone, creating this Special Subcommittee on Air and Water Pollution.

—There was for all practical purposes no environmental constituency, except the traditional conservation organizations like the Izaak Walton League, very interested in water pollution and fish. Not people, but fish. Ralph Nader was testifying on highway safety, and was being shadowed by GM, and had absolutely no interest in the Clean Air Act. Well, Muskie's not one to sit around on his ass. He started holding hearings all over the country, started creating a constituency—in '63, '64, '65, in Detroit, New Orleans, Kansas City, New York, San Francisco, Atlanta, just all over the goddamned place. I wasn't here then, but I went back and read a bunch of that stuff because I figured I'd better learn something in a hurry. One woman came to the New Orleans hearing, wanted to put a fence down both sides of the Mississippi River from top to bottom to keep people from throwing beer cans into the goddamned river. That was the kind of testimony they were getting.

—The Clean Air Act of '63 started with virtually no support. The Clean Air Act of '65, with the first motor vehicle emissions standards, was a very modest thing. They were primarily the Senate going along with the hard work of Ed Muskie. He dug into the issues like

[3] This was 1966. Billings' salary today is roughly $38,000.

he does every other goddamned thing, and he dug and dug and dug. It's one of the reasons he sometimes gets bored with it now, because nobody's caught up with him. He still knows more than most people, including me.

—The most fascinating thing I find about the guy is his intellectual process. I began seeing it right after we got the Dickey-Lincoln School project authorized by the House and Senate. I hadn't really had too much contact with Muskie, and subsequently found out that that's not terribly unusual. I went into his office one day and was standing there, you know, looking for a hole in his attention, and finally he looked up at me and said, "What do you want?" I said, "Well, you've got to call Mike Mansfield." He said, "I've got to call, I've got to call! What do you mean, I've got to call? I don't *got* to call *anybody!* You guys are always telling me what I've got to do." I said, "Well, you've got to call Mike Mansfield—" You know, ninety per cent of his crabbiness is style, and ten per cent of it's real. The question is whether you can judge which is which, and if you can judge it properly, he's not too difficult to live with. But anyway, I said, "You've got to call Mike Mansfield for four reasons." And I gave him the four reasons. He started to blast them apart. I was god-damned near in tears. Then he says, "Well, get Mansfield for me." So I called Mansfield, and Muskie gets on the phone and says, "Mike, I want you to talk to Allen Ellender[4] about Dickey-Lincoln School for three reasons." And he recited three of my four reasons almost exactly as I'd presented them. Obviously he'd rejected the fourth. He never told me why he rejected it because he never told me he'd accepted the other three. He gave Mansfield perfect arguments for why those three reasons were important. That was it, and I left. The funny thing is I felt wonderful. Three out of four!

—I think Muskie feels that the staff responds best in a highly pres-surized situation. He knows that's how *he* responds best, and I think that's what he expects from us—if the situation is easy, the prepara-tory job will be inadequate. I know it's worked for me. I used to be very sloppy, not just in my thought processes but in my work, my formulations, my analysis and so on. Because of the way he tests any idea by tearing into you and tearing you apart, it forces you—you've got to stop and think, Jeez, what kind of question is he going to ask

4 Former Senator from Louisiana.

so I can be ready to respond to it? It really improves the quality of the staff.

—I've got a bit of a reputation in his office as one of the few people who dishes it back to him. It's been suggested that there are certain basic biological incompatibilities between me and Ed Muskie, that when I walk into a room his blood pressure rises. Oh, I remember a dishing-it-back session. It was just before these markups began and I went over to show him a mockup of a print of the bill and how we were going to present the agenda of critical issues, and he just went bananas. He was very tired, felt put upon. He said, "What are you showing me this for? I just want you to raise the issues." And I said, "All right, one of the issues is how far the deadlines for the statutory standards for CO and HC and NOx should be delayed." He said, "That's not an issue!" And I said, "Well, some people think it is." He said, "Well, I'm not going to raise the son of a bitch!" And I said, "All right. So you *don't* want me to raise all the issues." He said, "I want you to raise the damned issues that are *relevant*." And I said, "All right, let's go over to health. One of the issues is whether we should modify the health standard." And he said, "I'm not going to raise that damned issue!" Well I just got pissed as hell, so finally I said, "What you want me to do is formulate the issues in such a way that nobody can accuse us of having formulated them in a prejudicial manner, but at the same time you don't want me to formulate any issues that you don't want to have raised. Right?" And he just stared at me. And that was one of those times.

—Something I learned a long time ago, Muskie doesn't dish it out to people he doesn't like. I don't think it would be possible to drive a wedge between me and Muskie after these almost ten years, because what exists between us exists. The only potential concern would be that Muskie—I don't think that Muskie likes to be well understood. I don't think he likes to perceive of himself as being well understood. I think that he likes to maintain a certain amount of mystery about his personality.

Monday morning, June 23

As threatened, Majority Whip Byrd kept the Senate in session late Friday. Instead of Muskie catching his 4:50 P.M. plane to Maine or the six-thirty "backup" flight for which Gayle had providently reserved, he had to take an eight-ten to Boston. A staff man from the Portland office drove down to pick up his boss, drove him to the family summer house at Kennebunk Beach, where Muskie arrived, undined, close to midnight. At 9:30 A.M. Saturday he was off to address the state American Legion convention.

Last night Muskie flew to New York so he could appear this morning at the crack of dawn on ABC's coast-to-coast "A.M. America" in an interview by John V. Lindsay. Lindsay is having all the Democratic presidential prospects in, and Muskie willingly puts himself on view among this group to deny his candidacy but to affirm his availability.

I'm on his calendar for a chat at 11:30 A.M. When he arrives from the airport and we settle down for our talk, Muskie quite relaxed in shirt sleeves and his big stuffed chair, I try to elicit from him some intimate observation of how he manipulated Montoya last Thursday and got just what he wanted. Muskie not only won't bite, but I don't think he's aware that I'm offering bait.

I can't think of a disparaging comment I've heard Muskie make about anybody. But it goes beyond that. He rarely describes anyone in terms of motivation, rarely judges or even characterizes anyone. He describes an action, or something said, or a vote cast, or a political person's general position—something observable and factual. As far as I can see, Muskie sees a person not as a bundle of passions but as a performer of external actions. Even someone who persistently gets in his way is accepted as a fact to deal with, pointless to complain about, like paying the mortgage.

Whether deliberate or not, this is a useful style of mind in the Senate, where a relatively small community of one hundred must live together for years and years, where one may team up with another as a partner one day and heave a wrecking ball to crush the other's position the next. I began now to understand Muskie's surprising and surprised observations of the Senate made in his little book, *Journeys,* published to promote his 1972 presidential campaign: "Before going to the Senate, I had the notion that members would meet on a continuing basis and discuss profound questions of public policy, debating in public or over lunch or perhaps over a drink in the afternoon. It turned out to be not that kind of place at all. You don't see the other Senators very often and you rarely get a chance to discuss many serious issues with them. . . . You rarely have more than one or two Senators sitting with you during the hearings. Days can go by when you don't run into more than one or two Senators."

What Muskie doesn't say but what becomes more clear with each hour of observation here is that Senators, while always grandly courteous with one another, are rarely chummy. No time to be? Perhaps. But more important, they can't afford to be, don't want to be. A Senator can't trust a single one of his colleagues on the next issue called up. Senators resist getting closer to one another than arm's length lest it mitigate their freedom to fight. They refer to one another promiscuously as "my good friend" because the term has little meaning in the Senate; they are not friends as others understand friendship: with loyalty, trust, love. These limitations on personal relationships wear easily on Senators since, by nature, politicians appear not to penetrate deeply into the lives of their "friends" and families, nor do they allow others to penetrate deeply into theirs. Thus their personality flaw is institutionalized in the Senate, and indeed becomes an operative strength.

The distance between Senators has another dimension. Because they are one hundred men[1] each with a colossal ego fattened daily by

[1] The repeated reference to members of the Senate as "men" is not thoughtless male chauvinism—at least, not on the author's part. The Senate has included numerous (although not enough) women in the past and presumably will have many more in the future. But the Senate of the Ninety-fourth Congress is one hundred per cent male.

staffs and supplicants, yet daily subject to challenge and possible defeat by colleagues, the Senate seethes with perilous potentialities that its members go to great lengths to keep restrained and unrealized. They are the potentialities for combat, disorder, personal humiliation, hatred, and vengeance. Thus the Senate has a written rule, violation of which is punishable by censure or expulsion, that a Senator may not, directly or indirectly, impute to another Senator any conduct or motive "unworthy or unbecoming a Senator." Even that broad rule is not sufficient to control the peril. So the rule is fortified by a custom. In debate, no Senator refers to another by name; thus the frequent references to "my good friend," "my learned colleague," "the distinguished junior Senator from Delaware." This is the senatorial equivalent of the Mafia hit man, while holding a gun to one ear of his victim, whispering in the other, "Nothing personal."

Who ever invented the preposterous idea that the Senate is a club?

A CONVERSATION WITH SENATOR MUSKIE

I had the feeling, after Montoya's subcommittee meeting, that, no matter how simply and how often you explained your countercyclical bill, Montoya was not going to get it.

—I was just trying to educate him to my proposal without trying to push it too hard. Sometimes a fellow who still resists something at the end of a session like that will go off and think it over and begin to revise his view. So I wouldn't say he's a hopeless case.

—For that matter, I'm not sure how the full committee will respond to it. The trouble is that three of the Republicans [Buckley, McClure, and Domenici] are also with me on the Budget Committee, and their votes on the Budget Committee would indicate that they're going to be very reluctant to add any new anti-recession programs.

Do you know that you'll have a better climate in the full Public Works Committee? Does a chairman—in this case, Jennings Randolph—so control the affairs of a committee that he can determine a bill's climate?

—It can have a bearing. Randolph likes to go to the floor with unanimous committees if he can. He'll go quite far to do that. And he doesn't like to break with me on an issue.[2] I haven't discussed this personally with him, but his inclination might well be to try to encourage the marriage of the bills. It will all depend on how he reads the President's mind. If he thinks a veto is more likely to be avoided by keeping the dollar amount down, he may well conclude that my proposal makes too big a package. On the other hand, if he agrees that my program adds to the merits of the bill, that the President would at least have a different case to consider, he might tend to go along. There are some indications—for example, Brock's support— that the White House may approve of the countercyclical approach. I don't like to assume that the Republicans on our committee or the President will be against my proposal simply because it originated with a Democrat. I like to bridge the party gap and concentrate on the issues. After all, the conservative-liberal line cuts across the party line. If you don't put a label on things, you can get people to look at the merits. As governor, I didn't label my programs as Democratic programs or as New Deal or liberal programs. Maine people aren't oriented that way. I talked about problems, practical options. What do you do about this problem? What do you *do* about it? Is

[2] I didn't ask Muskie to amplify this statement, but the probable explanation is derived, as they say in the Senate, from a look at the record. Randolph and Muskie, numbers one and two on Public Works respectively, were both elected to the Senate in 1958, both as labor-supported liberals and New Dealers. In understanding Randolph, it is important to know that he first came to Washington as a Congressman in 1932—in time for Franklin D. Roosevelt's first term! —and was here before any member of Congress serving at the time of publication of this book. So he is the most authentic current example of the "old school" of congressional style, politics, and gentility. After fourteen consecutive years in the House, Randolph was defeated by a Republican sweep in 1946, staying in Washington as a Hill lobbyist. While his chief retainer was Capitol Airlines, one of his major involvements was with the American Road Builders Association, a kingpin in what is known reverently in the halls of Congress as the highway lobby. In the early 1970s, long after Randolph entered the Senate, the Public Works Committee—and chiefly Randolph's Subcommittee on Roads —became the eye of a titanic storm: a struggle to break open the multi-billion-dollar Interstate Highway Trust Fund and to make off with some of those billions for mass transportation. The highway lobby (and Randolph) defended the fund as an issue of life and death. Leading the assault on the fund within the committee was the champion of the environment and enemy of highway pollution, Edmund Muskie. In a fearsome joust, Muskie lost within the committee through a tie vote—and then won by a surprising margin in the Senate. Ever since, the two men have engaged with most delicate solicitude, elaborate consideration, highest mutual respect and affection—and always at a cautious distance.

this a sensible approach? So they adopted a lot of ideas which they might have rejected if the ideas had been labeled.

—People don't require labels—that's the point. Only politicians and political activists do. Once they sell something politically with success, they try to pin a label on it so they can sell everything else under the same label, like selling a line of canned goods. But it's true, if those labels are used over and over again, people start to measure programs after a while in terms of the label. The trouble is, the meaning of a label starts to change, and then where are you? The Vietnam war converted Hubert Humphrey, in the public eye, from a liberal to a conservative. Nonsense. Liberal and conservative had nothing to do with that. Then the anti-war people were labeled the "new left," without reference to other issues.

—I remember when I ran against Congressman Clifford McIntire in 1964. He's now dead as a result of an accident, God bless him. He was a conservative Republican and the ACA—Americans for Constitutional Action—brought out some ratings to compare us on fiscal responsibility. Mine wasn't very high, of course, and McIntire's was about eighty-seven per cent. My people up home got alarmed. I said, "What are you worried about?" They said, "My God, that's a hard one to fight up here in Maine." I said, "The answer's very simple. Why don't you just spread the word that even the Americans for Constitutional Action found that Congressman McIntire is fiscally irresponsible thirteen per cent of the time." They're so ridiculous, those ratings.

—I suppose my unhappiness with these labels reflects my desire to get down to the substance of things. I'm receptive to any idea that will work. It's a pragmatism that's— Take Franklin Roosevelt. He was no ideologue at all. Not at all. I remember a famous story of his trade policy. Cordell Hull was for protective trade barriers and Ray Moley was for free trade. Opposite principles, and each brought in a paper to support his position. Roosevelt said, "Now you two fellows lock yourselves in that room and don't come out until you marry those two ideas." I'm partial to that because I think you need broad consensus to get stability in this system. Oh, not that there isn't room for bold, controversial, new ideas. They often come along through crusaders and third parties. That's all to the good. The system's flexible enough for that. But as you move forward in bringing a program to life, making it work, you've got to have a consensus.

Monday afternoon, June 23

Tomorrow's markup on clean air has been canceled. In fact, all markups on all bills, all hearings, have been canceled until further notice. Committee meetings of any kind can be held while the Senate is in session only by unanimous consent of all members. To expedite the Durkin-Wyman controversy, the leadership has been scheduling Senate sessions starting at 9 A.M. (more usually they start at noon). To break what they call the Democratic filibuster, the Republicans are withholding unanimous consent—therefore, no committee meetings; therefore, terrific pressure on the Democrats, who are already under criticism, as the majority is every year, for running a "do-nothing" Congress. So just when Muskie's Environmental Pollution Subcommittee is about to get rolling full steam, its agenda discussed and understood by members, it is stopped dead in its tracks.

At two-thirty today Muskie is to subject himself to some real, honest-to-God, live lobbying, receiving two vice-presidents of Commonwealth Edison of Chicago, the largest utility in the nation. It's not the size of their company, however, that got them on his calendar. It's their lawyer. Les Hyman is a young lawyer on a rapid rise in Washington. He has ambition, nerve, a smart wardrobe, a pocket notebook full of the right names, and a talent for knowing the right conversations in which to drop them. A simple trick for becoming a superlawyer in Washington—easily described but not frequently performed with suavity and skill—is to do something significant for a Senator or Congressman for free, out of sheer public spirit, personal admiration, belief in his future, devotion to his cause; then, having won his gratitude and obligation, to sell the access thus gained at a high legal fee.

Les Hyman is Muskie's "presidential man." At least for the time being. There are any number of more prominent personages who would like to see Muskie the Democratic candidate next year, but they are either not in Washington, or they can't come out too early, or they're too busy, or whatever. But there are chores to be done: keeping tabs on what people in what states might be the bones of an organizational skeleton, talking to newsmen and influentials at Georgetown parties to make sure that Muskie's non-candidacy but availability is widely noted, answering letters and writing letters to stir up a movement for a presidential candidacy over the "objections" and "refusal to co-operate" of the non-candidate. Non-candidacies don't come out of nowhere.

That kind of effort becomes conspicuous, at least among other lawyers and other President-pushers. So when word buzzes around lawyer circles that such-and-such client needs access to Ed Muskie, word soon buzzes back that Les Hyman has it. Every Senator has— must have—his Les Hymans. If not as President-pushers, they work their way in as speech providers, bill writers, brokers of all sorts, campaign organizers and fund raisers in the home state. For a lawyer, it's a very good thing to hold a pawn ticket, no matter how small, on a Senator.

Some major corporations, foreign nations, trade associations, or interests of whatever structure have as many as twelve Washington law firms on retainer. Not that they have that much law work, God knows, at least not in Washington. But they find it worth the price to have this group of firms on tap for reaching Democrats, that group for reaching Republicans; within each party, this law firm for its ready access to Chairman So-and-so of Committee Such-and-such, that one for getting to the regulatory commission, and on and on. The biggest interests who need and can afford the biggest lawyers go for the likes of Clark Clifford, Abe Fortas, Cyrus Vance, as impresarios for a sympathetic hearing before top Democrats; Charls E. Walker (a banking specialist, not a lawyer), Undersecretary of the Treasury in the Nixon Administration, to impress Republicans.

What is the debt so many Senators owe to, say, Clark Clifford? Nobody remembers any more. Clifford has been an adviser or administration official to every Democratic President since being assigned by the Pentagon to become Harry Truman's naval aide in 1946. When you advise Presidents, you represent access to Presidents. You no longer have to go to Senators; they come to you. That level of reputation, the status of governmental guru, magically fattens and flourishes even while feeding on itself, long after anyone remembers how it got started or who owes what to whom.

Les Hyman, still on his first steps down the road toward such superlawyerism, is dressed sportily in loafers and summery light blue suit which, while out of harmony with the electric-company gray of his clients, emits a message of breezy at-homeness in Muskie's office. With faintly ingratiating smile at both host and guests, Hyman introduces his clients to the Senator: Hubert Nexon, a Commonwealth Edison senior vice-president, and Byron Lee, a junior vice-president. Muskie and Leon Billings greet them with heavy-lidded reserve. They'll listen from a great distance, somewhat itchily mindful that this meeting has been—well, there's no other word for it— *purchased,* with a legal tender honored throughout the Senate: the right lawyer trading in previous obligation for access to the right Senator. A perfectly understandable practice—if the lawyer and Senator are on your side; evil, if they're on the other.

Sitting on the couch and without referring to notes, Nexon pleads his company's case smoothly and knowledgeably. The most anguishing issues of air pollution from stationary sources are involved.

There are two ways to assess air pollution, and the method required by the new environmental laws is about to cost Commonwealth Edison—and therefore its customers—tens of millions of dollars more than the other method. You can measure pollution in the *ambient* air—that is, loft a monitor to count particles of filth in the air of a general region, without knowing for sure where the filth came from or where it's headed. If the count is too high, somebody blows the whistle for all polluters to curtail or shut down operations until a fresh breeze comes by. This system is reinforced by requiring tall smokestacks, thus preventing most pollution from threatening human eyes and noses, and use of low-sulphur coal, otherwise known as "clean" coal. The trouble is, coal that is naturally low in sulphur is in short supply, and technology for removing sulphur from coal cannot be widely available for at least ten years. The foregoing combination of safeguards—low sulphur, high stacks, and shutting down when the air is bad—is called "intermittent control systems." In a speech, Muskie once referred to them as the "rhythm method" of pollution control.

The other, far more expensive, way is the installation of "stack gas scrubbers" to remove sulphur pollutants. Measuring poison in the ambient air, say scrubber proponents, is not good enough. The pollution must be controlled at the source. "Scrubbers" suggest huge brushes, but that's not what they are. The most widely used scrubber is a gigantic tank of lime or limestone in a watery solution. When sulphuric emissions are driven into the tank, the lime reacts with sulphur dioxide to form salts, primarily sulphites and sulphates. What comes out are colossal quantities of useless sludge which, utilities claim, present a huge, land-wasting disposal problem. There are other methods that produce little or no waste, but they are new and relatively untried. Installation of scrubber systems costs fifty dollars to sixty-five dollars for every kilowatt of a plant's capacity. Nationally, this would cost electric companies—and, inescapably, consumers—about $5.4 billion, according to EPA. It would run costs up fifteen to twenty per cent in those plants. Since only thirty per cent of the national coal-burning capacity would need scrubbers, however, the increased cost to consumers might shake down to as little as three per cent.

The electric industry argues that scrubbers are too expensive for the good they'll do—not cost-effective—and, besides, they are cranky, unreliable contraptions. The Federal Power Commission agrees. On the other hand, an EPA study charged that "most utilities seem content to raise the problems and wait for other utilities to solve them." If the best available way, scrubbers, is not good enough, implied EPA, it's the utilities' own fault, since they have spent less than one per cent of their revenue on research and development, and research on scrubbers took "only a small but undetermined portion" of this shortsighted one per cent.

Nexon of Commonwealth Edison is now pleading for exceptions in the law to cover two major plants in Illinois. One of these plants stands in virtual isolation from all other pollution sources, he points out, and therefore intermittent controls are feasible. The other is located in the city of Pekin (well known in the Senate as Everett Dirksen's hometown). Pekin is a gray, smoky, industrial city, and Nexon has a plan whereby his company could keep from making matters worse—without costly scrubbers. When the ambient air shows dangerous levels of pollution, Commonwealth Edison would be willing to shut down its plant temporarily, thus leaving other plants in town free of blame and free of penalty for the electric company's filth.

Furthermore, Commonwealth could assure its customers—and Muskie and the Senate—that such a temporary shutdown would not threaten a shortage of electricity, since the plant sits at the heart of the Mid-America Interpool Network (MAIN), a vast interconnection of electric companies that instantaneously can borrow or purchase power from one another.

Muskie asks a question here and there, points out that exceptions are difficult, almost impossible, to legislate, that yes, technology may soon be more efficient and effective. Two or three times he comments, "This is a frustrating business." At one point he says wearily, "Certainly, knowledge is incomplete. But it's always going to be incomplete. At some point we've got to say that we're going to make a decision. You've got to—we've got to—take some risks, and the question is whether we err on the side of public health or err on the side of what someone says is cost-effective. All the new evidence that we've been accumulating over the past twelve years indicates that the more we learn about health the worse the problem looks, and therefore we're better off erring on the side of protecting health than worrying about what is cost-effective. Also, if we opt for the least costly solution now, and ten years from now we find that we really do have a serious problem, such as acid rain, then the same people will be back here saying, 'Well, Gawd, we'd like to clean it up, but it's not cost-effective to solve that problem because we have to refit this and that and so forth.' "

Nexon nods and absorbs this rebuttal, commenting only that he hopes the Senator will think about his company's request and promising to put the plea on paper for the perusal of "you or your staff."

As Muskie closes the door behind his visitor, I think I hear him say, "They do have a case." (When I mention this later to Leon, he corrects me, "He said, 'They *may* have a case.' ")

Strolling across the street with Leon, I ask whether this presentation just gets lost in the wind and, if not, how does it have an impact? Leon replies:

"By the fact that it's been presented to him, it's been absorbed into his thought processes. When the issue is being hashed over in committee, Muskie, having thought this thing through, will be prepared to respond to someone else raising it, or he'll raise some of these questions himself to test them in his devil's advocate fashion."

Was there anything in the presentation that Leon or Muskie has not heard and already considered? Leon motions me into his office. He hands me a fat, paper-bound report called "Steel and the Environment: the Cost to the Fuel Industry," prepared by Arthur D. Little, Inc.

"This," says Leon, "is over a million dollars in lobbying investment. The power industry's report is three times the size of this. The petroleum industry has got fantastic color charts to go with their consultant reports. They're all here. They're prepared mainly for us to see."

Does anyone really listen to these people?

"We all listen to them. I listen to them. I've got to listen to them. We do a briefing analysis on all this material for Muskie and other members, trying to give the best summary of the facts. And it damned well better be good, because if Muskie suddenly gets hit with something we didn't prepare him for, it's our ass.

"You know, I have some degree of control over who sees Muskie, which some of these people resent me for. The Arthur D. Little people wanted to see him, and I felt it was important, so I put them on the list to see him and make their own presentation. These people don't particularly like me and think I withhold information from the Senator. I had to sit there and *pull* out of them the stuff that Muskie should have, saying, 'Why don't you tell the Senator about this? You forgot to mention that.' Basically, they're lousy lobbyists, and my job would be a lot easier if they did their jobs better."

When I return to Muskie's office, the Senator steps into the administrative office, looks at Maynard, at Dolores, at me, is about to say something, says nothing, disappears into his private sanctum. A minute later he steps out again, looks around nervously, then announces he's going over to S-199, the hideaway, to watch the playoff of the U. S. Open on television and asks if I want to come. As we charge down the hall he grumbles that this New Hampshire thing is now ridiculous:

"We have to hang around all day for floor votes, yet no Senate business can move. You can't schedule anything. No markups, no committee meetings. They're holding up the whole country, and when this is all history it won't matter a bit which one of them gets the damn seat.

"I don't know how long they'll stay tonight. Ask if there'll be any more roll calls, and nobody knows. Oh, what the hell, I'd just have to go home to an empty house anyhow."

I almost forgot that his family's away for the summer. I mention that, since markups are canceled, Dolores has been trying to compress tomorrow's schedule so he could take the morning off, but apparently there are going to be some floor votes.

"That would have been nice," he responds as we climb aboard the front seat of the subway car to the Capitol, "because I have so much yard work and there's laundry to be done."

Is he doing his own laundry these days?

"Well, I *have* to. You have to see that your underwear is clean. Of course, shirts aren't bad these days because you just launder them and hang them out. These permanent press shirts are kind of easy, just wash them and hang them out. But the rest of that stuff, you've got to go through that whole process of the washer and the dryer. . . ."

I've heard it said again and again—but it's not true—that he never talks small talk. He does, and with feeling, but only inside the family. Family? Me? The other day a long-time Muskie staff member told me of a curious incident in a car one night driving with Muskie to Bangor from some remote outpost in northern Maine. Muskie was explaining the necessity of having put the staff man on the spot in public, and commented, "But after all, you're a friend, and a friend should understand that." The staff man blurted out, "I'm not a friend." He immediately regretted the blurt and was about to profess his loyalty as a devoted employee and admirer, which, in his mind, are quite different from friendship and its implication of equality. But the hurt on Muskie's face looked so deep and unreachable that the aide just let it go.

Friendship, intimacy, trust are confusing items around here. Entering the little world of the Senate, you have to redefine them. Most Senators, Muskie among them, rarely socialize with their staffs, unless an office Christmas party is to be called socializing. They socialize, in a manner of speaking, with other Senators but, of course, can't trust them. An exception is Senator Lowell Weicker of Connecticut, one of his staff members has told me; Weicker rarely social-izes with other Senators, except on the tennis court. Most consider him arrogant, and he considers most his moral inferiors. He relaxes best not with "equals" or members of his family, who stay behind in Connecticut, but with his staff. They party together a lot, joking, sip-ping, the admirers circled around the admired to rechew the cud of the day's events. Whether Senators hold their staff people at a pro-tective distance or wrap their staffs around themselves like a warm cloak, the psychological current running between them is highly charged, each dependent upon the other as a constant reminder of identity. In that sense, maybe the transaction is deeper than friend-ship.

What politics and the Senate do to the concept of friendship is not unique. Public life of any kind twists it into something else. Someone once reconstructed for Howard Cosell a conversation with Muham-mad Ali in which Cosell was described as "your good friend." Ali said, "He ain't no friend." "Don't you like him any more?" "Sure I like him. He interviews me, and that's good business for me and good business for him. We get along fine. But that don't make him no friend." According to the anecdote, when Cosell heard of this conversation he was disturbed, disbelieving, slightly shaken. As topics changed from this to that, Cosell, distracted, kept coming back to it and asking, "Did Ali really say that? Are you sure?" Maybe Cosell shouldn't have dropped his openly stated ambition to run for the Senate after all.

Tuesday, June 24

Last thing every afternoon Dolores types a sheet of paper with several carbons, mounts the original on an easel on the Senator's desk, and distributes the carbons to key people around the office. It is his schedule for the next day. Today's, with four commitments, is more crowded than usual. Some days he has only one or two.

On today's schedule the first appointment seizes my attention:

SCHEDULE FOR SENATOR MUSKIE
TUESDAY, JUNE 24, 1975

---

11 A.M.   OFFICE APPOINTMENT
               SENATOR BUCKLEY
               RE: CLEAN AIR ACT

12:30 P.M.   DEMOCRATIC POLICY COMMITTEE
               LUNCHEON   S 221

2:30 P.M.   UNITED WAY OF AMERICA
               WASHINGTON TRAINEES   S 128
               RE: REVENUE SHARING
               STAFF: AL FROM
               (SEE CONGRESSMAN UDALL'S LETTER
               ATTACHED)

4 P.M.   SENATOR MC INTYRE'S OFFICE
               1215 DSOB
               RE: NATIONAL ENERGY POLICY
               FRANK ZARB, REA
               STAFF: DAVID JOHNSON [OF IGR
               STAFF]
               (SEE LETTER ATTACHED)

James Buckley, the Conservative-Republican of New York, brother of TV's eyebrow-arching interviewer, editor, and columnist William Buckley, is the ranking Republican member of the Environmental Pollution Subcommittee. This could very well become the meeting where, as they say around here, they "cut the deal." I get Leon Billings on the phone.

"I sounded Muskie out on a meeting early last week," says Leon, "and then suggested it to Hal Brayman. He's sort of my counterpart on the minority staff, Buckley's man, a former newspaperman, good fellow. It seemed time for Muskie and Buckley to find some common ground, and I proposed a couple of things to Muskie. We spent about forty minutes on it, him trying to tear it apart, me trying to defend it, same as he's done for years, until he was satisfied it would hold up. Then there was some back-and-forth between me and Brayman, a series of trial-and-error-type things, until we felt we had something the two Senators could be reasonably happy with.

"The meeting can be important because Buckley's, frankly, a swing vote. This is the kind of thing that Muskie likes to do, finds very effective, because it's hard to find anyone who wants to be to the right of Buckley and to the left of Ed Muskie. So if they reach an agreement, there's an awful lot of room for people to be comfortable. Number two, this year Muskie does have to think about Maine regarding everything and, I don't know if you know it or not, but there's a tendency up there to think of Muskie as being too partisan,[1] and that's because Muskie built the Democratic Party in Maine singlehanded. So at a time when Maine is worried about partisanship, it's pretty good for Muskie to protect his strong environmental position by making it bipartisan."

Why would Buckley want a common front with Muskie?

"Buckley is a strong conservationist, always has been, so he works fairly well on this with Muskie. And remember he's up for re-election next year too. Air pollution is a significant issue in New York, and the state has no stake in the auto industry. Buckley is a free enterpriser, but he recognizes that there are certain kinds of decisions that free enterprise is incapable of making, one of which is a decision to do something that doesn't make a profit. So he understands that there are areas in which government has a legitimate responsibility to intervene, and air pollution is one of them."

Hanging up the phone, I tell Dolores that I'd like to sit in on the Buckley meeting.

"As soon as he gets here, I'll clear it with him."

Isn't Muskie in his office now, waiting?

"Oh, not *him*. I'll have to ask Buckley. My standing orders are that the other party is always to know that you're here to write a book, and if it's okay with them, that's it."

[1] Clearly, Maynard Toll has called together all of Muskie's key people, committee people as well as senatorial office people, to brief them on trouble spots in the poll. So the resources of three Senate committees are at work to fix cracks in the image before Election Day, 1976. Such are the advantages of incumbency.

In a few minutes Dolores answers a buzz from the reception room. Seconds later she's showing in Senator Buckley, always surprisingly slight and prissy of walk, and a chap with white-blond hair and glasses, Hal Brayman, followed by Leon. Dolores crooks a finger for me to follow. Buckley didn't say no!

Inside Muskie's office, Buckley, smiling warmly, introduces himself to me. His fluttery eyes are not campaign-warm but personal-warm, a genuine greeting, which around here is a rare happening. This is the fellow, devoted environmentalist though he is, who's among the first to propose a bombing solution to almost any diplomatic crisis, who tries to augment almost any bill affecting a welfare mother with an amendment forbidding abortion, who condemns food stamps as a satanic temptation. The way he comes on—at committee meetings as well as here—just as gentle and full of kindliness as a hospital chaplain, you can't help but like him. *I* can't help but like him—and I have this feeling I'm supposed to feel guilty about it, somehow taken in.

"On auto emissions," Muskie begins, scarcely above a mumble, "I wanted to see how you react to some of these points. Maybe you have other ideas."

"I find myself increasingly confused," Buckley confesses, a boyish smile.

"It's hard when you've got to bat these damned figures around," allows Muskie, shaking his head wearily, sympathetically. "I want to find some way to change these statutory standards, make them a bit more achievable and practical, make the whole law more credible, yet not throw out the baby with the bath water."

Buckley nods.

These two men aren't bargaining. They're not probing for each other's weaknesses and strengths. At least they don't appear to be. Except for the tight jaws and watchdog eyes of their two staff men, the air is free of tension.

It slips in so quietly, I'm not sure who brings it up first, but they are suddenly discussing a 1978 standard of 1.0 grams per mile for NOx. That's a retreat! The present law requires .4 by 1978. The environmental purists will holler, "Conspiracy! Sellout to the auto industry! Two politicians are deciding to let old women and little children die!" On the other hand, auto companies will still shout, "Impossible! 1.0 is technologically unattainable." The auto makers insist on freezing the present 3.1 NOx standard through 1982, claiming any reduction will wreak havoc on fuel economy, intensify the oil crisis, further raise the price of cars, cut auto sales, spread unemployment, and bring on bankruptcies.

Buckley looks at Brayman, then at Leon, doesn't even word a question, and Leon starts to answer:

"The industry claims that they *can* achieve 1.5 NOx, but with a fuel penalty. They'll admit they can go to 1.0 without a fuel penalty, but that means new technology."

Buckley asks for a review: to 1.5 grams *with* a fuel penalty, and down to a cleaner 1.0 *without* a fuel penalty?

Yes, Leon responds. But achieving the cleaner 1.0 requires for larger cars a three-way catalyst, a new kind of add-on technology. Detroit doesn't like the three-way catalyst because the part itself adds significantly to the price of a car and, worse, it requires expensive retooling of the engine block. Furthermore it contains a sensor for a precise electronic mixing of fuel and air. If that sensor goes bad, the resultant incorrect mix ruins the catalyst. But it looks like that sensor problem is licked, says Leon. If forced to, General Motors will go with the three-way catalyst.

Another route is the stratified charge engine. A spark ignites a rich mixture of fuel and air in a tiny combustion chamber. Its flame, in turn, ignites a lean mixture down below, in the cylinders. The result is a far more complete burn, less waste, which means simultaneously less pollution and higher efficiency. Honda uses a stratified charge engine in its subcompact CVCC. Ford is making progress with it for somewhat larger cars.

The diesel engine can achieve 1.0, but it has a lot of problems: technological shortcomings as well as market resistance. For example, it's a balky starter in cold weather. And people don't like its stink. They assume it's an air polluter, although the offensive emission happens to be virtually harmless.

"Those are the choices?" Muskie asks, knowing full well that those are the choices.

Leon nods.

Buckley nods.

With those nods, the majority and minority heads of the subcommittee silently agree to retreat from the standards set in the 1970 law, dooming .4 as a short-range target and substituting 1.0. What they are agreeing is that Detroit is so adamant that .4 cannot be achieved—and most Americans are so insistent on big automobiles that make low pollution goals unachievable—that to insist on .4 threatens to make the Clean Air Act ridiculous through universal non-compliance. They are also agreeing that 1.0 *is* achievable, yet with such difficulty that auto engineers will be under pressure to find a better way of complying, preferably through a wholly redesigned engine.

The nods also signify something else. They are agreeing that they are willing to stand on the Senate floor, be confronted by the scare impact of Detroit's arguments, answer them point by point, and that they believe they can hold the Senate in line to pass the new standard. That political estimate is the critical and decisive judgment.

"Now let's take up," says Muskie, "the two-car strategy."

The conversational exchange soon reveals that this "strategy" offers car makers a "bonus" for achieving fuel economy. As worked out by Billings and Brayman (and presumably already considered by Muskie and Buckley), vehicles that achieve an efficiency target of twenty or more miles per gallon of gasoline would be permitted a year's delay in reducing NOx. Thus those models of cars would be permitted to continue belching 3.1 NOx, the present standard, until the '79 model year.

"This would be a nudge toward fuel economy," muses Buckley aloud. Then doing to Muskie, but ever so gently, what Muskie does mercilessly to Leon, Buckley challenges Muskie with the sword of his chairman's pet standard: "But how do you justify the sacrifice of health?" He goes on to suggest the answer (which Muskie would never do with Leon): "A pragmatic trade-off?"

Muskie responds, "Maybe we're giving away too much."

"What you're saying," Leon puts in, "is you'll give an emission subsidy for cars under 3,000 pounds." Thus Leon pinpoints why Detroit will choke over this "bonus." For all the esoteric talk by Detroit executives about research into engine efficiency, Muskie and Billings have become flatly convinced that fuel economy is essentially a function of an automobile's weight. Strip and shrink a Cadillac down to the size and weight of a Volkswagen and you have a Caddy with VW "efficiency." American cars are "inefficient" simply because they're too big and too loaded with heavyweight gadgets. European and Japanese auto makers, spurred by the high price of gasoline in their prime market places, have mastered and exploited the manufacture of small cars. Detroit has resisted smallness because (1) small cars with small price tags produce small profits; (2) the American consumer, accustomed to an abundance of gasoline at a low price, has preferred bigger cars; and (3) Detroit and its advertising agencies have spent hundreds of millions to insure that the American consumer persists in that preference. Now, under the pressure of the fuel crisis, Ford and General Motors are trying—not too successfully—to compete against small foreign cars with their Pinto and Vega, GM about to introduce an even smaller car, the Chevette. No doubt Ford will match the entry. The investment is stupendous, the risks staggering for any company, even for such giants.

Hal Brayman, although a co-conspirator in this proposal, appears troubled. "Wouldn't this be too big a burden on Chrysler? Would Congress be in the position of doing them in?"

"Good question," responds Leon. "They're busting their ass to get out a small compact, but with the financial shape they're in, they may be in no position to compete, even to get the car out. The question is whether it's Congress' job to save Chrysler."

Again, with scarcely any words of agreement, just the shorthand of phrases and nods, the Senators agree on the two-car strategy. They further agree that by 1981 even those cars getting 20 m.p.g. or better would have to comply with the same emission standard as other cars.

"Well," says Muskie, wrapping it up, "we'll have time to digest it this week, thanks to the New Hampshire stalemate, before the markups start again, before we have to run with this and start defending ourselves." Turning to Billings and Brayman, he asks, "Could we have this put together, not in legislative language, but as sort of an agenda statement for debate? That way we won't freeze the ideas too soon."

Fluttering his eyes appreciatively, Buckley concludes, "Good point."

One thing to be said about Buckley, the free enterpriser: he's a free enterpriser all the way. I learn later in the day that as they leave Muskie's office Brayman, still troubled, remarks to Senator Buckley, "You know, the effect of this thing may be to increase foreign car sales." Buckley replies, "Well then, the issue is whether our companies can compete or not. And if they can't compete, then they don't deserve to have anyone try to protect their sales."

At 4 P.M., I go over to the office of Senator Thomas McIntyre, the New Hampshire Democrat—in fact, until the interminable controversy is settled, the *only* member from New Hampshire in this Senate of ninety-nine—for the meeting with Frank Zarb, Federal Energy Administrator. Dolores tells me that all New England Senators have been invited. Also, it's open to members of their staffs. It's on that ground that I decide to crash the party. Fran Miller has arranged for the sergeant at arms to issue me a white card identifying me as an intern, a status I share with hundreds of high school and college teenagers who overrun the Hill all summer.

At any rate, if I'm bounced out of Senator McIntyre's office, the card will help me preserve my dignity, claiming it was an honest try.

No problem at all. I just ask for the energy meeting and a handsome Yankee woman warmly waves me "right in there." Right in there turns out to be Senator McIntyre's private office. These offices in the Dirksen S.O.B. are smaller than those of the Russell, thinner-and plainer-walled, no carved paneling. It's the functional modernity of a Holiday Inn as against the marbled, spacious, wasteful, lovely sprawl of the Plaza. In this compact room the chairs are jammed together in a tight horseshoe fanning out from McIntyre's desk. And in every chair a Senator: Ted Kennedy and Edward Brooke of Massachusetts; Claiborne Pell of Rhode Island; Patrick Leahy of Vermont; Abe Ribicoff of Connecticut; and Hathaway and Muskie of Maine.

Zarb, beside McIntyre's desk, has a most incongruous match of light gray-blue eyes under heavy black brows, giving him an intense look that could be taken as suspicious, sinister, penetrating, or compassionate, depending on what you want to see. I am starting to think that a public man, of necessity, must have some distinctive physical feature—the elongation of Ed Muskie, or the thick crop of prematurely gray hair quarreling with the baby face of Pat Leahy—and the thought quickly vanishes with a look at thin, balding McIntyre. Passing him in the halls, I always know I've seen him somewhere but can never remember who he is.

Ten or so staff people are leaning against the walls and the window recess, ready to take a note if his or her Senator promises, "I'll get the information for you," or says anything else noteworthy.

This is historic. The country is sitting on the saber's edge of an energy crisis. The worst of it is in New England. Here is the White House and here is almost all of the New England Senate delegation, face to face, eye to eye, behind a closed door, no stenotypist, no public, no record, no inhibition against stating flatly how it is, what each side wants from the other. The President has already vetoed one energy bill and Congress is tearing itself to pieces trying to produce another. In this kind of large-scale drama, how do these men talk with one another in private?

Kennedy, as always, talking rapid-fire, face reddened as though the colors in a Kodak print have come out slightly exaggerated, is banging away at Zarb with the perfectly well-known fact that the Northern tier of states in the United States are colder than those in the South, and that New England has no supply of home-heating gas, therefore is totally dependent on home-heating oil, and that any national policy *must* take into account New England's special need to solve the problem of home-heating oil and industrial oil—

"Now, wait a minute," Zarb breaks in. "That's not peculiar to New England. The shortage of home-heating oil, okay, but don't throw in industrial oil."

Kennedy gives in on the overstatement—and loses the floor.

Important point Kennedy makes. But it's been made in meetings as unprivate as "Meet the Press."

Ribicoff relies less on appeals to justice and more on the sanguine business of what-we've-got-and-what-you've-got, stating in effect: "Look, if you propose a decent bill, we have twelve votes. We can round up our people to support it. But you've got to give us assurances that we can get our home-heating oil, and get it at a decent price. We'll go along on anything reasonable—but we must have the oil."

Muskie introduces a note of annoyed passion, Kennedy jumping in to help, telling Zarb that the White House's position of trying to save energy by slapping an excise tax on imported oil—conserving gasoline by raising its price—is unjust to low-income people and a stupid way to approach the problem. A potent argument, but again right out of "Face the Nation."

Zarb takes it all, blue-gray eyes attentive, sympathetic, unflinching.

When he's sure the anger is all spent, he intones his well-prepared lines, which might be heard any Sunday on "Issues and Answers": "Look, the White House has no interest in having a confrontation with the Senate on this. The President is willing to work with you on any kind of decent bill. On the House side, Al Ullman [the new successor to Wilbur Mills as chairman of the Ways and Means Committee] has tried to do a fine job, just a fine job, but what finally came out is something that just won't save a gallon of gas, just a totally useless bill. We just look to you people to do better. . . ."

Convinced that I missed some important, subtle manipulation or shifts of positions or whatever, I ask Muskie on the way back what he made of it. He bats his hand in a mild gesture of boredom and disgust: "These goddamned meetings, going around and around the same material, the same phrases. Zarb came to see if he can get by just giving these guys assurances, and if he can, there's a substantial block of twelve votes he can count on."

Not twelve. Eleven, counting only one from New Hampshire. And nothing's going to happen about energy or anything else until *that* problem's straightened out.

Wednesday, June 25

No markup this morning. No progress on clean air. No progress on the floor about New Hampshire. The dispute drags on before a virtually empty chamber, mostly between Senator Howard Cannon representing the Rules Committee, Senator Lowell Weicker representing righteousness (in the form of sending the issue back to New Hampshire), and Senator James Allen, siding with the Republicans, having a great old time binding his fellow Democrat Cannon hand and foot with every parliamentary rope trick he knows. And there's none he doesn't know. While a relatively new Senator—elected in

1968—Allen is the only person ever to have served two terms as lieutenant governor of Alabama, 1951–55 and 1963–67. That required presiding over the state Senate, and the Alabama state Senate governs itself by the parliamentary rules of the United States Senate. He trained himself in what has become his favorite form of combat: cool, quiet, paralyzing tactics of parliamentary guerrilla warfare. Other Senators have admired his skill, but he's employed it too often and too well, and with the stretch-out of this New Hampshire controversy, much of it due to Allen's delaying tactics, he's starting to bug his colleagues.

Early this afternoon, following the unusual experience of devoting most of the morning to quiet study, Muskie nods approval to his press secretary, Bob Rose, who brings a request by a Boston *Globe* reporter, Bob Lenzner, for a telephone interview on the Clean Air Act. I am now conditioned to expect a grumpy response to any request that intrudes on his schedule. I'm going to have to recondition myself, because he does not grump when the request is from a Maine newspaper, a Boston newspaper (Boston circulation spills thickly into southern Maine), a TV network program or national news magazine, or a paper of national influence. Publicity seeker? Of course. It's the imperative of his trade.

"Yes, that's the auto industry's argument about cost effectiveness," Muskie says into the phone after listening to a question. "If we accepted that cost-effectiveness argument we wouldn't be where we are. We determined in 1970 that we ought to reduce emissions by ninety per cent in order to meet the health requirments of the country. Now you might well ask, 'Wouldn't eighty-nine per cent do just as well?' I suppose I'd settle for eighty-nine per cent. Then you'd say, 'How about eighty-eight per cent?' Then if I said yes to eighty-eight, you'd take me down to eighty-seven and pretty soon you'd have me down to fifty, because if you're considering one per cent at a time, and weighing it against its cost, how do you justify the expense of an insignificant one per cent of progress toward clean air? That kind of argument is what, in debating, we used to call *reductio ad absurdum*. But if you go from eighty-five down to seventy-seven, then from seventy-seven to seventy, you're suddenly talking about a difference of fifteen per cent. And I think even the automobile industry would agree that fifteen per cent is significant. That kind of playing around with numbers is just rhetoric to embroider their basic argument, which is that they'd like to be left where they are now, coasting along on current standards until 1982.

"What you have to understand is that people are worried about this mileage thing, and the companies are trying to make air pollution controls the scapegoat. But the problem in gas mileage *isn't* air pollution controls. It's *weight*. The average automobile today consumes twice as much energy as the average automobile in 1947, and the principal reasons are weight and power. I bought one of the last cars sold before World War II and one of the first ones sold after World War II, power plants of only a hundred and fifty or so horsepower, and about a thousand to fifteen hundred pounds lighter than today's, and they were damned good automobiles, I tell you that. I was a bachelor then, and you know how young bachelors feel about their automobiles. Then the manufacturers began adding all that weight which they're now peeling off, not only on the small cars but on the big cars. One of the biggest sellers is that new Cadillac—what's it called?—the Seville. They've shortened it and they've peeled off weight, and they're going to keep on peeling off weight until they get the energy consumption reduction they've promised the President. It's a very easy thing to do. They peel it off the same way they put it on. That's the way I ought to work on my pawt,[1] you know. You *can* if you make up your mind to it. But don't make any reference to my pawt in your story."

Chuckling, he says good-by.

Later in the afternoon Muskie is scheduled to appear before an all-day "seminar" sponsored by the ADA for a dozen or so liberal businessmen meeting across the Hill in the Rayburn Building. The schedule says that Jim Case, the quiet young lawyer, will "staff" the engagement. In this case, "staffing" amounts to getting Muskie's car out of the subterranean garage, driving it to the Capitol steps to meet the Senator following a floor vote, then driving the rest of the way across Capitol Park so Muskie will have his car handy at day's end.

As I ride with Jim to the steps, he tells me that Muskie accepted this engagement because it was requested by Don Fraser, the Minneapolis Congressman who last year was national chairman of ADA. No doubt another reason that attracted every member of Congress

---

[1] I could make no sense of this until I observed that he was patting himself in the region of the belt buckle.

who helps fill the all-day program is that these businessmen are rich and are national campaign contributors. The left has its fat cats too.

Soon Muskie's big, dark-suited figure is descending the great white steps of the Capitol in the steamy sunshine, looking strained. He's psyching up for an audience that expects him to say something important, provocative, something he'll intimate to *them* but wouldn't tell just *anybody* ("When I was in Washington, Ed Muskie told me . . ."), something beautifully coherent, and something memorable. Squeezing himself into the front seat of the car, he mutters, "I hate these goddamned speeches."

As we enter the big hearing room, where seminar participants are seated around a quadrangle of tables, Fraser and Representative Brock Adams, Muskie's counterpart as chairman of the House Budget Committee, visibly stir at Muskie's entrance. Henry Reuss of Wisconsin, chairman of the House Banking and Currency Committee, is speaking. Seeing Muskie, he says deferentially, "I see Senator Muskie is here, and we know how valuable his time is, so I'll hasten my remarks." That politeness in reverse—a Senator saying it in the Senate Office Building upon the arrival of a Representative—would be unthinkable. So much for the oft-touted "equality" of the two bodies of our bicameral Congress.

Reuss is relieved to wind it up anyway. Involved in his financial explications, referring to charts and tables, he's having a hard time, because he's lost a cuff link and every time he reaches for a chart his cuff flops open, he grabs for it with his other hand, an awkward, handcuffed way to try to be engrossing about monetary policy.

Muskie talks briefly about the Budget Committee, the need for a planned deficit as a self-levitation escape from the recession, and the discouragement to congressional Democrats of President Ford's record-breaking string of vetoes. He concludes with a time-tested item from his inventory: "We have an old Maine saying that you shouldn't speak unless you can improve on silence. I've probably breached that already."

The first question, from a graying, thin fat cat, is, How can all these well-informed congressmen have produced so little in a year when the people need so much? Essentially, it's the same question the teen-age Republicans put to him the other day. And Muskie goes at it with renewed vigor:

"There is a notion that Congress should be a substitute for the

President. But Congress cannot be. Congress is supposed to be a protection for the people *against* an arbitrary Executive. We have five hundred and thirty-five disparate voices. Not one voice. Five hundred and thirty-five.

"It's this institution that finally exposed Watergate, that brought the government down. Yet the very virtues that enabled the Judiciary Committee to bring down a President are the very virtues that make it impossible for Congress to *be* the President.

"I don't find that alarming. I find it rather reassuring.

"This has been a hard-working Congress. I know all the criticism about recesses and absenteeism and all the rest of it. But this is not just a legislative body. It is a representative body. If we're to be representative, we've got to get back to our people. In recent years we've developed the habit of twelve-month sessions. We were not able to get back to our people, so members were going when they could in order to protect themselves, sometimes missing votes. This year the leadership said, Let's schedule those trips home with recesses. The result has been that the average attendance for votes in the Senate has gone up dramatically this year. I've spent sixty days back home in Maine so far this year, working hard, and my voting attendance is ninety-four per cent, the highest in my senatorial career. That's the kind of Congress this has been.

"With respect to economic policy, I think the record of this Congress is superb. Before the end of March we enacted the most complicated tax bill since I've been in the Senate. In March, usually we're just beginning to spin our wheels. In House committees and Senate committees, we already had under way the many stimulative programs which we passed, one by one, and which the President has vetoed, one by one. I doubt that there's been a Congress in the history of the country where there have been so many vetoes so early in the first session as we have seen this year. Proof that the Congress has been working hard and effectively is that the President has had so many major bills to veto. We've produced an agricultural bill that he vetoed. We produced an energy program that he vetoed, a farm price support bill that he vetoed, a housing bill that he vetoed, an emergency employment bill that he vetoed. All these were produced in the same time frame as President Roosevelt's famous First Hundred Days. Now what more do you want of a Congress? Congress is responding. It can't do it as decisively or as quickly or as cohesively as a President, but I think you can trust this Congress to do what the country requires us to do. Now that's a longer answer than I'll give to other questions."

The same questioner persists with another possible theory to explain the country's disaffection: "People don't understand what you've just explained. Maybe it's a problem of communication."

"You know, I can't think of any institution in America made up of more people willing to communicate than the Congress of the United States. Part of the problem is that we are not given the same forum as the President. Newton Minow has written an excellent book on this. It's his argument that television, in effect, amended the Constitution by giving the President enormously greater power than the founders ever contemplated in the original balance, only because of his access to the people via television, one that Congress can't match.

"Back in 1970, I think, Mike Mansfield appointed me chairman of an ad hoc committee to work on the networks, to get them to give a congressional voice the same kind of platform they give the presidential voice. We've made some progress. The leadership on both sides has been able to agree on spokesmen. I've been selected a couple of times, and so have the Speaker, and Senator Humphrey, Senator Bentsen, Senator Jackson. But the networks have never yet agreed to give us simultaneous time.[2] If you're on only one network in a given half hour, all the viewers will turn to the other two. You've got to capture them, you know, to make them listen to a political speech, especially a reply to the President, no matter how articulate you are.

"I'll say this, that one thing we ought to do in the Congress is move into live coverage of our floor debates. We've been too skittish about that. We're worried that the country will see empty chambers and a lot of limelight grabbers. My own view is that if you expose us to national television our performance will improve. I think the House Judiciary hearings last year are testimony to that possibility, that we would organize our presentation of the issues better, that there would be better attendance. I don't mean wall-to-wall coverage. God, I wouldn't want to inflict on the country daily live telecasts from the floor of the two houses. But we could select the great issues,

[2] In January 1976, after this entry, the Democrats were given simultaneous time on the three major networks to reply to President Ford's State of the Union Address. Senator Muskie was the party's chosen spokesman.

the important debates, give the country a chance to tune in on us. I think we have the capacity to impress the country with our performance, our knowledge. On the Senate side we've opened the doors to our budget seminars—we don't have hearings but seminars. We've never had a closed session. And the reaction I got from some of the press, some of the old toughies, has been, 'My God, I never realized that Senators went into these things with such depth, that they debated things with such comprehension.' We enhanced our credibility simply by doing what we were always doing, but doing it in the open. If we did it on the Senate floor, maybe the objectives of a particular Congress, even though they weren't articulated by one man or one voice, would emerge."

SCHEDULE FOR SENATOR MUSKIE
THURSDAY, JUNE 26, 1975

9:30 A.M.	GOVERNMENT OPERATIONS MARKUP PRODUCTIVITY BILL EF 100
11 A.M.	INTERVIEW PAUL DUKE (OPPOSITE HOUSE STEPS) SEE MEMO ATTACHED
12:30 P.M.	LUNCHEON S 199 AL BARKAN, DEAN CLOWES, CHARLIE MICOLEAU
3 P.M.	FEDERAL GOVERNMENT ACCOUNTANTS ASSOCIATION PRESENTATION OF AN AWARD AND HONORARY MEMBERSHIP

Thursday, June 26

Until now I've been watching Muskie experience the Senate through *his* issues. This morning he is confronted with a problem about someone else's issue. Watching him react, I get an insight into how some Senator far removed from the Environmental Pollution Subcommittee—but deeply involved in some other important business—probably reacts to the puzzle of 1.5 grams of NOx per mile versus 1.0 grams. He knows he can't properly study what's involved. He knows it is important. He knows he must cast a vote. The difficult question is not whom to follow but on what basis to choose whom to follow. Is it the kind of question with which you just go along with your party? With your region? With a chosen expert? With someone who holds an IOU over your head? With someone from whom you want to pick up an IOU?

At a few minutes after nine Al From, the IGR staff chief, and one of his bright young assistants, Dave Johnson, arrive, urgently needing to see the Senator, who is in his office alone. There was supposed to have been a clean air markup this morning at eight-thirty, but Leon canceled it late yesterday upon learning that attendance would be insufficient. Now Al is urging Muskie to attend a markup of the Government Operations Committee. It's listed on his daily schedule (at Al's request) but Muskie did not expect to go. Muskie is not interested in Senator Charles Percy's productivity bill, topic of the markup, which he has already described to me as "meaningless, cosmetic." From's urgings are not over the productivity bill but, to my puzzlement, something about drugs and Bill Hathaway, Maine's junior Senator; something of Byzantine complexity and next to no importance.

It seems that when Senator Harold Hughes of Iowa, the ex-alcoholic who turned to religion, left the Senate, his chairmanship of the Subcommittee on Alcoholism and Narcotics (of the Committee on Labor and Public Welfare) was turned over to Senator Hathaway. Under Hughes, the Congress created an "action office" in the White House on drugs—just two people—as though to symbolize that the President himself was not going to let the drug abuse problem out of his sight for a minute. The White House office was to exist for three years. Hathaway has had the Labor and Public Welfare Committee approve a bill to reauthorize the "action office" for an additional year, perhaps to show that he is no less interested in drug abuse than Senator Hughes was.

That's where this morning's trouble begins. It seems that one of Senator Hughes's people must have forgotten to tell one of Senator Hathaway's people that Labor and Public Welfare's approval was not enough, that Hughes's original bill was a joint effort of Labor and Public Welfare *and* the Government Operations Committee. So now Government Ops must approve the renewal too. The ranking Republican on Government Ops, Senator Percy of Illinois, however, just won't have it. Percy, who is often attracted to actions that have more symbol than substance, feels strongly that elimination of this symbolic office would symbolize reduction of waste and inefficiency. The complications go deeper. The number two man on the Republican side of Government Ops, New York's Jacob Javits, would like to go along with his number one man. But he's caught in an embarrassing bind. For Javits is the number one man on the Republican side of Labor and Public Welfare—and in that capacity has already voted to approve Hathaway's bill. When you're caught on two sides of a question, the best thing to do is don the mantle of Henry Clay: propose the sage compromise that will heal the breach and bring the irreconcilable parties together. That's exactly what Javits is now about to do. Kill the office? Extend it for a year? Javits is going to suggest cutting the extension exactly in half: to six months. Hathaway wants to insure the success of this compromise by going through the motions of pressing for the full year—with the added weight of Muskie's towering presence on his side.

Muskie is smoldering, looking furious at Al's request.

"Why the hell *should* I go? I don't know anything about it."

"You said you wanted to help Senator Hathaway on this."

"I said I didn't want to go against Senator Hathaway on this. That's not the same thing."

Muskie swivels his chair, turning his back to Al, then gets up and looks out the window across a park toward Union Station. He is not shouting down Al's argument, not assaulting it with testing questions. He is really troubled, something beyond his minor outbursts. After a long silence he says, quietly, out of weary protest, aloneness, almost helplessness:

"I *can't* be everywhere. If you start getting involved in things you don't know about, how do you engineer what you do know about?" More silence. "It's a question of priorities. Am I supposed to do this thing that I know nothing about or am I supposed to prepare for the Paul Duke interview?"

Al just stands there, face reddened but ready to take more, like the hired sparring partner. Finally, throwing up his hands to end it, he says, "It's up to you." He and Dave leave. Muskie continues looking out the window. After a few long seconds, embarrassed, I leave too.

Outside his door, I'm astonished to find Al and Dave waiting—obviously for Muskie. Sure enough, in a few seconds he appears and silently we all walk together to the subway car and the markup in a Capitol meeting room near the Senate floor.

The meeting zips through on oiled ball bearings. In the subdued light of the chandeliered meeting room sit Chairman Ribicoff and ranking member Percy; William Roth of Delaware, with a reddish-brown, side-combed carpet of hair that seems sudden and must be a toupee; young Sam Nunn of Georgia, short, plump, solemn, private, whose lower face is always slightly ballooned in the manner of sneaking a burp; plaid-jacketed Lawton Chiles of Florida, who campaigned for his seat in 1970 by walking 1,003 miles from Pensacola to Miami (a campaign ordeal later emulated by others), which probably has nothing to do with his most distinctive attribute, walking hunched, loose-armed, and with an amused menace in his eyes, like an amiable gorilla; and Montana's Lee Metcalf, weather-worn, craggy, stubborn jaw, warm eyes, and shaky hands.

Ribicoff, who always looks worried, says worriedly, "I wish Senator Percy would consider an extension."

Percy, with a deep, cultivated voice straight from high atop Chicago's Congress Hotel overlooking Lake Michigan where we take pleasure in bringing you from coast to coast the danceable rhythms of Whoever and his Merry Men, intones, "Well, I'll go along with six months, although I prefer an immediate termination."

Ribicoff looks to the key man, the compromiser, but Jack Javits' chair is empty. His staff man announces that Senator Javits will "go along with the compromise," which all the parties know he invented. Just then Javits bustles in busily, gets briefed by his man that he has just gone along with his own compromise, and nods confirmation to the chairman. Javits' main problem of getting along in the Senate is that he always makes his entrance a little later, a little busier, a little more importantly than anyone else's.

That is it, and the committee turns to Percy's productivity bill. Muskie remains for a polite minute while Percy delivers a short, up-beat, organ-toned talk about the goodness of eliminating boredom on the job and of increasing productivity for the benefit of all. His talk fails to clarify what continuation of a small agency with a small appropriation, essentially for "research" and conducting meetings, seminars, and dinners with "experts," can accomplish to make the Detroit assembly-line worker or the New York garbage collector less bored and more productive. As soon as he can, Muskie leaves, followed by Al and Dave, followed by me. In the marble rotunda I ask Al if Muskie's presence had any effect.

"In this case it turned out not to matter," he says, "because Hathaway finally agreed to this extension of only six months. I didn't know that Hathaway agreed until Javits' guys told me. But it could have been that if Muskie wasn't in the room Percy might have insisted on no extension at all."

Did Muskie's resistance, his making a scene about going, bother Al?

"It used to really bother me. But the bottom line is whether he'll perform. More often than not he makes the right decision—and then performs well."

So the Senator earns a pat on the head. I've heard almost those same words in the same tone from other staff people, including staff people of other leading Senators. The trained dog comes through for his trainers. He barks and balks a little, but in the end does his trick, and performs it better than the pets of other trainers. In this status-conscious circus, where there are clear rules for assessing the relative status of pets (particularly the rule of seniority), the trainers compete for status too. It's very important in that competition to be identified with a performer who not only gets there but performs well when he does. While Senators bow to acknowledge the applause of the crowds, their uncelebrated staff members, behind the curtains in the wise and intimate world of those who know how it really works, take bows before one another. Identification with a good performer makes it worth while to take all that crap.

As we stride across the marble circular hall away from the meeting, from behind a thick column Rick Bayard suddenly appears and hands Muskie a memo, explaining there's about to be a vote on a compromise on a housing bill. Taking it, Muskie, looking surprised, comments, "I didn't know there *is* a new housing bill." Only yesterday President Ford vetoed a housing bill and the House failed to override it, thus killing it. Heading for S-199, nearby, where he can study the memo before his scheduled interview with Paul Duke for the Public Broadcasting System network, the Senator mutters, "My staff people are waiting around every damned corner." The complaint is halfhearted. He's especially fond of quiet, efficient Rick, whose job, fortunately, has nothing to do with scheduling or asking the Senator to go somewhere and work out something dreadfully unimportant with somebody.

In his big brown leather chair he fixes on the memo. Watching him read a piece of information is almost an aural experience. His eyes X-ray it, his face freezes with attention, and I swear I hear the inside of his head buzz. He does this every time Leon or the "Budget Boys" bring him a major statement or letter for approval. He takes the paper, leans in on it, his eyes and brain snap to attention, and there's a wall between him and the rest of the room.

Feeling like an intruder on an intimate act, I leave him to his reading and head out to the east lawn of the Capitol—"opposite House steps," as the schedule said—in search of Paul Duke. The program, to be broadcast July 16, will be a documentary called "Uncle Sam, Can You Spare a Dime?" and will deal with the need of big cities for federal money.

Television people are wonderful to look for in a busy place. You know them so well, although you've never laid eyes directly on them. As I arrive Duke is holding a mike, looking earnestly into a camera and introducing Hubert Humphrey. Of course, Hubert Humphrey isn't there, but presumably he will be later. A director, standing well off to the side and behind a control panel under a tree, calls, "That's just fine, Paul. Could you do it just once more?" Paul does it just once more, just as earnestly. A pretty girl in a loose shift comes out from under the tree and suggests in a British accent, "Paul, if you can just pat down your hair on the left side just a little bit." He waits a moment for the dying of a breeze and pats down his hair.

To strike a relaxed pose, Duke has one foot propped up on a low stone parapet bordering the grass. During his third introduction of the absent Hubert Humphrey, a Congressman walking by on the sidewalk destroys the performance, calling out, "Hey, Paul, only a politician's supposed to straddle a fence like that." Paul waves, smiling, and begins introducing Humphrey again. Earnestly.

Muskie arrives, chats with Duke off camera, feels for the knot in his tie, pats down his hair, and answers some on-camera questions about countercyclical assistance to the cities. Some tourists have gathered, among them a family from Maine. Muskie poses for a snapshot with the wife and kids, taking a minute to talk with the kids.

In midafternoon, after lunch in S-199 with two labor lobbyists who were invited and scheduled, and a third who was not, Muskie receives a delegation of government accountants who give him an award and an honorary membership, as well as an awesome pile of literature about their organization, presumably all to honor him for leading the new congressional budget operation. Seconds after they leave, Doug Bennet and John McEvoy, the "Budget Boys," arrive to get a piece of paper approved. The Senator piles on them the framed certificate, the membership card, and the literature. Bennet scrutinizes the certificate and says in mock satisfaction, "It's good to see that at last you're qualified."

Muskie is feeling good. Tomorrow the Senate shuts down for a July Fourth recess of ten days and he'll soon be off for Maine. He lights a cigar and blows out a long jet of smoke.

The Senate world's "happy hour" is between about six and nine-thirty and takes place in the spacious and noisy bar and lounge of the Monocle on D Street, a block away and around the corner from the two Senate office buildings, or at Club Two, a block farther away. Of course *some* people regularly leave their Senate offices before six o'clock, but those are the dull ones who take their home lives seriously, or those whose work at the Senate is of so little consequence that they don't feel the compulsion at the end of the day to "unwind" and talk loudly and late into the night with other Senate people about the Senate.

To the Monocle, people come in twos, threes, and fours, which sometimes expand to eights and twelves. Big names and big gossip are blown around like smoke puffs, indeed shouted because that's the only way you can be heard above the din from the surrounding tables, and you're always worried that the next table is listening, which it is, and your partners are only half listening to you because they're also busy picking up names and phrases from the other table. A stranger dropping in just for the show is handicapped in one important way. With no trouble he'll hear why Hubert is supporting Teddy's bill on the floor, at the same time scuttling it behind the scenes, and how everybody at last Friday night's party was so relaxed and having a good time until the phone rang and it was Marvella demanding to know, "Is Birch there?" and Senator Bayh had to leave. The problem arises when the storyteller keeps saying "the Senator"—no name. "The Senator" means the Senator who employs the storyteller, and if you don't know who the storyteller works for, you're dead. Also, in keeping with a delicate code of conversational respect, "the Senator" may also identify the other person's Senator, a kind of shared reverence, which further handicaps the innocent eavesdropper.

Anyway, I'm at the Monocle for this evening's "happy hour," in the company of a veteran and keenly observant staff man whose judgment and detachment I have learned to admire, and who has said, "Sure, I'll tell you how Senators rate Senators and, sure, you can take it all down and use it as long as you forget my name and my Senator's." It is possible, although not common, to choose a table at the Monocle away from the crowd—a "secure" table—and it's one of those we choose.

"Well, I think there may have been a club at one time," he begins skeptically, "when Southerners ran this place because they had lifetime seats and their seniority guaranteed them just about all the chairmanships. But when the old Southerners began dying, and Southern blacks began voting, and the new Southerner, to survive, had to become somewhat liberalized, the core of the power structure of the Senate just withered away. I haven't seen anything that can be construed as a club that we've been part of, and my Senator would be considered part of it if there were one. But you could find widespread agreement about a group of Senators—crossing ideological lines, because ideology has very little to do with prestige and power and respect around here—who are considered to be, one way or another, the movers, the heavyweights of the Senate."

Who would they be?

"I could go right down the roll call, if I had the roll with me."

From my briefcase I draw out a handy, pocket-size "Congressional Directory" published and distributed around the Hill as a public service by lobbyists of the American Medical Association for just such moments as this.

"Right off, you pretty much have to list all committee chairmen, although on closer look you might make a couple of exceptions there. First in this list, I'd say, Howard Baker is important. Others watch him, want to know what he does, what he says, where he's going to position himself on this or that."

Other Republicans?

"Other Democrats too. I'd say Lloyd Bentsen is rapidly working to that position, particularly among conservatives in both parties, or *was* until he went on the road to try to become President."

People will hold that against him?

"They don't hold it against him—well, some people will hold against him that he's going on the road, that he'd rather be anywhere than in the Senate—but the fact of the matter is that your ability to exercise influence and power in the Senate is diminished to the extent that you're off and running around the country. Brock has been an important figure, the more conservative of the two Republican Tennesseeans, Baker and Brock, but always thoughtful and well prepared when he chooses to have something to say, and he chooses those spots carefully, a good explicator of his views, never disagreeable to disagree with, and a very reliable supporter when he agrees to agree with you. Buckley is harder to judge. He's very important from your man's point of view because Muskie deals with him on a lot of things, but I have not detected his major influence within Republican circles. Robert Byrd, obviously. He's the Whip. Howard Cannon, obviously, he's Rules. Church—"

Why is Cannon "obviously" important as chairman of Rules? On the House side, Rules is important because it controls the flow of bills to the floor. But that's not so in the Senate. What is Cannon's power here?

"Rules' foremost leverage over the Senate is in passing on committee budgets. So it's internal, but very threatening, very powerful. Rules also handles all sorts of things having to do with internal housekeeping, a power that Wayne Hays on the other side uses so tyrannically as chairman of the House Administration Committee. Cannon is by no means the Hays type, not the bully, but there's a lot of fighting that goes on over little things, rooms, equipment. You take the Muskie office. He has six rooms down there, right? He's supposed to have five. I happen to know that his people had to prostrate themselves before Cannon to get that extra room. Senator Bible had that suite before Muskie, and somehow he wangled that sixth room, probably because he was from Nevada as Cannon is. Two Senators from the same state and the same party frequently don't get along well, but also they frequently develop gentle blackmail of one kind or another over one another. You can probably find signs of that between Muskie and Hathaway. Well, when Muskie took that suite, Cannon's staff tried to right the wrong and get that room back, and Muskie's people had to go and fight for it, maybe Muskie directly with Cannon.

"Church has been around here for a long time. He came as a boy wonder, so it's easy to think of him still as a young member, but he's been here as long as Herman Talmadge, as long as Jake Javits. He's next in line to be chairman of Foreign Relations, a uniquely powerful and prestigious position in the Senate. And when I say 'next in line,' bear in mind that John Sparkman, its present chairman, is going on seventy-six years old. Do you think he has a prayer of running again in '78, possibly against George Wallace?

"Cranston, Alan Cranston of California, not well known or considered one of your colorful figures in the world outside the Senate, is making himself very— You know, when you were talking about the club, one thinks normally of 'the club' as comprising moderate to conservative Senators. More and more this place is becoming liberal. Some of the liberal people are now becoming club-type respectables.

Cranston is one of the most effective floor operators around. He's noted as the best vote counter in the Senate. When he's interested in an issue, he's calling up staff, counting votes, keeping tallies on that long, narrow piece of paper of his. He's a work horse, a legislative work horse. For that reason, he's considered one of the candidates for Majority Leader. And many people say he'd make an an ideal Whip if Bobby Byrd quit or were elected Majority Leader. Make no mistake, being a work horse like Cranston is a route to power in the Senate.

"Eastland, obviously. Great seniority, chairman of Judiciary, although I don't know who's friendly with Eastland. The liberals just find him impossible. Goldwater, of course, is very powerful in Republican circles. No powerful's the wrong word, he has great prestige. Griffin of Michigan, of course, he's the Minority Whip. McGovern is an outcast."

Why has Goldwater survived his humiliating loss while McGovern has not?

"Because people don't like McGovern. He's regarded as preachy, self-righteous, arrogant, abrasive. Goldwater's considered a nice fellow. He lost with grace, even with humor. And after losing his Senate seat in the bargain he fought his way back to the Senate first chance he got. That got him high marks, as it later did Humphrey."

What you say about McGovern is also said constantly about Lowell Weicker.

"Yes, Weicker is disliked for very much the same reasons. He may be creating friends right now for taking the burden of leadership on this Wyman-Durkin thing, but people don't like these noisy, flailing, holier-than-thou types. They like dignity, reserve. Hubert Humphrey, without seniority—he lost the seniority he had, as well as his claim to good committee assignments, because of his four years as Vice-President, running for President, and two more years until his election back to the Senate in 1970—Humphrey has made an extraordinary comeback in a short time. He's used his chairmanship of the Joint Economic Committee, which has no legislative power and could have been a big nothing, used it skillfully and effectively as a personal platform. In the Senate, with no major official standing, he's gotten into almost everything and people look to him for leadership, for articulation, for persuasion off the floor and on the floor. He's very good at cultivating and helping young Senators, which most old-timers wouldn't bother with, and the newcomers appreciate it, and don't think Hubert doesn't know how to use their appreciation. A remarkable man, came here tattered after that raggle-taggle presidential campaign of his, and he's everybody's favorite again. The rival of every ambitious man around here, but it's almost impossible not to like him.

"Jackson, obviously, has long been a sort of central power, not the kind of man anybody likes or, for that matter, dislikes, although a good number hate him, which is something different. He's absolute master of how to use a committee chairmanship. In every way. Membership on Armed Services used to be his big thing until he became chairman of Interior and discovered the glories of chairmanship. He calls meetings and refuses to call meetings purely for his own purposes. Runs markups with the democracy and participation of the Politburo, reaches out for every jurisdiction he can lay his fingers on, the latest grab being practically anything to do with energy, and he always knows the shortest route to the television camera. His latest is creating and appointing himself chairman of a Special Subcommittee of Legislative Oversight. Would you like to try demarcating the boundaries of that? His other art, matched only by Ted Kennedy, is that of winning Senate approval of fat budgets for his committee, which can only mean one thing: a tremendous staff, then using that staff as a personal empire.

"Then there's Javits, who certainly fits in this list. Javits is disliked but respected. Javits is very smart, very quick, and has won very high regard, but only among liberals. He just sends conservatives up the wall. They can't stand him, whereas these same conservatives might be much more tolerant of other liberals. It's something in that fast, preoccupied New York style of Javits' that offends people. And some of it's jealousy, because he's so energetic and involved in so many things and considered so bright. He's also abrasive and does not suffer fools lightly, so he's not a popular guy. And, of course, as 'club types,' after having persuaded you that there's no such thing, I have to include powerful old-timers like Magnuson, Mansfield, McClellan. The more I think of it, the more I have to say that the Javits and Weicker types—and it's Mathias here who reminds me of this, because he's of the type—are outcasts, like McGovern. You can be of either party to build respect and power around here, but making a display of systematic independence of your party does not contribute to your good reputation.

"I'll tell you a typical old-school Senate type among the young members. Someone who'd be really up and coming in the club, if there were a club, is Sam Nunn of Georgia. But, of course, he was a protégé of the quintessential club type, Richard Russell. Nunn was a grandnephew or something of Carl Vinson, who was chairman of the House Armed Services Committee, it seemed forever, and toward the end of Vinson's service he appointed Nunn—he was then about twenty-four years old—to be the committee's legal counsel. Everybody knew Russell was coaching Nunn for a future here, and then an irony happened. When Russell died Governor Jimmy Carter of Georgia appointed a very liberal, Harvard-educated lawyer, David Gambrell, to fill the seat, giving him a leg up for the special election that fall. I don't want to say that Gambrell was too good for Georgia, but I guess he was too educated to hit it off in those small country towns. So Nunn challenged him in a primary and beat Gambrell. He's a guy who has gained tremendous respect around here by the old rules, by focusing on a select number of issues instead of trying to open his mouth in every goddamned debate, being known for doing his homework. When he opens his mouth he speaks authoritatively and is moderate, conservative in his style. Those were the old rules of the Senate club. Armed Services has been his basic issue and he's become sort of the Senate's foremost expert on U.S. troops in Europe, a leading voice in opposing cuts in those troops. He's also on the Budget Committee, which is becoming very important very fast.

"Percy's a bit of an outcast. It's his manner; that sonorous self-righteousness, that cultivated voice of his drives people crazy. Also his goody-goody Christianity bugs people because everybody knows he's very self-centered and aggressive. On one of his committees the staff calls him 'Charging Chuck.' Proxmire, who gets a lot of publicity and who all my friends at home think must be a Senator's Senator, is regarded here as an eccentric. Actually, he's regarded by fully half the people around here as a certifiable maniac. I've never really decided for myself what I think about him, his jogging across town to and from work every day, the hair transplant and all that. He's just a fiercely independent guy, and some of the things he does, you really have to hand it to him. Very good at highlighting a lot of waste. He's been an effective voice, but mostly on the outside. He's sort of opposite from the Senate club type. People are afraid to deal with Proxmire because you can't deal with him according to the normal rules. You can't ask him for a favor or ask his help or remind him that you once helped him, because everything for him is some kind of crusade or he doesn't want to bother with it. Really, a very serious guy. Randolph—he's been around forever, powerful, but not what I'd call respected. He's canny, wily, he'll count the number of followers before he'll lead a parade. For that reason he's rarely counted on to lead one. Ribicoff. Why don't you ask Muskie about Ribicoff? They've had a few gorgeous battles over the years. Not about policy or philosophy but jurisdictional issues within the Government Operations Committee. The way I've heard it, Ribicoff was trying to rip off some areas of jurisdiction for his Executive Reorganization Subcommittee that Muskie felt belonged to *him* in Intergovernmental Relations. They had a knock-down, drag-out match one day that you could hear out in the hall. People don't go for each other's necks around here over issues. Policy is for gentlemen's debate. What draws blood around here is jurisdiction, who *owns* what issues. Possession of issues means television time, newspaper space, staffs; and to a great extent all those, especially staffs, add up to power within the Senate.

"Stennis, of course, is a classic club type who is very tough to oppose in any debate on armed services because he knows his stuff so well. He's respected by all sides, except the really nasty liberals who really hate his courtly act. Sparkman—I don't know what to say. By virtue of being a committee chairman, especially of Foreign Relations, of course, he's—but he's just considered a sweet old doting man at this stage, a kind of caretaker between Fulbright's reign and Church's takeover. Strom Thurmond is thought by outsiders to be some mighty power because he's so Southern and for that Dixiecrat run for President of his, but he's really considered somewhat eccentric, what with his party switch from Democrat to Republican, which is respected on neither side, and for not knowing that his brand of extreme racism doesn't work here any more. Tower, extremely powerful, but only within Republican circles. If Hugh Scott should retire from the Senate, as some think he may do next year, Tower could be the new Republican leader.

"As for your man, if I may call him that, in a way he perfectly embodies what works extremely well here. The work of the Senate has thrust on him certain issues, which he may not have chosen, but he's never been heard to complain that they aren't glamorous enough. He knows more about those issues than anybody else, so his friends can rely on his leadership, and his adversaries think several times before bucking him. On his issues, especially the environment, he's towering, overpowering, impossible to ignore, but on everything else, quiet, disciplined, and knows how to get along. He's had a crummy deal in the Senate all these years, those crummy assignments, Public Works and Government Ops, until the Budget Committee was invented last year. It's becoming very important, central, and it's perfect for Muskie. His time has really come."

It's hard to believe, I interject, that Muskie's "crummy deal," which he's endured for seventeen years, is entirely attributable—yet apparently it is—to a single sentence uttered during his first week in the Senate to Majority Leader Lyndon Johnson.

"What sentence was that?" my friend asks. I'm amazed he doesn't know, that I have a bit of Senate lore to tell *him*. Every Senator's office, including his, abounds in so much lore, true or apocryphal, exaggerated and embellished, and stories just wished into belief, that no one has heard it all.

The Muskie story—as its victim tells it himself—is that Johnson was welcoming the ex-governor of Maine to Washington, explaining sympathetically how difficult the first years can be, especially becoming one of one hundred after having held personal sway over an entire state government, and how a single vote can sometimes involve a terrible complex of conflicting principles and obligations to colleagues. "Many times, Ed," the imposing Majority Leader is said to have said, "you won't know how you're going to vote until the clerk calling the roll gets to the M's."

Johnson then began outlining the legislative menu for the new session. Of special importance to him was a plan to change the rules for breaking a filibuster. Southerners and conservatives were determined to retain the old Senate rule of a two-thirds vote of all members of the Senate required for terminating debate. Senate liberals were pressing for a three-fifths rule (which, in a Senate of one hundred, is a difference between sixty-seven votes required under the old rule for cloture as against sixty required by the liberal proposal). That narrow difference was night versus day in either maintaining the South's stranglehold on the Senate through the filibuster and breaking it to permit majority rule. Johnson, the great peacemaker, compromiser, consensus taker, was determined to deliver a measure of "victory" to both sides with a rule of ending debate by a vote of two thirds of *members present,* cutting the fine difference even finer. His impassioned explanation of his stand was unmistakably an instruction as to how the new Senator was expected to vote. At the end, Johnson looked at Muskie, waited, then said, "Well, Ed, you don't seem to have much to say."

In his thoughtful, non-committal way of a Downeaster, Muskie, intending no impertinence, replied, "The clerk hasn't gotten to the M's yet."

Well, that was that for that smart-ass upstart from Maine. Johnson ignored Muskie's request for membership on the committees on Foreign Relations, Commerce, and Judiciary. He was banished to his fourth choice, Banking and Currency, and to the Siberias of Public Works and Government Operations. Muskie's relations with Johnson, while becoming somewhat more cordial in later years, remained forever distant and guarded.

Tuesday, July 8

Muskie is due to return from Maine today at 1:30 P.M. He's had a heavy schedule of flying and motoring around to campaign events, but his schedulers have been kind enough to give him a couple of days off during the ten-day recess for loafing at his shoreside house at Kennebunk Beach and for a round or two of golf on the course that stretches out from his back door.

The time has been anything but quiet. I am up to my waist in newspaper clippings, long lobbying letters, and detailed Leon memos on auto emissions, all reaction to the Muskie-Buckley "deal." The series of explosions erupted first at the White House, in response to a letter sent to all members of the Environmental Pollution Subcommittee, dated June 26, the date of my last entry. I suppose the letter was composed jointly by Billings and Hal Brayman; it was signed by Muskie and Buckley, and says in part:

> Honorable Gary Hart
> Committee on Public Works
> United States Senate
> Washington, D.C.
>
> Dear Gary:
>
> We had hoped to bring to your attention this morning a proposal regarding auto pollution that resulted from discussion we had earlier this week. Unfortunately the business of the Senate does not permit a meeting today. But we would appreciate your looking at this suggestion and thinking about it. . . .
>
> The essence of our proposal is an interim "two-car strategy." We would not alter the current standards for 1975–76. To provide continuity, we would extend the current standards through 1977 by changing the oxides of nitrogen number from 2.0 to 3.1 grams per mile. We would propose to hold that 1975–77 standard through the 1979 model year for those cars that achieve 20 miles per gallon or more on the urban driving cycle. Cars that fail to achieve 20 miles per gallon would meet the statutory standards in 1978. Those statutory standards would be the same now required for 1978 model cars, except that the NOx standard would be set at 1.0 grams per mile. Beginning in 1980, all cars would meet this statutory standard. . . .
>
> We want to emphasize that we have put this proposal together to stimulate discussion and focus your attention on the issues before us. Since the schedule of the Senate may constrain any early discussion within Committee, we wanted to bring this proposal to your attention so that we might move more quickly upon the reconvening of our markup.
>
> We look forward to your comments and your suggestions.
>
> Sincerely,
>
> JAMES L. BUCKLEY, U.S.S.   EDMUND S. MUSKIE, U.S.S.
> Ranking Minority Member   Chairman, Subcommittee on
>   Environmental Pollution

I didn't learn of the White House reaction until reading of it in the New York *Times* the morning I arrived home in Connecticut, Saturday, June 28. The story reports the White House going along totally —and not just passively—with the auto industry. The other fascinating wrinkle is that, now that Muskie and Buckley have stolen the fuel economy issue, the White House is making its argument on *health* grounds. The *Times* story reads in part:

Ford Asks 5-Year Freeze on Auto Emission Curbs

by E. W. Kenworthy

WASHINGTON, June 27—President Ford asked Congress today to amend the Clean Air Act of 1970 to give the automobile industry the five-year freeze on auto emission control that it has requested.

The President's request to Congress was announced at a White House news conference conducted by Frank G. Zarb, head of the Federal Energy Administration; John R. Quarles, deputy administrator of the Environmental Protection Agency, and John R. Barnum, Under Secretary of Transportation. . . .

In a development yesterday that may have prompted the suddenly called White House news conference today, Senator Edmund S. Muskie, Democrat of Maine, who is chairman of the Senate Public Works Subcommittee on Environmental Pollution, and Senator James L. Buckley, Republican-Conservative of New York, who is a subcommittee member, sent a letter to other members of the subcommittee proposing relaxations of the time schedules in the 1970 act. But their proposals were more modest than those recommended by the President. . . .

[EPA Administrator Russell] Train gave as his reason [for his proposal last March of a delay in standards, but not as long a delay as the auto industry—and now the White House—is demanding] that E.P.A. scientists had discovered that the catalytic converters used for the first time on 1975 models to oxidize carbon monoxide and hydrocarbons into harmless carbon dioxide and water also oxidized the small amounts of sulphur in the gasoline into sulphur dioxide which, in contact with water, turned into highly toxic sulphuric acid mist and other "sulphates." . . .

"Although there is some disagreement," [the President] said, "on the data and conclusions, there is general accord that it is impossible to accurately predict the adverse impacts likely to result if we move to stricter automobile pollution standards now."

Interesting that Russell Train himself was not at the press conference to explain the White House position, which scuttles his own.

A few days after that press conference Senator Domenici, after making an inquiry of the Ford Motor Company's Washington lobbyist, was startled and flattered to receive an answer from none less than the company president himself, Lee A. Iacocca (who sent copies to all members of the subcommittee). A nifty flourish of thoughtful lobbying. The letter runs four single-spaced pages and says in part:

On June 27, 1975, you asked our Washington Staff to give you our reaction to the proposal by Senators Muskie and Buckley for amending the motor vehicle standards sections of the Clean Air Act. As you know, Ford Motor Company has consistently urged a five-year moratorium . . . as being the most reasonable course of action because of the energy crisis and the economic situation. . . . On the basis of that position, we are opposed to the proposal set forth by Senators Muskie and Buckley.

. . . The idea of giving carryover emission levels only to the cars attaining 20 mpg on the urban driving cycle would amount to a massive government "give away" to the foreign imports. Only Ford Pintos or similar vehicles with our small engines, which are estimated to be less than 24 percent of our product line, could meet that fuel economy standard, but the Volkswagens, Toyotas, Datsuns, Hondas, and other foreign imports would get the benefit of less stringent emission standards and, as a result, receive a major cost benefit. . . .

A law weighted so heavily in favor of foreign imports obviously would be damaging to domestic automobile manufacturers and certainly would be injurious to American working men and women who are in direct competition with foreign workers for jobs.

The standards suggested for "all other" vehicles of .41/3.4/1.0 contain the same peril as do the statutory standards in that no auto manufacturer, domestic or foreign, has been able to meet these standards on a production vehicle capable of meeting the 50,000 mile criteria. In addition, those standards, if attainable, would substantially depreciate fuel economy. . . . In [an earlier] letter to Senator Buckley, we challenged the need for the one gram NOx standard. We do not think it is justified nor is it required to attain the air quality the nation is seeking. Further, we do not agree that the statutory standards for HC and CO (.41 and 3.4) are necessary. . . .

And the opposite side has staked its position too. All subcommittee members received a letter yesterday from the National Clean Air Coalition, signed by the lobbyists of Friends of the Earth, Ralph Nader's Public Interest Research Group, and the Sierra Club, who sit together or exchange significant glances at the markups. Their two-and-a-half-page argument declares that the two-car strategy and its concession to fuel economy "would be harmful to the public health and contrary to the Clean Air Act's basic premises. . . . Such a proposal merely sets the stage for future auto maker propaganda designed to permanently weaken emission standards by continuing the 'energy scare' tactics of the past year." The coalition also protests relaxing the NOx standard from .4 to 1.0. "Dr. Haagen-Schmidt, the most respected air pollution researcher in this country and the discoverer of the auto's role in smog formation, at the May 5, 1975, NAS conference said that the NOx standard should not be higher than 0.6 g/m because areas outward of the central business district would otherwise suffer from excessive oxidant formation. He stated the fear that smog might not be controlled in his lifetime because control strategies did not emphasize NOx control. . . ."

To open their two-thirty briefing at Muskie's desk, Leon Billings announces to the Senator, "Both the environmentalists and the auto companies are opposed to the Muskie-Buckley agreement. That means we've either got a bad bill or a very good one."

Having arrived from Maine only an hour earlier, the Senator is wearing brand-new tan suede loafers and a beige sport coat. Most Senators are drifting into town this afternoon following their recess, although the Senate has been "meeting" since early yesterday, a handful of participants keeping alive the Wyman-Durkin filibuster. A clean air markup was scheduled for this morning, but when the Majority Leader's office announced in advance there would be no floor votes on opening day, that finished off hope of collecting a quorum this morning. So Leon notified Muskie to stay in Maine an extra night and get in a morning round of golf.

Leon hands Muskie a two-page memo on reactions to Muskie-Buckley and delivers an oral briefing of his written briefing. Listening and reading without expression, Muskie asks how Leon thinks the committee will react. Leon goes through a partial rundown, starting with the Republicans:

Baker just seems to be worried about a Muskie-Buckley provision defining the "useful life" of cars at 100,000 miles, which Baker thinks is at least twice too long. Leon comments, "You'll happily give that away if you have to."

Stafford's "staff guys seem to be all right."

Domenici is dreaming up a proposal to tax the manufacturer $50, $100, or $150 for any car, depending on its year, that doesn't meet the standards. "It makes no sense at all."

McClure "may take the Administration approach," which means the auto industry approach voiced in the White House statement.

On the Democratic side, Montoya and Gravel would probably go along with Muskie, because they usually do.

Gary Hart and Culver will go along with the Muskie-Buckley stance, although their staffs have implied that those two would like to stay with tougher standards.

He doesn't mention Chairman Randolph, who is always a puzzle; or Quentin Burdick of North Dakota, who is not a member of the subcommittee; or Robert Morgan, the newcomer from North Carolina who rarely comes around to clean air markups; or Lloyd Bentsen, who sometimes does. (After the meeting I ask Leon if I missed his comment on Bentsen. He replies, "I didn't say anything about Bentsen. I think Bentsen will stay with the White House.")

Leon covers himself, emphasizing to Muskie that these are just speculations, no hard information, just a general feeling, but he anticipates no problems.

Outside the Senator's office, I ask Billings how the schedule looks for final disposition of the bill.

"It looks blique. That's spelled b-l-i-q-u-e."

He explains that the Wyman-Durkin stalemate is causing a terrible jam-up of all Senate business. (I can't recall a Senate year that hasn't had a jam-up like none anyone could remember.) The Senate is going into session at 9 A.M. or 10 A.M. daily, which bars 10 A.M. markups. If that continues, says Leon, Muskie and he will decide whether to urge upon other subcommittee members 8 A.M. or evening markups.

"That may push us past the August recess for getting a bill to the floor," says Leon. "That's the great danger. The longer it takes to develop a piece of legislation, the more opportunity for erosion. I mean, erosion by lobbyists, by industries interested in eroding this provision and that provision."

Rick Bayard strolls by, telling us he has to notify the Senator there'll be a 4 P.M. vote on cloture, a hopeful—but not too hopeful —attempt to shut down the Wyman-Durkin debate. "It'll be close," says Rick, the outcome somewhat dependent on whether the Republicans and the dwindling band of anti-cloture-on-principle Southerners can get Senator Eastland to the floor. He's broken a rib and they may have to wheel him in. Leon remarks that the outcome may not hang on Eastland voting against, but on whether the labor lobby can succeed in breaking Senator Schweiker of Pennsylvania away from the Republican bloc. The Democrats need one vote. Leon asks Rick if Eastland ever voted for cloture. Rick says, "Yes, to end a filibuster by liberals against an anti-school-busing amendment. There is no member of the Senate today who has not voted for cloture at least once."

Shaking his head sadly, Leon says, "No virgins any more. I never thought I'd live to see the day when there'd be no virgins in the Senate."

Maynard Toll has called a 4 P.M. meeting of all the top staff people of the three committees and subcommittees Muskie chairs. It's to take place in Al From's office diagonally across the street, the rundown brick building that used to be the Carroll Arms Hotel, historic trough for thirsty Senators, lobbyists, and what was then a relatively small Senate staff. Maynard tells me that the meeting is to review all current energy bills before the Senate, and to try to pull from that mountainous junkpile a perspective on Maine's interests and what Muskie's general position ought to be. I'm terrifically impressed by this far-seeing staff initiative and decide to attend.

Within minutes the real agenda of the meeting is clear. It's about what Muskie's position on energy should be in his re-election campaign. More prominently, how and where to state pieces of that position for maximum publicity.

Is this electioneering on government time, at government expense? Try to prove it.

Is anything wrong with it? Surely an outsider who wants in—a potential challenger for a Senator's seat—may feel so. But as for the rest of us, who want only to be well represented in Washington, as good a case can be built for defending the practice as for criticizing it. Voters want a Senator to be thinking about them every time he casts a floor vote. They want to keep him constantly fearful of possible punishment through retirement if he forgets them. When a Senator or a staff spends "company time" worrying over how to appeal to a voter next year, that may be the most reliable way to insure that they're worrying about how to represent a constituency well *this* year.

Anybody who has a clear, simple prescription for separating a Senator's public duty from his political self-interest is nibbling the leaves of the artichoke and missing the meaty heart. The beauty is in the paradoxical ways we get our national business done.

Wednesday, July 9

Two or three times a week Majority Whip Robert Byrd distributes a "Dear Colleague" memo about action that can be expected on the Senate floor. In immense letters at the top of the sheet it is rubber-stamped "Whip Notice." Since a Senator usually has his eyes focused on the progress of his own bills through his own committees, without the Whip Notice he would be at sea regarding the flow of the Nation's business to and through the floor. Today's Whip Notice is an interesting example:

Dear Colleague:

There will be cloture votes today and tomorrow on the New Hampshire election dispute (S. Res. 166). No other cloture votes will occur this week.

In addition to the New Hamsphire election dispute, the work load ahead is heavy. For this reason, the necessity of Saturday sessions during this month of July is becoming increasingly apparent. An examination of the business to be disposed of during July will indicate why the necessity for Saturday sessions confronts us. In addition to various other measures which may reach the calendar for floor debate, the following measures will be ready for action during the month of July, but they will not necessarily be called up in the order stated:

1. The New Hamsphire dispute (which continues before the Senate, and on which future cloture votes may be anticipated);
2. Clean Air Amendments;
3. Appropriation bills (especially the Transportation Appropriation bill, and the Treasury, Post Office Appropriation bill);
4. The Energy Allocation Act extension, S. 1849;
5. The Fuel Efficiency for Automobiles measure S. 1883;
6. The Outer Continental Shelf Act;
7. The Elk Hills measure;
8. Coal leasing and coal conversion legislation;
9. ERDA [Energy Research and Development Act];
10. The Energy Production Board;
11. Deregulation of natural gas, S. 692;
12. The extension of the Voting Rights Act, H. R. 6219;
13. Senate Resolution 160, which has to do with Diego Garcia;
14. S. 349, a bill to amend the Federal Trade Commission Act;

15. S. 670, a bill to regulate commerce and to prohibit unfair or deceptive acts or practices in commerce, and for other purposes;

16. S. 644, a bill to amend the Consumer Product Safety Act to improve the Consumer Safety Commission, to authorize new appropriations, and for other purposes;

17. H. R. 4222, an act to amend the National School Lunch Act and the Child Nutrition Act;

18. S. 963, a bill to amend the Federal Food, Drug, and Cosmetic Act; and

19. Various conference reports.

The leadership hopes to have the understanding of all Senators as the Senate tackles this difficult schedule which it is imperative that we follow, with early and late sessions expected daily, and with rollcall votes to occur daily, including Saturdays.

Robert C. Byrd
Extension 42158 or 42297

A striking aspect of that list of bills is that numbers 2 through 11 on Byrd's list all relate to energy. The list dramatizes the fact that the country has no energy policy but a dozen separate, overlapping, sometimes conflicting energy policies, trickling out of an assortment of congressional committees, each not necessarily knowing what the other is doing.

The leadership appears to have relented. The Senate goes into session at its normal noon today, permitting morning markups. Committee chairmen must have screamed from every direction.

Leon shows up in the Senator's office about nine-fifty to escort the boss to the clean air markup, which means he sees some issues hanging on thin threads. To the rhythm of vigorous strides through the basement corridors, building to building, Leon rebriefs Muskie on yesterday's oral briefing of his written briefing. He was indignant yesterday, and still is this morning, over news brought him last week by General Motors' lobbyist, Bill Chapman. It seems that GM's president, Elliott M. (Pete) Estes, told Muskie last May 14—and has since widely publicized—that GM is making a three-billion-dollar investment in new designs of cars that will be fuel-efficient, cleaner, and strong competition against Japanese and European subcompacts. Leon (and apparently Muskie) acquired the clear impression that Estes meant small cars. This was the crux of Estes' plea for a five-year freeze: If they could have time to develop new designs, new technology, the clean air and energy rewards would be great, and the American car industry and its workers would be saved from the foreign menace.

Last week Chapman told Leon that the Muskie-Buckley two-car strategy—separate clean air standards for gas-guzzling big cars and gas-efficient small ones—was "the most destructive proposal I've ever seen." The discussion brought out, Leon's memo says, that GM "does not intend to spend the $3 billion . . . on producing high mileage cars but rather to take weight out of big cars." Ford, too, after using the Japanese "threat" as the reason they need time to design new cars, now also intends to fight the Japanese by reducing the weight of overweight Fords, says his memo.

"It's clear now they had no intention of spending that three billion on small cars," Billings says between the huffs and puffs of their hurried journey. "They'll take a few pounds out here and there, pick up two or three miles per gallon here and there. What they really want to do is build a base for an advertising campaign to say, 'Look, we've got a Chevrolet Impala that gets twenty miles to a gallon.' But it's still going to get just twelve or thirteen in the city."

Muskie takes it in, wordlessly weighing, absorbing.

For the subcommittee's first reaction to the Muskie-Buckley proposal, only Senators Muskie, Domenici, and Stafford are present. Co-author Buckley is in New York, laboring early for re-election. Blond, mountain-shouldered Senator Culver drops in a few minutes after the call to order, and soon leaves without participating.

Muskie introduces the proposal in a meticulously evenhanded, detached tone: "I would like to present the questions raised by the environmentalists on the one hand, by the industry on the other hand, so we may examine those issues, maybe form some judgments."

The committee is struggling in a painful and frustrated way with questions of technology, physics, and chemistry. These Senators are not technological experts but mostly lawyers, and when they went to experts for answers the experts were either divided or just plain didn't know. Since the 1930s the American people have acquired the habit of depending upon Congress and its committees to address virtually every public problem and come up with a "solution." But this time it won't work. The technology will not necessarily give in to an up-and-down vote. And legislators are not accustomed to that frustration.

"Mr. Chairman, I want to comment," breaks in Senator Domenici nervously, uncertainly. "I just would like to talk about going to 1.0 NOx. I would favor leaving it at .4 rather than just arbitrarily plucking 1.0. That is just what this is—arbitrary. There is no evidence whatsoever that there's any more justification, healthwise, technologywise, fuel economywise, achievabilitywise, to put it at 1.0 than there is to put it at .4."

The committee table, the entire room is alerted. Domenici? The New Mexico Republican, the new pen pal of Lee Iacocca of Ford, suddenly siding with the most extreme environmentalist hard line? Muskie and Billings eye him carefully.

"We are not going to get any alternative engine development at 1.0 any more than we are at .4," Domenici continues. "So I think we are kidding ourselves to say we're making some substantial concession to energy conservation or alternative engines by putting in 1.0 instead of .4. I honestly believe that. I'm somewhat prepared to say that, if there's a health risk in NOx which we're learning more and more about, we may as well leave the standard at .4 as go to 1.0. I don't know if anyone would agree with that position."

"So you are for leaving NOx at .4?" Muskie asks, peering over his Ben Franklin reading glasses, looking for the other shoe.

And comes the other shoe immediately: "I would favor leaving it at .4—to be achieved four, five years hence. And with other conditions that I think would favor the domestic automobile industry versus this proposal which I firmly believe is extremely favorable to foreign import cars. I think it also totally disfavors those who need a larger car. I have some facts on that that are incredible. Twenty-five percent of American families have five people or more in them. I'm not talking about a life style but a need.

"When you first sent out this proposal I was intrigued. But the more I look at it the more I think it is extremely dangerous when we have an American automobile industry that is on the verge of bankruptcy. I think there are other ways to make them make small cars and make them conserve fuel. But I don't think this is going to do it."

"I'm not wedded to the two-car strategy," says Muskie righteously, extracting Leon's briefing from his mental file, reworded but quite intact. "But it's clear from the industry's reaction to this proposal that their answer to the energy problem is not the small car. It's reducing the weight of the big car. They are going to avoid any new technology. They just want to continue to feed the present habits of the American automobile owner. Mr. Iacocca had a meeting with me and Senator Buckley and the three other company presidents. They told me that they were committed to a small-car strategy. Once we surfaced this proposal, they backed off from that. They didn't back off from it, they never *meant* it. All they are going to trade off is weight.

"All along the line they have urged changes in the Clean Air Act that will minimize the pressure on them for achieving technological breakthroughs." Muskie's voice is now rising from his inner caverns, his lips taut, indignation misting in like a storm cloud. "I am prepared to be sympathetic, because the health of the American economy is at stake, the jobs of American workers are at stake. But I don't think that surrender to *them* and to *their* version of what the policy ought to be is the answer, even the answer in *their* interests." At *their*, his big open palm slams the committee table and his gray eyes ignite. "My own feeling is if they pursue their own policy line of foot-dragging against the future, the result will be an increasingly vulnerable American automobile industry, not a healthy one.

"Now is the time for them to address themselves to two points: the American people want more energy-efficient automobiles. They don't want some half-baked technological compromise. They want an energy-efficient automobile. I think the American industry can produce that, and that when it begins to, it will begin to be healthy again, economically. I think that is consistent with cleaning up the air.

"What was that statistic they kept throwing at us all that day, and we kept listening to them? Twenty-one per cent. Twenty-one per cent penetration of foreign imports into the American market. They kept waving that number in front of us and I was impressed with that number. But they made their point more effectively with me than they did with themselves. They were using it to influence us, but *they* were not influenced by it.

"It's not the intent of this proposal to hurt the American automobile industry. It's not the intent to compromise health standards. I don't know what numbers are holy. I've seen all kinds on NOx: 3.1, 1.5, 2.0, .6, .4, now 1.0. I would submit that 1.0 is as valid as any of the others. Somebody pulled all the others out of the air. The .4 was pulled out of the air. The .6 was pulled out of the air. The 1.5 was pulled out of the air." Eager to shore up the respectability of the Muskie-Buckley 1.0, Muskie asks Billings: "Where did that 1.0 come from? We didn't originate it in this proposal."

"From the National Academy of Sciences."

"Isn't it true that the industry has been trumpeting the merits of the National Academy as a source of enlightenment on this question?"

"Yes, sir. The industry requested the Committee on Public Works to engage the National Academy of Sciences."

"That is right," checks defense lawyer Muskie. "Senator Domenici was a leader in the committee at urging that National Academy study. It took a year and a half and a million dollars. Is there any indication of why *they* picked 1.0 as one of their numbers for analysis?"

"I think primarily because below 1.0 you begin to exclude engine alternatives, like the diesel. And you constrain the stratified-charge engine."

"Mr. Chairman," says Domenici, voice low, leaning forward, anxious to redeem himself with his chairman. "First, I hope that we've said enough on these committees for you not to think that I don't agree with you on about ninety-five per cent of what you have said about the automobile industry. I think you and I have given this, in my couple of years here as compared with your many years, as much of a working over as we could."

"You do pretty well, Senator."

"I agree they probably haven't done what they should have done over the past years. I see great merit in pushing the automobile industry and its customers to move toward a car that will conserve gasoline. We seem to have an American kind of thing going, that people who want twenty-five miles a gallon are people who like the foreign car. Ford produces one like it and they are not selling. It doesn't have that sort of intrigue, somehow. I also find—I read that General Motors is going to spend about three billions dollars in the next three or four years to produce a little car. If they are going to do that, how much more can we have them do, and how many will they sell if we put this in? Aren't we just going to add fifteen, twenty per cent more on foreign cars to the market? That is the part that concerns me.

"The other thing that disturbs me is that there can be no doubt that the smaller car is an urban car. The urban community is the polluted community. Wyoming is not yet polluted. New Mexico is not yet polluted. Out there, where life doesn't permit using little cars, you are saying, 'You buy that bigger car and it's going to have to meet a more stringent clean air standard."

"Pete, I would like the basis for your conclusion that the small car is just an urban car. I come from a rural state."

"I didn't say 'just.' If I did, strike it. I want to say this and I want it for the record. I certainly do not believe you intended to promote the foreign car over the American car as a thrust of this proposal. I don't mean to imply that."

"Just one comment, Mr. Chairman," calls Senator Gary Hart, who has arrived only minutes earlier. "In response to the earlier observation by Senator Domenici, New Mexico may not be polluted and Wyoming may not be polluted, but Colorado is. Denver is the fourth worst city in the country for NOx pollution, and in three years it will be the third worst. It's not just an L.A., Chicago, New York problem as far as we're concerned."

Domenici's concluding response sheds light on his unrelenting concern for the fate of the big car: "We have more children in New Mexico than you do in Colorado."

It's the talk of the Senate, usually accompanied by eye-rolling wonderment, that Senator Domenici has fathered a wagonload of eight.

Thursday morning, July 10

After yesterday's hair-pulling markup, this morning's was a downer: just sorting out, separating, and agreeing on a discussion agenda of the auto emissions issues. It was held under the gun of an 11 A.M. call for a caucus of all Democratic Senators. Senator Thomas Eagleton of Missouri had lobbied Mike Mansfield and Bobby Byrd to get around finally to doing the perfectly obvious: hold a party discussion on a dozen or so pending energy bills to see if anything resembling a party policy could be shaped.

This opened an opportunity to talk with Senator Buckley, and luckily a meeting was arranged on short notice. This slight, twinkly-eyed, crew-cutted New Yorker, with the quick, soft walk of a librarian and precious shaping of syllables is enshrouded by his image as the unyielding ultraconservative. I want to get a clearer picture of how his lifelong devotion to the environment—and, more immediately, his readiness to join hands with Muskie on auto emissions squares with his ideology. Is it an aberration in an otherwise definable, predictable pattern, like Senator Bob Dole, the Kansas Republican, being soft on food stamps?

It seems fitting that Senator Buckley's office is in the Russell Building—the *old* Senate Office Building—while most first-term Senators are in the sleeker Dirksen. Room 304, his reception office, has the cluttered look of a campaign headquarters, desks and shelves piled with stationery, out-of-date Congressional Records, reports that no one's decided where to file. Its walls are in bureaucratic green. A square of framed campaign photographs on one wall is the only attempt at decoration. Two young women interrupt their work to receive a visitor—"greet" is hardly the word—both devoid of make-up or chic. The room has the grimness that hangs over headquarters of causes. In a way, it's the friendliest reception room I've seen here, in that it's by far the least intimidating.

Senator Buckley's private office, in contrast, suggests a drawing room, no plush upholstery, but a grouping of chairs with delicate legs and arms. The Senator sits alertly, facing his visitor directly, the ever present staff aide, in this case, a full-bearded young man, deployed to one side. Unlike that of many public figures, Buckley's warm gaze appears to focus outwardly on his visitor rather than inwardly on himself, his mind fixed on the subject, its intricacies and intellectual fascinations, rather than as a mine field through which to tiptoe gingerly, lest a misstep blow him sky high. The visitor feels he has Buckley's full attention nine seconds out of ten, that tenth snatched away by a wall clock directly facing him, to which his hyperactive eyes repeatedly flit.

A CONVERSATION WITH SENATOR BUCKLEY

As one who is prominently identified against a great deal of federal regulation, why do you support this most intrusive kind of regulation?

—I believe my position on this act is a conservative position. Two things: I believe that there are certain problems that can only be handled at a national level. This happens to be one of them. You'll find that I'm not at all enthusiastic about federal government getting into solid waste disposal. That's because solid waste doesn't roll across from New Jersey to New York. And I also feel that the conservative community generally has not sufficiently awakened to a totally new phenomenon, namely that we are injecting into water and air huge quantities of totally artificial chemicals that didn't exist until after World War II. They have not educated themselves enough to accept that this is a problem.

—You asked about ideology. I have a certain sort of ideological approach here, mainly internalizing costs. Internalizing external costs. In other words, a commodity in being produced has used the air, in effect, as a free garbage disposal. When the cost is internalized, the purchaser is required to pick up the cost of keeping that public nuisance from being created.

The cost is internalized in the price of the commodity itself?

—Yes. I think it's appropriate and it's fair.

—But when we try to make these decisions on more stringent emission standards, however, there are so many complex factors. The obviously higher cost of the automobile when you internalize the cleaning-up cost is one factor. That doesn't bother me all that much. Then the energy trade-offs, which get us into a real debate with the scientific community as to, number one, whether the standards are realistic in terms of the law's ultimate objective. Number two, are we creating new pollutants that may prove to be dangerous? Such as sulphates and some other catalyst products that people are now beginning to talk about—such exotic things that I can't even remember their names. But I do know that there are people at EPA who are beginning to worry. So my instinct, at this stage, is to start to go slowly, because, first of all, the momentum of improvement is going to stay with us for a while.

—Another thing that worries me is the ability of a group of laymen, no matter how well motivated, to grasp and fully understand the kind of evidence being submitted to us. I mean the Senators themselves. I just don't have any confidence that we can come up with the ultimately wise decision because we don't have the competence to judge the conflicting arguments presented to us. I must confess that—of course, this is why we threw the ball to the National Academy of Sciences, but when the NAS threw the ball back to us, there weren't any clear directives. There was controversy within the NAS as to what this all meant.

—It makes me interested in a proposal that Dixy Lee Ray came up with—you know, she was at the Atomic Energy Commission—saying that there ought to be a court to judge technological matters. People who are scientifically qualified. I'm not sure that I would buy that as a solution, but it seems that this is one of the problems that we are facing in this act. And I think it's necessarily going to be faced in the Clean Water Act in due course, and other legislation of this complexity that reaches out into so many areas of our total national life.

—Another factor that concerns me is that I wonder if we can live with the basic criterion of the act, which is injury to health. Instead of having a precise, scientifically determinable standard onto which to hitch the regulatory statutory criteria, we find that one doesn't exist. It's a sliding scale.

With no thresholds at all.

—That's right. And therefore, what this suggests to me is that ultimately we're going to have to do explicitly something that nobody wants to do explicitly, which in other areas we do implicitly: to say, in effect, that there are trade-offs that involve health. That if somebody is highly susceptible to air pollutants the solution may be not to cause Los Angeles to have zero pollutants in its air but to suggest to this individual that he move to Arizona.

Or wear a gas mask.

—Or wear a gas mask. And when I say we have this implicit trade-off in other areas, we know we kill fifty thousand people a year in automobiles and we haven't said, "No driving." So at some point, as we see the costs of the incremental gains in pollution control getting high, high, high—I'm talking not only in monetary costs but also in social costs—we ultimately are going to face the fact that so long as we have an industrialized society there are going to be some areas that are unhealthy for some people.

—My educational process was with the water quality amendments, which I was in on from scratch. That's where I learned we cannot ignore economic factors. I have enough confidence in our ingenuity to feel we can make steady progress toward necessary environmental goals at acceptable costs. But if you try to force it too fast, or without sufficient knowledge, you get unnecessary costs and risk a backlash effect.

—Finally, there's another area in this whole thing that I'm beginning to find more and more appealing. That is to see if we can't search out, you might say, some automatic economic incentives that will inspire the creativity we're looking for. Some way of penalizing a polluter at least to the amount that he saves by not internalizing the cost of cleaning up.

So that he has no economic benefit by virtue of polluting.

—Right. I'm thinking of that sort of thing as an alternative to trying to stimulate development of technology through these iron deadlines, which don't seem to be producing sufficient—

—When these standards were set, they were known to be arbitrary but you had to start somewhere. And it has forced the development of technology. There's no doubt about it. But we realize now that the standards written into law for the next few years cannot be achieved at any reasonable cost. Therefore they must be modified. Then the terrible uncertainty of what's the most intelligent way to do it.

The auto industry hasn't distinguished itself by any appearance of commitment.

—It hasn't.

It appears they'll do as little as the law allows them to do.

—I agree. Except that if they perceive that the fight is not given up, perhaps they'll devote more of their research and development to finding some alternatives.

With your other committee responsibilities—the Budget Committee, Commerce, Joint Committee on Atomic Energy, other Public Works subcommittees—how do you try to make sense of getting your homework done?

—One of the problems that you have observed is the proliferation of congressional work and you get this vast absenteeism at committee meetings. When I think of the number of hours I've wasted at meetings, this committee, other committees, just waiting for other people to turn up to have a quorum . . .

Is there any organized effort to reform the operation of the Senate? Have you been in touch with, say, Senator Culver, who seems especially concerned with reform?

—We've had informal meetings of the classes of '69, '71, and '73, and have had some reforms that have grown out of our talks. But these have been principally housekeeping reforms. I've made a couple of proposals that have not excited much support. One of them is that I'm sick and tired of being called to the floor to vote on something of great importance that was issued out of committee only the night before. Something for which the report isn't yet available. In other words, you're voting blind.

—The recent legislation reforming pension funds is a great example of something that was a great idea, something that needed to be done, but nobody who had any experience—the banking fraternity, pension planners—had a look at the final version before it was adopted. As a result, we have just dozens of provisions in it that are greatly increasing the cost, causing some employees just to have no pension. Because the provisions of this bill weren't up there long enough in public view for people to dissect it, we ended up with an inferior product.

—Right now, we have a three-day rule. What I propose basically is that legislation should be in the public domain at least six weeks before it is voted upon, and any amendments thereto be three weeks. So that people who understand these things and have a stake in them can try to point out their flaws. I don't think it would delay the work at all. If it has to, let it. We suffer not from an insufficiency of legislation but from too much bad legislation.

Following his Democratic caucus meeting, Muskie heads for S-199 at the Capitol. He loves that room, feels as relaxed there as anywhere, which may seem strange considering its proximity to the floor, the action center of the Senate. He also likes using it to impress people, which is its purpose today. Muskie, Maynard Toll, and Charlie Micoleau gather there near midday to meet with—and impress— Senator Hathaway and a couple of Hathaway's most influential campaign friends, visiting from Maine, for the purpose of generating enthusiasm in the Hathaway camp behind Muskie in his expected race against Billy Cohen.

Late in the meeting Charlie says, "We need everybody's help and have to put on a campaign that's not only very energetic but *looks* energetic. Let's face it, Cohen is young, good-looking, aggressive, the living image of political energy. So we've got to counter it with our own image of aggressiveness and energy."

The others nod agreement and turn to Muskie for his reaction.

Muskie, who's had a rough morning, is blinking his eyes to fight dozing off in his beloved stuffed armchair.

Later I ask Maynard whether a purpose of this show of Democratic solidarity in Maine is to help discourage Cohen from running.

"No, it really is to steam those guys up for the campaign." Suddenly Maynard laughs. "If Hathaway thought his presence would discourage Cohen, he probably wouldn't have come. Hathaway would love for Cohen to go against Muskie."

Has that much rivalry—jealousy—developed between the two Maine Senators?

"Oh no. It's just that if Cohen doesn't go this time against Muskie, he's going to go in two years against Hathaway."

Thursday afternoon, July 10

Late today the revolution that has lain in ambush beneath the drab cover of something called the Budget Committee finally breaks out.

The air holds no hint of the surprise skirmish when Muskie fails to return to his office after the S-199 gathering. Dolores assumes, correctly, that he decided to stay near the Senate floor for upcoming votes. At about 4 P.M. the Budget Boys—Doug Bennet, Budget Committee staff director, and John McEvoy, committee counsel—show up at the office for a scheduled briefing.

Bennet looks the part of staff director of something as ponderous-sounding as a Budget Committee. He wears gold-rimmed specs and pin-striped suits, talks in a deep voice of cultivated sonority, and would look perfectly at home among the gray heads of the governors of the Federal Reserve except for two disqualifications: he walks very fast; and he's only thirty-seven, and looks it.

McEvoy, about the same age, has a tough street-Irish face and the combative crouch of a bantamweight. He was Maynard Toll's predecessor as Muskie's top aide, left to join a law firm to make some money, couldn't stand what he found to be the hollowness of that quest, and grabbed the opportunity of the formation of the Budget Committee to return to the Senate.

"The Senator just called," Dolores informs the Budget Boys. "He said, 'I have to stay on the floor to protect my budget resolution' "—the Budget Boys look startled—"and that you should go to the floor to meet him."

Like a shot they are out, and like a shot I follow, totally in the dark as to what this is about but totally certain that it is important. Almost at a gallop we leg our way down the familiar marble hall, down big marble stairs, through a basement rotunda where the clicks of heels echo like handclaps, and to the two-track station of the little trains of open subway cars. Neither train is there and, impatient, we hoof it to the Capitol along a side walkway.

"I assume," huffs McEvoy, "that H. R. 4222 is the bill that's up. It's the bill that authorizes the school lunch program. It came out of the Senate Agriculture Committee in good shape, within the budget resolution figure. Senator McGovern, who is chairman of the Select Committee on Nutrition and Human Needs—that committee can't act on bills, it's just advisory—is personally proposing an amendment to increase the number of families eligible for subsidized school lunches, the effect of which will raise the cost of the program by $200 million. That amount is clearly beyond anything anybody contemplated in the budget resolution. This bill wasn't supposed to get to the floor until tomorrow. It must have suddenly been called up."

What's the Senator's position on it?

"That's what we've been waiting to find out. He's never opposed school lunches in his life. The program is very important to Maine, and to him. He's caught between his Maine interests and his committee interest."

Just what is this Budget Committee interest?

For one thing, Senator Muskie views his chairmanship of the Budget Committee (which is still in its trial year and may yet die in infancy) as dwarfing his chairmanships over Environmental Pollution and Intergovernmental Relations. Senator Sam Ervin, who took the lead with Muskie and Senator Percy in creating the committee, flatly stated that the Budget Reform Act of 1974 was the most important piece of legislation he had ever worked on in his long career in Congress. Although its procedure is complex, the Budget Committee's purpose is so simple and so large that it is easy to miss. Perhaps the Congress itself did when it passed the Budget Act with little debate, only six dissenting votes in the House, none in the Senate.

On the surface the Budget Committees of the Senate and the House seem to be the latest gimmick in the annual show of seizing control of spending. And that is no small cause. One basic reason that spending has run out of control is not because supporters of Pentagon spending are unable to discipline themselves or because liberals are incapable of saying no to succoring the oppressed, but simply because Congress has had no system whatever for setting limits on its outgo. As Senator Ervin explained: "Congress never decides how much total expenditures should be, nor . . . whether the budget should have a surplus or deficit. The total seems to just happen, without anyone being responsible for it." Senator Muskie has singled out one fateful effect of this non-system: "Congress has seen its control over the federal purse strings ebb away over the past fifty years because of its inability to get a grip on the over-all budget. Meanwhile, the Office of Management and Budget"—the budget agency directly serving and controlled by the President—"has increased its power and influence."

But the importance of the new congressional budget procedure transcends a mere method of keeping the books. It thrusts to the heart of what Americans believe in, where they want to go, and how they want to use their government, because it is a system for *making choices*. A catch phrase of true believers—activists for conservative causes, liberal causes, causes of every bias—is that the country "needs to reorder its priorities." To reorder priorities, by simple definition, is to say that this, which has been neglected, is more important than that; and therefore, by implication, this should get more and that should get less.

The concept of more of something at the expense of less of something else, of course, implies another concept, that there is a limit, a total. These concepts, considered together, define a budget. In that sense, the American government has never lived by a budget. It has never been compelled to eliminate the costs of bad past decisions because it wants to try something new that looks good. It simply has added the new choice to the old ones, and whatever they added up to —that was the total.

This scarcely touches on another fundamental purpose of the Budget Reform Act, that of deciding in advance whether the budget shall provide a surplus or a deficit. Without that decision, there is no national economic policy, just policy by accident. The Budget Act sets up a Budget Committee within each house of Congress and a Congressional Budget Office composed chiefly of economists to feed data and advice to both. Early in the year each Budget Committee studies the state of the economy, the President's budget recommendations, their probable impact on the economy, then determines its own opinion of how it wants the national economy affected by the national budget. (Chiefly, that means whether it wants a budgeted deficit or a budgeted surplus.) Then comes the revolutionary part: by April 15 each Budget Committee recommends a "target" of spending for the upcoming fiscal year. It also recommends a target of taxation. Setting those targets enables Congress, for the first time in history, to *plan a deficit* as a means of revving up the economy or *a surplus* as a means of cooling it down.

Control of a spending sum, however, is futile without control of its parts. The spending target is divided into seventeen categories. These are defined by how they affect human life or a function of government, *not* in the old bureaucratic way of which department does the spending or which Senate committees do the authorizing.

Some of the budget categories and Senate Budget Committee target recommendations for 1976 are:

National defense ($101 billion);　.

International affairs ($6 billion, including outlays for the Peace Corps, Food for Peace, and non-military foreign aid, as well as the operation of the State Department, foreign information and exchange activities);

Science, space, and technology ($4.7 billion);

Natural resources, environment, and energy ($13.4 billion);

Agriculture ($4.3 billion, mostly for price supports and loans to farmers, but not including food stamps and food for foreign aid);

Commerce and transportation ($9.5 billion);

Community and regional development ($6 billion, including disaster insurance and relief and Indian development projects, as well as grants and loans to local governments and individuals for resource and economic development);

Education, manpower, and social services ($20.7 billion);

Health ($32.6 billion, of which 77 per cent is for Medicare and Medicaid);

Income security (by far the most costly category, $138.5 billion— 34 per cent of all federal spending—including Social Security and unemployment insurance, retirement systems for federal and railroad employees, aid to families with dependent children, aid to the disabled and blind, and other assistance programs for the needy, such as food stamps and public housing);

Veterans' benefits and services ($17.6 billion, covering military re-

tirement pensions, disability compensation, GI bill education
benefits, and medical and hospital care);
   Law enforcement and justice ($3.3 billion);
   Revenue sharing ($7.3 billion);
   Interest on the public debt ($35.3 billion).

These category allotments are called "flexible" because the April
15 budget resolution does not give them the force of law. They provide watermarks for Congress and all its committees to observe as
bills parade through the legislative process from spring to fall. In late
summer the Budget Committee of each house takes another look at
the state of the economy; gets one more chance at adjusting the
planned surplus or deficit upward or downward, and one more
chance at reordering the priorities among budget categories (although fattening any budget category may be at the cost of another).
Then by September 15 each house must approve its Budget Committee's second—and final—budget resolution before a new fiscal year
begins on October 1. After passage of that final resolution, a proposed appropriation that would exceed the budget can be blocked on
the floor by any Senator simply by his raising a point of order.

Actually this budget process—as law—doesn't go into effect until
the fiscal year 1977, which begins October 1976. By common consent, however, Congress has "agreed" to conduct itself this year as
though the Budget Act were already in effect, a "dry run" except that
the "point of order" rule is not yet in force. This rehearsal may contain a mortal hazard. Congress, practiced in disciplining the White
House, the states, cities, the nation's mass of citizens, does not often
vote to impose discipline upon itself. Unlike a citizen who may decide to break a law at the peril of penalty, if Congress decides it
doesn't want to be confined by its Budget Act, all it needs to do is re-
peal it. The hazard of the "dry run," therefore, is that the trial year
may provide Congress with an excuse to start forming the habit of ignoring the discipline instead of learning to accept its restrictions.

Muskie has been worried about that.

And now, with exquisite irony, the first threat to break the budget
—and to start dismantling the whole budget process—comes through

a proposal to expand the number of children eligible for low-cost school lunches, on which the children of Maine, in greater proportion than of many states, have come to rely. (And on the eve of Muskie's re-election year!)

As our hurried stride through the subway tunnel brings us near the Capitol, I remark to McEvoy that it's a pity the potential budget buster has come from a Democrat, from an ally, making it especially painful for Muskie.

"That's where it will always come from," John responds. "Muskie's problem is which way to be the son of a bitch. He could vote for McGovern's amendment and say, 'This far but no further,' meanwhile setting the example of how to scuttle the budget process. Or he could vote for the school lunch bill as budgeted, praising the program, but against McGovern's amendment expanding it. That protects the budget but won't help him much in Maine, where they understand a ten-cent lunch much better than the Budget Act."

How do McEvoy's staff colleagues get wind that McGovern is going to introduce his budget-busting amendment directly on the floor after losing his battle for it in the Agriculture Committee?

"Three ways. One is that frequently a Senator prints an upcoming amendment in the Congressional Record, with a statement to alert other Senators. So we'll pick it up from the Record. A more frequent method is that he sends a letter around to other Senators, soliciting co-sponsors. But in this case it was personal contact. Jim Storey, our Budget staff guy who follows up all legislation in the budget categories of income security and health, was on the phone with somebody downtown, I guess at the Department of Agriculture, who is engaged some way in administering school lunches, who mentioned that he learned from someone on McGovern's Nutrition Committee that it would be coming up as a floor amendment. Under the Senate rules, anybody can introduce an amendment even if it's been turned down in committee. All he has to do is get recognized."

We go charging up the "up" escalator that connects the subway and the Senate elevators in the Capitol basement. Doug and John leap out of the staff elevator at the second floor to join Muskie in the chamber. I go up to the third floor and take a seat in the gallery: my favorite spot, in the front corner to the presiding officer's right.

Barry Goldwater is presiding (the onerous duty of playing Vice-President is spelled off every hour, but usually by Senators far more junior than Goldwater). For a moment I'm confused because stone-eyed James Allen of Alabama is droning forth, and I wonder how his filibuster on Wyman-Durkin spilled over into the school lunch bill, until it becomes clear that Allen is managing the school lunch bill as chairman of the Subcommittee on Agricultural Research and General Legislation. A roll call is defeating an amendment by Carl Curtis of Nebraska, and some Senators—more than a dozen—remain on the floor, possibly because they've heard, or just sense, that a storm is about to break. Muskie is in his seat in the back row, engaged in casual but sustained conversation with his left-side neighbor, Tom Eagleton of Missouri. (There's a status group of Senators who have staked out that back row over the years, not observing the custom of moving forward with seniority. Ted Kennedy is there, at the same desk his brother John chose as his permanent position, where John outfitted his chair with a cushioned backing. Others in the row are Ernest Hollings of South Carolina and McIntyre of New Hampshire; between Kennedy and Muskie sits Phil Hart of Michigan; beyond Muskie are Eagleton, Cranston, and Gale McGee of Wyoming.)

Is Muskie lobbying Eagleton for support in the bold move he's about to make? Or sounding out Eagleton as a test of whether to make the move?

"The bill is open for further amendment," Goldwater routinely announces after declaring the Curtis amendment defeated.

"Mr. President," confidently calls McGovern, on his feet, "I call up my amendment No. 672. . . . Mr. President, this amendment does two things: first, it raises, by twenty-five per cent, the income eligibility level for reduced-price lunches, and second, it mandates that schools offer this program. . . . This amendment has been unanimously accepted by the House. In practical terms, if this provision becomes law, a child from a family of four that earns between $5,000 and $10,000 per year will be eligible for a reduced-price school lunch. Reduced-price lunches cost the student no more than twenty cents. . . . At the present time, in order to receive a free lunch, children must be from extremely poor families . . . $5,000 for a family of four.

"By using the proven mechanism of school lunch, families can be given some support while their children's health and well-being is protected by receiving a nutritious meal. And this can be done without establishing a new federal program or new bureaucratic structure. . . . Mr. President, I believe that this amendment represents an intelligent and serious attempt to improve existing law. Congress has shown great leadership in beginning the reduced-price lunch program. I think now is a very good time to improve it and help our school children."

"Mr. President, will the Senator yield?" The big voice is from little John Pastore, the Rhode Island orator.

"I yield." There are different kinds of interruptions, a good number being scheduled, put-up jobs to help reveal support, and clearly this is one.

"I compliment the Senator for his amendment. I hope that for the purpose of the record he will be a little more specific. . . ." And he draws McGovern through a catechism to detail the expanded eligibility, finally wrapping it up with a rhetorical question: "This is not a free lunch—this is a reduced-price lunch?"

"This is a reduced price. . . ."

"I thank the Senator. The amendment is worthy of support."

"Mr. President, I think the intent of the amendment is clear. I do not see any point in belaboring the argument." McGovern is either supremely confident, with his implication that debate would be a waste of time, or he wants to rush this to a roll call, avoiding further debate.

"Mr. President, will the Senator yield?" calls Bob Dole of Kansas, a member of both the Select Committee on Nutrition and the Budget Committee, who asks McGovern what the cost of the amendment would add to the bill.

"This amendment, I say to the Senator from Kansas, would cost, nationwide, an estimated $150 million. Even if the Senate adopts this amendment, the Senate version of the bill still would be $125 million below the level of the House-passed school nutrition bill."

"But, as I understand it, it still would be about $200 million over the budget."

"Yes. When we consider the other add-ons, if this amendment is adopted, the Senator is correct. . . . I stress again to the Senator that this assistance would go directly to families now getting nothing, yet who are in a very low-income category. I think the families in the country that are having the toughest time now are those in the range between about $5,000 and $10,000, with a family of four. This program does not put them on charity. It still requires that the child pay something toward the school lunch, but it does give them a reduced price."

Give and take between Dole and McGovern brings out that the House bill is a bigger budget-buster than the McGovern amendment because it provides a five-cent federally rebated price cut for every lunch served a child who does *not* qualify for free or cut-price meals. Apparently there is an "agreement" in the House that the five-cent subsidy will be dropped in a conference committee of the two houses, the House conferees "compromising" by insisting on retention of the McGovern provisions in the final bill. For those to whom the McGovern provisions are paramount, this is an effective maneuver. For those to whom the budget resolution is paramount, this "compromise" is no compromise at all, but a threat to the infant budget process. Dole is caught in the middle:

"I think the efforts of the Senator from South Dakota make a great deal more sense than giving a nickel to those who do not qualify under the program . . . [and might] make it possible for some of us to support the amendment. . . ."

Muskie picks this moment to request the floor.

"Mr. President, I rise for the purpose of explaining the impact of the McGovern amendment on the first concurrent budget resolution. I think the discussion between the distinguished Senator from South Dakota and the distinguished Senator from Kansas has already disclosed the dimensions of that impact, but I think I should, as chairman of the Committee on the Budget, spell that out in more detail.

"Mr. President, the school lunch program is among the most successful human resources programs ever devised by the federal government. . . . When the Budget Committee met in April to develop the first budget resolution, we were confronted with the President's budget for child nutrition programs that assumed legislative reductions of about $600 million. . . . However, the Committee on Agriculture and Forestry advised us that the President's proposed legislation would *not* be enacted, so the budget resolution assumes an extension of current law. . . . Since that time, the Department of Agriculture submitted a new estimate based on congressional intent to extend current programs. The Department's estimate is $100 million higher than the figures used by the Budget Committee. For the bill before us today, H. R. 4222, the Agriculture Committee estimates the cost at $200 million over and above the estimated cost of extending current law. This puts the bill $300 million over the spending level assumed in the budget resolution.

". . . The Senate Agriculture Committee, while reducing the cost of the House-passed bill by $300 million, nonetheless has added $200 million to the cost of simply carrying the *existing* program. While I would have preferred that the budget target be adhered to, in this case I intend to support the committee's recommendation. I will vote for this bill.

"However, I must oppose amendments to the bill which will further increase its cost. . . .

"There is no question that many children, including some in my own state of Maine, where incomes tend to be lower than in some other states, would be aided by this measure. The cost of these changes, however, would bring the cost of this bill half a billion dollars higher than the budget resolution we agreed to just eight weeks ago.

"Mr. President, I will cast my vote against these amendments reluctantly. Like every other Senator, I wish that we could meet each newly identified human need. The painful reality that led to the enactment of the Budget Act is that we cannot meet *all* our needs *all* at once *all* the time. We must establish priorities. . . . Through the budget process, we have managed to lay before Congress a sound fiscal plan with emphasis on job creation and meeting human needs. It substantially reduces"—he turns to look directly at McGovern—"the portion of the budget the President requested for armaments. . . . It increases the amount of the budget for this very program, the Child Nutrition Act, by $600 million more than the President requested.

"If the Budget Act is to mean anything"—his arms are now aloft and his gaze scans to reach a slowly enlarging attendance of Senators—"it means that at some point we must say, 'This much and no more,' and on this bill we are at that point. . . . We cannot do everything in addition that is attractive, or that we would like to do, or that can be justified on one ground or another, that would appeal to any of us or all of us. We have to say no occasionally, and I regret that this is one of those occasions that I must rise, as chairman of the Committee on the Budget, to say no to this amendment.

"I wish it were not the case but if we breach the budget on this we are simply opening the door to further breaches on other worth-while programs. So I urge my colleagues to consider that this is a significant, important breach of the budget resolution.

"Just this week, stories in the Maine press reported that Maine is among the five poorest states in terms of family income in the country. We have twenty per cent of our people under the poverty level. Our people feel the pressure of inflation and unemployment greatly. But they are also concerned about the integrity of our economic system. If the budget reform legislation is to mean anything, it has to mean that we are willing to accept its *discipline*"—he lets that word suspend and seep in—"not only with respect to those programs which we may *not* be enthusiastic about, but also the programs that have real heart-plucking implications.

"*Discipline* is *discipline*." His eyes are alight now, back of the hand slamming into palm. "It cannot be directed only at the defense budget—or only at the space budget—or only at those programs that have no relevance to our own states and our own needs. Discipline has to be across the board when we are talking about $365 billion of spending in a fiscal year.

"It is that spirit, may I say to the distinguished Senator, my good friend from South Dakota, who has been the real champion of these school lunch and food stamp programs—it is in that spirit that I present this factual report to the Senate."

"Will the Senator yield to me just a moment?" McGovern asks.

"Yes, I do yield."

"Mr. President," breaks in Majority Whip Robert Byrd, "before the Senator propounds a question or makes a statement, I ask unanimous consent that I may proceed for one minute without the Senator who has the floor losing his right to the floor."

"Without objection, it is so ordered," responds Goldwater.

"May we determine in some way whether we can complete action on this bill today? . . . Will the Senators be agreeable to a time limit on the pending amendment?"

McGovern seizes the opportunity. The Democratic-majority Senate simply does not turn down amendments like this, and he wants to get this vote over with: "I say to the Senator from West Virginia, I am ready to vote on it *now*. I think the issue is understood by members of the Senate. I do not wish any additional time."

Senator Clifford Case, New Jersey's liberal Republican, a co-sponsor of McGovern's amendment, does want his moment: "I appreciate fully the purposes for which the Senator from Maine has just been addressing himself. He is doing his duty as he sees it and, as I think this body wants him to do it. I think in this instance the purpose of the amendment overrides the considerations he has suggested. I fully support the amendment. I think it is an excellent one."

"Mr. President," pleads the single-minded Majority Whip, "would the Senators agree to vote on the pending amendment no later than 6 P.M. today?"

"No," bawls Allen of Alabama.

"He would not," Byrd mutters in resignation.

McGovern continues, his self-assurance undiminished, yet with a conciliatory tone that may suggest he senses trouble:

"Mr. President, I just want to take a minute to say that I feel that I understand the point that the Senator from Maine has made as the chairman of the Budget Committee, and he really has no other recourse than to draw the attention of the Senate to the fact that this amendment does go beyond the budget guidelines. I think it is important that we be alerted to that, and we have to make a judgment as to whether there are larger and more fundamental considerations that have to be applied.

"I think in this case it would probably give some reassurance to the Senator from Maine . . . that there is some maneuvering room there in conference where further reductions might be made in other respects of the bill as passed by the House. . . . I, for one, if I should have anything to do with the conference, certainly would be prepared to look at the possibility of some economy moves on the version of the bill as it emerged from the House, and that would perhaps make it more acceptable to the Senator from Maine and his committee."

"I appreciate that statement from the distinguished Senator from South Dakota," Muskie recites ritually but edgily. "Let me make this point: there are a lot of upward pressures on the budget, and a lot of them are in what are often described as uncontrollable areas, and the biggest such area is in the income security field. What is involved here is on the order of $125 to $130 billion, including Social Security payments, SSI payments, unemployment compensation payments, food stamp payments, and they are so uncontrollable that the budget, by and large, reflects simply the latest estimates of what the case loads will be. There is no opportunity to control them beyond that.

"And if the economy continues to deteriorate in terms of unemployment, whatever else happens in the so-called bottoming-out phase of the economic cycle—about which we have heard a great deal from Administration economists—if unemployment continues to deteriorate, then these uncontrollable costs are going to rise. Food stamp costs are going to rise. Unemployment compensation costs will rise. This is the one area, the one big area in the whole federal budget, where we are riding a horse that is almost out of control. I do not say that in any denigrating sense. I am not suggesting that we take action to cut back on the authorizations that allow cost-of-living increases to Social Security beneficiaries, and so on. As a matter of fact, this budget rejects the President's notion of a ceiling on those kinds of payments. It lifts his five per cent cap to the real cost-of-living increases. We have done that.

"But to do *more* than that is a decision that the Senate ought to look at carefully in the terms of what the final consequence will be. Because it is my hope that, when this first year's exercise under the Budget Act is completed, we will have demonstrated the capacity of discipline in spending. If we can demonstrate that capacity this year, then we will have a handle on the budget, not simply for *cutting* spending"—again, the dramatic aiming of his words toward his own side of the House—"but for *directing* spending into the areas which we consider of most importance to the country.

"So establishing that discipline this year, I think, is terribly important. . . . There is a need for carefully targeted programs directed to the highest priority needs. The Senator's amendment addresses a problem that is a high-priority need, but we cannot do them all this year. As chairman of the Budget Committee, I will make that point as eloquently as I can."

Support now comes Muskie's way from the bill's manager, stone-face, stone-age Jim Allen:

"Sometimes I think those who are pushing these tremendously escalating costs are not going to be satisfied until these nutrition programs are pushed up in size, and the defense program pulled down in size, to the point where they meet. . . ."

Ordinarily a Senator is grateful for support from any corner. In this case, however, I suspect Muskie is experiencing a certain tightening of the innards. He is asking his fellow liberals to break a habit, to look at money, politics, the function of government, in a new way, asking them to sacrifice a "heart-plucking" measure for the broader goal of reaffirming a budget procedure, a priority-choosing procedure. When he gets "help" from an unpopular, tightfisted standpatter who attacks McGovern's amendment in all the tired old ways, the difficult change he asks of his colleagues is not made easier.

"I think this amendment," Allen drones on, "costing an additional $180 million, is an example of our fine humanitarian impulses outrunning our ability to pay. . . . This proposal, though paraded as an anti-poverty, anti-recession measure, is actually a partial implementation of a universal reduced-price lunch program. The logic for offering meals at token prices to families making $10,000 per year can be easily stretched to families making $11,000, then on up the income ladder until all the upper-middle and upper-income families are covered. Then the argument will shift to one of uniformity, and it will be proposed to offer token prices to all children regardless of need, or even free meals. That proposal is waiting in the wings, I dare say. That is what we are heading for."

At this perfect psychological moment a McGovern ally unsheathes a powerful weapon for coaxing liberals into line behind the amendment: a recorded vote. What liberal wants to explain at a rally back home his vote against needy kids? Is he to stand there, at a public meeting, and try to explain the budget process? Gaylord Nelson of Wisconsin, McGovern's committee mate and closest friend in the Senate, gets recognition:

"Mr. President, I ask for the yeas and nays on the pending amendment."

Majority Whip Byrd announces a list of Democrats "necessarily absent," presumably getting a Thursday evening start on a weekend of traveling and speechmaking: both Bayh and Hartke of Indiana, Mansfield and Metcalf of Montana, Eastland of Mississippi, Symington of Missouri, and Tunney of California. Also, surprisingly, he adds Pastore of Rhode Island, who lauded McGovern's amendment less than hour ago. Minority Whip Griffin announces the lone Republican absentee, Pete Domenici.

The clerk commences his foghorn call of the roll:

"A b o u r e z k. . . ." McGovern's protégé as South Dakota's jun-

ior Senator. But also a member of the Budget Committee. Abourezk
goes with McGovern: "Aye."

"A l l e n"—predictably, "No."

"B a k e r"—a Republican moderate, "No."

The roll proceeds through Bartlett, Beall, Bellmon, all Republicans, and Bentsen, the Texas Democrat, all voting "No"—with the
Budget Committee, against McGovern—and there's still not the
faintest hint of how this vote will go.

"B i d e n. . . ." His vote will show something. This young Delaware Democrat—elected in 1972 at only twenty-nine, explaining
again and again during his campaign that he'd reach the Senate-
eligible age of thirty before January—has won admiration not only
for his directness but for his personal fortitude. Days after his election, Joe Biden's wife and infant daughter were killed in an automobile accident, leaving him with two small children, and for a time
there was some doubt as to whether he would take his seat. Biden is
an articulate, tough-questioning member of the Budget Committee.
But now—where is he? His slim frame and distinctive long cut of
light brown hair are not to be seen on the floor.

"B r o c k"—the conservative Tennessee Republican of course votes
"No."

"B r o o k e. . . ." A pivotal vote—and Muskie loses this black
liberal Republican from Massachusetts.

Then Buckley, of course, "No."

Dale Bumpers, the handsome former governor of Arkansas who
brought down the career of William Fulbright in a Democratic primary, perhaps a bellwether vote: No answer. Bumpers is standing
right there, a few feet from his seat, but declines to respond to his
name. Burdick, the maverick North Dakota liberal, votes with his
South Dakota neighbor.

Harry Byrd of Virginia, the non-partisan professional miser, pipes
his high-pitched "No." Bobby Byrd, like Bumpers, standing scarcely
six feet from the clerk, pretends not to hear his name, but that's not
necessarily significant since West Virginia Byrd frequently with-
holds his vote till the end, delivering it to where it may have trading
power in the futures market.

And so it goes, suspensefully, yielding little hint of its direction—
until Tom Eagleton calls a loud "No" (McGovern, who supported
Eagleton "one thousand per cent," then dumped him from the na-

tional ticket, is in numerous small ways, here and there, repaid in kind). Then John Glenn: "No." The two liberal Harts, Gary and Philip, go against Muskie. Daniel Inouye of Hawaii has elbowed through the swinging door from the cloakroom and heads straight for Muskie for a quick exchange of words. Inouye calls "No." Pat Leahy of Vermont sides with Muskie, voting "No," and so do Gale McGee of Wyoming, McIntyre of New Hampshire, Montoya of New Mexico, Moss of Utah, Proxmire of Wisconsin—a Democratic tide is swinging to Muskie. But he's lost the votes—and influence—of Humphrey, Jackson, Kennedy, Magnuson, Mondale, Pell. Abe Ribicoff of Connecticut must have timed his entrance to the calling of his name. He plunges in through a side door, calls "Aye," slackens his pace not the slightest, crosses the well of the chamber and, at the precise cadence with which he entered, makes his exit at the opposite side. Is the chairman of the Government Operations Committee, which mothered the Budget Act, reluctant to linger—and face Muskie?

If Democratic liberals are delivering a split for Muskie, the Republican liberals are an almost total loss: Brooke is followed by Clifford Case of New Jersey, Mark Hatfield of Oregon, Javits of New York, Mathias of Maryland, Percy of Illinois (who takes bows in all directions for "co-authoring" the Budget Act with Sam Ervin and Muskie!), and the unpredictable twins of Republican independence, Schweiker and Weicker.

The floor is crowded now, more milling, more hubbubbing by Senators than is common during a roll call. An unusual number have not answered to their names, although present. After the alphabet is completed, hands are raised, here, there, in every corner, a signal to the clerk to repeat the calling of a name. Adlai Stevenson III of Illinois calls "No." Randolph, a veteran senser of the direction of a parade: "No." Bobby Byrd: "No." And some younger Democrats: Morgan of North Carolina, "No." Dick Stone of Florida, "No." Sam Nunn of Georgia: "No."

Joe Biden is on the floor. He's talked to Muskie. He votes "No." Bumpers votes "No."

All through the jittery proceeding Muskie sits hunched in a huge heap at his desk, expressionless, eyes wandering. A stranger might think him daydreaming. Toward the end McGovern is standing ramrod straight at his desk. Occasionally he says something abbreviated, urgent, to a passing Senator. His eyes dart about, expectant.

And then the final tally is announced:

The Yeas—29. Nays—61. The amendment is rejected.

Without a word, not even to a paper-drowned aide seated behind him, McGovern strides sternly to the nearest door, beneath where I sit, and disappears.

The gallery buzzes. The Senators who did the amendment in, still milling, seem slightly awed by something imponderable they have just witnessed: the Senate, *this* Senate of the overwhelming Democratic and liberal majority, *does not defeat school lunch bills.* How did this remarkable event, totally unforeseen by anyone just two hours ago, come about?

At the opposite end of the gallery, across the Press Gallery section which occupies front center, I see Rick Bayard rise to his feet in the section reserved for Senate staff. As he leaves his corner of the gallery I leave mine to head back to the office to wait for Rick. What I observed on the floor from my viewpoint may not be the same as what he saw as Muskie's legislative eyes and ears. In a few minutes Rick ambles in with his gentle dignity and scuffed shoes. At my mention that I want to glean some of the detail of his triumph, there is that subtle acknowledgment one sees only at rare moments in reserved souls: the faintest change of temperature in the eyes, a current of joy. With feet on the desk, we shake our heads and smile at what the world would do if it ever found out how impromptu, often so sudden and accidental, are the crucial acts of public figures to whose every move we attribute meticulous planning and plotting and cunning.

A CONVERSATION WITH RICK BAYARD

How did you first hear that the McGovern amendment was coming up?

—Jim Storey knew it was coming, but we didn't expect the bill till tomorrow. Jim had drafted a memo explaining his reading of the bill's effect on the budget. It was a short, very judicious memo: As chairman of Budget, you stand this way; as Senator from Maine, you stand that way. The same as what I try to do in my memos on bills coming to the floor.

—Muskie was having a two o'clock meeting in S-199 with Maynard and some people from Maine. Suddenly this afternoon I learned that the school lunch bill was on the floor—I didn't find out until about ten minutes after it came up. Jim Storey and I went to the Capitol together. He was going to monitor the floor situation while I talked to Muskie about the statement. Since his meeting was going on, we both went to the floor to try to find out what time the McGovern amendment would come up. With this bill there had been no unanimous consent on time limits on amendments, any restrictions like that, because people figured the bill wasn't too controversial and wouldn't take very long. So we had to make a guess. When we thought it was pretty near to being called up, we went back down to S-199, and fortunately the meeting was just breaking up. At this point Muskie didn't know a thing about the bill. He didn't know anything about its budget implications, and he didn't know anything about what we were going to recommend. He had scanned our memo once during the meeting he had with Maynard, but that's all. Now we sat down and he read it over. As he really read it this time, he arched his eyebrows and glared at me and said, "Am I going to be the only one voting against this?"

—He realized what a touchy decision this faced him with. It's an emotional, popular program and one that one does not vote against. Now this amendment was not all that extravagant, but when put together with the amount that the bill was already over the budget, it would have amounted to a half billion dollars too much, a major attack on the budget resolution. The built-in excess, the $300 million, was mostly through uncontrollable growth, since this is an "entitlement" program. The law just says that a child is entitled to something, in this case a free lunch, if his family's income is such and such. It authorizes spending without naming a specific appropriation. Whatever the cost of an entitlement bill comes to, the government's got to pay. It's the same with veterans' pensions, aid to dependent children, food stamps, Medicaid, the cost-of-living increase for Social Security—all "entitlement" bills that have sent the income security portion of the budget through the roof. The budget is stuck forever with each of these past actions of Congress. Each year each entitlement grows larger, and somebody's always introducing some new entitlement bill, usually something irresistible. Income security is suddenly by far the largest category in the budget, way above defense, and still growing.

For many Senators this vote presented a difficult choice. They can't possibly have thought long or deeply about it, since Muskie himself didn't know he was going to make a fight until minutes earlier. How do those Senators make that spur-of-the-moment decision?

—I venture to say that most Senators, on this issue as well as others, hear about it either from other Senators around the door as they come in, or from the people who work for the Secretary of the Majority—or of the Minority. The Secretary of the Majority is supposed to sit at that big roll-top desk near the front door—yes, I guess it'll be known forever as the Bobby Baker desk—and he's got his staff of cloakroom people, and they frequently brief Senators on what's going on.

How does one of these people brief a Senator in just a few seconds, without sounding like he's telling the Senator how to vote?

—These are sharp guys. They know a Senator's past record, his philosophy, his constituency. They might say, "The other Senator from your state voted this way," or "Mr. Byrd or Mr. Mansfield voted that way." Now you take Joe Biden. Biden frequently has a staff person who meets him at the elevator and briefs him on the vote. The individual—in this case it's a girl—would have told him very briefly what Muskie had said. Biden came on the floor and walked right over to Muskie and asked him something, and Muskie shook his head. I saw that from the gallery. Biden voted no. Inouye did the same thing—walked directly to Muskie. Inouye wasn't there for the debate. He'd heard from someone outside about the amendment, and that Muskie had stood up and said, "I have to oppose it." So he went right to Muskie and talked to him briefly, and that was that. He voted no. This may look like Senators just take orders from other Senators, but that's not it. This was such an unusual vote, and it's so unusual to hear in the hall that Muskie is opposing something like this, that they want confirmation of what they'd heard.

From my spot in the gallery, I thought that at the end of today's vote McGovern looked stunned.

—That was certainly my assessment. Stunned. Stood at his desk on the floor, amazed, shell-shocked.

—You have to understand that this was chairman against chairman, liberal against liberal—on a liberal issue. McGovern didn't expect Muskie to oppose it. Muskie had given no indication that he was going to oppose it. And even after Muskie was finished, McGovern thought he had the votes. That's why he wanted to call for a vote when Byrd asked how long this was going to take. If the vote had been taken then, McGovern might have won, possibly—probably. Because word still hadn't gotten around, and people hadn't had a chance to digest what a significant thing this was for Muskie as a liberal to be opposing a liberal on a bill like this. You could tell from the tone of his voice and his demeanor that McGovern was confident until he started to bargain with Muskie, which is very extraordinary. Remember that business, McGovern saying if he got on the conference committee he'd try to get the House version cut down? McGovern was bargaining—with Muskie. One does not bargain with anyone other than the manager of the bill. Muskie wasn't the manager of this bill. Allen was. I've never seen that anywhere before—never. At that point McGovern was nervous. And Muskie ignored him roundly, which was perfect. Then McGovern started to get more and more nervous.

At what point of the roll call do you think McGovern began to realize what was happening?

—I don't think he realized he was going to lose—he must have thought it was close until the very end. I'll tell you how I know. He walked over to Pat Leahy, a liberal from Vermont, and tried to get him to change his vote. Leahy said—I could read his lips and his face—he said, "If you really *need* it." They walked together to the tally sheets, and I saw Leahy shake his head, saying, "Sorry, it's not going to make any difference." And they walked their separate ways. But that was the most interesting thing I saw McGovern do: try and get someone to change his vote right on the floor. He was willing to get himself indebted to young Leahy, whom he'll have to deal with for years on the Agriculture Committee, a new and impressionable Senator, a liberal, and he couldn't get him to go along.

—After the vote he just walked out stunned, couldn't talk to anybody. He didn't go over and say, as they often do, "Congratulations, Ed. Your point carried the day." Maybe he was angry for not having been warned in advance.[1]

Do you suppose Muskie regrets not having warned him?

[1] This is later contradicted by Senator Muskie.

—No. This makes it a stronger—you know, Muskie could have gotten more votes if there had been advance notice. On such short notice, I thought he'd lose, but not by as many votes as he thought. Let me tell you this: right after the vote, I came down from the gallery and walked up to him on the floor, and I said, "I guess you're as surprised as McGovern was." And he laughed and said, "Yes." Later, as we were coming back, he said, "You know, this is the most important thing we've done so far to establish the budget process. After this, anybody who comes up with a big-spending amendment is going to have to say, 'Better get in touch with the Budget Committee and see what they say. What's that guy Muskie going to do?' "

Muskie was talking a fairly long time with Eagleton. Would he have been working on him?

—They sit just two seats apart, and the reason why they chat, generally, is for Muskie to listen to Eagleton's jokes. They both enjoy a joke.

Do you find it true that McGovern's prestige is shot in the Senate?

—No, that's not true. It's just that he's never been a very effective Senator in terms of getting legislation through. And that's either because he'd propose flaky things like $1,000 a person or because he was—well, he was sort of a flamer in the early days—

Flamer?

—Yeah, you know, the kind who'd rather go down in flames defending something whole and pure than going for part of it and winning. Like he'd be the only guy in the whole Senate to vote against something, or he'd offer amendments that had no chance of passing, all for show. It just pissed people off. He didn't work well with other people in committees during his early career. Muskie does. And that makes a big difference. Maybe McGovern's a little frustrated with a committee's pace, and not willing to compromise his particular principles as he sees them.

Muskie's door is slightly ajar. Sometimes during this suspension between day and evening he's in there walking around in his shirttail and undershorts, meticulously hanging up a suit, laying out another. But I take the liberty of peeking in. The Senator is behind his desk gazing into space. Looking up, he doesn't scowl at the intrusion, which is virtually an invitation.

"That was quite a show," I offer. "You stuck your neck out and I wanted to congratulate you."

The Senator's face transforms with unconcealed pleasure. I suddenly realize I've never heard any member of his staff say, "Congratulations." They take his achievements, his triumphs for granted, exactly as he takes their initiative, their intelligence, their hard work. And he's as starved for praise from them—from anybody—as they from him. Clearly he wants to hear more, so I press a few questions.

"You had no time for any phone calling, any lobbying on this at all, just went in cold?"

"Oh yes. I expected to lose."

"You were sitting with Eagleton for quite a while. Did that help bring him over?

"Oh, we were just—I just told him that it was a budget-buster."

"Did you happen to notice Humphrey's vote?"

"He voted for the amendment. Jackson voted for the amendment. Ribicoff. This is a real heartbreaker. That's why—you know, I could have let this slide by, picked it up on some later issue and said, 'We've gone over the budget by so much with this and this and this.' To get the liberals to support the budget process on a cut in defense spending—that's easy. But if I want to have credibility on the floor, the Senate has got to understand that I will vote to hold down spending on programs I'm very favorable to as well as programs I'm not so favorable to. This is very important. *Very* important."

"Do you suppose McGovern resents not having been warned?"

"I warned him. I did warn him I was going to do it. I told him at the Policy Committee the other day. I said something like, 'My job is to keep your feet to the fire and I'm going to do it. You may not like it. You may be uncomfortable, but I'm going to do it. Because either this thing is going to *work* or it *isn't* going to work. And you're a *part* of it.'"

"I wonder how often you'll have to give today's sermon."

"This thing today did it. I think, up to now, they've not really been conscious of the Budget Committee. From now on, they know that the Budget Committee's got clout and will use it."

"I don't think the significance of the budget process has dawned on many people outside of Capitol Hill or outside of Washington."

With a mischievous gleam, he confides, "I don't believe so either."

Thursday evening, July 10

Jim Case, the blond, efficient lawyer, whispered to me this afternoon, before the school lunch outbreak, that he's having a few people over tonight "for hamburgers," and could I come. I accepted
gladly. These people, with whom I have been spending all my days,
are becoming friends and, in a sense, office mates, and I'm curious to
see them in other settings. We head across the Potomac to Alexandria
where Jim, his quiet, creamy-skinned wife Cathy, and their baby
daughter live in a small, comfortable, rented house.

Two guests are young men visiting from Maine, both staff
members of the state legislature in Augusta, the rest all from
Muskie's office: Charlie Micoleau; Estelle Lavoie, Jim's co-worker
on constituent "cases," and Bob Rose, the short, dark, introverted
press aide. Except for me and Charlie, who is barely over the line,
nobody in the room is over thirty. For the full first hour of natter
and banter, the marvel takes place—I really came to believe it was
impossible—of Senate people not talking about the Senate or their
Senators or Senate politics. What do they talk about? They talk
about Maine politics. Mostly directing questions at the two visitors:
how's So and So, and how did the feud between So and So and
Whatsisname ever work out, and if So and So decides to run for such
and such, who's going to run for his present such and such?

Maine politics are interrupted by the arrival of not hamburgers but
a generous platter of barbecued chicken. On the coffee table a big jug
of low-cost California wine is emptying, and a growing collection of
empty beer cans has something to do with an affectionate glow that
takes over the room. And when the panning of Maine runs out of
yield, the conversation wanders back to familiar ground. Washington. The Senate. The Senator.

They all, or most of them, have this great big dominant fact in common: the Senator. Identities that flow from him. Loyalty to him, belief in him. Occasional humiliation because of him. And what they would hesitate to admit, hostility toward him. He is, after all, their parent, their commanding officer, their warden, their employer, and he stirs the love-hate that those roles imply. Somewhere, sometime, the pressure has to leak out. And now the wine, the beer, the fresh audience of outsiders, and the trust that these are friendly, reliable outsiders, and the common ground that they, too, are focused on the Senator as Object—all this helps loosen the flow. Charlie is explaining to the three outsiders what can be fully appreciated only by his appreciative audience of insiders, the rigors of character required by a staff member of a Senator when, no matter what you bring him, whether responding to a question or a request for a piece of paper, his immediate reaction is some kind of dissatisfaction. I reach for my tape recorder, put it on the floor in front of Charlie, in the center of the rapt circle, and to general laughter I switch it on with a flourish. Rather than inhibiting him, it eggs him on:

"One time Dolores gets a call, rolls her eyes like it's really important, and hands the phone to Maynard. Maynard listens awhile, then hangs up and goes in to tell the Senator, 'Senator, Henry Kissinger would like to have breakfast with you tomorrow morning.' And the Senator says, 'For chrissake, with all I have on my schedule?' Maynard says, 'There's nothing on the schedule at breakfast. You can have an early morning meeting.' And the Senator blows up. 'Well, damn it, you could schedule something at six o'clock in the morning, and of *course* I'd be free!' And somewhere along there he mutters, 'All he wants to do anyhow is lobby me on Turkey.' Finally Maynard just has to ask, 'Are you going to go?' And he never does get an answer. So Maynard just calls Kissinger's office and tells them he'll be there.

"Like tonight, we needed an answer on whether he approved a particular line in a letter. Jim finally came back and said, 'Well, I got the answer. He laughed.' That meant yes."

"Do you think," I ask, "that the Senator's resistance may be based partly on a feeling that he's not up on all the details of the Turkey situation and doesn't want to be snowed by Kissinger?"

"I'm sure he didn't want to be put on the spot by Kissinger to make a commitment yet. Actually this happens all the time. I wanted him to call some lawyers in Maine on the no-fault insurance issue, just two or three, just to talk to them about it, give them the feeling he was listening to their opposition to it. Not saying he was opposed or in favor, but just to get their views personally. His attitude was, 'If I call them, they're going to try to press a commitment out of me that I'll oppose the thing, and I don't want to put myself in that position.'"

"But isn't it his style to" (why am I defending him? I begin to wonder as I'm still framing the question) "to preserve—"

"Preserve that flexibility. Ed Muskie's political genius over the years has been his ability to fight battles on *his* terms, not somebody else's. And one of the ways you achieve that is you don't get into the battle early. You wait. Not to see which way the wind is blowing, because I don't think he operates that way, but you wait until people have committed themselves to a position. And while his position may be opposed to theirs, they're locked in. He can stake out the strongest position against them. He's fresh. He's new.

"I don't think he's a very good politician, but he's a great tactician. One on one, he overwhelms an opponent with his intelligence, his oratorical skills, and his adversary capability. He makes it almost impossible to survive. And that's both good and bad. He can be absolutely wrong and never change his mind. He goes off the wall sometimes. He's on one of those things now, just repeatedly keeps saying the Congress does have an energy policy, that of opposing Ford's tax increase. That is *not* an energy policy. But nothing's going to move him from that. I think he's making a serious mistake in that it's an implied defense of Congress, and I don't think you can really defend Congress on this.

"But on this business of why he reacts the way he does, there are other reasons. How would you like to have your life run by a piece of paper? How many years has he been going through this? Twenty-five years of that daily schedule. And his old daily schedules are nothing like he's had in the last ten years."

"But most executives live by their calendars and it's not that much of a hangup for them, is it? I wonder if a half dozen out of the ninety-nine Senators feel that strongly about being pushed around by their schedules."

"I don't know how many actually have to live that way. But for him, it's more than a hangup. To him, the schedule is an intrusion.

The other side of that, though, is that he couldn't live any other way. I mean, it's all a fraud. You sit around thinking what would happen if you really believed him about the things he'd want to do if he only had the time, if you just left him alone. Say he was in his office and you brought him a piece of paper and left. I'm convinced you could leave him there a week, and you'd open his door, and there'd be cobwebs over the guy and that piece of paper still there. He never bothers to call anybody and ask them to come in. He'd just sit there. He's a passive guy.

"Leon has this description of him, I guess it's in the Nader report on Congress. Leon describes Muskie's creative processes, where he just absorbs information and proposals like a sponge in an adversary sort of way, fighting it tooth and nail. But he absorbs them. You keep feeding him, and all of a sudden it's like a catalytic reaction. Suddenly he'll begin to create. He'll take bits and pieces of what somebody told him a month ago, a year ago. I've seen this in Maine, where he'll take something that happened twenty years ago, he'll wrap it into something that's happening now, and all of a sudden he'll start to create. And the end product will be more than the total of the pieces that went into it.

"He plays on people. A very satisfying thing, from the staff point of view, is that by the time he's reached the point of accepting one of your ideas he's raised every objection, totally explored every nook and cranny of it. In terms of mental discipline, let me tell you this makes you refine your thinking, refine your proposals a great deal before you submit them. You don't walk in there with an awful lot of proposals."

"How do you know when an idea doesn't interest him at all?"

"Dead silence. That would be lowest on a scale of Ed Muskie reactions. The signals I look for, moving up the ladder of communication from dead silence, are 'Humph,' and then going beyond that, you get 'Why?' These are indications of the beginning of interest. He really starts when he looks at you accusingly and says, 'You think I ought to do *that?*' Then you know he's listening, he's heard what you said and is going to focus on it. When he actually starts quizzing you—'Who said that? What's *this?*'—then you know you're really off and running."

At a few minutes after one there is unanimous consent that there's a hard day at the office ahead and everybody better get home.

Friday morning, July 11

The sixth attempt to shut down the Durkin-Wyman controversy through cloture failed yesterday by six votes. Allen of Alabama, one of the handful of Southern Democrats siding with the Republicans, is most responsible for dragging out the talkathon for weeks, pausing only occasionally to let a few bills slip through. So yesterday the Democratic caucus decided (spurred by Eagleton, with Allen not objecting) to go on a two-track system. After a few hours each day of the New Hampshire debate, the Senate will spend an additional few hours taking up, one by one, that hodgepodge of energy bills, aiming to act on them in the three weeks before Congress recesses for the month of August. Whether that patchwork of bills, coming out of several committees, comprises an "energy policy" remains to be seen.

At about nine-ten, I arrive at the office, immediately sense a strangeness in the air, and realize the place has been invaded and taken over by a superior outside force. Three men in blue jeans and ski jackets and heavily armed with cables, lights, and sound equipment have driven Muskie from his own office and are giving orders to Maynard and Dolores, which they carry out docilely. It seems that "CBS Morning News" is preparing a short feature on the budget process, and as part of that short feature they want Muskie's talking head to answer a question about the "scorekeeping" method—the system of tracking bills in process.

For one question, maybe thirty seconds on TV, all this!

Where's Muskie? When Dolores tells me, I'm sure she's kidding, but I go back there to check. Verily, he's in the last office of the suite, crouched in a small wooden chair between the Xerox copier and the signature machine that signs "Ed," gazing at a chart while Doug Bennet and John McEvoy brief him. Something besides the Senator is out of place, something incongruous, almost comic. Actually, two things:

1. This man, who can seethe at the intrusion when a staff member approaches him in the hall with an urgent question, appears totally uncomplaining about this forcible eviction from his own nest. I cannot recall ever witnessing so sincere a tribute to the power of TV.

2. In the weeks I've been here—and, people tell me, for months and months before that—Muskie has not once been moved to walk the length of his assigned real estate to favor his staff with a glimpse of his living self, or vice versa. And his reason for doing it this once is not improvement of employee relations but an appearance on "CBS Morning News." (In defense of Muskie's Olympian aloofness, it should be said that staff morale can be affected just as negatively by a Senator's visitations. There's a persistent story around the Hill that Hubert Humphrey prowls his suite after hours almost nightly, poking into wastebaskets, rummaging through carbon copies to check on what's really going on. Fritz Mondale prowls by day, believing it important to see and be seen by staff. Staff would just as soon he stayed holed up. Like the other day, so a story goes, on his shoulder-patting tour, just to show a little interest, he reached his hand into an "In" basket to sample what the troops are hard at work at. He came up with a letter from a constituent that had remained unanswered for all of eight days. That ruined his good-will tour. Face flushed, he shouted, "Isn't *anybody* around here interested in what happens to Fritz Mondale?")

When the technicians are finally ready with their wires and lights, they send word through Dolores that the Senator may return now. He settles into his big swivel chair behind the desk while they study shadows and flesh tones. Muskie feels low behind his desk, not towering and powerful. Two technicians spin the swivel chair to raise it. Muskie tries it again, then reaches for a straight-backed armchair and feels better. He passes time by chatting with the technicians, asking questions. Finally Doug asks, "When do we get started?" The cameraman replies, "We're waiting for the talent."

The "talent," in the person of Bruce Morton, soon makes his busy entrance. The arrival, like the throwing of a switch, electrifies and activates all the lesser participants, the lighting man, the sound man, the cameraman, and the United States Senator. Morton, from the couch, out of camera range, asks his question, and Muskie, aglow under focused light, responds coolly, with succinctness, thoroughness, and low-key force. Hum of camera ceases. Lights out. Morton rises, extends hand, smiles with a distant warmth, saying, "Thank you, Senator," with the same concealment of condescension that Senators use on constituents, and he busily departs, leaving the others to restore the office, and leaving Muskie to wait until they restore it.

After the one-question interview, Doug Bennet hustles back to his office, and I hustle with him. He occupies a corner room in the former Carroll Arms Hotel, possibly the only government building where the lowliest staff member has ready access to a private bath with shower. Bennet's office is slightly larger than most, no doubt once a honeymoon suite. His voice is authoritative, deeper than seems natural, masking an underlay of anxiety. When taking an important phone call, such as from Muskie, he nervously paces a wide arc around his desk, with each turnaround adding another twist to the hopeless snarl of his phone wire. From a box atop his desk, he pops Pine Bros. glycerine lozenges.

"I don't know how I ever became a budgeteer," Bennet protests with an amused shake of his head. After earning an advanced degree in medieval Russian history, he went to work for a Connecticut neighbor, Chester Bowles, in the American Embassy in India. Upon returning to the United States, he became administrative assistant to Senator Eagleton, then to Connecticut's Senator Ribicoff. In 1974 he entered the Democratic primary for eastern Connecticut's seat in Congress, to be beaten by Christopher Dodd, son of former Senator Thomas Dodd.

A CONVERSATION WITH DOUGLAS BENNET

Much as the Budget Act may change procedures, can it really change the way Congress behaves?

—I have a sort of apocalyptic view of that. If this doesn't work, I think you might as well give Congress to the Smithsonian and forget it. If Congress can't make this work, it means that a legislative body can't make the kind of decisions, can't use the kind of foresight that you need in a modern society. An important thing that's happened in the United States is that we've moved out of the era of unlimited resources. There was a time when there was enough room, enough air, enough minerals, enough energy, enough everything. No matter what you did, no matter what your political system did, there was always more. One of the big things you never had to do, therefore, was plan. The only problem was how to get your hands on what you needed. Now the problem is how to clean up after yourself, not only in physical terms but in economic terms—how to deal with the consequences of economic acts. The Budget Act, with its built-in system for determining mid-term and long-term costs of any new commitment, is the first real effort to look ahead in economic policy making in the United States. And that goes for the executive branch as well as Congress.

When you say we've reached the limit of resources, do you mean dollar resources, or do you mean we've reached the pollution limit, or do you mean some form of social cost of technology?

—The limit on expendable dollars is simply an expression of the others. And I'm not talking about the recession, which may be short-term. We still have on the books of this country's laws—well, just take the case of depletion allowances. We still have on the books laws designed to encourage people to go out and dig things up—dig coal and ore, pump oil. We don't encourage people to recycle things. In steel, for example, you don't get a subsidy for running a junkyard, but you get a depletion allowance for taking stuff out of the earth. The Interstate Commerce Commission reaffirmed just a few days ago a long-standing decision that the rate is higher for transporting scrap than for transporting iron ore. It just doesn't make any sense at all. It's just left over from another era.

What is the new budget process most likely to founder on?

—Inability to get discipline, that's number one. You don't have to discipline individuals. It's a question of disciplining the aggregate. You have to expect that individuals are going to introduce big bills. They come from different parts of the country, have different classes of constituencies and different legitimate needs. I think the real trick is to get them to understand how each specific need relates to a portion of the budget. If the Congress has decided that they're going to allocate *x* for health, they're going to have to decide on the most efficient way to achieve their health objective, within that portion of the budget, and give up individual items in that portion of the budget that are less effective.

—You have to understand, it's extremely important in understanding this budget process, that the Budget Committee does not weigh one line item against another line item. Under the defense category, for example, it's not the Budget Committee's job to quibble over going for the B-1 bomber or not going for the B-1 bomber. That's the Armed Services Committee's job, and later, the money for the B-1 becomes the job of the Armed Services Subcommittee of the Appropriations Committee. Our job is to recommend the total of what defense ought to be versus what health ought to be or versus what any other national need ought to be. That's the priorities factor.

—That priorities factor, I would say parenthetically, is not something that the executive branch does very well. It has too many internal political pressures. Momentum is a bigger factor in the executive than it is here. By momentum, I mean the way the President's budget gets put together, all the guys who run little tiny programs adding their little pieces in. By the time you get to the apex of, say, the health function, there's so much momentum behind all those pieces that it's very hard to stand back and take a general look at the whole thing and say that we should shift emphasis from health to something else, or to health from something else. The momentum of what already exists is too overpowering. On the Congress side, we don't directly feel the pressure, the burden of all those minutiae, all that momentum.

—The second thing we could founder on is the tendency to expect too much out of analysis. There's a tenacious feeling around here that if you only study a thing long enough and hard enough you really can come up with a cost-benefit analysis on something like education. Or a cost-benefit analysis on something more tangible like a weapons system. And I'd say you can't—ever. You assemble as much information as you can and then, by God, you've got to go out and make a judgment. And that's tough. But that's what you have a legislative body for.

Are there promising signs that you're going to get this thing you call "discipline"?

—Much more—and much sooner—than we expected. I can't figure out why. Senators are calling us up to ask what a given bill would do to the target. They ask Muskie all the time what a given piece of legislation will do, or what his estimate of the economy is, meaning is the planned deficit likely to go up or down, making room for additional spending or forcing a reduction of spending.

—A great danger would be if Muskie or someone on the committee has to stand up every day doing a Horatio at the bridge every time a budget buster came around the corner, the way Muskie had to do yesterday for the first time on the school lunch bill. Instead, what we've tried to do is keep track of what's happening in every committee, if possible, every subcommittee. We have a staff specialist for every budget category, and each specialist has a staff of his or her own. Instead of that dangerous Horatio tactic, what we've tried to do is just very, very quietly, very, very early in the game, catch bills at the subcommittee level that might bust the budget. We just talk with sponsors, with staff people and so forth, and already this is working surprisingly well. It'll probably work even better after what they saw yesterday.

Monday, July 14

Muskie arrives from Maine in the early afternoon. The important item on today's schedule is a meeting at four-thirty with Leonard Woodcock, the UAW president. Muskie doesn't accept a shred of Woodcock's belief that the added cost to an automobile of pollution control equipment is a significant cause of the collapse of auto sales or the hundreds of thousands of layoffs by auto companies and suppliers. Yet he views Woodcock's position with sympathy. Partly because he likes the man. Strong, private men, which both these men are, often communicate actively in a language of silence, of empathy, to which wordy people are deaf. Mostly, however, Muskie does not associate Woodcock with what he considers to be the industry's deliberate "stonewalling." Woodcock's anxiety over his members' joblessness is deep-felt and honest, even if his linking it with clean air is, as Muskie feels, misguided.

Woodcock turns up promptly at four-thirty, seconds after Muskie has disappeared for a floor vote. Dolores hands Leon the precious key to S-199, where the Senator will go from the floor. So the labor leader proceeds to the Capitol with his companions, David Ragone, the University of Michigan's dean of engineering who is Woodcock's adviser on pollution control, and Jack Beidler, chief UAW lobbyist; also, Leon and me.

Woodcock is visibly impressed by the Capitol hideaway. Muskie arrives at four fifty-five, greets the visitors, picks up from a side table a glass-covered cross section of a cylindrical piece of hardware, and lays it on the coffee table between Woodcock and himself, murmuring, "Should we have half a catalyst as a centerpiece?" Turning to Leon, he asks, "What's new?" Leon starts to catch him up on the past few days' developments, which, besides imparting information, conveys the message to Woodcock that he's a friend, an insider, liked and trusted. This gesture is a Muskie Valentine.

Hart has sent around a memo, begins Leon, with an alternative proposal to Muskie-Buckley. It would go to 1.0 NOx in 1978, as Muskie-Buckley does, hold it through 1981, thence to .4 NOx, which the Muskie-Buckley position abandons as a statutory target. Hart, too, has a two-car strategy, but a different kind, exempting—up to ten per cent of a company's production—from the tightening ratchet of NOx standards those cars outfitted with "innovative technology," which Hart's proposal does not clearly define.

"This is *Gary* Hart," Muskie twits Woodcock, a constituent of Phil Hart. "I wouldn't want you to get mixed up."

"I have my Harts in the right place," Woodcock assures him.

Leon continues: Domenici is preparing another substitute proposal involving fines—per car; say, $50 the first year, $100 the second—for failure to comply with standards. In theory, that should insure that failure to comply is because a company can't, not because it doesn't want to.

"If it weren't for the fuel-economy problem and the employment problem," Woodcock mutters, almost apologetically, "we wouldn't be yacking about it. I worry about Chrysler and American Motors. American Motors has now made a deal with Volkswagen for a four-cylinder engine. Don't tell anybody I told you that. I hope Chrysler can come in on something like that."

"Have you given any thought to our proposal?" Muskie asks mildly.

"You mean yours and Senator Buckley's. The trouble with it is you deal out anything above a compact. It gives a terrific leg up to the imports—and to GM, because they have the capital to retool. On that Domenici thing, it means you can have the delay if you can afford to buy it. That's no help to Chrysler and AMC."

Talk ambles toward various fuel-economy bills pending in both houses and how fuel economy is suddenly a popular goal after years of gasoline squandering, and how the Administration is under great pressure to reduce oil imports.

"I told Henry Ford," Woodcock continues, "that the only way he's going to get anything on emissions—any delay—is to come up with real fuel economy. He says, 'Okay, we'll get on it.' First thing you know, his lobbyist, Markley, is at Burning Tree playing golf with Markley's good friend the President, and we're back at square one. Markley brought half the message. Gerald Ford comes out for an emissions freeze without setting any condition of fuel economy."

Muskie chuckles. They communicate by silence for a spell, then Muskie says aloud: "It's hard to say where this thing will go in committee. There are various proposals and I'm treading water waiting to see what we can work out. *My* mind's not made up. This is the toughest legislative problem I can ever remember. Not only the political problems but the technical. It's hard to build an automobile by law. This is tougher than the original Clean Air Act—by far."

"I would agree with that."

"We tried deadlines, but that's tarnished now because technology wouldn't listen to the deadlines. If you have to start shifting the deadlines you lose credibility."

Muskie shakes his head at the difficulties. Woodcock nods his.

Both men stand. The meeting is over.

Did I miss something? Did one of them proffer something that the other accepted—or refused? Who won? Who lost? Even if they tied, on *what* did they tie? Is this what happens around here when power confronts power?

After Woodcock departs, Leon tells Muskie there may be still more proposals and counterproposals at tomorrow's markup. The combinations of standards for the three regulated pollutants, and varieties of possible deadlines, could become a snarl of yarn, impossible to unravel. But with a conspiratorial leer, Leon advances a suggestion: "Why not vote on standards first? Final standards only, with no deadlines. After that's settled, then vote on dates."

Muskie ingests the suggestion expressionlessly.

An hour or so later I run into Leon leaving the Dirksen Building. How does he assess the meeting?

"I just had a call from a friend at UAW," Leon says, "to tell me how pleased Woodcock was."

Why? Nothing was decided. Hardly anything was discussed.

"Maybe just because it was friendly. Last time Woodcock and Muskie got together they both got pretty hot. Or maybe it was just that Muskie said his mind wasn't made up."

Tuesday, July 15

With an 8 A.M. clean air markup ahead, Muskie rises at dawn in his family-shorn house in Bethesda, and before making a huge breakfast, which he once told me is his favorite meal, he prepares for the day by opening his black, loose-leaf clean air briefing book to a memo dated July 10, last Thursday, from Leon Billings and his staff lieutenant, Karl Braithwaite.

It sums up the substitute for Muskie-Buckley to be proposed this morning by Gary Hart, which Muskie hopes to get out of the way through a vote before 9 A.M. when the markup must end. The memo concludes:

"The proposal has an attractive feature: It retains the health basis of the Act by keeping the .4 [NOx] standard, but recognizes the value . . . various standards have to stimulation of technology. . . . [But] this proposal would allow numerous opportunities for the auto industry to come back to Congress and request a revision of standards, since the deadlines stretch out through 1986. Its basic concept has some attractiveness, and perhaps it could be modified into some acceptable form if the Muskie-Buckley proposal is not successful."

It annoys Muskie, surely, that Hart, a newcomer, is striking this stance of environmental absolutism—of moral superiority—by pressing for the statutory goal of .4 grams per mile of NOx, knowing its political—and possibly technical—unfeasibility. Muskie has decided long ago that the key principle to making the Clean Air Act strong is its credibility. The word "credibility" is central to everything he thinks and does. By his way of thinking, if the act is so "strong" that it invites either widespread non-compliance or repeated revision of standards and deadlines, the act will be disrespected, weak, and will contribute to a prolongation of foul air.

Yet, in a way, he welcomes Hart's proposal to retain .4 NOx in the law. By comparison, his (and Buckley's) target of 1.0 NOx—which Detroit also considers intolerable, but which *is* known to be achievable—is now the moderate position, more feasible to sustain politically. Muskie loves nothing more, after committing himself to a difficult position on an issue, than to maneuver so that his is the "moderate" position. Leon's favorite Muskie quotation—and I've heard Muskie state variations of it—is, "If I could control the positions of the extremes, I could control where the middle is—and always win."

Overnight, Muskie has decided that, yes, in accordance with Leon's suggestion, a good way to untangle the auto emissions mess is to vote first on what the ultimate standards should be, and then to vote on deadlines for achieving those standards.

At the markup, after Hart reviews his substitute proposal, there ensues the usual wrestling, this time among Hart, Domenici, and McClure, over whether the National Academy of Sciences did or did not state that .4 NOx is essential to health, whether NAS said or did not say that .4 NOx is or would soon be achievable, and whether NAS said that the diesel could or could not comply with an emission standard of 1.0 NOx.

Then McClure becomes aware of an implication of Leon's plan to vote separately on standards and deadlines. A sly glint emanating from his eyes, McClure asks Muskie, "We are not voting on the timetable now, or on interim standards? We are only voting on emission standards?"

Muskie assents.

"In that context," asserts McClure, swallowing a canary, "I support the .4. But with a different timetable than Gary's."

Senator Domenici catches the glint—and the implication. And for reasons as numerous as the Senators who have now filled most of the places around the table, the Hart proposal (without deadlines) has become extremely attractive. It's a way of going on record with the strongest possible environmentalist vote—in favor of .4 NOx—in a most harmless way, without saying when it must go into force.

Barry Meyer, the Public Works Committee counsel and chief clerk, starts calling the roll.

Bentsen and Buckley vote "No." A good start for the survival of the Muskie-Buckley target and schedule. Then successive "Ayes"— for the substitute—from Culver, Domenici, Gravel, Hart, McClure, Morgan, and Stafford, interrupted only by Muskie's "No."

So the substitute proposal of freshman Hart—his standards only, not his deadlines—has won the day, and the Muskie-Buckley position has been kicked aside.

With Hart's proposal now the pending business, McClure next presents his timetable as a substitute for Hart's. McClure proposes stretching out the current 1976-model standards, relatively permissive ones, for all three pollutants, hydrocarbons, carbon dioxides, and NOx, through 1979, then two years of an easily achievable .9 for HC, 9.0 for CO and 1.5 for NOx. Finally in 1982 he goes to Hart's tough standards of .41/3.4/.4—but with a catch. After completion of new analyses by EPA and NAS, Congress is to "review" whether the 1980–81 and the 1982-and-beyond reductions are actually to go into effect. This virtually gives the auto industry the five-year moratorium it wants—ample lobbying time to erase that 1982 target of .4 NOx.

At five minutes past nine the markup ends before taking a vote on a timetable, because Muskie and most of the members must reassemble themselves as the Economic Development Subcommittee of the Public Works Committee. Following that—at ten o'clock—the Budget Committee is to have an exchange with three economists in what the Budget Committe likes to call "seminars" instead of "hearings" or markups. And after that Muskie has a meeting of the Water

Quality Commission in the Capitol, of which Vice-President Rockefeller is chairman and Muskie vice-chairman. And at two-thirty a reception in the Caucus Room for Alexander Solzhenitsyn, which I
doubt he'll squeeze in, and at five-thirty a "social" for labor officials
in S-199 (more pregame warmup for next year's campaign), and tonight, back to the Rockefellers' Foxhall Road place for dinner with
the Water Quality Commission members and staff. Leon knows it's
hopeless to try to get consulting time with the Senator today. He returns to his office and settles for a memo:

> Today's vote establishing an ultimate .4 NOx standard has the
> fortunate effect of sending a message to the industry that the
> Committee is serious about achieving health-related air quality.
> Unfortunately, it will permit the industry to continue to argue
> that certain kinds of technology are precluded at the .4 NOx
> level, and thus only catalyst technology will be pursued. . . .
>
> I am also afraid that a vote for .4 NOx is a cheap pro-environ-
> mental vote, the effect of which will be to weaken the possibility
> of going to statutory standards in 1978. Senator Buckley seems
> to be wavering on the question of the 1978 standards. He is
> afraid that the industry may not be able to meet .4/3.4/1.0 in
> two years and does not want to be the sponsor of an unachieva-
> ble standard. . . .

Early in the afternoon I ask Leon if he thinks that Hart realized
his purist insistence on .4 allowed him to get sandbagged by
Domenici and McClure.

Leon responds, with a gleam that is part hurt, part gloating, "He
does now."

More distant from the Capitol than that of any other Senator's is
the office of Gary Hart of Colorado. He is at the end of the northern
corridor of the top floor of the Dirksen Building. His reception room
is a desk-crowded working room. From a side corridor appears his
amiable secretary, Elsie Vance, daughter of Cyrus Vance, who informs me that the Senator is not back yet—when is a Senator ever
back yet?—but he's expected soon. Hart is indeed under extraordinary time pressure for a new member. Despite his strong devotion

and campaign commitment to the environment, right now the Public Works Committee is the least of his three committee concerns. He's on Armed Services where, among other crises, there's one having to do with whether the United States has a legitimate national security interest in defending Diego Garcia, a tiny island in the Indian Ocean. (Shades of Quemoy and Matsu!) More conspicuously, he's on the special committee, chaired by Frank Church, investigating the CIA, putting out supersecret documents and televised hearings.

Soon Miss Vance reappears and leads me through that narrow passage where Hart distractedly greets me. Ignoring the major part of his office dominated by his desk, he sits in a straight-backed chair near the door, showing me to a straight-backed chair opposite him. He sits erect, enduring the present, resisting some urgency to charge into the next thing. His posture of attention says, "Deliver to me your questions so I can get on with delivering you my answers." His eyes, directed toward his visitor, make no contact. My previous sense of some unresolved conflict in this man, suggested by the uncomfortable, tender way he walks the marble floors on the balls of his feet in his macho cowboy boots, flares up again with his tension at the prospect of conversation. He can scarcely sit still for an exchange, I've noticed, even with his clean air staff aide, Kevin Cornell, of whom he'll ask a most cryptic question upon arriving at a markup, then start nervously nodding, too impatient to wait out the answer. Yet he makes a display of his relaxation and informality by having his staff call him "Gary."

A CONVERSATION WITH SENATOR GARY HART

How do you manage to keep up with the intricacies of clean air while the CIA and armed services are so demanding?

—I could not have kept up with it, even participated in it, without excellent staff help. I've been the beneficiary of very capable staff assistance, in the form of Kevin Cornell, who is a Ph.D. in physics. He came to me through a fellowship program which provides a year on the Hill for free, no cost to my budget, and he selected our office, thankfully. He's a broad-gauge fellow. He does a little economics and he can also bat and catch right- and left-handed.

—In addition to which I would just add that I was in the Interior Department in '65 and '66 under Stewart Udall when the original clean air and clean water legislation was being drafted and debated in the Johnson Administration.

What were some of your surprises about the Senate?

—I would say minor surprise impressions. First of all, I would say the historical burden. I feel very strongly above governmental institutions. What I think fell upon me most in starting out were the predecessors—the Websters and the Clays and the La Follettes—the giants. And their ghosts still haunt the place, at least for me. Second, I'd say the contemporaries, the intricacies of personality of a lot of them. These are very complex human beings, by and large. Those that aren't complex aren't very interesting, but the bulk of them are extremely interesting human beings. Russell Long. Phil Hart. On and on. The challenge of the give-and-take with dominant, highly capable personalities is fascinating to me. I think the third thing would be the opportunities. The ball game is really changing—has changed. A new Senator doesn't need to just sit. I campaigned on this. Everybody said, "We mustn't lose the seniority of a two-term incumbent. You're too young, and it'll take you too long to learn." I said, "Nonsense." Sure, even as recently as Lyndon Johnson it was probably important—committee assignments, logrolling, pork-barreling, all those things. The longer you were around here, the more goodies you could get for your state. But now that's a political myth that still hangs on in the public mind. Across the country it becomes a political issue whenever a new person runs, and we dealt with it during the campaign. I said it was nonsense—and I found out I was right. If you're of a mind to be kind of a front bencher, moving up and introducing legislation, you can—just the other day three others and myself, all of them senior to me, began working on an oil divestiture bill to break up the oil companies. Something like that was relatively unheard of—

Who are the others?

—Abourezk, Phil Hart, and Gaylord Nelson. But the fact that a first-term person, six months in the Senate, can be involved in that kind of thing if he chooses is, I think, a very important change in the institution.

The whole business about keeping your silence during the first term is gone?

—It used to be the first six years. You sat in the back and earned your spurs. You didn't open your mouth and you didn't put any bills in. Well, that's all gone.

You don't feel the frustration that most others have described about their first years here?

—Oh, I feel frustration. For example, that filibuster that's going on now. Business is stopped, energy is stopped. The way a handful, even one individual can—

But that's a frustration of the whole Senate, not the special problem of the junior Senator.

—No, I don't feel frustrated as an individual. I really don't. In fact, I see just the opposite. I see this vast land of opportunity.

As one of two top people in the McGovern campaign, inheriting an image as a superliberal and a non-compromiser, then coming into this house of accommodation and compromise, did your thinking have to shift?

—The impression was wrong. I came into politics as a disciple of John Kennedy, and one of the things I admired about him was his, if you will, pragmatic liberalism. That was a very sadly erroneous press image about that campaign being run by radical, unbending, anti-party types. Anybody who knew me, say, in my home state, and what I had done in the party there, knew that that was just not true. But there's no way to counter it once that line gets going. No, I have understood all my life how the political process works—all my adult life, since I got interested in it in 1960. And I haven't changed. I think the image was just wrong. But I must say, the image preceded me. In subtle ways it was apparent that a lot of the, say, more conservative people here, even in my own party, expected me to be a furniture breaker and a bomb thrower.

And yet on clean air this morning you took the most far-out position, for .4 NOx.

—I believed in it. It's very important in my state, and I think in this country. So I take just the opposite view on this issue from, let's say, the majority of the people here. First of all, I don't think it's a liberal or conservative issue at all. I consider myself not an environmentalist but a conservationist—which obviously has the same derivation as "conservative." It means to shepherd and steward the resources, use them wisely. That's a conservative point of view. Most people say we've got to relax environmental standards now because of economic conditions. I take just the opposite view. I think that, because health and safety problems have grown, environmental concerns are no longer a luxury that you can take or leave, as we thought in the sixties. They're a necessity now. I think we're talking about saving lives, saving the air and water. I mean preserving them for future generations. So that became a motivating factor. Plus Kevin Cornell's assurances to me, based on the evidence, that the technology could do it. I wasn't just starry-eyed.

Getting back to the learning process, any surprises there?

—I've said some fairly complimentary things about the caliber of the people here—higher than the average citizen would believe in terms of intelligence and energy and so on. But on the negative side, I'm somewhat dismayed that there are Senators who go into committee meetings, or on the floor, who are not prepared. They don't know what the issues are about. They ask their friends how to vote. Or they're a drag on procedures. They don't take the time to work hard and stay up late at night and read the documents, or hire the right kind of staff—whatever it takes, a combination of several things, to be prepared. And therefore one person, not only because of the rules but because of the comity that goes on around here, can determine the speed and the level of discussion, and I reject that. No, I resist that. I think that's too bad, and it galls me.

To hold up progress that way, would the offending member have to be a senior member or a chairman?

—No, it may be a freshman member who doesn't know what's going on, who hasn't gotten himself surrounded with the right kind of staff, who doesn't do his homework, then comes in and says, "Mr. Chairman, I don't fully understand this issue, can we put it off until tomorrow?" Well, that means that I stayed up late for nothing, and that galls me. It happens too often. And of course you see it on a different level on the floor, in the debate, or in watching people vote who haven't been briefed, who haven't insisted that their staff give them an independent judgment. They go on the floor and trust their friends in the cloakroom to tell them how to vote. I see more of that than I would have hoped.

Yet one might say that, in a sense, Kevin is telling you how to vote on NOx.

—That's one thing you do when you hire a staff. I didn't hire a guy out of the cloakroom. When you hire somebody, part of what you're doing is hiring their judgment. But you'd be surprised as to the number of times I've heard him out and gone against him. So it's not just that I swallow everything he tells me.

Presidential candidates, cabinet members, foreign heads of state can stroll through these halls as routine visitors, virtually unnoticed. Recently I saw George Wallace wheeled down a corridor of the Dirksen Building, noticed by few, and even they were alerted more by his wheel chair than his famous face. Bring in a different kind of celebrity, however, and this place goes high school. My memory remains vivid of the filming here of the movie *Advise and Consent*. Crowds gathered to watch a corridor scene played by Walter Pidgeon and Don Murray. Senators lurked sheepishly behind office girls to watch actors play Senators, Eugene McCarthy lingering longer than anybody. And how flattered the junior Senator from Mississippi was when Charles Laughton, playing an ancient Southern safe-seater and having difficulty turning a line precisely as it should be, walked up to him and asked, "How do you say that in Stennis?"

Something approaching that excitement occurred early this year when opposition to a White House nomination of a new Secretary of the Interior was lobbied by, of all people, Robert Redford. Never have secretaries been so solicitous of a supplicant trying to get on a Senator's calendar—or Senators so ready to clear time for a lobbyist.

A special event this afternoon is Alexander Solzhenitsyn's address to members of the Senate and the House in the Caucus Room. I discover, next door to Muskie's suite, a sizable and excited crowd outside Senator Jackson's door, and learn that Solzhenitsyn has been spirited there after his talk. As he has a reputation for doing with issues and committee personnel, Jackson seems to have seized control of Solzhenitsyn. While some of the crowd are young men and women from nearby offices, others, toting note pads and tape recorders, are obviously newspeople. A couple of TV film cameras are shoulder-poised for action. A door opens, the crowd rushes to it. It's a Jackson staff person, checking on whether the crowd's still there. The door shuts. A distant door opens, a few male bodies surge out. One of the groupies, a slim blonde in a skimpy cotton dress and eyes that seem to have cried all night, shrieks, "There he is!" and she is first in pursuit, dragging a TV cameraman by the shirt. She's Catherine

Mackin of NBC News, swept up in the now-or-never anxiety and indignity of a news stakeout. The Soviet refugee is rushed—virtually
carried—by his escorts down a circular staircase to the basement, the
stage-door Johnnies and Janes in furious chase, then out a side door
where the escorts cram the author into an aged red convertible with
District of Columbia plates and thunder him off.

Wednesday morning, July 16

Not one but two clean air markups are scheduled for today, the
second at 6:30 P.M. Muskie is determined to resolve auto emission
standards and get on with other headaches of the clean air bill.

At eight this morning lobbyists and observers from law firms fill
the folding chairs of the Public Works chamber, some gobbling
Danish-and-coffee breakfasts out of carry-out boxes from the basement cafeteria. Buckley is back from his urgent precampaign campaigning in New York. On opposite sides of the rectangle of tables
McClure and Hart wait, sip coffee from porcelain cups. Eventually
Morgan, Gravel, Stafford, and Domenici stroll in. At eight-fifteen
Muskie gavels the group to order, announcing he can stay only until
nine-thirty. (He's scheduled to meet seventy Maine children attending a school for the deaf that Muskie, as governor, was responsible
for building. In a pinch, that could be delayed and cut short. But at
ten there's a markup of the full Government Operations Committee
to take up his countercyclical anti-recession bill. That can't be
missed.)

More than half the allotted time is taken up with another go-
round, for the benefit of Senator Morgan, on whether or not .4 NOx
will inhibit development of new engine designs, and whether there is
indeed a direct conflict between clean air and fuel economy. Morgan,
the diminutive freshman from North Carolina, rarely seen at clean

air markups, is chairman of the Public Works Subcommittee on Buildings and Grounds, a time-consuming bondage. A reporter from his state has confided the opinion to me that Morgan "is not a Senator yet, because he hasn't learned to focus on three subjects in the same period of time."

The session then swings into its most interesting part, when Muskie starts banging away, with the hammers of new facts and figures, at the assumption "that you can't get fuel economy without sacrificing clean air and that if you insist upon the Clean Air Act standards, you will get no fuel economy." If the auto industry can put that over as the choice facing the Congress, believes Muskie, the Clean Air Act teeters at the edge of destruction.

Asserting again that vehicle weight, not pollution control, most determines fuel economy, Muskie cites estimates that if only four per cent of the auto market each year were to shift to the next smaller vehicle size—from large cars to medium, and medium to small—by 1980 fuel economy would improve by a remarkable twenty per cent. If engine performance were curtailed so that a fully loaded car required eighteen seconds to accelerate from zero speed to sixty miles an hour—instead of twelve seconds, the capability of most American cars now—fuel economy would improve ten to fifteen per cent. He cites other savings that would come from a modification of a four-speed automatic transmission, from reduction of wind drag through body design, use of radial tires, accessory-power thermostats on air conditioners, and more. These all add up, he asserts, "to a conclusion that a fuel-economy improvement of over forty per cent can be achieved by 1980 with no change in engine concepts whatsoever.

"Yet they keep saying, 'The burden, Senator Muskie, is on *you*. To save gasoline, we are going to ask *you* to sacrifice your clean air.' That is the argument I hear over and over again from the press, from the Congress, and from the industry. Is it more important to hold onto that six seconds of acceleration than it is to maintain the highest possible clean air standards?"

Thus, almost imperceptibly, he swings the debate back from the technical to the essentially political. Is the Congress ready to legislate certain mandatory changes in the American life style? Is it willing to intrude on the love affair between Americans and their high-powered cars? Is it willing to impose upon Detroit economic sacrifices that may result from that intrusion?

Senator McClure springs at the cue. Day after day he and Muskie and Hart and Domenici and Billings quibble over the validity of the decimal-point numbers, all pretending that their interpretations of science mold their legislative decisions. But state the choices as *political* choices—defining responsibilities between consumers and profit makers and government—and suddenly the argument pulses with new enthusiasm, the participants on familiar home ground.

"Do all those things," McClure taunts, "and you may end up with a car that is mandated but that nobody buys. People may opt to keep their old ones. Then, I suppose, the answer will be, 'We'll *make* them buy the new one.'"

"What you're saying, Senator," rebuts Muskie, "is we're not going to move toward either fuel economy or clean air unless the manufacturers judge that they can continue to sell cars in accordance with past practices."

"No, I'm not saying the manufacturers judge. I'm saying whether the purchasers judge."

"It's the manufacturers who *form* the present judgments as to what consumers will buy. You're saying, let them continue making the same judgments that have led us into this mess."

"No, not at all." McClure is smiling. Muskie is not. "I am saying that the purchasers are the ones who make the ultimate judgment."

"Do you have proof of that?"

"Perhaps it ought to be our view that we shouldn't produce ten million automobiles a year, that that is wasteful, that we ought to get it down to five million automobiles a year."

"Senator, I'm not arguing that at all," frets Muskie. "But if we carry your argument to its logical conclusion we should make everything—clean air, fuel economy, everything—voluntary with the companies, relying on *their* judgment as to what the consumer will buy. I don't know, what other conclusions does one draw from that argument?"

"Not at all," soothes Senator McClure. "You misunderstood what I said."

"You misunderstood what *I* said."

"If you will listen to me, I promise I will listen to you. . . ."

"Mr. Chairman," breaks in Senator Hart, "that's one of the theses behind my proposal yesterday, that we are being presented a phony alternative: clean air versus a sound economy. Let me also say that the intention of the .4 standard I proposed is not in any way to discourage innovation or discourage any particular technology. I don't believe it will. . . ."

"I can't give assurance," says Muskie, now turning on Hart, "as to what the automobile industry would do even if they *had* the same motivations we do, and obviously they don't. One of the most difficult things to write into legislation is incentives or disincentives that will move big elements of our economy in directions that we think the public interest requires. We run into these frustrations with tax policy. You think you've written a tax policy to move somebody in one direction. You find it moved him somewhere else.

"We achieved, in this case, a result we didn't want. We achieved the catalyst when all our previous testimony for six years was negative on the catalyst. When we wrote the 1970 act we didn't mandate the catalyst. What we did was leave it open. We said, 'We are not going to try to design this car. What we are trying to do is move the industry into new technology.' As of now, they've moved only into the catalyst, which they've since brightened up and polished and refurbished, so that maybe that's what we're going to end up with indefinitely. . . . Simply listing the things you would *like* to see the industry experiment on doesn't mean they are going to."

"Mr. Chairman," re-enters McClure, "I see a difference between your position and mine that might help us focus on the problem. It is your feeling that by setting strict standards you impel them to try different technologies. My feeling is just the opposite. It is your conclusion that we didn't mandate the catalyst. I think we, in effect, *did,* although we didn't write it into the statute. We set standards they thought were surely achievable only with one technology. So they went into that one technology to make sure they got there."

"Jim, I see it looking back not just to 1970, but I have been dealing with the problem since 1963, when we thought we could clean the air without pressuring them by specific deadlines."

"I understand that."

"I know what their reaction to our doing nothing was. They did nothing."

Senator Buckley steps in: "I think Senator McClure is saying that Senator Muskie is insisting on a standard, so tight that there is only one safe approach that the industry will follow. Whereas if you have something a little less tight you give them several options."

"Aren't our motivations identical?" demands Muskie. "You want to stretch the industry to do as much as it is reasonable to ask them to do. And that is exactly my position."

"Then the difference," responds McClure, keeping his distance as smoothly as quicksilver, "comes in how much pressure is productive, and when does additional pressure become counterproductive. Upon that judgment, we have some difference."

"Mr. Chairman," says the wry Vermonter, Senator Stafford, "I would like to try to explain what I think all three of you are saying." The room roars appreciatively. Deciding to quit while he's ahead, Stafford says, "It's nine-thirty. Time to vote."

The vote is on the extremely lenient McClure timetable, but including an ultimate target of .4 NOx, adopted yesterday. Barry Meyer starts to call the names.

Bentsen, absent. Buckley, No. Culver, absent. Domenici, No. Hart, No, adding No for Culver, by proxy. Gravel, No. McClure, Aye. Montoya, absent. Morgan, No. Muskie, No. Stafford, No. Meyer announces that McClure's substitute loses, 8 to 1.

"You and I have had similar success," Muskie teases McClure. "In fact, yesterday I came out one vote better."

And auto emission standards remain up in the air.

After a brief shoulder-squeezing visit with the deaf children in a meeting room on the top floor of the Russell Building, Muskie rings for an elevator, hurrying to the Government Operations Committee in the Dirksen.

"Is this elevator for Senators only?" asks a man with a briefcase.

"No, this is public."

Obviously recognizing Muskie, the man says with a flourish of deference, "I didn't want to invade anyone's rights."

"We have no rights," grumbles Muskie. "Only privileges."

In the Government Operations hearing room, Chairman Ribicoff approaches Muskie to congratulate him on the countercyclical bill.

"I didn't read it till last night," Ribicoff almost whispers. "It's a fascinating concept."

"Will we have a quorum?"

"For the vote, we'll call Senator Glenn. He promised to come."

Before taking up Muskie's, the committee disposes of another bill. This committee, compared to the workmanlike atmosphere of Public Works, seems a colony of movie stars. Javits, arriving busily and late, imperiously challenges Ribicoff on minor procedures. The New York liberal Republican and Connecticut liberal Democrat each clearly resents the star on the other's dressing-room door. Senator Percy, the ranking Republican, lets the boys be boys for a moment before stepping in to settle things in his bass tremolo. Although the name plate of an absent Senator is usually not displayed, whoever sets up the table for Government Ops meetings always puts up the I.D. of "Mr. Jackson," as though forever hopeful his eminence will consent to a cameo appearance. I have yet to see him show.

Javits announces that he is "enthusiastic" about the countercyclical idea, except that he'd like to see a couple of changes. The bill establishes that one locality may receive no more than ten per cent of its state's money allotment. Javits would raise that limit to twenty-five per cent. Muskie, seeing the basis of a broad, bipartisan support —he knows he has Bill Brock, the committee's most conservative Republican—accepts Javits' change.

John Glenn, who has just arrived, leaning his head for the whispered fill-in by his committee aide (the only black person in that role I have yet seen here), injects that the Javits amendment has the clear look of a bail-out for New York City's fiscal problem at the cost of smaller communities. It will lose votes on the floor for the whole bill, says Glenn, and for that reason he opposes Javits' change. Javits quickly comes back with a counteroffer of fifteen per cent. Glenn accepts that. So does Muskie.

Percy also blesses the bill, pointing out that the congressional budget resolution can accommodate the two billion dollars of this bill in its allowance for public works.

Muskie picks up that cue to mention for the first time that he "would like to marry the two bills"—the public works bill and this countercyclical measure. He does not mention his expectation that this bill, as a separate Government Operations bill, will die in the House committee, that he is putting it through this committee mostly to enlist the prestige of Government Ops behind it, and that his hope for the bill rests on its sneaking through both houses as a piggyback rider to the public works bill.

As the discussion rounds the turn toward a vote, a staff type rushes in and hands a note to Ribicoff, who announces, with worried amusement, "All Senators are required on the floor for a quorum by order of the sergeant at arms." The Durkin-Wyman filibusterers are up to mischief again. Afraid that his quorum in committee might never find its way back from the floor, Ribicoff says bravely, "Let the sergeant at arms exercise his privilege of bringing us there bodily." Soon, another call, another message. Senator Brock points out that ignoring the order could endanger the privilege of committees meeting while the Senate is in session during the Durkin-Wyman controversy. Bravery collapses and they go.

No sooner are they back than Lawton Chiles of Florida, in a red plaid jacket, says he must leave. Staff members of two other Senators urge him to stay. Torn, he draws an orange card from his shirt pocket, studies it, shoves it back, and slumps in his chair. Whether orange or white or powder blue, that schedule card is in every Senator's pocket, and he lives under its tyranny.

Senator Roth, the Delaware Republican with the red hair that lacks credibility, opposes the bill, makes his argument that it costs too much and will accomplish too little, and, except for his opposition, the countercyclical bill is voted the formal approval of the committee.

My luncheon companion in a restaurant at the Capitol is Eliot Cutler, an uncomfortable lobbyist. In his thirties, mustached and corporately groomed, Cutler was until a year or so ago a Muskie employee, right-hand man to Leon Billings. Deciding to use his law degree more remuneratively, he became the Capitol Hill voice of the International Council of Shopping Centers, convincing himself that that connection did not corrupt his devotion to the environment. Owners of shopping centers favor strong pollution control of automobiles, although for reasons not altogether altruistic. One section of the Clean Air Act is on "land use and transportation controls." Mainly this section authorizes the EPA to limit the size of parking areas (a power that could strangle shopping centers) and impose bridge tolls in urban areas to discourage unnecessary driving, another threat to retailing. Cutler and his shopping center landlords argue for getting rid of pollution before it escapes from the auto tailpipe: shove the burden onto the auto manufacturers, keeping it off the backs of his clients. And since that position gives Cutler a coincidence of lobbying interest with the environmentalists, it also keeps him on the side of the angels. But Cutler is uneasy about having turned lobbyist,[1] and much prefers to talk about law and the legislative process, and how they may best serve the ends of social justice.

That is what leads him into making some points I have not heard in any of the markups or any previous conversation about them. I ask whether he thinks the Senate committee is spending too much time and scrutiny on the decimal points of auto emissions. Traditionally, laws turn those decisions over to the experts in regulatory agencies. The subject enlivens Cutler:

"I think statutes ought to be as detailed as possible. They ought to leave as little question as possible for courts to interpret as to Congress' meaning and intention. The most delicate and difficult kind of balance in legislation is setting this relationship between Congress, the administrative agencies, and the courts. Very difficult question. Another difficult question: how do you work the courts into the process so that they don't actually make the law but only review the law Congress made and decide whether the agency is properly carrying it out?

"Muskie is very, very conscious of that difficult balance and where it has too often gone wrong. You take a look at the Clean Air Act and the Water Pollution Control Act. Those are two of the most detailed statutes ever written by the Congress. The reason is because Muskie insists on it. Writing detailed statutes—and getting broad political agreement on them—is much tougher than writing broad statutes and saying to some agency administrator, 'You take care of the problem. You make the decisions.' Especially when there's not a lot of experience behind the statute.

"My view is that Congress has really abdicated its responsibility horribly in the last generation by writing more and more general stat-

<hr>

[1] Before this book is published, Cutler forsakes lobbying to join the campaign staff of vice-presidential candidate Walter Mondale, and after the election is rewarded with appointment as associate director of the Office of Management and Budget, overseeing the sectors of energy and the environment.

utes and relying on more and more agencies to figure them out. It removes people from the political process. Muskie feels that way. That's why, when the subcommittee was reviewing the agenda and started talking about land use and transportation controls, Muskie said, 'You know, all we gave them, the EPA, was just that five-word phrase in 1970. That wasn't enough. They've abused the discretion, and now we've got to be very specific.' And when you get specific, that's when people start raising questions about cost, about impingements, about political problems, and so forth. That's when the going gets tough, but Muskie seems determined to get them through it.

"It goes to the guts of the Constitution. Remember, the Constitution never mentioned administrative agencies. It certainly never mentioned the regulatory commissions that the New Deal created. It never contemplated the growth of the federal bureaucracy or the degree to which the bureaucracy would make the kinds of decisions which the Constitution writers thought would be made by Congress.

"What Congress is doing now, by deciding the numbers and the decimal points, is taking responsibility for the political heat. When an administrator enforces this law, nobody can haul him into court to challenge his authority. He can say, 'This is the law as Congress wrote it.' Muskie recognizes that there are limits to how specific Congress can be, how tough a job it is to be specific, the incredible amount of time and effort it takes, and how the more specific you get —the more people you affect directly—the more political risks you encounter. But, goddam, it's really tragic that nobody has ever recognized that this is one of his great talents. This is what makes him, in my mind, damned near a genius in this area. He never talks about it enough, either.

"What we're talking about here is a tide of counterreformation that is, I think, beginning to swell. That term, at least for liberals like myself, means examining the effects of all the reforms we have instituted since World War II, certainly in the last ten or a dozen years. It means that a lot of those 'reforms' have, in fact, not reformed the process, that they have distorted it, that they have created a gap between government and people. It means simply that government's actions, regulations, rules, no longer are solving problems, no longer are understood by people, no longer therefore carry any real force and effect. And they're being ignored. It also carries the implication that you can't solve problems by throwing new money after old money. Counterreformation to me is a liberal's understanding of some of the liberals' mistakes. I think it is important to understand that counterreformation does *not* imply rethinking government's responsibility to insure individual liberty, insure the protection of human rights. But we can't go on with our legislative bodies saying broadly, 'We must do this,' then creating a bureaucracy with virtually no instructions as to methods for solving the problem, but merely giving them a lot of money to hire so-called experts."

At this point I observe that only one other Senator, regarding almost every issue of the act, constantly asks: Shouldn't we review this issue in a couple of years, rather than leave it permanently in the lap of the administrator?

"Buckley," Cutler says, nodding. "That's right. Buckley and Muskie are relatively close on this score. Buckley may be the only other guy who understands it, but I'm not sure he has the balanced view of it that I think Muskie has. I'm not even sure McClure really understands it, although McClure's very smart."

It's sometimes said that a Senator's office resembles the Senator. The office of James McClure, one of the three or four most consistently conservative members of the Senate, is confidently neat, with no pretensions to style. There's an Idaho travel poster and two postcard-type color blowups of Idaho mountaintops framed in rough-hewn wood. It could be the office of a town clerk. His private office is no more artistically stimulating, but cozier. We face each other across a mid-floor coffee table. Mike Hathaway, McClure's aide for environmental and energy issues, sits beside his boss. A big leather couch is ignored. Without being ingratiating, McClure gives himself to his visitor warmly and totally, especially through his good-humored eyes.

A CONVERSATION WITH SENATOR McCLURE

—One of the interesting things about the Clean Air Act is that it goes beyond what Congress usually does in delegating authority. It sets exact numbers for air standards, which Congress would ordinarily authorize an administrator to do.

How do you feel about that?

—As a matter of fact, I like it. It's extremely difficult, and that's why we're going through all we're going through. Senator Hart, for instance, in one or two sessions, has said, "We shouldn't be dealing with numbers. We ought to be dealing with general policy instead of dealing with numbers." I don't agree with that. If it's difficult, that's tough. That's our job. We can get out of it only be delegating it to a bureaucracy and then complaining about the results.

One of Muskie's former staff people was just telling me that Senator Muskie believes one of the reasons executive agencies have grown so large and so powerful is that Congress has not always faced up to the tough political decisions.

—Exactly. Exactly. I have not heard Senator Muskie articulate that, but I certainly agree with him. It's one of the frustrations people have developed about government. You run into all these regulations set by some bureaucrat somewhere whom you don't know, you never see, never have a chance to talk with. You never know what went into his decision. You have no opportunity to react by voting against him. Yet he does the thing that directly impinges upon the citizen's action.

—How many times have you heard a member of the House or Senate say, "That's not what I intended when that law was passed"? I can think of a dozen good examples of a major author of a piece of legislation saying in frustration, "The bureaucrats are twisting that!" Sometimes they are. But I'm afraid, for too many politicians, it's become a convenient out: insulating himself from political heat and pointing a finger at someone else, rather than confessing that the law was not well drawn.

Don't you feel a conflict over your ideology here, telling industry what it can and can't do in ways they've not been told before?

—That end of it doesn't bother me. If we expect industry to take steps for the public good that are unrelated to the direct corporate good, we should set the rules and expect them to live within those rules. I don't expect corporations voluntarily to try to achieve broad social goals. That's not their function. If we expect them to do that we're going to be disappointed. If they try to do it they're going to have lawsuits from their shareholders, saying, "You have no right to do that." Now they can—and I hope they will—be enlightened enough to look at the benefits of being able to say, "This community is a good place for our workers to live," and all that sort of thing. But if we expect them to achieve more than that, it's up to us to tell them what it is they're all to achieve, and write the rules so they all have the same rules to live by. It's up to us to see that one business moving in this direction doesn't find itself in a competitive disadvantage against others that don't. So I'm not troubled by that.

—We have all kinds of restrictions in society on individual liberty. Whether you're liberal or conservative, we nevertheless cherish individual liberty and recognize that there must be restrictions on each of us in order to maximize the areas of freedom of everyone else. As long as there are any two people rubbing shoulders at all, the areas of their freedom become somewhat restricted. So you try to set the rules so that each has the greatest possible amount of freedom.

What has troubled you most in this clean air bill?

—Our failure to come to grips with scientific evidence of what is and what is not attainable. The evidence, of course, is conflicting. If you set goals far beyond what companies can attain, they simply cannot do it and they start doing irrational things in an effort to—you've frustrated them beyond reasonable limit and, among other things, you've greatly increased the cost to the consumer.

—For instance, the stack scrubber. The stack scrubber does not work. The laboratories' answer is that in small pilot programs it does. But it does not really work in commercial application at this time. Yet we're about to require everybody to go that way. By doing so, we're going to achieve progress and we *are* going to develop scrubbers that do work, but before that we will have wasted hundreds of millions of dollars by forcing use of the technology before it is proven. I would rather go a little slower. Not for the benefit of the company forced to use them, but because this is a social cost. You can't invest money in non-productive enterprises without reducing the standard of living of all of us. So when it's a massive expenditure like this, I say go a little slower, force them to go only as fast as we know they can go. But *do* force them to go as fast as we know they can go, and maybe set goals a little bit beyond our known technology. I think we've exceeded that.

Do you see a counterpart of this in the auto emissions issue?

—Yes, definitely. When we set the original goals we didn't know what we were doing in terms of, Was it achievable? I think the standards were written the way they were largely because General Motors had developed catalyst technology, and Ed Cole, at that time GM's president, decided that that was the way he was going to take GM, and the standards were written in a way that Cole thought he could live with. The other auto makers, foreign and domestic, then had to fall in behind GM's strategy. At that time it was absolutely predictable that the catalyst strategy was going to create a sulphuric acid and sulphates problem. The simple chemistry of the catalyst said so. It also was very obvious that the catalyst was going to have a heat problem and some reliability problems. But we set standards which nothing else but the catalyst could possibly achieve, so everybody had to go in that direction whether they wanted to or not. They had no option for pursuing alternative technologies—in the short run.

Have you found the level of lobbying on this bill high or low?

—The thing that has impressed me is that the company reps stationed here in Washington are terribly inept. The staff people who come in from lower levels from Detroit to work with our staff and the committee staff are very competent people. Occasionally the company hierarchy—their presidents and vice-presidents—fly in and want to reinvent the wheel. They want to tell us from the beginning what their problem is. It's a terribly wasteful exercise. They sound like they've never heard of the problem before, like they've memorized somebody's briefing, and they assume we've never heard of it before.

[McClure is handed a message by his secretary and he leaves the room. Mike Hathaway, his aide, an engineer whom McClure recruited from the space program, uses the absence to say, "Just to set the record straight, I agree with his position on the Washington lobbyists, but there's one man who has done an extremely competent job, in my personal opinion, Bill Chapman of General Motors. I think people who know Bill realize he's a fair man, extremely competent and hard-working, and he knows his stuff, and he doesn't try to snow you with a bunch of bull." I ask what Hathaway wants from a lobbyist. "First of all, exactly what his company's position is. It amazes me to call a lobbyist for industry in Washington and they can't tell me what their company's position is." Am I correct that the Ford lobbyists' approach is just to pout? Mike nods. "They can't believe it's happening." McClure returns and, requiring no prodding of a question, resumes the subject of lobbying.]

—When I started in the Idaho state legislature in 1961, I replaced a guy who complained constantly about lobbyists, always protesting they were in there applying pressure and seducing him one way or another. There's got to be something behind complaining like that. I always suspect a girl who seduces too easily, and I suspected the same of him. He seduced a little too easily.

—I personally believe lobbyists have a very useful role. If you want to find out the real information, if you want a breadth of opinion, call the lobbyists who are for it and the lobbyists against it. You'll get an education in a hurry. They'll give you all the best arguments on both sides. I think that system works.

Do you expect to be able to support what you sense will come out of the auto emissions discussions?

—Well, I'm not sure I can sense what will come out. I could not support the action we seem headed for now. The subcommittee seems on its way to setting standards that are unrealistic, unattainable, so far from a realistic standard that I think we'll probably back up and take another cut at it before we're through. I don't think the full committee will vote out the standards that the subcommittee seems ready to vote out. Because of that, it's difficult to say that I'll support the bill because I don't know what the bill's going to be.

The Senate still being in session at six-thirty, with roll calls expected, the subcommittee holds its evening markup near the floor, in one of the Capitol's paneled and chandeliered rooms, S-207. A crowd of staffers, lobbyists, and observers fills most of the room, separated from the committee table only by a respectful moat. The irregular hour and a few recent martinis at the Monocle bar contribute to a gaiety in the crowd's conversation.

After a daylong session of the supersecret, superglamorous CIA Investigating Committee, Gary Hart is an early arriver, pitter-pattering in on the soles of his slippery boots. In a pinkish-gray Edwardian suit, he heads for the committee table, slightly bowed and weighted down, opens a briefcase, removes a document, and sinks into homework reading. Senator and dude, a striking man. The next few seconds bespeak his identity conflict. A young woman from the crowd, addressing him as "Gary," hands him a periodical, pointing out a passage. He puts it down to his right, continuing to read from the typescript to its left. He switches his attention to the periodical, then back again to the document. Then, fed up, back to the periodical. I peer over his shoulder. The typescript, no doubt a document on the CIA, is rubber-stamped in a loud, stern voice, "TOP SECRET." The magazine is *Rolling Stone.*

At six forty-five Muskie gavels, reviews the parliamentary situation: to go with the set of standards proposed by Senator Hart, and already adopted, Hart has further proposed a schedule of deadlines, to which Senator McClure offered a substitute. McClure's was defeated, therefore Hart's is the pending business. The Muskie-Buckley schedule is yet to be considered, except that Senator Buckley is abandoning that partnership and will offer a substitute of his own. Senator Stafford has announced he will have a compromise substitute and so have Senator Gravel and Senator Domenici. This review, and fragments of discussion it ignites, becomes more than a review. With the help of two roll calls on the floor, it becomes the whole meeting, which adjourns, with generally shared frustration, at five past eight, to reconvene at eight tomorrow morning.

"Just in time. You miss *Nashville,*" Leon remarks sympathetically to Senator Hart.

"Yeah, what a way to blow a movie."

On the broad steps of the Capitol in an orange haze of summer twilight, Leon boisterously calls across the Capitol plaza to a staff man climbing into a car, "When is John Culver going to have his compromise?" The man calls back, "There's one other guy who hasn't had one yet." And both men break up as they call in unison, "Montoya!"

When Stafford said inside, just a few minutes earlier, that he'd have a compromise, everybody laughed. The situation scarcely needed cluttering by another "compromise," and least of all, a few observers thought, from Stafford, who has taken little part in the proceedings. Leon now remarks to me before disappearing, "Don't laugh. Stafford's isn't a bad one. It may wind up being the rallying point."

I loiter on the steps, waiting for Senator Muskie to make a last check of the floor before we go off "for a hamburger." Down the steps, collar and tie jerked open, jacket slung over shoulder, strolls Senator Kennedy, heading for his faded blue, aging convertible. Senator Percy, climbing the steps, passes him. They exchange nods, briskly, distantly. To pass the time, I chat with a man whose face I've seen at the markups. He turns out to be John R. Blizard, a lobbyist for Corning Glass. Why would Corning Glass be involved here?

"We make the substrate for catalytic converters." His speech is gentle, personal, cultured. "It's a ceramic structure on which the platinum is plated and it's important in the catalysis."

"What do you say," I ask, "to the companies' claim that the standards can't be achieved?"

"I'm saying that they claim it can't be done because they don't want to have to change anything. They have an enormous investment in tooling and capital equipment that makes the car the way it is today. And they don't want to have to obsolete that equipment by making the car in some different way. They're delighted to add anything to the car that sits on the outside and makes people in the showroom say, 'There is a sexy, interesting car.' Like the disappearing headlights, or the vinyl top, or the opera window, or the engraved designs on the opera window. You don't *see* a catalytic converter. People don't mind when these other things, these sexy, visible things, make the car cost more, as the catalytic converter does. In fact these things are usually optional, and people gladly buy them. Actually the catalytic converter can make the car cost less in the long run because it uses less fuel if they put in the proper type of equipment. But if the auto makers do it in a halfhearted way, with the least possible addition of technical equipment to the engine, it uses more fuel. So, in that way, the auto makers can hold down the sticker price slightly, making it easier to sell, but they thereby increase the lifetime cost of the car."

Corning is a major supplier of window glass for automobiles. Does the company, I ask Blizard, suffer internal conflicts when it tries to enhance the market for catalytic converters by lobbying for tough clean air standards—in direct opposition to the auto companies—while at the same time trying to cultivate auto makers as customers of window glass?

"We thought a lot about that, yes, but it's more or less been laid to rest. I've been a glass man, still am, and I know these auto company people in Detroit very, very well, and I'm a great friend of many of them. When I was given this assignment I said to one of my best auto friends, 'Max, my job from now on is going to be to get as much of this stuff—catalytic converters—on your cars as I can, and I know you want it off.' They know what we're doing and they know why we're doing it. And, after all, other suppliers of theirs, manufacturers of catalytic converters and other things, are lobbying for their positions, so our position on this will be pressed whether we do it or not. We are friendly adversaries. We talk to each other."

"This fear that Detroit will lose a dangerous proportion of its market to imports," I ask Blizard, "do you think it's a reasonable fear?"

"I think our sales *are* being diverted to imports, and to a large extent it's because of fuel economy. More and more people will buy our small cars if we have better fuel economy."

Then the clean air factor is irrelevant to that problem.

"I think it's somewhat irrelevant. Small foreign cars have to meet the same clean air standards that American cars do. But if people are going to go to economy cars, I think they may be choosing foreign cars for other reasons: their workmanship, size, and maybe for status, to some extent. We'll have to learn to produce a small car that can furnish those attractions."

Muskie finally appears and we slip into the front seat of his car. It's a big Chrysler, several years old. Maine license plate USS-1.

"Where do you want to have a hamburger?" he asks with a hint of distaste. I reply that I suggested a hamburger only in its generic sense when he complained earlier that the evening markup didn't even permit time to get a hamburger. Looking relieved, he points his car toward Rock Creek Parkway and his favorite purveyor of huge, saucy spareribs, Arbaugh's on Connecticut Avenue just beyond the Shoreham Hotel. About to turn into Connecticut from Calvert Street, he is confronted with a huge "No Left Turn" sign. Momentarily startled and confused, he hesitates, then mumbles, "What the hell," makes the left turn, and parks.

The unprepossessing restaurant is almost empty, and two women on duty, a cashier and hostess, leap to flushed attention on recognizing him, at the same time trying to mute their excitement because appearing excited over a Senator is not a Washington thing to do. The waitress, too, tries to cover her flutters with routine disinterest, as we both order vodka martinis and ribs.

Being alone at home all summer, Muskie comments, is now just part of his annual cycle. It comes down to a choice between just the loneliness, which he says he hates, or accepting dinner invitations proffered by friends who are overeager to "help" him out. He usually prefers the former. "I can wind up with three or four engagments a week that are hard to get out of, and then I have to crowd my schedule around that. And those things are hard to leave right after dinner, and they become just obligations rather than relaxation."

Small talk soon runs out. If conversation is to flow, it has to return to politics and government, which it does. Yes, the congressional budget process passed an important first hurdle the other day. A good start. After decades of progressively surrendering fiscal initiative to the White House, perhaps Congress truly wants to win back its constitutional prerogative.

"But pretty soon," Muskie says with a light, slow, mark-my-words tapping of the finger on the table, "maybe not this year, but if not this year surely next, we're going to need a test. Then we'll know how secure the process is."

I wait for more. When it doesn't come I prod, "You mean a real budget buster."

"That's right." Long pause. "I hope it's not something like Social Security, some big raise of some sort not provided for in the budget resolution, that the majority won't dare go on record against. But we do need a very severe test that will put the budget figure under tremendous strain, and then we'll know how seriously Congress takes its pledge to hold the line it set for itself." Another pause, and he says, "It could come toward the end of this year."

Through emergency anti-recession measures? Public works? A defense increase?

"No, the thing it could be is national health."

But isn't that pretty well dead for this year?

"It is dead for this year, but it could come up with an eye toward next."

How costly would that actually be?

"It could be forty to sixty billion dollars a year. But the trouble is something like only a third has to go into the first year, because it takes time for the cost to settle in and for the system to develop. So it has the appearance of just a twenty-billion-dollar expenditure. But then, like Medicare, its costliness explodes, and there's no real way to control just how much."

If the issue of national health insurance is to be forced in the next year, I assume it would be forced by Ted Kennedy, chairman of the Health Subcommittee of Labor and Public Welfare. Would Kennedy, I ask, force it even if it threatened wrecking the budget procedure? Muskie responds with neither word nor facial expression, which is a response. To encourage a frank answer, I try another tack: "How do you get along with Kennedy?"

He gets up to lead us out of the restaurant. I'm about to give up on getting an answer when he says, in a sort of way affectionately, "The trouble with Kennedy is all he can think of is spend, spend, spend. Maybe when you're brought up that way, it's the only—" His voice drifts off.

Kennedy's compassion appears genuine, I comment. At that New England energy meeting in McIntyre's office, while other Senators talked in high policy slogans, only Kennedy spoke in the vivid terms of low-income people who can't afford to buy storm doors and fix their roofs.

"He *always* does that," Muskie says, quickly adding, "Not that he doesn't mean it."

It's almost eleven. As he crowds his big frame through the car door Muskie remarks that he's got to do some reading tonight for tomorrow morning's markup. When I look a little surprised he says, "The staff keeps saying that I'm such a quick and thorough study. They don't know I have to sit up every night reading all their damned stuff."

Thursday morning, July 17

If things go at this morning's 8 A.M. markup as Muskie hopes they will, the numbers game of auto emission standards may be settled, the haggling at last ended. At least until the subject is reviewed by the full Public Works Committee. At eight-thirty Muskie gavels to order Senators Hart, Buckley, Stafford, McClure, and Domenici.

"My suggestion," he says, "is that we proceed rather quickly to vote on all these deadline options that have been presented. The Hart proposal is the question before us. Pending is a Buckley amendment to the Hart proposal. When we broke up last night Senator Stafford warned us that he had another proposal. Is that a substitute to Buckley?"

"Mr. Chairman," says Stafford, "it is being further revised at the moment."

"Then why don't we take a crack at the Buckley amendment?"

"Before you do that, Mr. Chairman," interrupts Domenici, "I had a proposal pending. I want to offer a new one, much simpler than the old one. But at some point later."

"Is the one we know about inoperative at this point?"

"It's not too much different, except I'm getting rid of the penalties."

Muskie asks Meyer for a roll call on the Buckley amendment, titled on an explanatory sheet passed out to Senators, "Senator Buckley's Variation on Muskie-Buckley." Essentially, it abandons the 1.0 NOx position of Muskie-Buckley, substituting 1.5, then going to .4 in 1982. Buckley loses 5 to 2, only McClure joining him.

"I think we all rank about the same," observes Muskie dryly. "There hasn't been a proposal that has gotten more than three votes. Are we ready to proceed to the Hart proposal?"

"I've been talking last night and this morning," reports Hart, "with Senator Stafford. I prefer to wait and hear his proposal. In fact, I think when Senator Domenici hears it he might be interested in it also."

"The next logical one would be the Gravel one, but he isn't here."

Domenici then launches into a long, sincere, convoluted rehash of his reservations about this proposal and that, and the technological reasons for each reservation. His monologue appears to serve the proceeding perfectly well because Stafford's staff man and Hart's staff man are whispering and scribbling furiously, until Stafford interrupts. "Mr. Chairman, I realize this is out of turn, but if Senator Domenici will yield to me, I will just describe what I propose to do. We have copies now that we will get around."

Sheets are passed among Senators and their staff aides. "Mr. Chairman," says Stafford, arranging himself formally in his chair for a pronouncement, "I will present the proposal which I have worked out. You all now have copies of it, I think. This has been prepared after consultations with Senator Hart. I think it meets with his agreement."

Eyes dart to Hart, who blinks assent. A surprising alliance in a series of surprising alliances. Presumably this will now replace the Hart schedule of deadlines. "It would follow the same route everybody has through 1976 and '77," says Stafford, "but would allow the EPA administrator to waive the '78–'79 standards for up to fifty per cent of each manufacturer's production in those two years. Then in 1980 and '81 the standard of .41/3.4/1.0 for all cars for two years and the tougher standard of .4 in 1982, which would give the industry and the Congress a five-year look at the situation before the requirement of .4 in NOx emissions. That, very briefly, is the proposal."

As the Senators study their sheets, Stafford, a licensed pilot, adds, "This proposal is sort of like the Japanese airplane designer in the thirties. He borrowed a little bit from everybody to see if it would fly."

Muskie peers over his reading glasses and nods approvingly at Hart. After a few minutes more of exchange and clarification between McClure and Stafford, Muskie directs Meyer to call the roll. All "yes," except for Domenici and McClure. The Stafford-Hart compromise carries the day, 7 to 2.

Standards and deadlines are settled!

At least for now.

So the freshman, Senator Hart, is the hero, opening a path that attracts a majority of the subcommittee, then making the key compromise. Late in the afternoon I ask Leon what he thinks Hart has learned from the last couple of days.

"What I'm afraid of," says Leon, "is that he hasn't learned anything. I don't think he knows how bad a proposal he's got. The environmentalists think it's a better proposal than the Muskie-Buckley because it keeps that ultimate .4 in there. But fifty per cent of the cars are exempted from the standards in 1978."

Who is to decide which cars may go into which fifty per cent?

"That's a good question. For instance, what happens with Rolls-

Royce, a single-engine line? It's easier when you have twenty-four model lines. You can have twelve in and twelve out."

Does the fifty per cent apply to model lines or to the number of cars a company produces?

"Another good question. The only way you could logically do it is by model line. General Motors has already told me they'll probably put the technology on the little cars and let the big cars pollute. Under the Muskie-Buckley proposal, we have an emissions waiver for small, fuel-efficient cars. Under the Hart proposal, you can have an emissions waiver for big cars, and that's stupid. Of course, the auto companies will apply the waiver to the big cars."

Why did it go through without a real fight?

"What else was there? It was the only train leaving the station. Muskie and Buckley both voted for it. It was time to go on. As Muskie said on our way to the elevator, 'Nobody wanted to take the lead in relaxing the standards. Nobody wanted to be the person out front.' That Hart proposal of .4 in 1982 is asinine. It has nothing to do with anything. It's seven years off. It's not going to be achieved even then and it's going to be changed."

Why go into the full committee with a bad bill?

"I'm not sure we're going in with a bad bill. We're going in with a bad proposal, one part of the bill. It's a response to the frustration of not being able to get together on anything else. I told a reporter this morning that we're not likely to replow any fields. I don't expect this will be undone in subcommittee. But everything will be subject to review in full committee."

You've said that you must get the bill out of subcommittee by recess—only two weeks away—to get it through committee and to the floor in September before Muskie gets tied up with the budget resolution. Can you still do it?

"No. It's out of the question."

In the cafeteria I encounter Hal Brayman, the blond-haired, blond-browed, quiet Leon Billings of the subcommittee minority. A question has lingered in my head ever since the first time I met him at the meeting when Muskie and Buckley "cut the deal." Just how did that meeting come about? How and when did Buckley decide to join Muskie in the position that was supposed to settle emissions standards, a position abandoned by Buckley during the last twenty-four hours?

I ask who invented the two-car strategy idea that was at the heart of that agreement.

"I ascribe it to Leon," says Brayman modestly. "We kicked it back and forth, but essentially it was his idea."

"Did Buckley consider it in some detail before the two of you got to Muskie's office?"

"Oh yes. Prior to that meeting—the day before, or maybe two— we had a meeting in the Vice-President's Room, a ceremonial office just off the floor that's vacant nearly all the time. Howard Baker was there and Buckley and McClure, and I think Stafford. I don't think Domenici was there, but Lee Rawls, his staff man, came. Buckley made the case that Muskie would probably settle for a final 1.0 NOx standard and reducing the 100,000-mile warranty. Buckley asked what they thought of it. And Baker, as I recall, said, 'If you get Muskie to buy that, it should be something we can all live with.' So Buckley was encouraged to meet with Muskie.

"We were about to go into markups. Both he and Muskie felt that they had come up with something that deserved to be floated. Perhaps we could solve the auto thing just like that. Well, of course, things didn't turn out that way."

"What killed it?"

"Mainly the auto industry screaming bloody murder, saying the only things that would sell would be foreign cars. I don't think anyone on the committee believed that was necessarily true. I think they all thought the argument was overstated. But nobody had any real response to it. I know the hue and cry certainly had an effect on Domenici. I'm sure it had an effect on McClure. It probably had an effect on Buckley—and Muskie. So they had to give up what they intended as their fair and equitable approach."

"So the lobbying was effective even if poorly grounded?"

"Yes. Of course, it could be that the proposal was poorly grounded."

Thursday evening, July 17

About a week ago Leon phoned from home in midevening, a little breathless. "Say, could you come to dinner next Thursday?"
"Sure."
"I think the Senator's going to come. And a few others."
"Fine."
It was a little surprising. I have not heard of another instance of a staff member having the Senator to his home, except for an office party.

Joking to both Leon and Dolores today about the Senator's three dinners out this month—two at the Rockefellers' and one at the Billings'—I am able to put together, from their responses, how Leon engineered the evening. Once he and Pat decided they wanted to have the boss, Leon told Dolores that the Senator was coming to dinner and that he wanted an open date. Dolores gave him the seventeenth. Then, at a relaxed moment, Leon told the Senator that he and Pat would like to have him for dinner. Silently, Muskie absorbed the suggestion the way he absorbs advice on a parliamentary maneuver. After almost ten years of advising Muskie, Leon knows that not getting a "no" is an invitation to interpret the non-reply as a "yes." Yesterday Leon told Dolores that the Senator was coming Thursday, so please put it on the calendar. When Muskie got to his desk this morning the schedule on his desk easel informed him that he's to be at the Billings' at seven.

When I arrive at the modern house in a woodsy acre in the Kensington district of Silver Spring, Maryland, Muskie is already there in tieless shirt, blue sweater, and relaxed in the contentment of this morning's vote and a fistful of vodka martini. During the afternoon he's had his hair cut. The style is modern campaign compromise, full sideburns, locks embracing the rims of his ears, but not shaggy. He's very pleased that I notice and like it. Also arrived are Tom Jorling and Jim Smith. Tom, an environmental expert, is on the faculty of Williams College and a consultant to the subcommittee staff.[1] Smith is deputy director of the Water Quality Commission and, like Jorling and the Senator, a summer bachelor in Washington. In a few minutes we're joined by Don Alexander, a former staff assistant of Leon's, who is now an assistant attorney general of Maine, and his wife, Barbara Reid Alexander, whom I have seen at the markups. She is environmental quality chairperson of the Maine League of Women Voters and has been retained by the Sierra Club to station herself in Washington as its lobbyist on the Clean Air Act. As everyone knows, a fat-cat corporation will pay lavish fees to a Washington lobbyist because he has social access to the right Senator, say, chairman of the subcommittee that has life-and-death control over a corporation interest. So of course non-profit groups like the Sierra Club purchase access exactly the same way, but on a lower budget.

In minutes it's clear, however, that Mrs. Alexander is no fawning, ingratiating cultivator of influence. While Don and Leon and Tom corner the Senator with shop talk, Barbara crowds herself into the end of the couch. Her eyes are intense and she wears thick glasses that magnify her intensity. For a conversation opener, I ask what she considers to be her main function as a lobbyist.

"To establish lines of communication with our friends." Only with friends? "With people who will listen to us." Whom does she see? "Senator Hart, Senator Culver." Personally? "Senator Culver's office. Senator Muskie's office, Senator Domenici, Senator Stafford's office. I've had very good success in getting to Senator Gravel's staff. They're open to us, willing to listen to us, and I can get my information to his staff and through them to the Senator. And I get a personal reaction from them." Senator Buckley? "Staffwise, yes. Personally, no."

But that's only part of it, she adds. She works under a lobbying umbrella called the Clean Air Coalition, which includes two other groups with full-time lobbyists, Friends of the Earth and Ralph Nader's Public Interest Research Group, and many affiliated organizations around the country. Each member group has a key person, she explains, who understands the provisions of the Clean Air Act. "It's a whole network," Barbara says, "and when we turn on that

[1] Jorling is later named by President Carter as EPA's assistant administrator for water pollution.

network we get a response from these local organizations of phone calls to Senators and Congressmen, of letters coming in, and visitors coming in." I have not seen or heard reference to any "grass roots" lobbying on the environmental side of the clean air bill. Is the network effective? She replies with certainty, "Very."

We are called to dinner. At the candlelit table I mention to Muskie my surprise that Stafford, who has taken so little part in the markups, who has given no hint of having a grasp of the technical issues, should be the one to identify the point of compromise. With unconcealed pride Muskie says, "You've got to watch out for those quiet, canny northern New Englanders. But it's often that the man who knows least has the detachment to find where the area of agreement is."

Someone else comments that he doesn't think of awkward, shy Robert Stafford as exercising power.

"Power, power," says Muskie impatiently. "People have all sorts of conspiratorial theories on what constitutes power in the Senate. It has little to do with the size of the state you come from. Or the source of your money. Or committee chairmanships, although that certainly gives you a kind of power. But real power up there comes from doing your work and knowing what you're talking about. Power is the ability to change someone's mind. That is power around here." Then making clear, through flicks of the eye, that he's directing his message to Barbara Alexander, an unyielding zealot for .4 NOx, he sums up, slamming a flat palm on the table: "The most important thing in the Senate is credibility. *Credibility! That* is power."

The table slams startle five-year-old Erin Billings, goddaughter of the Senator, who is struggling to preserve her poise while helping her mother distribute servings of a tempting meringue dessert. Glaring squarely into the face of Muskie, Erin commands, "You mustn't *do* that."

By the time the laughter subsides, we've moved with our coffee cups into the living room and I ask Muskie what constitutes credibility in the Senate.

"When someone gets up to say that something is so, and if you can have absolute reliance that he's right, *that* is credibility. And that is power. If you've done your homework and know what you're talking about, that is power. It takes time to build up. Over the years that is one thing that has not changed in the Senate. One of the things that *has* changed is that the floor is not the place it used to be for changing minds. There was a time, not many years ago, when a good debate would attract a good number of Senators, and some would make up their minds on the basis of what was said. Today, hardly anyone has time to go to the floor except for votes because the work load has proliferated so much. So many more issues, so much more committee work to take care of, to become expert in."

Then the power to change minds, someone observes, is evident only in the cloakroom.

"The cloakroom!" Muskie scoffs. "In committee, not the cloakroom. Nothing happens in the cloakroom. Nothing. The cloakroom is where you go to rest your ass."

When conversation drifts back to the technical haggling on auto emissions and what a marathon it was, igniting a gleam in Mrs. Alexander's eyes, Muskie defends the subcommittee and what he calls, with a tone of reverence, the "legislative process." It took that much time, he argues, to bring out the disagreement. The seeming chaos of drawing out disagreement in Congress is an efficient process. It's when it does not happen that Congress becomes inefficient. Disagreement, asserts Muskie, lifting his vocal sonority—he's elaborating his central theme—disagreement, the clear defining of disagreement, and the eventual reconciliation and resolving of disagreement is what makes for good legislation, and therefore is efficient. When a law goes through this process, particularly the reconciliation part, it comes out a piece of strong and good legislation. A lot of Senators, he says, can't see beyond confrontation politics. Their imaginations can't handle anything beyond pitting strength against strength, one position merely outvoting another, defeating its valid points along with its less valid ones. That characterizes a lot of what happens in committees. It may take less time, Muskie concludes, but there's nothing efficient about it.

Just the other day in Maynard Toll's files I came across a similar thought, written for the Boston Sunday Globe by Charlie Ferris, Mike Mansfield's canny right-hand man:

If efficiency means swift action, then it should not be a primary objective for the Congress. It is a mistake to equate, as is often done, efficiency with effectiveness. In a sense, the Congress was efficient in passing the Gulf of Tonkin resolution. . . . I sense sometimes that Congress is operating most effectively when it appears to be functioning in total chaos. When members of Congress are in fierce combat over an issue either among themselves or with the Executive branch, the Congress is operating as it should, performing at its best.

The Civil Rights Acts of the '60s are perfect examples of Congress operating effectively but not necessarily efficiently. In 1964, the Senate spent approximately 85 days considering the Civil Rights Act and nothing else. The great success of those Acts—the ultimate acceptance of those judgments—can be attributed in great part to the fact that the opponents had their day in court—that the action was taken deliberately after a full discussion. This was Congress operating effectively if not efficiently.

Friday, July 18

A fiery clash illuminates the Senate today. Yes, illuminates, because it makes visible the design of Senate rules as a protection of the minority against a possibly ruthless majority, the weapons the majority can use when the minority abuses the rules, and the uses of parliamentary wit and maneuver as tools of political achievement—tools at least as effective, and perhaps as legitimate, as debate itself.

Two weeks from today the Senate goes into recess for the entire month of August. The date is set by law. With a huge list of "must" bills the Senate is convening early, staying late every day. They will meet tomorrow, Saturday. In the rush, the filibuster over the vacant New Hampshire seat has evaporated, the issue remaining unresolved. A new filibuster is openly and widely threatened, to defeat a ten-year extension of the voting rights bill. It will be led by—guess who— James Allen of Alabama. Even before the debate begins, a petition for a cloture vote has been drawn up.

To start the parliamentary grapple, Majority Leader Mike Mansfield contrives a way to outsmart Allen. The Judiciary Committee has just approved the voting rights bill and it's expected to come to the floor next week—when the time pressure will be fierce, just two or three days before the recess, and blocking its passage through quorum calls and procedural motions will be easy. As it happens, the House passed an almost identical voting rights bill weeks ago, and Mansfield has been holding that bill in the drawer of his desk. Today, rather than waiting for the Senate Judiciary Committee to prepare its report, Mansfield plans to surprise the Senate by calling up the House bill for ratification.

But the move is not a surprise to wily James Allen. Divining Mansfield's plan, Allen sends a note to the presiding officer, who, during that hour, happens to be his fellow Southern conservative, Jesse Helms of North Carolina. The note asks for quick recognition when Allen rises for it. At the first pause in discussion, Allen rises. So does Mansfield. Senate tradition establishes the leader's prerogative to be recognized first when several Senators ask to speak, but Helms gives the floor to Allen, who calls for reconsideration of a vote just taken on the consumer product safety bill, a motion that opens rich opportunities for dilation.

Furious, Mansfield recesses the Senate for an hour. On its resumption Dick Stone of Florida is in the chair. He recognizes Mansfield, who calls up the House bill, immediately followed by Majority Whip Byrd, who introduces the petition for cloture which, if passed, would limit debate to one hour per Senator. Then Mansfield unlooses an impassioned speech on the history and meaning of cloture, that it is designed to protect the minority, that bringing debate to a halt is so serious a matter that it requires "nine more votes than the maximum that is necessary for the Senate to declare war. . . . The fact is that there is no other cork large enough in the Senate rules to stop an endless drivel of irrelevance. . . . If cloture does not mean 'stop,' then there is not anything that means stop. . . .

"I would point out that Rule XXII specifies—I repeat, specifies—the inadmissibility of what is 'dilatory' once cloture is invoked." Then, in an unusual but unmistakable warning that punishment may come down upon Senator Allen, Mansfield declares: "So I serve notice now that if and when cloture is obtained . . . and if there is resort to tactics thereafter to go beyond this liberal allocation of one hour of time for each member in an effort to frustrate the preponderant will of the Senate, the Senate will be asked by the leadership to confront the issue squarely and without delay. It will be for the

Senate to decide whether to submit to the indignity of procedural pranks. I would urge members, therefore, who are inclined to vote for cloture to gird for a subsequent prospect—the prospect of having to deal also with the secondary issue of dilatoriness after the adoption of cloture."

In defense of Allen, Senator William Scott of Virginia protests that the Senate was not "on notice" that Mansfield would call up the House version of the bill. Byrd replies angrily:

"The leadership did what it had to do under the circumstances. The distinguished Senator from Alabama did not put the leadership on notice—Mr. President, may we have order in the Senate?—that he was going to attempt to call up another bill from the calendar. The distinguished Senator from Alabama seized the reins. He seized the leadership reins when he did that. The leadership cannot put itself in the position of going to Mr. Allen—and I use his name with great respect—and tell him what the leadership plans to do when we know that Mr. Allen is not going to come to the leadership and tell us what *he* plans to do. . . . When others play hardball, sometimes the leadership has to play hardball too."

The one-hour recess began at 4 P.M. A few minutes later Gayle Cory begins to revise Muskie's weekend schedule. The original schedule calls for him to leave the office at four-ten for National Airport and Maine. Gayle phones him in the cloakroom to ask, "Are you going or not going?" He replies, "I don't think I can. We're in a parliamentary wrangle and I don't know what's going to happen. They say there could be several votes." She asks, "Are the votes important enough to mess up the weekend schedule?" "It's not the importance of the votes but the number of them, and that's unpredictable. If I should miss four votes, it'll take a hundred to make up for them."

Maine newspapers, Gayle explains to me, are finicky about the percentage of votes missed, and surely Muskie's opponent next year would make much of a record that falls below, say, ninety-five per cent.

As matters turn out, Gayle arranges for Senator Mansfield's chauffeur and limousine—often just called "the Senate car and driver"—to race Muskie to the airport in time for a 6:35 P.M. flight.

Thursday, July 24

Muskie's scamper for the plane last Friday was not for naught. His weekend campaign schedule brought him Sunday to Aroostook County, a large slab of northernmost Maine that makes up in potatoes what it lacks in population. What people it has, however, take their politics seriously, and "the County," as Aroostook is called, has long been a Muskie stronghold. From a town only three miles short of the Canadian border, today's mail brings the Fort Fairfield *Review* and this report:

Perhaps the most talked about topic in political circles in Maine is if Bill Cohen is going to run against Ed Muskie for the U. S. Senate next year. . . . .
One event at last week's Maine Potato Blossom Festival gave Cohen an opportunity to tip his hand. . . . The pair participated in a contest for the world's championship potato-picking title. Staged in front of the post office, it was watched by a large number of people.
Muskie, as confident as a rooster in a chicken coop, generously conceded Cohen a handicap by starting to pick from a standing position, but he very quickly learned that his six-foot-four frame and erect stance left his hands too far from the ground, and potatoes were really flying into Bill's basket. An old pro at the art, Bill was down on his knees and piling up points rapidly.
Maine Potato Queen Pat Cyr of Madawaska, quickly taking in the situation, threw caution, political affiliation and personal sympathies to the winds and went to Ed's rescue. The result was an obstacle too great for Bill to overcome. . . .
Cohen, not taking a bit kindly to what had happened, termed

the incident the "Fairfield Fix." He didn't say it over the radio or TV, but bitterly complained to anyone who would listen, and there were a pile of people around. The second district congressman was overheard telling his tale even to some Democrats.

Muskie's reaction to the "fix" accusation was: ". . . If I had known how Bill felt about the contest, I'd have allowed him to win."

Today's crowded schedule portends a fragmented, confusing day for Muskie. Clean air markups have skidded to a dead halt. Members are not showing up. Lacking quorums, meetings all this past week have been stillborn. In desperation, Muskie and Leon called one for last night, postponed it until 8 A.M. this morning, now delay it until 4 P.M. today. At ten today, a Budget Committee seminar. At noon an office appointment with the chairman of the board of Johnson & Johnson, whose New Jersey factory is in trouble over pollution regulations; Senator Harrison Williams personally requested the meeting, so Muskie has to do it. At twelve-thirty, an unusual luncheon in S-199: with his daughter Ellen, who is married to an auto mechanic and service station owner across the Potomac, and with her son Ethan, who is celebrating his fifth birthday. (On his way to the budget seminar, Grandfather Muskie directs Dolores to find some birthday candles, an anxious quest that ruins her morning until Al From's secretary locates some in a supply closet of the Armed Services Committee.) At one forty-five he's to see the Senate physician because of a persistent pain in his arm. At three a couple of Maine businessmen—one a reliable contributor—are to urge him to vote against the common-site picketing bill, which would permit workers engaged in a labor dispute against any subcontractor of a construction project to picket the chief contractor and any other subcontractor of that project. For several days contractors pouring into the Capitol to oppose this bill seem to have outnumbered tourists. The AFL-CIO has designated passage of the bill as its number one priority of the year. For anyone who must have labor's support next year to win and who opposes this bill—curtains. But Muskie has to hear out his contractor friends and satisfy them that he has an open mind. Then at 4 P.M. the postponed markup. Enough?

Bobby Byrd has served notice there'll be roll calls all day, just as often as Senator Allen will permit less controversial bills to interrupt his filibuster against voting rights.

Having disposed of auto issues, Muskie's subcommittee is trying to settle—or, by persistent absence, to avoid—the extremely difficult business of "non-degradation," the complexities of which could fill another book. The problem is to try to clarify the principle that no new pollution shall be permitted in an area that would degrade the quality of the ambient air. For one thing, that implies that a plant can't be built with a new, polluting smokestack until the pollution from old smokestacks is cleaned sufficiently to "make room" for the new. At least as troublesome for many states in the country, the principle involves special protections for national parks and wilderness areas—not only in or near these areas but long distances away if prevailing winds might blow pollutants into these areas. Clarifying that principle is headache enough, but trying to translate the intention into workable, real-world regulations is a brainbuster.

While the subcommittee is deciding—or avoiding—nondegradation, the all-settled auto emissions issue goes on, unsettled. Someone has rung the White House fire alarm over the subcommittee's new standards. Last Friday Federal Energy Administrator Frank Zarb, reflecting President Ford's extreme sensitivity to the concerns of the auto industry, sent a hand-delivered letter to Chairman Jennings Randolph. It draws conclusions from the subcommittee bill that ought to guarantee scary newspaper copy. The subcommittee standards, says Zarb, "will cost the Nation 420,000 barrels of oil a day in 1985. . . . The consumer will have to pay $300 more per car for the emissions control systems . . . and [the new standards] will halt work on developing promising alternate engine systems."

That's a remarkably quick, alert White House response to a subcommittee action taken only the previous day. One can't help but recall that on the day Gerald Ford was sworn in as President newspapers listed his four closest Washington chums and golfing companions. Ranked first was Rodney W. Markley, Ford Motor Company's Washington vice-president and chief lobbyist. Did Markley give the President a jingle? After twenty-five years in a Michigan seat in the House of Representatives, Gerald Ford probably needs no prompting on the interests of the auto industry.

Leon Billings and other staff members collaborate on a reply, knocking down "clear distortions of fact" one by one. In the artful strategies of communication between Congress and the White House, the letter is signed not only by Muskie, as subcommittee chairman, but by Senators Stafford and Hart, a Republican and Democrat, co-authors of the finally adopted standards.

The late afternoon markup in a Capitol room near the Senate floor progresses fitfully. All through it, Morgan of North Carolina is in and out. Buckley and McClure are in and out. The center of action is in the other ring, the floor. Eventually Muskie surrenders, adjourning the markup. I head for the gallery, for the main show and for what turns out to be a long evening.

Cloture has been voted to end the filibuster against the voting rights bill. In these closing hours, with no purpose any longer served in stretching time by blowing wind into it, the debate has turned earnest. It's for real.

This is the Congress, the Senate that, having voted the money that brought us to the moon, must soon knuckle down to assess other futuristic, high-technology goals: nuclear energy, solar energy, Lord knows what others. Yet today, no less than it was a hundred years ago, even forty years ago, drama in the Senate is highest and most in character when it is the old drama, the postslavery drama, the year-after-year, bloodied, unbindable cleavage of North versus South, brown derby hat versus black string tie, free suffragist versus poll taxer, the La Follettes and Wagners versus the Bilbos and Huey Longs. In the Senate, the body of Congress that represents all states equally, far more than in the House, the states have battled through the trials of Reconstruction, over the ban on poll taxes, over making a federal crime of lynching, over the Civil Rights Act, and over passage in 1965 of the Voting Rights Act, according to some, the most important of all.

The voting rights law expires August 6, little more than two weeks away. The law names seven Southern states to be patrolled by federal election officers, policing them against a re-enactment of past sins. These states regard a ten-year extension of probation as humiliating. To mitigate the oncoming embarrassment, Majority Whip Bobby Byrd devised—and two days ago the Senate passed—a sop for the South, an amendment reducing the policing period to seven years. Opponents of that amendment are still protesting it on the floor today. Their complaint is that now the Senate bill differs from the bill already passed by the House, which still provides for a ten-year extension. So now voting rights will have to go to a House-Senate conference committee, probably delaying a final vote of approval until the last hours before the Congress recesses, reopening a new possibility of filibuster, even opening the possibility of a pocket veto by President Ford during the recess. By introducing that amendment and shepherding it to passage, they are charging, Bobby Byrd has endangered this bill and all the bills lined up behind it requiring passage before recess. He has botched up the Senate calendar.

Surely Bobby Byrd is as assailable on some ground or other as most men in the Senate. But if a critic wants to keep some shadow of credibility, he doesn't go around saying that Bobby Byrd has botched up the Senate calendar. Any fool knows that if there's any god that Byrd has worshiped since acquiring his whipship, it's been the god of the Senate calendar and Senate schedule. As Lyndon Johnson and Alben Barkley and other Southerners and border staters have done upon moving from state to national responsibility, Byrd has transformed himself from regional tub thumper to Senate harmonizer, facilitator, lubricator, devoted totally to greasing the skids of legislation, getting bills to move *on schedule*. So craftsmanlike has he become in this new devotion that Majority Leader Mansfield has called Byrd "the best Whip the Senate has ever had." In fact it's commonly said that if Mansfield should retire at the end of his present term, which expires next year—and many think he may—Byrd is his most likely successor.

That's quite a metamorphosis for one who, a quarter century ago, organized 150 of his West Virginia hill neighbors into the Ku Klux Klan, became their Kleagle, and thus launched his political career—a start which Byrd has since conceded was a "mistake," pointing out that "back in that time and in that part of the country, a lot of people, respectable people, were members." He has recovered from that lapse so well that he declared his candidacy for the 1972 Democratic presidential nomination. While the boom for him never boomed, it's expected he'll do so again in 1976.[1] Some canny Byrdwatchers confide that these hat-throwings are merely to impress West Virginians or perhaps to give him a national aura as preparation for a Majority Leader race. A reporter has asked if he thinks he has the charisma of other potential candidates. Byrd replied, "Maybe not, but can any of the others play the fiddle?" And anyone who questions Byrd's ideological broadening should hear him play duets to the blue grass guitar of Senator James Abourezk of South Dakota, one of the Senate's farthest-out liberals.

Nobody puts down Byrd any more for lacking a college diploma. In fact nobody has taken him lightly in any way ever since he unseated Ted Kennedy as Whip in 1971. He won that post by spending endless hours, which Kennedy did not, seeking out and looking after the floor needs of Senators, seeing that their amendments were properly introduced, finding co-sponsors for weak-kneed bills, recording his colleagues' "unavoidable" absences in the Congressional Record, scheduling floor debate for a bill at a time convenient for its chief sponsor and opponent, writing thank-you notes on the slightest pretext, always managing the availability of an extra pair of tickets to a Bullets basketball game. And every favor extended so courteously and generously has been recorded in a memory cell behind Bobby Byrd's high, wide forehead.

To understand the craftsmanship of Bobby Byrd is to open an important window on the character of the Senate. Muskie, a potential rival for becoming Majority Leader of the Senate, has observed about Byrd: "I must say, he's been damned effective. In any organization —a social club, the Boy Scouts, or the Senate—when a guy is ready to go out and do the dirty work, the legwork, it's a good case for advancement. He wheels and deals for us. He's a service organization all by himself and a very efficient one. I remember when he first handled the D.C. appropriations bill as floor manager, his very first presentation. I was sitting in the chair, presiding. He had the whole thing memorized. He didn't look at a note, an amazing performance. Not just blind memorization, but he had thoroughly mastered it. That's power. When anyone does that kind of a job it's convertible to power. Respect and leadership come whenever a member of a group steps forward and does something and does it well."

[1] He did.

No, Bobby Byrd does not introduce amendments—and organize majorities to pass them—as a way to botch a schedule. That voting rights amendment, he repeats today as he argued the day it was debated and passed, was to heal the breach between North and South, to insure the voting rights bill's passage. Seven years, after all, is time enough to give the Congress another chance at seeing whether federal supervision of seven Southern states continues to be necessary.

Just as the protests subside, a young page in uniform of white shirt and black pants brings Byrd an envelope, which he opens and, suppressing a gloat, reads to the Senate. The timing is theatrical. The letter is from House Judiciary Chairman Peter Rodino and a subcommittee chairman, Don Edwards, saying that since Byrd's seven-year amendment is the only difference in otherwise identical bills, they would simply recommend that the House endorse the bill as the Senate has amended it. Thus a conference would be unnecessary, and the bill would go to the White House the moment the Senate passes it.

But that is only the beginning of the evening's entertainment. Older Southern Senators feel old stirrings of old Senate wars, and the running of adrenalin makes them young again. Younger Southerners bridle at the bill's naming their states as stepchildren. Hasn't the South outdone the North—with more sincere resolve and far more impressive practical results—in desegregating schools? Hasn't the rise in black voting in their states created a "New South," indeed has it not brought many of these young faces to the Senate? Do the North and West insist on showing no respect for the pride and sovereignty and new spirit of great Southern states? Senators young and old argue into the evening that the seven states, so singled out because they averaged only 29.3 per cent registration of black voters in 1964, have lifted their black registration in some cases as high as the North's. How much proving is enough?

Senator Strom Thurmond (old) introduces an amendment to wipe out the feature of "pre-clearance" by a federal court in Washington. It loses 72–22. Virginia's Republican William L. Scott (old) sponsors another, to free a state from federal supervision if its registration for all voters has risen above fifty per cent by 1972. A loser, 68–26. Another by Scott, to shift the "pre-clearance" decision out of Washington and into local courts. Beaten 57–38.

Then the young Senators of the New South take the stage. Robert Morgan, North Carolina's former attorney general, and Sam Nunn, Georgia's candidate for one day becoming the new Richard Russell, present an ingenious and arresting amendment that would equalize the status of Southern states with that of all others, yet provide a pre-clearance procedure that might be more workable than battling it out in court after court. Theirs would require the U. S. Attorney General to "pre-clear" the election laws of every state and county in the nation, regardless of whether discrimination has been previously shown.

Instantly, Jake Javits of New York rises to block the amendment on a point of order arising from the rules of cloture.

And instantly not only Nunn and Morgan but Lawton Chiles of Florida are on their feet. Furious, Chiles protests that he broke away from colleagues of his region to vote for cloture yesterday—and now the rights of those colleagues are shut out as the bitter reward of that vote. Morgan and Nunn and Chiles have all voted with other Democrats to obtain cloture in the New Hampshire election dispute. All three in turn, in virtually identical words, now bitterly warn: "It will be a long time before I'll vote for cloture again."

Alan Cranston is darting around the floor, making check marks on his familiar tally sheet. The liberal reincarnation of pre-Whip Bobby Byrd, Cranston is the volunteer vote counter, fixer of details, one-man service organization. He confers intently with John Tunney, his fellow Californian, who is floor-managing the bill. Tunney nods assent. Cranston dashes to Nunn, a quick exchange, and Nunn gives Cranston's arm an appreciative squeeze. Tunney announces to the presiding officer that he would welcome a vote on the Nunn amendment. This time no objection is raised against the irregular procedure. In the roll call, Cranston votes against the amendment. Tunney votes against it. A solid Southern bloc and virtually all Republicans except a band of liberals (Javits, Edward Brooke, Maryland's Charles Mathias) support the amendment. Nunn's amendment is defeated 48 to 41.

One of the liberal Republicans later tells a reporter, "We understood Cranston's game of placating the Southerners to hold their votes for New Hampshire, and we thought it was irresponsible to risk the voting rights bill for that."

But Cranston knew it was not a risk. He had counted the votes. The net gain was tremendous: by giving Nunn the courtesy of permitting his amendment to come to a vote, Cranston not only insured retention of three votes in the New Hampshire battle and in other battles unforeseen that might require a vote of cloture, but bound at least three Democrats of the "New South" more snugly into the national patchwork quilt that comprises the Democratic Party.

Why didn't Javits insist on blocking the amendment by repeating his point of order? That turned out to be just one of those things. Javits felt the parliamentary maneuver would be more effectively done by either Ed Brooke (a black) or Charles Mathias (a liberal border stater). They agreed. When the moment came for the objection, however, Brooke thought Mathias was going to raise it, and Mathias was waiting for Brooke to do it. When Brooke called for recognition, the "no objection" was already "so ordered." It was too late.

McClure's and Buckley's preoccupation at the markup with what was going on on the floor is explained by their active participation in supporting the Nunn amendment. With relish, they play the egalitarians, seeing no reason why any state or county should be discriminated against, no reason why the Attorney General should not investigate the fairness of every election board in the land if it's to investigate a single one. After failing to dilute the bill by "democratizing" it, Buckley and McClure support its passage.

Finally the voting rights bill arrives at its judgment and—who would imagine the anguish and the battles concealed behind the numbers?—passes easily, 77 Senators to 12. The time is ten forty-five.

Saturday, July 26

Today, all day, while the Senate is in session across a corridor, the Environmental Pollution Subcommittee starts meeting at 10 A.M. in Room S-207, a dignified, dark-paneled room with a great chandelier looming over the committee table and an original Gilbert Stuart of George Washington watching sternly over the subcommittee's members. All day, all day, until at about four-thirty the elusive beast of non-degradation is finally cornered.

For a man who, like other Senators, has spoken and written of his impatience in the early years of his Senate life after serving as governor when he could decide things, run things, command action and get it, Muskie has taught himself to be a remarkably patient man. To him, patience is not a surrender but an essential tool in guiding the legislative process. Like a leader of a Quaker meeting, he sees it as a form of *activity* to sit and wait, waiting for the participants to arrive at the "sense of the meeting," which not only brings agreement but makes every participant a defender of the agreement.

At about twelve-thirty today, when already bones are weary and minds fuzzy, the committee turns to a new question: since the bill authorizes each state to set certain air standards of its own, provided they are no lower than minimum federal standards, what if a state refuses to enforce its own standards? Who may sue the state to force its enforcement? The EPA? A citizen's suit? The committee, almost all lawyers, haggle and bicker and bicker and haggle. Finally Gary Hart, sitting as silently as Muskie but looking more bored, bursts out, "Can't it be one or the other or both? Is this a thing that a group of Senators should be spending a Saturday afternoon deciding?"

Either or both. Like men pricked awake, they decide, of course, that's the way to do it.

Leon quietly passes a note to Hart. It says, "Thank you."

The solution is obvious and Muskie, the only member present who has been on the subcommittee for more than a single term, could have dictated the answer, even chided the committee for dawdling. But he waits. And in the end gets a bill that is not only defensible but has a broad co-authorship for its defense.

The fits and starts of the committee's work all day, the interruptions, the comings and goings to and from the Senate floor, are best explained by yesterday's communication to all Senators from Bobby Byrd:

WHIP NOTICE

TODAY
Friday
July 25, 1975

Dear Colleague:

In view of the approaching August 1 recess, the program of business to be transacted today and tomorrow (Saturday) is a busy one. It is hoped and believed that at least the following measures (and possibly others) can be acted upon today and tomorrow:

1. H. R. 8365 (Transportation Appropriation Bill, being debated on the Senate Floor at time of Whip Notice preparation).
2. H. R. 8561 (Agriculture Appropriation Bill)
3. H. R. 8597 (Treasury, Post Office Appropriation Bill)
4. HUD Appropriation Bill
5. S. 391 (Mineral leasing)
6. S. 2173 (Naval petroleum reserves)
7. S. 1281 (Public understanding of depository institutions in home financing)
8. S. 963 (Diethylstilbestrol)

Time agreements have been entered into on all of the measures listed above. *Consequently, there will be rollcall votes tomorrow (Saturday)*, and I would anticipate that the Senate will put in a full day in an effort to complete work on all of the foregoing measures.

On Monday, the Senate will take up S. Res. 160 (Diego Garcia) and, after that matter has been disposed of, there will be a heavy workload during the week which will include the following, but the list is not complete nor will bills be necessarily called up in the order stated:

1. S. 521 (Outer Continental Shelf)
2. S. 1587 (Public works and EDA)
3. S. 598 (ERDA authorization)
4. H. R. 8121 (State, Justice, Commerce Appropriation Bill)
5. HEW Appropriation Bill

REMINDER: There will be rollcall votes today and tomorrow (Saturday).

NOTE: (1) Conference reports, being privileged, may be called up at any time and rollcall votes can occur thereon.

(2) The New Hampshire election dispute is still to be dealt with.

The leadership hopes that as many Senators as possible will be in attendance tomorrow (Saturday), especially in view of the fact that rollcall votes are assured by virtue of the time agreements on the measures to be taken up.

Robert C. Byrd
Extension 42158 or 42297

Monday, July 28

Muskie's fireworks are loud, but his bombshells can be so quiet, they're easy to miss. He sets one off today.

At the end of a hot, crowded, dreary markup in a Capitol meeting room that opens a new phase of the clean air bill, that of land use and transportation controls, he casually mentions a letter President Ford has just sent to the committee (addressed to Chairman Randolph, and an identical one to Representative Harley Staggers, chairman of the House Interstate and Foreign Commerce Committee). It refers to a "detailed" executive branch review of air quality, health, energy, and price implications of auto pollution control, and it concludes:

"I urge you to hold another hearing on this matter so Administration witnesses can present the findings."

The White House has also released a "fact sheet" on the "executive branch study," a repetition of previous arguments to support a five-year freeze on standards.

Subcommittee members, Republicans and Democrats alike, appear faintly amused by the President's request, which permits no other interpretation than as a device for further delay, thus forcing postponement of new emissions standards for another auto-model year and giving Detroit that extra year to lobby for a five-year freeze.

"Really," Muskie remarks upon gaveling the meeting to a close, "I don't care if we have a Clean Air Act this year. The present law specifies standards, and if they want to meet those next year, that's fine. There's *some* information that technology is available that *might* meet them. If the President wants to delay for more hearings, we're not going to be able to get through this bill until November, because a lot of us here are going to be tied up in the Budget Committee with that second budget resolution. So, if we don't get a Clean Air Act this year, I'm not going to be the first in line for the crying towel."

The committee becomes a freeze-frame of faces, each member transfixed in quick calculations and political estimates. Muskie is fingering a powerful weapon. After all, this is not a bill to impose tough new standards on the auto industry but to relax present standards. If the present law mandates standards for 1978 automobiles that are indeed unachievable by present technology—what a threat to the industry, holding over their heads the club of retaining the present law! What a way to scare the auto lobby, the White House itself, out of playing games of dalliance.

If this threat has previously occurred to committee members, you wouldn't know it by the exclamation points in their eyes at Muskie's shrugging remark.

Before the afternoon is out Leon Billings, Hal Brayman, committee counsel Barry Meyer, and minority counsel Bailey Guard are kicking around an appropriate tit-for-tat reply. They decide that Ford's morally impregnable position of calling for an open-hearing-so-that-all-may-know-the-facts is a game that two can play. Their cunning reply, to be signed by Chairman Randolph and Howard Baker, ranking Republican on the full committee, reads:

Honorable Gerald R. Ford
The President
The White House

Dear Mr. President:

We have discussed your July 26, 1975 request for a hearing on automobile emissions with the Members of the Committee on Public Works. There is agreement that a hearing could be held if you desire it.

If such a hearing is held, undoubtedly private and public groups would also desire to be heard on the information presented. We would be constrained to honor those requests. Such a situation would entail postponing further Committee consideration of other issues involved in the Clean Air Act. It had been our hope to begin Full Committee consideration of the Clean Air Act during the week of September 8 so that during that week and the following week, we could develop and report the legislation for Senate consideration.

By reason of service on the Budget Committee, Senator Muskie, Chairman of the Subcommittee, Senator McClure and Senator Domenici . . . will be required to address themselves to the Second Budget Resolution which must be considered by the Congress by mid-October. If the hearings you request are held, it is a reasonable certainty that the Public Works Committee could not conclude its deliberations on the Clean Air Act until late October or early November. This delay would, we suggest, cause severe problems for those who are regulated by the Act, including the automobile industry.

Mr. President, if you have further counsel to give us in this matter, we shall be pleased to receive it.

Truly,

Howard H. Baker, Jr.   Jennings Randolph

Tuesday, July 29

Byrd's Whip Notice lists the public works bill among those the leadership hopes to call up today. It is to this bill, of course, to which Muskie has planned to introduce the countercyclical assistance bill as an amendment. And sure enough, in midafternoon it is called up.

"Mr. President," says Senator Montoya, floor-managing the bill as chairman of the Economic Development Subcommittee, reading obediently from a prepared statement that opens with an arresting non sequitur, "it is a very late hour at which we are finally coming to deal with the economic problems that have been facing our people for a long time. . . . The President blames the Congress for inaction, the Congress blames the Executive. Surely, truth must lie somewhere in between. That truth is irrefutable. . . ."

An hour or so later the moment arrives for Muskie to open debate on his amendment and, immediately after his statement summarizing the proposal, he yields the floor for five minutes to Bill Brock of Tennessee, a move that compels attention. Tennessee's two Senators, Baker and Brock, both Republican, both "conservative," both personable and youthfully handsome, have been foreseen as bearers one day of their party's national banner, and each has been waiting for the banner to fall within his grasp. In the Senate each has what in theater is called "star quality." Of the two, Brock is regarded as the more conservative, analytical, and hard-nosed: an ideal ally for a liberal introducing an economic assistance bill.

The amendment, begins Brock, "is a remarkable piece of work and one in which I'm privileged to join . . . unique, because it is related explicitly to the economic hardship under which we now suffer —and only that. . . . In the twelve years I have been here, I have seen us place into law program after program which was needed at a particular time but which remained in effect no matter how long ago the need disappeared. This bill is a specific remedy that deals only with the problem and phases out when the problem is gone. . . ."

Montoya still considers this incomprehensible hocus-pocus called countercyclical assistance an intrusion on his turf, and the moment Brock sits down Montoya unlooses his irritation:

"What is this so-called Muskie amendment? What does it do? It is, in my opinion, another revenue-sharing bill. . . . I would probably vote for this particular amendment as a bill if it came here separately. But I say, Mr. President, that the amendment puts a burden on the bill and makes it subject to a presidential vee-toe. . . . The amendment does not create jobs. . . . No committee action has been taken on this amendment. Will it be an albatross? It is an ingenious way to get the matter before the House, but I regret that it is using the public works bill as a vehicle to get there. . . . I wonder, as I study the amendment before us, if it is not basically an urban bill. . . . I represent a poor rural state. . . ."

In a wide swing of the political pendulum from Brock, Muskie yields five minutes to Hubert Humphrey, whose ebullient voice, more like a razzberry than a trumpet, lifts the chamber:

"First of all, the Senator from New Mexico indicated that the amendment does not create jobs. Let me say what it does do. It *preserves* jobs. . . . The Joint Economic Committee has made a survey of American cities with . . . unemployment rates of 11, 12, and 14 per cent. This morning we heard testimony from New York City, over 11 per cent; Detroit, over 25 per cent; Phoenix, I believe, over 14 per cent. In city after city, from Providence to Wilmington to New York to Cleveland to Detroit, you find mayors and city councils compelled in the name of fiscal frugality to lay off workers. . . . May I say I commend the able Senator from New Mexico for an extraordinarily good job of legislative craftsmanship in bringing to us a bill which makes a tremendous amount of sense. The issue, of course, that has us worried here is will this provoke a veto? I think the Senate would be interested in knowing that only this morning as I was holding hearings as chairman of the Joint Economic Committee, Dr. Arthur Burns, one of the senior advisers to the President of the United States, and who is chairman of the Federal Reserve Board, responded to questions from Senator Javits. Dr. Burns said of this very proposal that we are now debating: 'The one proposal that makes sense to aid our cities is the countercyclical revenue assistance program.'"

Montoya rebuts by yielding five minutes of the time allotted for opposition to the amendment to Russell Long of Louisiana, who, as chairman of the Finance Committee, is warden of all bills that tax and, stemming from that guardianship, warden of revenue sharing. To Long, the issue presented here transcends national social policy —it is the holier matter of committee jurisdiction:

"The Senator from New Mexico has correctly said this amendment does not belong on a public works bill. It belongs on a Finance Committee bill if it belongs on any bill. I do not know why anyone would want to by-pass the committee whose jurisdiction includes revenue sharing.

"This is not a bill to build so much as a chicken coop. This is an amendment that would share revenues, 2 billion dollars, with the states. Now, I notice"—he gazes significantly around the chamber—"it does not follow the revenue-sharing formula. There are thirty states that make out a lot worse under this amendment than they would under the general revenue-sharing formula. To some states it will not make much difference. It will not make much difference to Maine, for example. It will make a lot of difference to Wyoming—"

"Will the Senator yield twenty seconds?" calls Gale McGee of Wyoming, a 1958 "classmate" of Muskie's. "I see Wyoming would get twelve times as much under the existing revenue-sharing formula. Would it be a stroke of statesmanship if I took a position favoring this amendment?"

By now, aides of Long have mounted huge charts on easels in the back of the chamber, illustrating through colored graphs how each state would fare under Muskie's six per cent unemployment formula as against the formula of general revenue sharing, which is not related to a state's or city's rate of unemployment.

Long thunders: *"Their* formula cannot begin to tell you what all the little communities are going to get, what the counties are going to get, what the small towns are going to get. Why not? Because this is a *big-city-mayor* bill. Those people figured this thing out in a way that helps each one to meet their problems. I do not blame them. If I were a big-city mayor that is what I would do." Then, aiming his knockout blow not at the bill but at Muskie, as budget chairman: "Mr. President, it is said this amendment would have very little budgetary impact because 2 billion dollars has been *budgeted* for temporary recovery programs. Well, Mr. President, that refers to public service jobs programs, where the objective is *more jobs*."

"If the Senator will examine the report on the first budget resolution," responds Muskie, "that 2 billion dollars is allocated for public works and for other anti-recession assistance to state and local governments."

"Well, it says additional temporary recovery programs, and I don't think anybody had this bill in mind when they put that language in there."

"That was precisely the bill that was discussed in conference. If the Senator has not examined the transcript of the conference, he ought not to presume what was said. This is *precisely* the bill that was envisioned by the language—"

"Well, I was not—"

"—of the budget resolution."

"Well, I was not in the conference, but I am a United States Senator, I was here, and I am familiar with the fact that I heard very little about this bill except in vague general terms, and I am still not hearing anything about it except in vague general terms. Nobody can tell me how much Winnfield, Louisiana, will get out of this bill."

Humphrey is on his feet. "The Senator will find out that all he needs to know is that any community that has six per cent or more unemployment will share in this bill. The reason we do not have information on Winnfield, Louisiana, is that there is no statistical evidence of how much unemployment they have. . . . May I also say that if the Senator has not heard about this bill it does not mean that it has not been discussed. As a matter of fact the main witness for the bill was the mayor of New Orleans."

"If we are going to adopt the standard here," enters Javits of New York, "that in every case, every bill, every state has to get its cut or it will not play, that will create insurmountable problems for any kind of targeted assistance . . . and if the Senate is going to run in that direction I can see nothing but anarchy ahead of us."

Javits' New York colleague, Senator Buckley, has problems over Muskie's bill. Perhaps his inclination is to oppose it. But he has already burned his fingers over the boiling issue of New York City's budget crisis. Buckley has indicated that City Hall ought to be left to stew in its own juice, and he must not get caught again in that position if he's to survive his 1976 campaign. But in anticipation of the Muskie amendment he's developed a remarkable acrobatic stance: "We have enacted many bills this year that attempt to ameliorate the effects of the current recession. . . . Much of this legislation is ineffective and based on disproven economic policies that will only serve to create greater distortions. . . . I have found one legislative proposal, however, which would help state and local governments adjust . . . [and that is] the Senator from Maine's proposal. . . . My support is premised upon the principle that the federal government should assume certain liability for conditions and consequences it causes. In other words, it should not, in this instance, leave state and local governments holding the bag when the recession, induced by wrongheaded economic policies followed by the federal government, cut deeply into tax revenues and budgetary commitments, especially as so many of these commitments have been mandated by the federal government in the first instance."

Muskie next yields time to Ted Kennedy, who is difficult to imagine on the same side of this bill as Buckley. Kennedy pleads a brief and routine case for the cities "where there is the greatest need for housing and education, for mass transit, for health care and other social services."

For the opposition, Montoya yields to Senator McClure, who as usual avoids ideological puffery, instead digging into the working innards of the issue, attempting to show it won't accomplish the desired results:

"I understand the motivation that has led the authors of this amendment to offer it. . . . I want to point up one or two fallacies. . . . It is premised on the idea that tax revenues to state and local governments have dropped off in this period of recession. . . . [Most unpaid local taxes are] simply deferred to some future year. Most state statutes of which I am aware allow local governments to issue tax anticipation notes so that they can borrow in anticipation of those revenues. So this revenue is not lost to them. . . . If this amendment is passed, they not only will collect under this because of the downward trend in revenues, they will get it back later when they actually collect those taxes. They will, in effect, have an added increment in their spending allowance because of the largess of the federal government. . . . The concern for the plight of local government is correct. I think they have a long-term problem. But this is not the way to address that long-term problem."

Muskie's Maine colleague, Senator Hathaway, is yielded one minute by Montoya. By Montoya? Is Hathaway going to oppose Muskie? Why only one minute?

"I regret that I have only one minute," Hathaway begins, "and I also regret having to oppose my distinguished colleague from Maine. I do not oppose him in principle, but I am in agreement with the chairman of the Finance Committee, particularly since I am the chairman of the Subcommittee on Revenue Sharing. . . ." Clearly he is earning a merit badge from Senator Long and defending his own revenue-sharing turf. When his minute is up he asks unanimous consent to have the rest of a long statement appear in the Congressional Record as though read, relieved that his uncomfortable minute is over with.

Muskie yields a minute to Senator Domenici, who goes overtime explaining his tortuous decision to support the amendment, his reasoning remaining unclear:

"Let me say to the distinguished Senator from Maine I am going to support the amendment. I do not want Senators to have any misunderstanding about my vote. I am going to vote for it because I think the concept is right. To cast a negative vote might lead some people to conclude that I do not think it is a good approach. I am not sure the triggering mechanism is right. Senator Montoya, my state's senior Senator, might be right, that we are burdening this bill. . . . The Senator from Louisiana has a good point, that it probably should have gone through the Committee on Finance. . . . This Senator is voting for it because at this particular time in history, as a concept . . . it is the best measure to hit the floor of the Senate. . . . If I vote against it later, I want the Senator [from Maine] to understand it will be in terms of the over-all budget and other factors."

Sensing the difficulty of the choice and the possible indecision of some Senators, Long decides to maximize his chance of killing the Muskie amendment by giving Senators a way to vote it down without going on record against it. He moves to table it. Muskie counters by asking for "the yeas and nays," a recorded roll-call vote. Long's motion to table is defeated, 58 to 36. Actually, that is a test vote for the amendment itself. Unless Long can conjure another parliamentary device for blocking it, the amendment appears sure of passage.

Long tries. He offers an amendment to substitute the revenue-sharing formula for Muskie's, which would destroy the anti-recession concept.

Meanwhile the roll call has enlarged the audience for the debate, which immediately resumes.

"I'm delighted," declares Muskie, "that there are more Senators present now. . . . This is not a revenue-sharing bill. . . . I think the Senator from Louisiana understands that, but he does not want the Senate to understand that. . . . If this is revenue sharing, so are all the education programs. So are all the health programs. So is any program of grants to states and local governments, because that is all this is. It is a grant program. It is *not* revenue sharing. The whole concept of revenue sharing is that state and local governments ought to share, on a continuing basis, a certain percentage of federal revenues generated within their borders. That is not this bill. . . . So do not confuse the two. If the Senators reject this one, do not reject it because somebody tells us it is a substitute for general revenue sharing. Reject it because they think states and cities do not need the help. . . .

"When the Senator from Louisiana stands here and tells us that this formula does not work exact justice, he is not making any new discovery. I do not find exact justice in many of the tax bills that he reports to the chamber of the Senate. I do not expect to. This is a legislative process, not a miracle-making process. . . . This is a very simple idea. It does not need to be distorted into the kind of monster that the Senator from Louisiana tries to make it out to be. . . . This was not some sudden surprise. . . . It was studied in the Committee on the Budget. It was studied in the chamber of the Senate when the budget resolution was before us. . . . We have held six days of hearings that were well covered in the press. We invited inputs from everyone. Our jurisdiction was never challenged until this afternoon. As the Senator is always willing to remind us, he is ready to receive testimony from us in the Committee on Finance—and we were ready to receive testimony from him in the Committee on Government Operations. This has been a well-digested idea, and no amount of ridicule can dismiss it."

Muskie is feeling annoyed and feeling good. Nothing stirs a Senator like an audience of other Senators, conscripted by a roll call and lingering in the chamber lest they miss a good show. Hubert Humphrey can't resist the temptation:

"Mr. President, I see we are having a little trouble deciding whether or not this is a revenue-sharing bill or an anti-recession bill. . . . We bail out the railroads. They come down here to Congress. We don't have any talk about revenue sharing." Humphrey's eyes are open wide in dramatic astonishment, his arms stretched from coast to coast, and he swings them, outstretched, as he peers from corner to corner of the chamber, from one Senator's face to the next, full of innocence, wonder, and indignation. "We do not have anybody getting up and saying, 'What is the jurisdiction of the committee?' *Noooooo*. Penn Central comes in, and we say, 'Get out the money scoop!'" From both sides of the aisle, an uproar of laughter. "We say we *have* to do it—that we can't afford to let Penn Central go down the drain. The Federal Reserve Board bailed out Franklin National Bank with a loan of $1.2 billion. Why? Because they said if it was not done the whole banking structure might fall apart. Look down the cities on the list here. . . .

"People say, 'Well, we have to argue about committee jurisdiction around here.' . . . Senator Muskie did not come around here and say, 'I don't want the Finance Committee to get it.' He came over here and did what we are supposed to do. He put a bill on the desk on behalf of himself and others—and I was one of the others. The *parliamentarian* said that the bill goes to the Committee on Government Operations. . . . But we are saying to ourselves, 'We are going to have a fight in the Senate about jurisdiction. You cities just wait. You cannot die now, because we have to have a little more time to find out which committee is going to handle this.' . . ."

And finally the allotted time of both sides expires. The roll call reveals that the amendment's prospects were tested exactly by the earlier test vote. Countercyclical assistance is voted to become part of the Senate public works bill, 58–36.

On the day I waited to meet Senator Muskie for lunch to arrange our understanding about this book, my waiting room was the hearing chamber for this bill. Its subject was incomprehensible; it was still in the early stage of going through subcommittee; of the members of the subcommittee only Muskie was interested enough to show up.

That was little more than two months ago. In the same period of time, hundreds of bills have languished on the shelves of dozens of subcommittees, unbudging. What transported this one so far and so fast, to the big time of the Senate floor, and to victory over inflamed opposition? I must look for Al From and sit him down to lay out for me the innards of this achievement.

The Senate is to stay late again tonight. After the public works vote I descend from the third-floor gallery to the first floor where the restaurants are, three in a cluster with a common menu and kitchen. The Senators' dining room is the most decorous, with ornate chandeliers and deep carpet. It is open only to Senators, the administrative assistant of each, and their guests. That rule is not enforced fanatically. Occasionally a staff member of lower rank calls to say he or she is coming over with "friends of the Senator." For select visiting firemen, lunch with their Senator amid this sea of faces of other Senators (and other visiting firemen, all of whom are assumed to be important) is indeed a story to take home. The second nicest is the "family dining room," really for staff members and their friends and guests and the lobbyists they're willing to have to lunch; this room, too, is carpeted, its chatter and clatter cushioned by tablecloths, although it's a little less heavy on the chandeliers. Between those two, and opening on the main Capitol corridor, is the public dining room, with a smaller off-room reserved for the press. Table tops are exposed plastic and floors are of linoleum tile. The dominant ornament is a huge cashier's counter laden with candy bars and smokes.

The restaurants stay open as long as the Senate is in session. In the evening the Capitol is virtually empty of tourists and I have the public restaurant almost all to myself, where I order the corned beef platter, which is excellent. In mid-meal, Senator McGovern drops by the counter for a cigar. He gives me a warm nod. No, he doesn't know me from Adam but assumes that I know him. Sam Donaldson, Cassie Mackin, and a couple of others from the TV gallery are in the off-room. They, too, assume they are known but don't nod at anybody.

The Senate is nervous about tonight because it's to take up a pay increase for its own members and members of the House. The increase would also cover more than 16,000 other high-level officials, including the Vice-President, members of the Cabinet, federal judges, and top-level federal appointees. Like a tiger riding the back of a kitten, the pay rise proposal is an amendment to a minor bill dealing with postal matters that the House has already passed. If it passes tonight with the amendment, the bill will have to go back to the House.

Members of Congress, judges, and federal executives haven't had a pay rise since 1969, a period during which the cost of living has risen 47.5 per cent. Congress is understandably timid about raising its own pay, particularly those members whose tenure must be renewed at the next election, a group that includes all 435 members of the House and a third of the Senate. With impunity, Congress could vote the increase for the executives and judges. Voting the increase for itself is what sticks in the public craw. So the only hope Congressmen have of some semblance of a race against their cost of living is to hold all the others hostage.

A member of Congress, whether Senator or Representative, presently earns $42,500 a year,[1] plus sizable allotments for office and travel costs. Senators from states with a population of less than two million, such as Maine, are allowed $392,298 for staff salaries. They are permitted to apportion that fund among their helpers any way they like up to a top salary of $36,000.[2] That top salary is generally reserved for the administrative assistant. (On committees, where salaries are paid by the committee budget, not a Senator's private budget, the same top salary is usually reserved for a staff director and/or committee counsel.) The staff salary allowance ranges upward, according to the size of state, to a maximum for states with more than seventeen million population (New York and California) of $751,980.

In addition to salaries for his staff, a Senator is given a "consolidated allowance" for telephones, telegrams, postage, stationery, subscriptions, transportation between his state and the District of Columbia, and so forth. A Senator from a small state, like Maine, is allowed approximately $39,000 a year. Until recently this allowance was not "consolidated," but it specified so much for phones, so much for stationery, so much for travel, etc. If a Senator scrimped on paper but, out of devotion to his constituents, flew home more often than provided for, the U. S. Treasury kept the saving on his paper

[1] Raised soon after this entry to $57,500 a year.
[2] Raised to a ceiling of $49,941 for administrative assistants to Senators; $52,000 for committee staff directors.

and the Congressman paid the extra travel cost from his own pocket. The "consolidated allowance," for which some members fought long and hard, was considered a major reform.

The cost of maintaining a single Senator does not end with that half million to a million dollars a year in salaries, supplies, and services. If the real estate value and maintenance costs of the Capitol and two colossal office buildings, plus their furniture and carpeting, and IBM Selectric typewriters, and signature machines, and computerized legislative reference terminals, and their underground garage, and their page boys and page girls and college-educated operators of push-button elevators, and dozens of doorkeepers to open every door for any Senator as well as to protect these elected officials from their electors, and all the committees and their staffs and their consultants and their travel costs—if all this were divided by 100, and to that dividend were added the cost of maintaining, supplying, and servicing up to eight offices in the Senator's home state, the resultant cost of maintaining a Senator might encourage some citizens not to vote in the hope that they might thereby avoid the expense of keeping one.

But for all that, the Senator himself may well be in serious financial distress. On a salary equal to that of a moderately successful salesman a Senator is expected to maintain a self-respecting home in Washington and another in his home state, dress like a chairman of the board, and entertain a constant flow of visitors who are accustomed to the high-style living of expense accounts (one perk that taxpayers, generous in many other ways, have not bestowed on their Senators). When a Senator flies (at government expense) to see his constituents, his constituents like to meet the Senate wife, too, but the government does not pay for that. Like other people between the ages of forty and sixty, Senators often have college tuitions to pay, sometimes two at a time.

A few days ago, on Senate payday, I was sitting at a desk near Leslie Finn's when she had just made out a deposit slip for Senator Muskie's salary check and was paying his personal bills. In a few minutes she said, with that sad sigh of frustration that any average householder knows, "I can't believe it. It's all gone, and I still have all these." I have not asked Muskie about how he keeps up with his household bills and don't plan to. But I do know that occasionally neighborhood repair men and other creditors phone the office of the chairman of the Senate Budget Committee to press for payment of overdue bills. Leslie, Dolores, and Gayle have their ways of handling these.

Muskie's problem—and that of many others in the Congress—is that his financial background is close to the ideal of what the public wants in a Senator. Financially, if not in other ways, he has resembled the average man. Back in 1946 his law office over a Waterville, Maine, dress shop (whose bookkeeper and sometime model he was soon to marry) was just beginning to turn a few fees into a living when a local Democratic leader invited Muskie to run for the state legislature. His election two years later as Minority Leader meant an almost total neglect of his law practice. In 1954 young Muskie had the idea that a vigorous and serious Democratic campaign for the governorship of Maine would be a real party builder, possibly increasing the legislative representation. Everyone agreed, but no well-known Democrat was about to have the bell tied around his neck. So bearing the penalty that comes to all those who dare make suggestions in committees, Muskie was stuck with running. And he ran. He ran like no Democrat in the memory of anyone in Maine ever ran. He slept in the spare room of some foolishly optimistic Democrat in every corner of every county in the state and all but wore out a good automobile finding Democrats of foolish enough optimism. When the votes were in, by a hairline, and to the astonishment of everyone, including himself, he was elected governor. And four years after that—in 1958—to the Senate.

The point of that mini-history is that Ed Muskie has never had a chance to make his pile, because the lure and thrill of elective office, and the privilege of composing public policy, got to him first.

There are others like that, some under such financial stress that they would go to extreme lengths not to let the news out lest the embarrassment tarnish their public images. It is known (but not widely) that several Congressmen use their private offices as their Washington sleeping rooms. For one reason or another, perhaps not wanting to tear children from their accustomed schools, they have not moved their families to Washington and can't afford a home away from home. One such Congressman plays a bit of paddleball in the House gym at seven in the morning so it won't appear odd that he showers there every day. Every day he sees four or five colleagues on the courts and wonders whether they're involved in the same dodge and the same cover, but wouldn't dare ask. He's a freshman, a bit shocked at the price to himself and his family of the glamor of being elected to Washington, and sometimes wonders if he ought to run for re-election. "But then, if I didn't," he says, "what about all those Bicentennial speeches I give about the need for people to participate in their government?"

Having lots of money not only eases life in Washington but it eases getting there. A candidate with a built-in campaign fund has an obvious advantage over one who spends two thirds of his campaigning time with hat in hand to finance the remaining third. So it is no surprise that more than half of the 100 members of the Senate can be classed as decidedly unpoor, and that 22 are millionaires. (Has it been ever thus? Apparently yes. The *World Almanac* of 1902 found 18 millionaires among 90 men who then composed the Senate, an almost identical proportion. And in 1902, before adoption of the seventeenth Amendment requiring the popular election of Senators, rich men commonly bought their appointments to Senate seats either by direct bribery of governors and key state legislators, or by the more refined means of lavish contributions to party campaigns.)

The assumption that a Senate of rich men is a Senate that turns its back on the lower classes—that money means conservatism—does not get impressive support in the current roster of the Senate rich. The wealthiest Senator, also one of the most liberal, is assumed to be Edward M. Kennedy, inheritor of a pot of ten million dollars. Another major inheritor is Claiborne Pell, Democrat, liberal, and member of the not-to-worry clan of Rhode Island Pells. Philip Hart of Michigan is not a big inheritor but married one, the former Jane Briggs of a lustrous family name in the Chrysler saga. Charles Percy, the Illinois Republican, considered a liberal (especially by illiberal Republicans), is a bootstrap millionaire, having first discovered the limitless promise of capitalist America through selling magazine subscriptions as a University of Chicago student, then doing far better getting other students to sell subscriptions for him, eventually becoming boy-wonder president of Bell & Howell. Abe Ribicoff, the Connecticut Democrat, not a great believer in financial disclosure, recently reported a one-year income of $175,000. His holdings, he says, are in a blind trust, and he doesn't know how much he is worth, although this far he'll go: "I am a man of substance, but I do not consider myself to be a millionaire." Minority Leader Hugh Scott of Pennsylvania, who both liberals and conservatives claim is often a captive of the other side, has put out a financial statement that doesn't show much that is readily spendable, listing real estate and securities but not their value. But his home in Washington is considered "expensive" and his collection of Oriental art is generally described as "priceless." Joseph Montoya of New Mexico, who deserves to be called a liberal on public works and revenue sharing —but a conservative on countercyclical assistance to cities—has extensive holdings in real estate and shopping centers, although he neither confirms nor denies that he is a millionaire. And Stuart Symington of Missouri did well in the manufacture of radios and other electronics, selling off or giving away more than a million dollars in corporate assets to avoid conflict of interest upon joining the Truman Administration thirty years ago.

Republicans and conservative Democrats, however, do outnumber liberals as millionaires. Hiram Fong, the Hawaii Republican, one of eleven children of a penniless Chinese immigrant laborer, worked his way through the University of Hawaii, went to Harvard Law School, then amassed a fortune in real estate, construction, insurance, and bananas. Lloyd Bentsen, Texas Democrat, coasted on his family's cattle and oil fortune to become a judge at twenty-five, a Congressman at twenty-seven (urging nuclear bombing of North Korea), then quit politics at thirty-three to start from a sort of scratch to become a millionaire in his own right before re-entering politics. Russell Long, the Louisiana Democrat, and Dewey Bartlett, Oklahoma Republican, have done right well in oil; Herman Talmadge, Georgia Democrat, in family land and converting a fine strain of local pig into Talmadge-brand hams; Bill Brock, Tennessee Republican, born into a successful candy-making family; Harry F. Byrd, Virginia independent, inheriting a newspaper and vast apple orchards from his famous Senator father; James Eastland, Mississippi Democrat, not only through farming but through sizable government checks for not farming; Robert A. Taft, Jr., Ohio Republican, another son of a famous Senator father, a family communications business; Howard Baker, Tennessee Republican, son-in-law of a famous Senator, Everett Dirksen, banking and real estate. Both Arizona Republicans,

Barry Goldwater and Paul Fannin, are scions of successful Arizona retailers, the Goldwaters in department stores, the Fannins in lumber, hardware, and bottled propane gas. Of the two, Fannin is far richer, believed to be worth more than five million. Clifford Hansen, Wyoming Republican, inherited a ranch and developed it into a popular ski resort. Paul Laxalt, Republican and former governor of Nevada, owns twenty-six per cent of the Ormsby House, a hotel and casino in Carson City.

A few Senators have indicated embarrassment at putting out a financial statement because of how little they say they own. Besides Muskie, among those believed to possess little more than their homes are Jake Garn, Utah Republican, former mayor of Salt Lake City; James Allen, Democrat of Alabama; and Dick Clark, Iowa Democrat.

One way an unrich Senator can pay his way through a comfortable standard of living—or, at least, through all those extra airline tickets and club membership fees—is by becoming a Senate star, wanted for banquets, conventions, school convocations, and religious fellowship groups as a platform attraction. In 1974, seventy Senators reported extra income moonlighting as lecturers. Senator Muskie, as a former national candidate, did very well, earning $28,800. But at least five others earned more. Senator Daniel K. Inouye of Hawaii who, during the televised Watergate hearings, collected many fans as the tough, suave Oriental wounded veteran, took in $29,550. Herman Talmadge of Georgia, another Watergate quizzer, made $32,165. Henry M. Jackson, Washington Democrat, collected $34,350, but reported that he turned every dollar over to charity. Hubert Humphrey, who didn't need Watergate to become a platform star, $40,750. Earning more than Humphrey, surprisingly, was Oregon Republican Mark O. Hatfield (not hurt, no doubt, as co-author of the McGovern-Hatfield amendment to dry up the Vietnam War by cutting off the money supply), who gathered $45,677 mainly from university and religious audiences. The Senate's top earner, at $49,650, was Howard Baker, who played Bing Crosby to Sam Ervin's Bob Hope on the Watergate television series. Baker set a standard speech fee of $1,750 and had no trouble getting it.

Other substantial earners were Edward W. Brooke, Republican of Massachusetts, $28,700; Harrison A. Williams, Jr., New Jersey

Democrat, $28,617; John V. Tunney, California Democrat, $25,450; Barry Goldwater, $25,190; and Bob Dole, Kansas Republican, $20,850.

While speechmaking for students and churchgoers is a nice, wholesome way to pick up those extra dollars without compromising senatorial independence, not all speechmaking is untainted. Why, for example, would Talmadge (whose name Watergate failed to make a household word) have done so well? Talmadge, chairman of the Agriculture and Forestry Committee, accepted $2,500 for a short appearance before the Fertilizer Institute, $2,500 from the National Forest Products Association, and $2,500 from the Quality Bakers of America. He also is second-ranking Democrat on the Finance Committee, which controls tax bills, and received $2,000 for a speech before the Ad Hoc Committee for an Effective Investment Tax Credit, and another $2,000 from the American Council on Capital Gains and Estate Taxation.

Vance Hartke, the Indiana Democrat with as flawless a liberal voting record as any Senator (and whose devotion to AFL-CIO wishes is so total that it has contributed to a Senate wisecrack, "Indiana has two Democratic Senators: one is Bayh, the other is Bought"), is chairman of the Commerce Subcommittee on Surface Transportation, which will soon consider deregulation of the trucking industry. This did not stand in the way of Hartke accepting $1,500 to address the Common Carrier Conference of the American Trucking Associations, and $1,000 from Atlas Van Lines, both of which bitterly oppose the deregulation of trucking fees that are now determined by government rather than by competition, and are set at high, sure-profit levels.

John Sparkman, Democrat of Alabama, the aged and amiable Foreign Relations chairman, has a side line as chairman of a housing subcommittee, and saw no problem in accepting $1,500 to speak before the National Association of Home Builders. Edward Brooke, ranking Republican on Banking's Subcommittee on Securities, took $2,000 and an expense-paid trip to Bermuda to speak to an investors' group. The same subcommittee's chairman, Harrison Williams, did slightly better, a fee of $2,500 for a talk to the Securities Industry Association, made up of stockbrokers directly governed by bills coming before the subcommittee. The American Bankers Association took still better care of Brooke, paying him $4,500 for two speeches, and only $2,000 to Williams for one speech. Two other Banking Committee members, Alan Cranston, California Democrat, and Bob Packwood, Oregon Republican, spoke to the ABA for $1,000 apiece.

While Senators were enjoying those goodies, some less discriminately than others, the Watergate pressure of 1974 was upon them, and the Congress has put a new leash on itself that some members, who carefully select their audiences for non-conflict and who are dependent on those earnings, now fear may be unfairly tight. Effective in 1979, members are restricted to a limit of $1,000 per speech and a maximum speech income of 15 per cent of the members' salary.

That leash chokes only the most popular Senators. But an estimated fifty per cent of all members of Congress are threatened by another form of attempted self-strangulation. About half the members keep an informal account they usually call a "constituent service fund," but which their opponents call a "political slush fund." When Richard Nixon, as vice-presidential candidate, appeared on television in 1952 with his dog Checkers and his wife's cloth coat, it was to explain away charges that he had accepted money from well-heeled individuals and "interests," not for campaigning but to support his government allowance so that he might "better serve" his constituents. Nixon pleaded the legitimacy of such a fund and asserted with altar-boy sincerity that not a penny of it ever went to his personal use. His opponents immensely enjoyed the embarrassment to the Eisenhower ticket, but Democratic Congressmen privately were almost as nervous and uncomfortable as Nixon. Because the Nixon "slush fund" and the non-personal use of it was a common Capitol Hill device—and still is.

Such funds are indeed what keep less than rich members of the House and Senate afloat while they do reach for the checks of eight or twelve dinner guests; do fly the Missus home for weekend political socials; do have an office cabinet well stocked with refreshment just in case a delegation of influentials happens to visit during the happy hour; do send a generous bouquet to a bereaved constituent; do maintain a Christmas card list numbering in the thousands; do thank supporters and home-state dignitaries for special favors by sending a flag that supposedly flew from the Capitol flagpole (actually it did;

there's a stunted flagpole in the back room of the stationery store, and these flags are "raised" and "lowered" in mass production before they're boxed and sold to congressional offices only, at $3.50 per); and, indeed, do often exceed their "consolidated allowance," and the excess costs of phone calls, newsletters, and travel have to come from somewhere.

Members dug themselves into a hole over slush funds not directly but by creating the Federal Election Commission to finance presidential campaigns and govern the financing of congressional campaigns. "Congressmen have suddenly woken up to the power that they gave the commission," a commission staff aide has intimated, "and now they're afraid that it can be used against them."

The power was boldly used against them just a year ago in the commission's first major opinion. With its six members ruling unanimously, the commission decided that the government's consolidated allowances to members "are for presumptively nonpolitical, legislative activities and, therefore, not subject to the limitations and prohibitions of the act. Accordingly"—and here comes the slammer— "additional monies not appropriated by Congress but raised independently by the members themselves or their supporters should be viewed as political and not legislative funds."

Based on that piercing logic, the commission ruled that Senators and Representatives must make a quarterly report, available to public inspection, of all their office accounts, which is not the worst of it. The worst is that contributions and expenditures passing through the slush fund are to be counted as contributions to and expenditures from the member's next campaign fund. And since congressional campaign funds, according to the same law, are now limited in size —for a Senator, according to the population of his state—the campaign fund limit would be reduced accordingly. Well now, that's fine if the Senator happens to come from, say, New York where he's permitted to spend about three million dollars to renew his seat. So he's spent $150,000 in six years through his slush fund being Mr. Nice Guy. You can hardly see the nick. But how about if you come from Nevada or Maine, where the legal campaign limit is more like $250,000? And suppose the Senator has "slushed" a modest $10,000 a year—totaling $60,000. He is now held to a $190,000 campaign, while his opponent can go all out with a quarter million. That difference can hurt.[3]

So there is some reason to believe that one of these days Congress may take a hard, icy look at the nine million-dollar annual budget it lavished upon the audacious commission that is now biting the hand that feeds it. Then we'll see who's in command around here.

A major reason that congressional tongues are hanging out for this pay-rise amendment is not only the cash in hand, but that this amendment may wipe out the need for Congress to go through future votes to raise its own pay. The pay-rise amendment is, of all things, an entitlement bill, the very kind the Budget Committee says it wants to do away with, although neither the Budget Committee nor its chairman is out to knife this one. The amendment provides that the officials covered by it would hereafter receive *automatic* cost-of-living increases in October, in the same percentage as the President recommends, under a previous law, for lower-level civil servants. By the guidelines of that law, this year's increase would range between 5 per cent and 8.6 per cent, with Ford expected to hold his recommendation to 5 per cent. The trouble with entitlement bills (also known as "backdoor appropriations") is that Congress surrenders control over the expenditures these bills provide, and there's nothing to stop the costs from running sky high if the "entitlement" so warrants. In this case, a "backdoor appropriation" is what Congress wants, not because of unbridled greed, but to escape, once and for all, the dread of voting on its own pay. No matter how justified a pay rise, the jeers of constituents make poverty almost preferable.

In tonight's debate the Senate's favorite Senator, Jim Allen, belly-kicks his colleagues again: "I do not believe we would be acting in the best interests of the image of Congress at this time of recession and inflation to try to rush in and set up a built-in annual salary increase for members of the Congress."

Allen's absence of known independent income does not strengthen the affection felt toward him for his statement. His motion to kill all

---

[3] In the spring of 1976 the Supreme Court, responding to a suit by Senator Buckley, former Senator Eugene McCarthy and others, removed all limitations on the size of campaign expenditures, on grounds of the First Amendment.

raises is beaten, 57–30. He follows up with a "compromise" motion, to let all the raises go through—except those for Congress. This is stomped out even harder, 61–25. Bob Taft of Ohio, who doesn't need the money, moves to let Congress have its cost-of-living raise this fall, but not the automatic follow-up in future years. It goes down, 74–12.

Finally, to sighs of deep relief, the Senate gets rid of the albatross, voting 58–29 for the pay rise and for a permanent ticket on the cost-of-living escalator.

Wednesday, July 30

Last night's tension over the Senate's pay-rise vote was a frolic compared to the jitters that hit the House today for the confirming vote. The House is always up for re-election, always feeling nervously accountable, always defensive, and slightly more so than usual this year.

The extreme jumpiness is made more obvious and dramatic by the new way the House votes. Members press buttons at their seats, recording their votes on an electronic "tote" board. But until the presiding officer gavels the vote to a close, votes can be changed (and often are, if a member favoring a bill thinks it will please his district to vote against it, and when the tote board clearly shows the bill will pass without him). The board for today's vote is to be "open" for fifteen minutes. The votes are hopping from "yes" to "no," "no" to "yes," like popcorn. At exactly fifteen minutes, the totals stand at a heart-stopping 214 for "no," 213 for "yes." Speaker Carl Albert (whose $62,500 salary equals the Vice-President's) just sits there impassive, determined to be blind to what he sees. He lets the corn jumble and pop until the board reverses itself to 214 for "yes," 213 for "no," waits an extra few seconds to make sure that whoever changed his mind last indeed means it—then hammers his gavel down thunderously. (Later, Albert says he hoped it would settle into a tie so he could cast the deciding vote in favor of the pay rise.)

From Muskie's office I go diagonally across the street to the former Carroll Arms, to the floor housing the Intergovernmental Relations Subcommittee, and the corner room, complete with bath, of Al From. Al buzzes for his secretary, Hanne Evans—a silky blonde, slender and always unexpectedly breath-taking, whose arrival awkwardly slows the conversation of men who don't know her, and after she leaves, as though to confirm that the crisis is every bit as grave as the stranger senses, someone always leans in to explain in a whisper, "She used to date John Tunney"—and Al instructs that he doesn't want any calls. For him, this is like pulling the plug on his own life support. Before Hanne closes the door he calls after her to say, "Except So and So." She nods. "And except So and So." This time she waits. "And if So and So calls, I guess I'd better take it."

As though suppressed by his introverted eyes, his voice is so quiet, so unprojecting, so private, that to catch his generous outpouring of detail I have to attach a tiny microphone high on his necktie. Al loves to tell all; his voice likes to keep secrets.

A CONVERSATION WITH ALVIN FROM

—I'm not a scholar of political science, but I tell you the process we operate with around here is so different from any college course, it's like night and day. The thing that matters around here is having a majority of the votes. There's no better example than the countercyclical bill.

How did you get here?

—I came in 1966 when I was still a graduate student in journalism at Northwestern. The journalism school started a program that had fifteen of us spend a quarter covering Washington for a bunch of small papers. Down here I ran into Ed May, whom I'd met when he spoke at Northwestern. Ed was with the Office of Economic Opportunity. I mentioned I was going back to take a job with the Chicago *Daily News,* and he said, "You don't want to do that. I've been in

the journalism business and you'll have more fun if you come here."
I wrote several Senators, one of them Joe Tydings of Maryland, and
got a job on the Senate D.C. Committee.

—Tydings got beat by Beall, then John McEvoy, our staff director, moved over to become Muskie's A.A. and brought me onto this
subcommittee in April of '71. I guess I've been staff director since
November of '71.

How did the countercyclical assistance idea get started?

—It was developed by Bob Reischauer, son of the former ambas-
sador to Japan. He was at Brookings and talked about it during our
presidential campaign in '71, but we didn't really pay attention to it.
After last September's President's Conference on Inflation, my basic
feeling was that the President was focusing on the wrong issue and a
recession was really going to hit. I asked the Library of Congress—
the Legislative Reference Service—to trace employment patterns in
state and local governments, and what we finally showed in our report, but with little help from the Library, was that state and local
government was the fastest-growing sector of the economy. A slow-
down in the growth of that sector would have grave economic implications. Then last January Arnold Packer, the Budget Committee's
chief economist, did a memo on the economy. One of his suggestions
for stimulating it was some sort of payment to state and local governments. Then I heard Charlie Schultze talk about it at the National
Conference of Mayors. Reischauer worked for him. Schultze has
been called the father of this by Muskie, but he's really kind of a
stepfather because Reischauer developed it.

—There are a couple of remarkable things about this bill, but the
most remarkable is that we took a new idea—something that only a
handful of the most sophisticated economists had seriously discussed
—and pushed it through the Senate in four or five months. We introduced our bill April 7. It passed the Senate the hardest way it could,
as an amendment that was opposed by the manager of the bill and
opposed by the chairman of the Finance Committee.

—At the time Packer handed in that memo, I said to Muskie, "I
think there's a growing issue of how the recession is going to impact
on state and local governments. I think I can get mayors to come in
and do a big show." So we did it. Fourteen or so mayors came,
through the Conference of Mayors. We had one panel of all the big
stars, like Ken Gibson of Newark, The Moon [Moon Landrieu] of

New Orleans. We arranged a bunch of tables into a kind of horse-shoe in the Government Ops hearing room. The TV cameras were there. When you do the mayors, even if you don't get national television there's great regional television, because the networks feed to their affiliates every day. It's their four o'clock feedout after they decide what's going to go on the national evening news, and all the stuff that's left over they send out to be taped locally. Mayors are one group that can focus on an issue better than anyone else, mainly because they're hurting and they make a lot more noise.

When you "do the mayors" and get them on TV, who is your target audience? Do you want the whole country? The voters in each mayor's own city?

—A primary audience, believe it or not, is other Senators, right on our own committee, even our subcommittee. It's a way of getting them to the hearing and getting them interested. This is very key. A good show, the chance of getting on television, attracts Senators who might not otherwise hear these mayors talk in a million years. If you schedule a United States Senator for two hearings at the same time, and one has cameras, that's the one he's going to go to. Besides, Senators find mayors basically interesting. They're both politicians and live in the same world. A most critically important thing for this bill was getting Senators to listen. And we had one other target audience, certain key reporters, like David Broder, whom Senators read. It's important to get your stuff explained in the *National Journal* which nobody knows about outside of Washington. It's like the trade journal of government, both legislative and executive. Reporters read it. Congressional staffs read it. An idea floats because press people and Hill people read about it in the *National Journal,* in Broder's column in the *Post.* Then other people start writing about it. Discussion starts.

—I said it's important to get other Senators there. Yesterday you saw that Bill Brock was a key ally. Brock's a bright guy, a perceptive guy. I've dealt with Brock on a couple of bills, and we went down the line with him, and he with us, in writing a budget bill that would work. I really have the highest regard for Brock. One of the things he did on the floor yesterday was to quote Mayor Gibson. At our hearing Gibson asked, "How can I tell my people who've been working for the city for years and years that I'm laying them off, then hire somebody else with no experience and no skill to do that same job because I've got special federal money that I can only use to hire the unemployed? How can I tell my people that? And this bill protects us from having to drop our regular people and making *them* unemployed." That quote is pretty close and it was that statement at that hearing that got Brock interested.

—A month later, in February, after we got all these people talking about our "bill," we decided we had to write an actual bill. So, with help from Reischauer mostly, and with a guy on Humphrey's staff over at the Joint Economic Committee, I got the Legislative Counsel to do a draft. That's an office of lawyers, legislative technicians, who work for the whole Senate. Any staff person can go to them and get a bill written.

—The Joint Economic Committee was finishing a study on the effect of recession on state and local governments. I put a college intern and one or two other people on the phone to help them finish their survey so they could present their findings at some hearings we were going to have May 6, 7, and 8.

—About this time I also was having discussions with Jim Lynn. He used to be Secretary of Housing and Urban Development, and now the director of OMB, the Office of Management and Budget. He kept saying, "If it came down here now, we'd veto it, but it's an idea worth discussing because of those attractive new features, the turn-off triggers and so on. It costs too much, but I tend to like the idea."

—In late April the American Federation of State, County and Municipal Employees brought in a bunch of its people from around the country. That helped create interest. Then on Thursday, May 8, the mayors testified again. After the hearing the Democratic mayors met with the leadership of both houses, with Carl Albert, Mike Mansfield, Bobby Byrd, Tip O'Neill, and some committee chairmen. By this time the bill had become the number one priority of the mayors, and all those guys, Henry Maier of Milwaukee and Joe Alioto of San Francisco and the rest, were in here to pressure the leadership. They knew the House was more favorable to public works. But they wanted to get the ball rolling on countercyclical, and they went to the leadership and did it. Speaker Albert promised the mayors he'd get Jack Brooks [chairman of the House Government Operations Committee] to hold a hearing on the bill. Bob Byrd promised his help in getting the bill to the floor. So the bill was starting to look alive, but we were pumping life into it basically out of this office.

By this time, did you know that you had the subcommittee behind you?

—I can't remember when, but it was shortly after that meeting that I decided we had five votes. And that's what I wanted. The members of the IGR Subcommittee on the Democratic side are Muskie, McClellan, Metcalf, Chiles, and Glenn. On the Republican side, Roth, Brock, and Percy. Five and three. All the time you work the members of your subcommittee. I'd talked to the minority counsel and found out that Percy was basically interested in the idea. Metcalf tends to follow our lead on all this stuff. McClellan never does anything on this subcommittee. I assumed Chiles would be opposed. He's very independent. He sometimes looks to be mean, but he's not. As things turned out later, Chiles fought this bill hard in subcommittee, very hard, but in full committee, once he lost his battle, he spoke against it for the record but not at any great length. Then he had a chance to kill the bill by walking out of the room and breaking the quorum. Instead, he told me, "I'm going to stay here to vote against your bill, but I'm not going to delay it by either walking out or trying to write a minority view for the report." That's a kind of senatorial courtesy that some observe and some don't. It says, I've had my fight and I've lost, so I'm not going to screw you up, because there's going to be a next issue where I'm going to beat you and I don't want you screwing me up on my bill. To be effective around here, you can't hold grudges against people because they differ with you. For example, this bill was to come up at the same markup as another one on intergovernmental personnel. Brock and Muskie were to lead the charge on countercyclical but fight at opposite ends on the personnel bill.

—So I counted the five votes we needed: Muskie, Glenn, Brock, Percy, and Metcalf. At that point I went to Muskie and asked if I could schedule a markup, which we did for Tuesday, June 10.

—The Thursday before the markup I got a computer print-out of just how the bill's formula would work in dollars and cents. It showed we were giving too much money to cities—restoring too high a percentage of their locally raised revenues. At the unemployment rate we were talking about, it came to four billion dollars and that was just too much money. I didn't want to be caught in a position of giving cities a quarter of their local taxes back. So I spent the whole weekend in here with a calculator and the print-out, and I was on the phone a lot with Reischauer. I'm not a mathematician but I can handle a formula pretty well.

—On Monday night I was really out of it because I'd stayed so late Saturday and Sunday nights. Muskie had just come back from Maine and he was dead tired. It was like talking to a wall. I said, "Senator, screw it. I'm going to give you the briefing book. If you get a chance, look at it tonight, but it's probably better for you to get a good night's sleep. I'll come in in the morning and tell you what our problem is and how we recommend solving it." Mind you, next morning was the markup.

Did Muskie know a great deal about the fine details of the bill?

—This bill was drafted by staff, by and large. It had to be. It's too technical and too intricate to be drafted by a Senator, because he just doesn't have the time. I'm talking about sixteen-hour days peering over a print-out to make sure the thing works right, figuring out percentages, figuring each allocation versus normal taxes, how it works as unemployment goes up and down, how it would work with different formulae.

—We decided Monday night—that is, the staff decided—that we had only one choice, and that was to cut the formula by half before bringing it into the markup—that Muskie would offer an amendment cutting his own bill in half. So I got up Tuesday morning at some ungodly hour, got in here about seven o'clock, and dictated a memo that I took over to him. I outlined the problem and said that both in terms of being within the budget resolution and in terms of having the strongest possible bill with the right amount of money we had to cut it in half and here's the amendment. Then I had to make some quick phone calls to people backing us, like the Conference of Mayors, and the National Association of County Officials, and the American Federation of State, County and Municipal Employees, to make sure they wouldn't go bananas. We didn't want to lose their support, but what I was more afraid of was going into committee and finding ourselves absolutely vulnerable.

—At the markup everybody was happy to make it for less money. As I expected, we had opposition from Chiles and Roth, and McClellan didn't show. Glenn had a couple of cosmetic amendments. It went through, 5 to 2.

—Right after that is when Dick Wegman, the Government Ops staff chief, and Barry Meyer, the Public Works staff chief, and I talked and came to the informal agreement that we'd look into the possibility of the bill becoming a rider to the public works bill. We all knew there was going to be a problem getting it through Government Ops in the House because it's chaired by Jack Brooks of Texas, and Texas doesn't have much unemployment and doesn't get any money under our bill. No matter how we tried to design the bill, we couldn't make Texas need money. The other problem is that L. H. Fountain of North Carolina is the chairman of the subcommittee, and he's a slow-moving guy. Not a bad guy, but we thought we'd never get a bill like this out of his subcommittee.

Why that strategy was good for your bill is clear. But why was Public Works, particularly Barry Meyer and Senator Randolph, interested in your bill and your victory?

—A couple of reasons. In the testimony before their committee on the public works bill, the mayors and the AFSCME told them they wanted our bill. We had the same strong constituencies, so they knew the support for public works would be stronger if the bills were combined. The other reason is that Montoya was the only guy who bought the argument that our bill would be a burden on theirs. More of them may have believed it at one point, but yesterday on the floor eleven of the fourteen members of Public Works voted for us. The other thing Barry saw was that public works alone was certain to be vetoed. It didn't matter how big or how small it was, any public works bill going to Ford was going to be sandbagged. But on countercyclical, I was getting Jim Lynn at the White House interested. So there was some prospect of avoiding the veto, or at least broadening support for an override of a veto, by combining the two bills.

And yet your bill did not become a part of the bill that the Public Works Committee reported out. You had to offer it on the floor. What happened?

—I decided that things didn't look too good at Public Works at that time. Public Works is made up mostly of people from rural states that weren't particularly impacted by the recession, and I thought it would be a fairly unfriendly forum. And with Montoya's opposition, it was hard to get a firm head count. People didn't want to go against him unless they really knew why, and they were new to this bill. It's not an easy bill to educate people about. The Public

Works Committee works differently than we do. We have staff meetings on bills. We put a finished bill in front of those guys and they know what they're doing. In Public Works, they sometimes write their bills in a long series of markups. They'd had no chance to study this bill, neither in subcommittee nor now in full committee. We hadn't had a chance to lobby them intensely because all this happened—the decision to go to Public Works—in only a week and a half. I figured Randolph would be with us. Muskie, of course. Gravel, probably Gary Hart, probably Bentsen. I wasn't sure of Burdick, Culver, Morgan—but I thought we'd get one of the three. I didn't know anything about the Republicans, but I was not counting on any help except maybe from Stafford, who tends to follow Muskie on a lot of economic stuff, and his staff guy said he liked the idea basically. I talked to staff guys, but clearly we hadn't done enough work on them. My gut count was that we'd either win 8 to 6 or we'd tie 7 to 7 in Public Works. Even if we won, that's a weak position for going to the floor.

—I talked to Muskie about seven o'clock Monday night before the Tuesday morning public works markup and said, "Senator, I don't think we ought to go tomorrow. We're just not set for it." He said, "All right." And that was the end of it. On Wednesday we were scheduled for the Government Ops markup, where I felt sure we'd come out 9–2, and I knew the Government Ops chairman and members would support us on the floor when countercyclical was offered as an amendment to public works.

How did you prepare for the floor?

—We had a meeting last Thursday, the twenty-fourth, with the Conference of Mayors, the League of Cities, the county people, and the AFSCME—maybe twelve people, all in this room. And it was really hot in here. This old Carroll Arms air conditioning doesn't work very well. We went down the list of Senators on tally sheets, the mayors taking some, the counties some, all the others some, and some we were going to hit two or three times. They reported back Friday night. And all day Friday Lee Enfield and Jane Fenderson of my staff were calling legislative assistants of Senators. I talked to Brock Friday morning and he told me he felt we'd get substantial Republican support. We left rounding up Republicans to him, and he did an unbelievable job, personally hooking people on the floor, in the halls, in committees. When those lobbyists came in Friday night, they'd won Morgan of North Carolina, Stone of Florida, Packwood of Oregon, and others.

When did you know you had it?

—You never know you have it. I had a feeling by Monday night that we were in pretty good shape. I told the AFSCME when we went to the floor yesterday that I thought we'd get fifty-eight votes and that's what we got. But I had some mistakes on my tally that balanced out.

—After a meeting Monday night, I went over to the floor to see Muskie. They were having some procedural fight and he was just sitting there. I went over the count with him, so he was apprised of where we were, and I told him that I thought it was important to get Randolph to speak for the amendment. Early Tuesday morning I did a note suggesting that he talk to Mansfield and Byrd about speaking for the bill. He called me about noon and said they wouldn't speak for it but continued to support it. They never speak for things like this. Their role is to make sure that Democrats know what the party line is, which they did very well. So Muskie was going to talk to Randolph, and he was thinking about talking to Cranston, the big peacemaker in the Senate, about talking to Montoya.

—About nine o'clock yesterday morning I called Dan Leach, who works for Mansfield and Byrd, and he said the public works bill was probably not going to come up. I started to dictate a memo to Muskie, confirming the tally and reviewing things I wanted him to do. Before I got through Leach called to say the bill would hit the floor at noon. More feedback came from the AFL-CIO and AFSCME. Votes were starting to really change, the count swelling to 45, 46 on our side, probably enough to win, and some of these new votes not guys I had on my list of likelies. But I was still nervous because you never know how good a commitment is. Sometimes staff will make a commitment without talking to the Senator, sometimes a Senator will make a commitment to a constituent without realizing what he is doing, then change his mind. At about ten-thirty I went to tell the Senator in a Budget Committee seminar that it was coming off, and gave him his floor statement, which he wanted cut down because it was too long. So we came back and did that. Meanwhile, I'm trying to juggle with Buckley and Glenn. Glenn had to leave at three o'clock. Buckley, who was now committed to support us, was not going to be back until three or three-thirty. And I wanted to make sure we got them both by juggling the time of the vote. AFSCME was doing an attendance check on other Senators.

—At about eleven I got a call from a leading staff guy, you'd better not print who, saying that Senator Hathaway was really going to fight us, and that surprised me. What Long and Hathaway did was underhanded, I thought, because yesterday they had charts up on the floor comparing their revenue-sharing formulas and ours. Obviously they had worked on it for some time. It wasn't an overnight thing. And they gave us no warning. The thing that bothered this fellow who called me is that there's a courtesy thing around here, if you're going to oppose somebody, particularly if you're from the same state as the guy you're going to fight, you let him know. We knew, for example, that Bentsen was going to offer an amendment yesterday. Bentsen's guy came over and talked to us about it. That doesn't mean that you don't try on occasion to surprise people. But if it's going to be a jurisdictional fight, generally there's some advance signal. So I told the Senator, who by this time was back in his office, I said, "I think you ought to talk to Hathaway." And he said, "Well, you don't know Senator Hathaway." As usual, he acted like he didn't want to do it, but later Muskie got hold of Hathaway and I heard that he really reamed his ass before we got to the floor, I mean he was really angry at him. It's unusual when a junior Senator opposes a senior Senator from his own state on one of the senior Senator's major bills. You remember that thing that we did for Hathaway to extend that drug office. We would never have done it, except as a personal favor.

—Okay, so we're on the floor and Muskie's making his opening statement, and I'd arranged for him to yield to Brock and then Humphrey was going to come on. Brock told me before we went on that he'd picked up Beall, Garn, and Domenici, and that any of them would speak for us if we wanted them. Domenici did. I'd seen Domenici on my way to the floor, and he said, "I'd really like to support you, but I'm just a little hesitant." Brock apparently nailed him between that time and the time the debate opened. I think Brock is as responsible as anybody for passing this thing, a terrific job.

—Then there was Long's motion to table the Muskie amendment. A tabling motion is very tricky because it reverses the way people vote. If you are for the bill, you have to vote "no" on the tabling motion, and a lot of Senators rush onto the floor and don't know what's

THE SENATE NOBODY KNOWS 259

happening. So I spent all of that roll call chasing down Senators who
voted wrong. Humphrey voted wrong. Percy did—we got him. I'm
not sure whether Beall did. I chased down three or four others.
When a bill comes up, usually the manager reads a list of staff people
and asks unanimous consent for them to have the privilege of the
floor, but you're not supposed to run around and raise hell like a
Senator. They have these little enforcers in the Senate who try to
make you sit down all the time, but whenever I heard a Senator vote
wrong I went after him, or I'd get Brock to get him, or Muskie if it
was a Democrat. I'd just go up and say, "Senator, are you aware that
that's a tabling motion and you voted to table?" Nobody took
offense.

*Why did both Nelson and Proxmire, both from Wisconsin, both
liberal Democrats, vote for Long's amendment to substitute the
revenue-sharing formula?*

—Nelson is on Finance, and there was a kind of a bond on the Finance Committee that they had to go with revenue sharing. But Nelson was persuaded by Humphrey and Muskie in the debate, and he
supported the Muskie amendment in the final vote. I think Proxmire
resents Muskie for his Budget Committee role. Proxmire likes to be
the fiscal watchdog of the Senate, and he doesn't like Muskie getting
up and making speeches on every appropriations bill. Besides, Proxmire probably just didn't like the countercyclical idea.

—I thought we were in trouble on the Long amendment. But some
guys who opposed our bill, like Bill Roth, helped us kill Long's
amendment. Roth is the ranking Republican on the IGR Subcommittee, and he's a decent guy. I said to him, "Senator, I think the Long
amendment is an underhanded way to kill our bill. If you want to
vote against the bill, that's fine. But if we're going to lose it, we'd like
to lose it straight out." And he said, "I'll help you." He voted against
the Long amendment, and then against our bill.

After the final vote, what was the first thing Muskie said?

—Well, first I said, "Senator, we did all right. I'm going to take off
now." And he kind of nodded and said, "Thanks."

I've been told that that's one thing he never says.

—He's not effusive, but he says it. Then Lee Enfield and I went
over to correct the Record, the text of the debate. Whenever your
Senator's in a debate, you do that. They have the transcripts in a little room behind the presiding officer within ten minutes after the

debate. The person who's taking the stenography goes back and types it up immediately after being relieved. Muskie's easy to edit, his sentences are so good. You ought to do it on other guys. Gibberish. But everyone has his bad passages. Muskie might say something like "public jobs" when he means "public works." Or the transcript might leave out a word. It might say, "This is revenue sharing," when he said, "This is not revenue sharing." Going over the Record doesn't take long.

Did you celebrate?

—Right after that I went out to the lobby, and the lobbyists I'd worked with had just come down from the gallery. So we all went over to the Monocle and the guy from the AFSMCE bought some champagne, and the whole gang from all the organizations went for dinner at La Bagatelle, and I wound up wandering home about twelve-thirty. My wife wasn't exactly happy about that, but I figured I don't pass a major bill but once or twice a two-year Congress.

From New Hampshire comes a startling piece of news that will unblock the Senate calendar more than all the decisions Bobby Byrd can make. John A. Durkin, the Democrat in the Durkin-Wyman stalemate, has decided that a Senate log jam that can't be broken after seven months of trying is not going to be broken. So yesterday he went home to New Hampshire, slept on it, and announced today that he is asking Senate leaders to declare the disputed seat vacant— which would permit a new election!

That, of course, is what Louis C. Wyman and Senate Republicans, without exception, have demanded all along, the Democrats insisting on the Senate's "constitutional responsibility" to decide such disputes.

The Washington *Post*'s Spencer Rich, the most digging reporter in the Senate press gallery, got Durkin on the phone and Durkin told him: "Last Thursday when the Senate was on the voting rights bill, I sat down with Alan Cranston at his desk at the back of the Senate and said, 'My analysis is that the constitutional trolley has run out of gas.'

"On Friday I talked with Cranston and [Rules Committee Chairman] Cannon. Cannon said the Republicans were offering various compromises. I said I thought I had a solution—let's send it back."

The New Hampshire election will probably be held on September 16, and on the seventeenth this Body of One Hundred will have one hundred bodies again.

Friday, August 1

The best time to have a relaxed, unhurried talk with Muskie is when his world seems most out of control but actually has moved beyond his control and there's nothing to do but wait. At such times he likes to retreat to the serene splendor of S-199 and sink into one of those big leather chairs. In those moments of waiting he likes to talk. While a man of privacy and long silences, he is supremely a man of carefully turned formulations, of talk.

Today is the last day before the month's recess. Muskie will be off to Maine for a few days with his family and for golf, and then three weeks of touring town after town after town, trying to put to death as visibly as possible the impression around his state that he's grown too big for his Maine britches, that his mind is too much on the world and the nation and too little on his neighbors. Toward the end of the month I'll join him.

Today is a day for the floor, for transforming bills into laws and appropriations, like squeezing in a few extra plays before the whistle blows. Muskie is waiting for the call-up of a House-Senate conference report on military procurement, a legislative item that sounds so deadly, I'm frank to say that I'm not aware, during our chat, of its special import; certainly not that its outcome before the day is out will stun the Senate's most powerful members and become a landmark in Senate history.

A CONVERSATION WITH SENATOR MUSKIE

What function does floor debate serve? Does anyone go to the floor to become educated about a bill before he votes?
—I do on occasion. Not as often as I used to, because I don't have the time. If something's coming along that I'm really puzzled about and I've had advance notice of and I really want to know who's for what and why, and if I can find time, I'll go.
Can you give me a recent example of that?
—There was one today, the Tunney amendment.[1] On the face of it, that looked like an amendment I would naturally support, it being the environmentalist position. I had a staff memo, not one of Rick's, recommending a vote against the Tunney amendment. I read the memo, which was about five pages long. Against the amendment? What the hell gives? So I went there and sat and listened to the debate until I made up my mind. And I voted against the Tunney amendment. Because, really, what's involved is a demonstration of whether the breeder reactor, one way or another, makes sense. Until we know that, we don't really know what the possibilities are, especially for New England, for energy resources. You've got oil, which is probably going to be a weak reed for New England. And coal, which is very expensive, so New England moved out of coal. And nuclear. So you can't just dismiss it. There are a lot of people in New England who don't like the idea of nuclear power, and I have my reservations about it. But this is a demonstration project. So I decided, what the hell is wrong with finding out what we need to know? That was a case where I decided to stay there long enough to hear Tunney explain his view, and Pastore explain his view, and that gave me a better perspective on the vote than the memo did.
What changed your mind? A particular thing one of them said?
—The debate didn't change my mind. It made up my mind. Mainly, Pastore's explanation of what the provision does that Tunney wanted to eliminate. It does not trigger commercial development.

[1] An amendment to the Energy Research and Development Administration appropriation to strike out an appropriation for an experimental demonstration of a breeder reactor. Tunney's case against the demonstration project was based on potential safety hazards of breeder reactors.

It's just a pure and simple demonstration. Tunney's argument, which was very well made, was addressed to the broader questions of the dangers of nuclear energy, the risks. Well, we all understand that. *I was in the gallery at the time and saw you at your desk reading something intently. Having a conspiratorial mind, I assumed your only interest was defeating that military conference report, and you were preparing to destroy the opposition.*

—I've been here too long to try any more to understand how people view this institution, but long enough to know they get a very distorted impression of what this place is all about. One thing I don't like is that, when most people think about the Senate and judge it, they go right to the matter of motivations. And they come up with bad motivations. Especially these days. They just assume that anybody inside these walls, a Senator or a Congressman, has bad motivations. If you cast a vote with which they disagree, they assume it was for venal or immoral reasons. It's not a difference in judgment but a bad motivation. That really bothers me, because I find most of the people I've served with in the Senate, they've been *good* people. Decent, good men and women who try to do their best.

Do you ever become awed by the responsibility of voting yes or no on issues that may cost all Americans heavily, yet with no certainty that what you do will produce the desired results? Is lawmaking sometimes frightening?

—There's no way of avoiding costs. The question is, what shape should cost take? The cost of more people getting sick if you neglect the problem? Of more people dying because you neglect the problem? Or of fifty to a hundred dollars more per car in order to deal with the problem? There are costs regardless: costs that affect the way automobiles are made, the way cities are built, costs that affect pocketbooks, and costs that affect health. We can't avoid costs, so you trade one for another, using the best judgment you can apply. Making these decisions, I understand their magnitude, but I've been inured to it for so long that I don't find the duty awesome. I apply my best judgment, then accept it, live with it.

—I just don't see laws as being that much of a cure-all. I don't think laws are that magical. Laws don't only deal with problems, they also create problems. They create bureaucracies, and bureaucracies tend to be autocratic and insensitive and callous. Not that there aren't good civil servants. There are, of course.

Is the growth of the federal government reversible?

—Well, the number of civil employees in the federal establishment hasn't changed in twenty-five years. In 1950 it was about two and a half million, and it's two and a half million now. The dramatic growth is at the state and local level, in part because federal programs are administered at the state and local level, and also because funds are now pushed in that direction. But government has to occupy itself with more and more things simply because problems become more complicated as society grows. I don't know how you stop that.

—Some of the means by which we've tried to achieve our good objectives were not well chosen. They may have resulted in more interference than help. This kind of growth of government responsibility has developed a momentum in the last ten years that ought to be examined. That's why I've been for converting grant-in-aid programs—funding specific categories of activity—to block-grant programs and revenue sharing, in order to get the federal government's cotton-picking hands out of the details of local life, out of decision making, and so on.

—On the other hand, you don't want to push decision making down to units that are too small for the problem. Mass transit—you can't build mass transit for units of 1,500 people, and you can't really develop housing programs in towns of 5,000. So there it is. Your government jurisdiction has to coincide with the solutions. You've got to move down from centralization at the national level and move up a little from the purely local village to deal with a growing number of problems. I don't want to see towns and villages disappear. But their school systems have to be looked at from a broader base.

The first time we conversed in this room, you said that having these talks might be fun, a chance to unburden. Unburden about what? What do you feel most misunderstood about? [I expect a long, thought-gathering pause. But no. The reply comes quite readily.]

—To put it in its simplest terms: I have an intellectual momentum of my own. I'm not just someone to be scheduled. There's an inside to me. I can think. I *do* think. These things that have visibility in committee meetings or on the floor of the Senate or in my office are a product of the thought process, and that process has to have a flow. What happens is that there are so many things and so many people that interrupt that flow. I mean, my thought processes develop momentum. If I get up in the morning and I'm driving down here, I think about things I've got to do, challenges I face. I begin to develop directions in which I want my energies to go that day. Then I get here and suddenly somebody wants to push me off down Road C when I'm traveling Road A. And I've got that little typewritten schedule to go by, and I say, "God!" It would be interesting to know how many productive lines of thought I've abandoned, never to find them again because—You know, there has to be a certain element of creativity to solve the kinds of problems we have, and when that creative mood strikes you, you'd like to enjoy it. You'd like to let it blossom out. You'd like to see where it takes you. And it's just snuffed out so often. Really. And you forget what it was. I have vague recollections from time to time, "By God, there was a hell of a good idea that I had back there a couple of days ago, and for the life of me I can't recall what it was."

Because just at that moment the phone rang.

—Yeah. And it's *so* frustrating. *So* frustrating. I always considered the telephone the rudest kind of instrument. A fellow can spend a month trying to get in to see you on some matter he considers important. He's finally there across the desk. He's got fifteen minutes or a half hour to present his case, and some guy on the other end of the telephone gets your ear on the phone and consumes all of this fellow's half hour. A rude damned instrument. I didn't invite him to call, to interrupt me in my own office. There's that kind of interruption all day long.

—As a matter of fact, the other day I was stepping into the bathroom in my office, the *bathroom,* when this girl whom I didn't recognize just walked in from Dolores' office, stuck out her hand, and said, "I'm So and So." Jesus Christ! Yes, I know who she is, and her father's a very good friend and a contributor, and she was visiting Washington, but Christ, they find every interstice in your damned day and *go* for it.

—It isn't just that they inconvenience you. The pleasure in this job, if there is any, is the challenge it gives to your ability to think, to create, to innovate, to put things together. But the structure of the damned thing is that it snuffs out that side of you, and there's nobody to protect that side of you. So that, more than anything else, is what stimulates my temper, and nothing else very much does. Nothing else. You've seen me sit for hours in committees, absolutely patient, because I'm uninterrupted. I'm in control. I bring everybody in. The creative process is under way. So I have absolute patience.

—Well, I guess I've made the point.

How do other Senators handle it?

—They may not be as bothered by it. A lot of people in this business are only interested in the frenetic side of it. They just like the game. Not all people feel that creative urge. Then you have somebody like Hubert, whose energy is boundless and can expand in every direction. I don't think it bothers him at all. I'm intense. When I'm concentrating on something I want to concentrate. I want to do *that* and only that.

Do you feel penalized as a politician because you're just not the kind to do as much glad-handing as some of these other fellows do?

—Well, in its time and place I do all of that. When I go home to Maine to campaign in the field, I enjoy it, and I think I can do it as well as anybody. Because that's what I'm there for. I enjoy it, and I set the time aside for that, and it really isn't that kind of interference down there. Once in a while a constituent comes in at an inconvenient time, but it isn't in such volume that it's a real bother. I don't mind those intrusions. But the socializing around in Washington, my wife and I, we just cut that to the bone. At the beginning we did all of it because we thought it was necessary.

And it must be good for the ego for a while.

—Yeah. But it kills you. It kills your health and kills your time and your energy and your ability to do the job. Too often when I go to an embassy party or somewhere else, all during the evening I'm worried about that bill that I'd like to be working on, or a problem I'd like to be tackling. When I get home and go to bed, I pile the books up beside it and read until I fall asleep. Well, that's no way to do business. Or get up at five-thirty in the morning.

Do you prefer early morning study? I understand you're a natural early riser.

—Oh yeah. I can do a lot of work at five-thirty in the morning. I don't mind it if I haven't been out all night. In the couple of hours between five-thirty and seven-thirty I can do more work than the rest of the day. My mind is fresh. I can plow through a lot of material and absorb it very fast.

—But then, having worked up a good head of steam, I come down to the office and hit a stone wall. [*A rueful laugh.*]

Getting back to where we began, about floor debate and so forth:
Is my growing impression correct that, whereas we think of one hun-
dred men in the Senate who pass bills, the true number is closer to
five or six, and that those five or six change from bill to bill? Today,
for example, those bills are going through here like an express train.
There's no possible way you can be authoritative on each of them the
way you'd like to be. So, in a sense, every vote is a poll of the "man
on the street," except that these are very intelligent "men on the
street," who are taking leadership from a very few, about ninety-five
following five who have really gone into it. Is that reasonably sound?

—Yes, it is. What you've just said is another description of what
we call "the committee process." In order to handle the volume of
legislation, committees divide up the legislative work, the spadework
as it were. So committee credibility is an awfully important thing.
For that reason, what you said ought to be modified. It isn't five
men, it's the committee. And within the committee, the men knowledgeable on any given bill will change, because of the composition of
subcommittees.

—And each combination of men has a different chemistry, so that
some committees more than others develop a reputation for
thoroughness, or comprehension, or reliability for fairness and accu-
racy, and for good judgment. That may be the most important—a
reputation for good judgment. A lot of members of the Senate will
arrive on the floor, and there's an amendment up that they really
haven't had a chance to look at, and they'll just come up and ask,
"What's the committee position?" And they'll follow that committee
position, meaning the committee majority, which sometimes may be
a unanimous position. The majority of a committee that backs a bill
is usually bipartisan, or at least crosses party lines. Once in a while,
like the New Hampshire business, it's straight party lines, but that's
increasingly rare. So it's the committee position, and the ability of
the committee.

—And the credibility of its chairman is an important part of that.
If you've got both the chairman and the ranking member, a Republican, both supporting a committee position, then that's a very powerful influence in the Senate. So it isn't just the four or five men who
may be debating a particular bill or who may be managing it. It's the
committee. If there's disagreement within the committee, even then
the way the committee divides will be determinative of how the rest

of the Senate divides most of the time. Nobody's taken any statistics on this, but my observation is that the habit of Senators has not changed much in the eighteen years I've been here, of relying on the committee. Not that the committee's never overturned. It is, on occasion. But the committee position is the first basic piece of information you want.

—In addition, of course, there's the Senator's staff. Rick analyzes every piece of legislation that comes through. There's a one-page or two-page memo for you, so I know what the basic thrust of the legislation is, what amendments can be anticipated so I won't be caught by surprise, and a recommendation based upon his knowledge of my philosophy and of my voting record. He does a very masterful job of digesting and pointing out the strong points, the danger points, and so on. Really, he's very, very good. In my early years I didn't have that kind of very useful service. I sort of had to jump onto the floor, standing there, trying quickly to get the gist of it myself. Very frustrating. This is much better.

When word comes by telephone that the military procurement conference report will be called up momentarily, ending our conversation, all I know about it as I make my way up the grand marble stairs to the gallery floor is roughly the following: Weeks ago the Senate passed a defense bill that conformed with the budget resolution, reducing by 9.8 per cent the President's budget request. The budget resolution ceiling target set by the Senate was $100.7 billion in appropriations of which $90.7 billion would actually be spent in the current fiscal year. The House "busted" the budget resolution ceiling with bills adding up to a higher figure. Then, in virtually the last minute, President Ford asked for an additional $60 million—against the advice of the Defense Department and his own Office of Management and Budget—to finance preliminary engineering plans for a $1.2 billion nuclear power cruiser urged by Vice-Admiral Hyman G. Rickover (who has remarkable standing in the House, although less in the Senate, and considerably less in the Pentagon). Muskie and others denounced this suggestion as a "down payment" on a huge "backdoor commitment." Once the "down payment" is made, they said, Congress will have taken a long step toward the purchase itself, the merits of which Congress has not adequately con-

THE SENATE NOBODY KNOWS

sidered. A House-Senate conference committee—wrangling for seven weeks!—settled the issue the way conference committees settle almost all money questions: they cut the difference in half. Muskie charges that the compromise figure for military procurement breaks through the over-all ceiling for the military budget category by $700 million.

Today Muskie is going to fight to reject that conference report—to force the conference committee to begin all over again. In doing so, he is testing his Budget Committee in the severest way, a battle to do what the Senate has not done in recent history: defeat a major defense bill.

Is he risking too much too soon?

It seems an insuperable venture. Only one reason is congressional fear of rejecting military bills. The other is that if this Budget Committee, in its infancy, whips back and tames Armed Services, it would become a clear and present threat to every old-line chairman of every old-line appropriating committee. Would they stand for it?

Muskie's opening sentences are quiet, factual, and unexpected:

"Mr. President, the Senate has pending before it two important conference reports which have major implications for the new congressional budget. I am compelled, as a member of the Senate and as chairman of the Senate Budget Committee, to vote against both.

"I will vote against the military procurement conference report. . . . I will vote against the school lunch conference report. . . . I hope other Senators will vote likewise."

The school lunch conference report is not before the Senate! I have not heard a mention that the conference has come to agreement, let alone that the issue is coming to the Senate floor before the recess. But by confronting the Senate with these two issues *as a pair,* Muskie challenges supporters of each budget buster to examine their zeal in the light of the other issue. If either issue is more important than the budget process, then so are both issues, or, for that matter, any issue over which any group of members feels enough zeal. And there will be no budget process at all. Responsibility for the nation's finances would be surrendered once again to the White House—this time, perhaps for good. The implication is immediate, clear, and electrifying.

"The Budget Reform Act," Muskie continues, "has two purposes —to control federal spending and cut waste, and to reorder our na-

tional priorities within an over-all spending ceiling. These two conference reports provide both guns and butter—more in each case
than Congress has targeted. Both should be rejected.

"What if we reject only one report and not the other? Are we
prepared to say to America's families and their children that we will
break the budget to buy bullets but we are going to cut back on the
budget at the school lunch counter? . . .

"My colleagues are aware that in October we will be voting on the
second concurrent resolution on the budget. If, at that time, we find
that we are over the $367 billion outlay target we set for ourselves in
May, and wonder what happened to our efforts to keep the deficit
under control, we can look to bills like this one and know the reason
why we failed. And the responsibility will belong to no one but ourselves."

Muskie yields the floor to Henry Bellmon of Oklahoma, the ranking Republican of the Budget Committee. Bellmon, of mild, round
face and thinning hair, exudes neither energy nor originality nor
charm. In fact, a total nondescript, he does not exude. But the impression misleads. In a state that has been remarkably faithful to
Democrats in state-wide races, Bellmon destroyed tradition to become governor in 1962, then Senator in 1968 after a brief period as
Richard Nixon's first presidential campaign chairman. Nixon,
through his presidential years, enjoyed no more ready and steady
Senate voice than Bellmon's. As late as the spring of 1974, Bellmon
declared that even if Watergate led to impeachment he would ask
Nixon to come to Oklahoma to campaign for him. Nixon's downfall
in August did not unseat Bellmon in November, as it did other colleagues who quit the sinking ship earlier.

The Budget Act was born of anger in Congress against Nixon—
particularly against his innovation of impounding funds appropriated
by Congress, refusing to spend them, sometimes virtually refusing to
execute whole programs. Hence, the full name of the law: the Congressional Budget and Impoundment Control Act of 1974. In the
context of that rebellion, it can be said with some fairness that Nixon
is as responsible as anyone for the new budget process and the determination of most members to make it succeed.

And whom does fate cast into the seat of Republican leader on the
Budget Committee? Lord save the process, Henry Bellmon! Yet, as
though politically blind, or choosing to be, Muskie determined early

in the year that Henry Bellmon had to be made an ally. In the way
that he has cultivated Buckley, Domenici, McClure into joint propri-
etorship of the Clean Air Act, he began nurturing Bellmon's commitment to the Budget Act, dangling its promise of spending control, a
concept which Bellmon may have held more dearly than that of priority setting. But as in the Clean Air Act meetings, Muskie did not
rush events; he waited for them. And the pivotal event, sure enough,
came of itself—in the form of a visit to Muskie's office by Senator
Walter Mondale of Minnesota. The Budget Committee had just
modified (downward) an economic stimulus package put forth by
Muskie. Mondale urged that Muskie fight on the floor to restore the
full spending package. Mondale pledged that he and other liberals
would labor to scare up every marginal vote, and they'd put it over.
Muskie replied that he was undecided. "The question," as Muskie re-
calls stating it, "is which is more important: to fight for my own position or to establish the integrity of the budget process." Then
through the often peculiar routing of the Senate grapevine (sometimes from Senator directly to Senator, but more often from, say, a
committee's ranking Republican to the committee's top minority staff
aide to the majority's top staff aide to the committee chairman, or
that route in reverse) Muskie learned that ranking member Bellmon
was undecided too. He had fought in committee to *reduce* the spending stimulus. Should he now put up a show on the floor for *his* position—the same old battle of less versus more—or was it more important to launch the budget process itself with a show of health and
strength?

Although Mondale may never have known it, his visit resulted in
Muskie inviting Bellmon in for a private summit chat—man to man,
no staff members. The chairman frankly laid out his dilemma. The
ranking member frankly laid out his. Seizing the moment, Muskie
suggested a pact: He, Muskie, would go to the floor and defend the
budget resolution as it emerged from committee if Bellmon would
pledge the same. The two standing together would make the resolution virtually unbeatable—and would insure the budget process
being safely born. Within committee during the next year, they could
fight tooth and nail over whether the budget ceiling should go up or
down, over how much should go for this category, how much for
that. But once a resolution emerges from the committee—*their* committee, in which Muskie was offering a "stock split," joint ownership,

joint responsibility—the two would stand as partners defending the
budget targets, opposing any budget buster that came down the pike.
They shook hands on it. (Later, Mondale offered on the floor the
stimulus package as originally advanced in committee by Muskie—
and Muskie's floor opposition defeated it.)

And now Budget Chairman Muskie, in a live-or-die moment of the
Budget Act's life, yields the floor to ranking member Bellmon:

"Mr. President," Bellmon begins gravely, "I find myself in a quan-
dary today. I am completely dedicated to making the newly adopted
budget process work. It is the only available means Congress has to
stop the irresponsible accumulation of one huge deficit after another,
as has happened every year since I have been in the Senate. This
plunge into economic chaos has to be stopped. I consider it to be the
greatest threat our country faces today, and therefore, while I have
always supported and still support a strong national defense, I intend
to oppose, and ask my colleagues to oppose, the conference report
on H.R. 6674, the military procurement authorization bill. . . . I am
absolutely convinced that this country must be just as strong economically as it must be prepared militarily. . . ."

Chairman Stennis of Armed Services takes it in, calculates, slightly
crouching, alert as a quarry. Spare, almost shrunken, yet formidable,
with sallow cheeks and piercing eyes beneath a huge skull, this
seventy-four-year-old's vigor gives no hint that not long ago he lay
near death from a sidewalk shooting by two teen-age muggers near
his Washington home.

If the Senate accepts this $700 million military budget buster,
Muskie suggests, the only way it can preserve its budget target is to
reduce the cost of military personnel: either cutting the size of the
armed forces or denying a pay rise promised them.

Stennis is indignant. The cost of manpower is the subject of a totally separate bill. What does *this* have to do with *that?* A fundamental concept of the Budget Act—combining all costs of a functional category, such as defense, into a single ceiling target—has not
made its way through Stennis' head. Or he finds it convenient to pretend it has not.

"We passed a bill here 9.8 per cent below the budget of the President of the United States," pleads Stennis, deciding that the stance of
a martyr is the strongest in his repertoire for today's need. "No one
else has [taken a cut] of that proportion, no other department

has. . . . What the Senator seeks to do today is to charge this bill with a great many matters from another bill. . . . They are changing the rules in midstream, bringing up all this about manpower. After all, how can one meet obligations about manpower? Take these people off the payroll?"

"We have not changed any rules," Muskie responds, his steam starting to rise. "This is not the Budget Committee mandating. All I am doing is holding up what the Senate did on May 15. It set a *target*." He hurls the word like an arrow at Stennis, and through lips stretched slightly to one side, his signal of loss of cool, Muskie thunders, "Uncomfortable, isn't it? You don't like it!"[2] To depersonalize the attack, Muskie unfastens his gaze from Stennis and casts it in a wide arc: "That is true of every Senator when that budget hits a program he is interested in. It is not *comfortable*. I told the Senator on May 15 that this was a tight budget—"

"Will the Senator yield?" calls Stennis.

"If I may finish."

"All right." The courtly Stennis retreats.

". . . Tight in the defense function, tight in every function. Of course it's uncomfortable. It is my job to hold that number up for us to see."

Stennis, in a new line of attack, turns to what really galls him and other chairmen. Going into conference committee, pitting the strength of the Senate against the strength of the House, trying to return to your own colleagues with the prestige of victory or at least a workable compromise, is difficult enough. But now comes this new complication, not only a crippling one but a demeaning one, as chairmen see it. After going through the torments of compromise, a chairman must go on bended knee to a fellow chairman—indeed the chairman of a mere babe among committees, the Budget Committee —to ask meekly, "Will this compromise be all right? Do you approve of the new figure?" Infinitely worse, Stennis now claims he *did* go through that indignity and Muskie would give him no answer! In fact, he went to Muskie *before* the conference to ask how high the Senate conferees could go in compromising with the House, where the Budget Committee would draw its line.

[2] This presses uncomfortably against the rule of impersonal debate. A Budget Committee staff member later edits the Congressional Record to read, "Uncomfortable, is it not? The Senator does not like it."

"The Senator has admitted he expressly refrained from giving us anything definite, any figure, that the Senator wanted us to come under," Stennis protests. "We did not know just where the line was. . . . We do not know yet where the Senator's line is. He said this morning he especially refrained from mentioning figures on different categories."

Muskie knows, of course, that if he were to indicate that a budget stretch of, say, $300 million would be acceptable, the compromise would most certainly come back at a minimum of $300 million. "In the debate of June 4," he replies, "I told the Senator specifically that the amount of that bill was tight and barely within the target. *That* was the number. What does the Senator mean that I did not give him a number? The amount contained in the Senate bill was the number." Muskie reveals his hand for a peekaboo moment: "Now, I expect the conferees are going to have to compromise. And realistically, they probably could not hold to that number. All I am saying now is, let us get closer to that number. Because that number is as much a House obligation as it is a Senate obligation. Try to get closer to it. Now, if the view of all Senators is that expressed by the distinguished chairman—that the numbers that are within the budget go out the window when his committee walks to the conference—we have got nowhere to go."

At stake here is more than the budget target, more than the sum for military procurement, more than the down payment for a nuclear-powered cruiser. At stake is the personal pride of John Stennis. Go back to the House? Ask to reconstitute the conference committee and admit to that less esteemed body that he could not carry his own colleagues along on a perfectly good compromise? That would be a humiliation for Stennis, from which John Pastore— Muskie's friend, Stennis' friend—now tries to save him:

"Mr. President, I have been here for twenty-five years. I have attended a lot of conferences with the House of Representatives. I congratulate the Budget Committee for the job it did"—his arms lift and fingers extend prayerfully—"but it can only seek to govern the actions of the Senate. It does not govern the action of the House of Representatives.

"Looking at this thing realistically, what are the chances of any improvements if we go back at this late hour? . . . The thing here is a question of pragmatism. If the gentlemen who have been making all the speeches here will go on the new conference, and see if they can convince the House conferees, well and good. But if we are going to send the same ministers back, the House has heard all the arguments we have, and they will not be able to compromise. That is exactly what we are up against—the realities of the situation.

"Frankly, it will be an exercise in futility. All of this will read nice on the front pages tomorrow. But if we go back to that conference after they have already compromised it, and they will not budge an inch, and you say, 'Well, the Budget Committee of the Senate said this,' do you know what they will do? They will laugh right in your faces.

"I am all for the Budget Committee. But the fact remains that we have to look at it realistically at this point. There is no need to castigate the Senate conferees. They tried hard to maintain the position of the Senate. But they had to listen to the position of the House as well, and they compromised."

Stennis picks up Pastore's cue: "I'm satisfied in my mind that this bill is the best that this group of conferees can do. I say this seriously —if the majority that votes down this bill will select conferees among themselves who will go to the conference and maintain the position of that majority, that is a step I would welcome strongly. Senators can tell by the way I speak that I am not being angry or vindictive. I have done all I can. I will welcome having someone else carry the load."

"I say to the Senator from Rhode Island," says Muskie, ignoring Stennis' threatened bow-out, "that this is not just the Committee on the Budget. This is the *congressional* budget process. The targets were set in a *joint* concurrent resolution agreed to by both houses as a result of a conference of both houses. If the conferees of the House of Representatives do indeed laugh at the Senate Committee on the Budget, they will be laughing at the new budget process and at any prospects of making it work, because one house cannot make it work."

". . . But it still is the budget recommendation of the Senate portion of the budget process," insists Pastore.

"That is not true," Muskie hurls back.

"What I am saying is—"

"It is not *true,*" Muskie presses.

"Well, it is not—"

"All time has expired," gavels the presiding officer.

"I mean the figure that the Senator from Maine recommends is the same figure that was recommended [by the House Budget Committee and rejected] in the House of Representatives."

Muskie calls for "the yeas and nays," a roll-call vote, unusual for a conference report, which usually zips by routinely.

A flurry of commotion erupts at a chamber entrance to the right of the dais. Two husky, athletic men, members of the Secret Service, hold the doors, looking rapidly, suspiciously around the chamber floor and scanning the gallery. Vice-President Nelson Rockefeller materializes, shakes a few hands, and bounds up to the presiding officer's chair. On a critically important vote that may be close, the minority leadership sends for him just in case a tie-breaking vote may be needed.

As the roll call begins, Muskie watches for signs, for the little surprises either this way or that, that tip off which way it may go. Abourezk, no (against the conference committee report, and with Muskie), no surprise. Allen, aye (against Muskie), no surprise. Bellmon's no is no surprise, but a comfort. It's followed by Bentsen's no, a good sign. Brooke's no, very good if it means other liberal Republicans will stand with the Budget Committee. Buckley's aye, coming from a member of the Budget Committee, is scarcely a surprise from a military hard-liner—yet a disappointment. Robert Byrd's aye is incomprehensible, but from a man difficult to comprehend. (Is Byrd, ambitious to become Majority Leader, already apprehensive of the Senate-wide power potential of the Budget Committee and its chairman? Or is he making points with committee chairmen in this critical vote, hoping that chairmen will remember him when he needs their support?) Cannon, aye, a member of Armed Services. Chiles, no, Budget Committee. Culver, no, defying Stennis, although a member of Armed Services. Dole, no, loyal to the Budget Committee. Domenici, same. Gary Hart, no, also defying his Armed Services chairman. Hathaway, aye; more clearly every day, his obligation to his senior Maine Senator ranks lower in his priorities than pleasing his Finance Committee chairman Russell Long, who would obliterate the Budget Committee without a twinge. Humphrey, no. Inouye, aye, member of Appropriations, strong pro-Navy constituency in Hawaii. Jackson, aye, a strong voice on Armed Services, a committee chairman, and no surprise. Leahy, no, although an Armed Services member. Mansfield, no, a big vote that could carry others to the Budget Committee's side. Mathias, no, another liberal Republican. Proxmire, no; although a member of Appropriations and although discomfited by Muskie's new role, as an enthusiastic Pentagon critic he could scarcely go the other way. Ribicoff, aye; the scent of that nuclear cruiser contract for New London's shipyards proves over-powering. And the final three noes are gifts from the Republican side: Roth (a member of Finance), Schweiker (Appropriations), and Stafford.

Amazing. The budget process wins over the military, 48 to 42!

"Mr. President," Muskie calls, "I move to reconsider the vote." A routine gesture: the manager of the winning side moves to recon-sider, an ally moves to table that motion, and the motion is tabled by unanimous consent, foreclosing the possibility of anyone else making a genuine motion to reconsider. It's a final procedural nail to seal a victory.

"Mr. President, point of order." The voice is Minority Whip Griffin's. Something is irregular.

Majority Leader Mansfield is on his feet, making the routine re-sponse to Muskie's motion: "I move to lay the motion on the table."

But Griffin won't be shunted aside: "Mr. President, is a motion to reconsider in order coming from the Senator from Maine?"

At the lower level of the dais, the parliamentarian swings around to Rockefeller and nods.

"The Senator is qualified to make the motion," Rockefeller an-nounces.

"Mr. President," Mansfield urgently repeats, "I move to lay that motion on the table."

The Senate's tiniest man with the tallest name, Tower of Texas, unhooks his microphone from his desk and announces, "Mr. Presi-dent, I ask for the yeas and nays." Roll call on a motion to table? Does Tower really believe enough Senators will vote "wrong" in the confusing switch of a tabling motion so that he can hold the question open, to be reconsidered after the recess? His true motive suddenly comes clear. The Senate has erupted into a chaos of aisle-scurrying, huddles, and hubbub, the exchanges more animated than I have ever seen them in this chamber of cut-glass dignity. Astonished that the Senate has rejected a military conference report, Tower and his Armed Services colleagues are actually lobbying—intensely—to produce instant change in the vote, at least to hold the question open for reconsideration.

Over the tumult, Rockefeller hammers his gavel and asks, "Is there a sufficient second on the motion to table the motion to reconsider?" He grins with amusement at the achievement of his own sentence. "There is a sufficient second. The clerk will call the roll."

"Mr. President," Gaylord Nelson of Wisconsin shouts over the din, determined to break up the Armed Services blitz, "there are members conversing in the aisles, and staff members. I think we ought to have order in the Senate before we proceed with the roll call."

"Let there be order in the Senate, please, before we proceed with the roll call," Rockefeller dutifully commands and gavels.

"Mr. President"—Nelson again—"there are members back here who did not hear the gavel, and some over there, too."

"May we have order in the Senate, please?"

Nelson remains insistent: "There is a member at the rear, at the door, who did not hear the gavel, Mr. President."

"I will give it to him again. I have a bigger gavel in my office," chuckles Rockefeller.

"There are two members on the other side, including the Minority Leader, who did not hear the gavel."

"Will the members [*bang*] please take their seats [*bang bang*] before the roll call continues [*bang bang bang bang*]."

"There are members, Mr. President, in the center aisle who have not heard the gavel."

"Mr. President," coaches Bobby Byrd, "will the Senator from Wisconsin use his microphone?"

"I think, Mr. President," booms the Senator from Wisconsin through his microphone, "that the roll call ought to be held—"

Rockefeller has had enough. "Debate is not in order during a roll call. The Senator has made the point. I shall hit the gavel once more and ask the Senators to please take their seats. Then the roll call will proceed."

The alert, last-ditch, almost desperate maneuver by Tower fails. The motion to table wins, 47 to 41. The only vote switched—from a vote against the conference report to a vote to reconsider—is that of enfeebled Warren Magnuson of Washington, caught between his memberships on the Budget and Appropriations committees. Was his change an error or a decision? When old Senators retire, they take answers to such questions with them. Senators Brock and Laxalt, both recorded as favoring the conference committee report, had to bolt the chamber to catch planes before the tabling motion was voted.

The Budget Committee and budget process, not yet graduated from their "dry run" year, will never again be taken lightly by entrenched chairmen. When Senator Muskie speculated only a few nights ago over spareribs at Arbaugh's that one day soon the budget process would have to withstand the test of a budget buster before earning its long pants, he clearly did not anticipate that it would happen this way, on a military rather than a social welfare budget buster, and he certainly did not expect it so soon.

Bangor, Maine
Monday, August 25

At a candlelit table of a private dining room in the basement of Bangor House, I find Senator Muskie winding up a luncheon discussion with about twenty lawyers. They have been urging him to vote against national no-fault insurance. Sympathetically, but non-committally, he promises to look into it carefully before he votes.

We climb into the car of Clyde MacDonald, head of Muskie's Bangor office, fortyish, a former professor of history at the University of Maine. His mind wiped clear of the meeting just ended, Muskie girds himself for what he knows he'll be asked on a TV panel quiz, next on his schedule. The program is "Follow-Up," the highest-rated interview show in Maine, today's tape to be broadcast next Sunday. "This morning at a press conference, the other day on TV up north, every damned place I go," he mutters, "all they ask is about Billy Cohen. Do I think he's going to run? Do I think it's going to be tight? I just don't want to get into that with them. I'm not going to spend from now till November of next year helping them build up Billy Cohen. But they won't let you out of it."

He glares out his front-seat window at the roadside speeding by.

"Can't you say," I ask—having begun a suggestion, it's too late to turn back—"can't you say, 'All I know is that I'm going to have to run against *somebody*. No matter who it is, I assume that he'll be the strongest they can find, and, of course, I'm going to run scared because I always do'?"

He keeps looking out the window. I kick myself again, not for the suggestion, but for identifying too strongly with the man about whom I write, supposedly with detachment.

In the big, dark, concrete barn of a studio, Muskie flanked by two political reporters on a brilliantly lit stage set, sure enough the first question is about Cohen—will he be Muskie's Republican opponent and is Muskie worried about it?

"I don't have the slightest idea," Muskie begins, "and all I can tell you is this: they're going to put *somebody* up against me, and whether it's the man you mentioned or somebody else, I assume they'll pick their strongest, and of course I'll run scared. I always do. Nobody should take public office for granted."

Unexpectedly I experience for myself what they've all been talking about—Leon Billings, Al From, Jim Case: the kick of his acceptance of your idea, picking it up and running with it in the Big Game.

We proceed to the town of Old Town, just northeast of Bangor, and the Marsh Island Senior Citizens Apartments, a modern, cheery place where cheery tenants, mostly widows, share coffee and cookies with their Senator, animatedly nattering about almost anything but politics. One lady boasts of being mother, grandmother, and great-grandmother of a tree of eighty-three descendants, and when Muskie displays broad astonishment, she invites him up to her room. And he accepts. On her wall, mounted on a huge board, arranged in family branches, are eighty-three photographs—her own at the pinnacle—each enclosed in a circular frame.

A male resident, sporting a Western-style neck cord with an Eisenhower silver dollar mounted on its slide, asks Muskie to explain why a change was made (I miss the details) in his veteran's benefits when a certain adjustment (I miss those details too) was made in his Social Security check. Muskie listens with an attentiveness to match the man's earnestness and says he can't offhand explain it but that he'll check into it and let the man know. MacDonald has been taking notes and there's no doubt that a well-placed official in the Veterans' Administration will soon go to some length to explain to a Senator's office the whys and wherefores—or an error will be straightened out.

Muskie admires the neck doodad.

"Would you like to have one like it? I have two," the man offers eagerly.

"Sure," responds Muskie with wide-eyed delight. The man disappears and returns, making a ceremony of placing it around the Senator's neck.

"What am I going to do with this thing?" Muskie asks in the car after we leave. "I didn't want to take it, but I didn't want to let him down." He instructs MacDonald to make sure a nice letter of appreciation goes to the donor. A personal thoughtfulness he has no time for in Washington appears to come easily—indeed, with some businesslike urgency—in Maine.

We swing by the Holiday Inn East, where Muskie stayed last night, so he can take a quick shower and shave before an evening meeting at a supporter's home in Bangor. In the lobby MacDonald learns the distressing news that the Senator was dispossessed of his room at checkout time because the hotel is booked full for tonight. With the self-protective resourcefulness of a good staff man, MacDonald dives for a phone booth to make an alternative arrangement before breaking the bad news. The alternative arrangement is that Mrs. MacDonald is to straighten out the house and get out of her hair curlers in twenty minutes flat because the Senator (whom she has never met) is coming to take a shower.

Clyde suggests dinner near the airport at a restaurant that serves an incomparable plate of spareribs and beans. It's a huge place and, walking behind Muskie, I observe a few double-takes, forks frozen in mid-air, wives whispering to husbands the news of who just walked by, yet all subdued, almost resistant. Our college-age waiter clearly does not recognize his guest. That poll must be right about young voters and Muskie. Then, handing us our menus, the young man says coolly, "Gentlemen, Senator Muskie, what'll it be tonight?" Clyde orders ribs and beans for us all. "Sorry," says the waiter matter-of-factly, "we're out of ribs tonight." After a long reorganizational pause, Clyde asks if we could have the steak special with the beans instead of the vegetables as listed. "Sorry, no substitutions." The three of us, clearly downcast, turn again to the menu. The waiter asks to be excused, then quickly returns to say that the steak-and-bean combination can be arranged. Even in Maine, concessions are sometimes made to the high and mighty.

Muskie has been making nostalgic references all afternoon to Campobello Island in the Bay of Fundy where he spent Friday night and Saturday. He is a commissioner of the U.S.-Canada park created where Franklin Roosevelt spent his childhood summers and contracted polio in his 40th year. He loves the place. Our privileged serving of beans sets him off on a detailed, admiring profile of a park founder, neighbor, and devotee, aging Sumner Pike, friend of F.D.R., naturalist and scientist, who has experimentally developed a bean especially high in nutrients and low in its generation of oxygen. Muskie engages the wandering attention of his two listeners by saying dryly, "You understand, don't you, that that means a fawtless bean."

He springs his repertoire of such Maine oddisms only when he's relaxed—which means only in Maine. One day he asked an out-of-state reporter accompanying him along the main street of Rockland if he'd ever seen a lobster hypnotized. When the outsider scoffed, Muskie stopped at an outdoor tank they were approaching, seized a huge one just behind its menacing claws, which were not yet pegged, and began to stroke its tail soothingly. Soon the tail folded down and the lobster quieted into a trance. Muskie gently set it on the sidewalk where it rested, immobile, on its head and claws. Then the hypnotist abruptly picked up the subject, releasing the spell, and the big claws snapped into angry action. Muskie smugly dropped the beast back into the tank. Greeting someone he recognized, he said, "Excuse my clammy hand. I've just been hypnotizing a lobster."

The unimpressed, efficient young waiter scribbles our check, lays it face down on our table, hesitates, and abruptly announces, "Senator, I guess a person doesn't have a chance every day to say this, so I just thought I'd tell you that I don't always agree with you but I admire your work." Sternly concealing embarrassment, he turns and strides away.

The evening meeting is at the home of Nick Albans, selected not for its owner's prominence (the house is modest, on a middle-class city street) but for the robust size of its living room. Twenty people sit in a large circle, about half from Bangor, half from outlying counties. Muskie opens with a frank report that polls and editorial comment show a feeling that he's been away from Maine too much and out of touch with the state's problems. He makes it clear he doesn't think that's true, but the impression must be dealt with. He knows he has a particular problem, he adds, with young people who are not interested in achievements of his earlier days and who are not highly aware of his more recent ones. Muskie asks for frank statements of other perceived problems and any suggestions of what might be done in the coming year to overcome them. The ensuing discussion keeps bobbing up the name of Billy Cohen, his strong appeal among the young, independents, even some Democrats, partly because of his physical attractiveness and that of his personality, partly because of the renown he won during the Nixon impeachment proceedings.

A state legislator urges Muskie to demolish Cohen by publicizing bold positions, especially on the environment. People in this state feel strongly about the environment, he argues with high enthusiasm, and supporters will crawl out of the woodwork if they are given strong positions to support. (The Woodwork Theory of politics reappears in some form in every major election. In 1964 conservative Republicans were convinced that voters would "crawl out of the woodwork" if a bold candidate like Goldwater were nominated. Similarly, George McGovern was to have been elected in 1972 by the woodwork vote. The theory holds that normal arithmetic goes out the window and political reality goes down the drain under the influence of a magical chemical substance apparently found only in woodwork.) Others at the meeting gingerly express doubt. One woman says she's increasingly hearing working people and labor union members, particularly in the paper industry, which accounts for a third of the state's manufacturing and fully one fourth of its labor force, repeat a saying that "saving a person's job is more important than saving a tree." A young man jumps in quickly to add that the construction industry, especially the building trades unions, is inflamed over fear that environmental restrictions will halt expansion of industry, thus severely curtailing construction. Whether that interpretation is right or not, the young man says, is not the point at the moment; the point is that Senator Muskie is seen as Mr. Environment, therefore as Mr. Unemployment, and a lot of people are ready to forget about our Senator's great record as a friend of labor and give him the knife next year. So, the young man concludes, he's not sure Muskie ought to step out front raising the environment issue because it just may split traditional Democratic support in half. A woman adds that if some old Republican fuddydud were running against the Senator it would be different. But a lot of people who normally are Muskie people are teetering between him and Billy Cohen. Raising a divisive issue, she says, might push just enough people over to Cohen to give him the election. The environment issue—she shakes her head worriedly—"I just don't know."

When the subject finishes its circle of the room, Muskie comments that one of his great concerns is that his poll shows a disturbing softness of support within the ranks of labor. "I'm sure there is a good bit of feeling that I'm more concerned about trees than about jobs, and some developing distrust of me as a result." He says he thinks it is essential that he answer any questioner or any opponent clearly and boldly on his stance on both the environment and unemployment, particularly that he is not trying to protect the environment at the expense of employment. That conflict, he says, has been invented to confuse the environmental issue. Therefore this is probably not the year, he concludes reluctantly, to go out aggressively making speeches on an issue on which there is considerable confusion.

Later at night, as we speed down I-95 to Waterville, Clyde Mac-Donald tells Muskie that before he worked for him he was in frequent touch socially with Cohen at the university, where Cohen taught a course. Cohen once told Clyde that when he decided as a young Bangor lawyer to go into politics he made a calculated decision to do so as a Republican. The Democratic Party was so full of talent and the Republican Party so devoid of it that clearly the GOP presented the more attractive possibility of a quick rise to the top. Muskie nods, acknowledging Cohen's perfectly reasonable and craftsmanlike decision. The irony is exquisite. It is an exact reversal of what Ed Muskie perceived twenty-one years ago—a poverty among Maine Democrats and an unchallenged concentration of power among Republicans. Muskie's capture of the state capital began the tidal flow of talent to the Democrats, which Cohen now seeks to reverse. In ebbs and flows, every consolidated victory clearing the ground for its own defeat, that's the way political history moves; that's what Muskie's nod calmly, unresentfully acknowledges.

Waterville, Maine
Tuesday, August 26

In a changing of the guard, I am picked up this morning at the Waterville Holiday Inn not by Clyde MacDonald but by John Delehanty, young, tall, self-assured son of a Lewiston judge, keeper of Muskie's Waterville office, who will be leaving the Senator's employ in a week to enter law school. We collect the Senator at the home of Jack Gray, brother of Mrs. Muskie and advertising manager of Waterville's newspaper, and head for the small town of Richmond, south of Augusta, which has experienced a population upsurge and, under extremely resourceful home-grown leadership and planning, has become a model of controlled development and historic preservation. We sit through a long morning of briefing for state and federal officials (who have either financed the Richmond plan or will be asked to, or both) followed by a sightseeing walk through town, and are rewarded by a tasty buffet of Russian delicacies, garnished with a display of Russian folk dances and Russian music. The town was largely settled by wellborn refugees from the Russian Revolution, and Russians still comprise about a fifth of the town's 2,500 residents. A buxom dancer, carried away by the music, sweeps up her Senator in an invitation he can't refuse, and he acquits himself on the dance floor with an at-home zest.

At one-thirty we depart, again for Waterville. As we park in the business district Muskie points out to me the over-a-store office where he used to practice law, and the dress shop, just a couple of doors away, where, in his thirties, he spotted Jane Gray, who succeeded in committing the preoccupied young state legislator to marriage and a family.

His present office, sustained by a Senate allowance, is a suite of four rooms up a long flight of stairs in a building that's not quite dinky but by no stretch grand. The dominant personage is its office manager, bubbly, grandmotherly Marge Hutchinson who, I am surprised to learn, was Muskie's secretary way back in his days as governor, and mentioning this to Muskie, I further learn that she served him before that, across the street in his not too prosperous law office.

Muskie's schedule says "Phone calls, Waterville office—John Delehanty has list," which could be a schedule euphemism for taking a breather. But Muskie indeed places a few calls around the state asking several prominent citizens to join his campaign "advisory" committee. (Although the committee may never meet or advise, some of its members will represent political factions out to murder one another but joined in happy harmony behind their Senator.) From Muskie's side of the conversation, it's clear that every callee, whether judge or commissioner or party grandee emeritus, is flattered to be asked and accepts on the spot. After a few calls Muskie starts poking through drawers of his ancient bureaucratic desk, finding old political cartoons, campaign polls, scribbled phone numbers of merchants of local power. He pokes and muses and reminisces, just idling and chatting the afternoon away in a manner I did not think he knew how to do. After a while Marge and her two office assistants bring out a cake with lighted candles to mark John Delehanty's farewell—a little premature, but most happily done while the Senator's here. Muskie leans back in a simple chair at the big table where newsletters are usually folded and enveloped, now the party table. He is totally at ease and at home, unpressed by time, unbadgered by duty, unharassed by issues. It's as though he were sitting around of an empty afternoon in the law office across the street, waiting for a house closing or a will to walk in.

At five o'clock, back to the world; specifically to the Hilton Hotel at the Bangor Airport and a large, dressy cocktail party of the Maine Women's Political Caucus to celebrate the anniversary of women's suffrage. Muskie's six feet four towers over the room of mostly women, attracting small clusters of beaming admirers. When Governor James B. Longley, the insurance man who defeated both Democratic and Republican rivals, enters, the cluster that gathers around him is noticeably larger, the buzz perceptibly buzzier. The governor, acquiring a reputation as unpredictable and eccentric—his critics simply call him "a nut"—is wearing a button with his immensely provocative but quizzical campaign slogan. Against a green background, it whispers in thin white letters, "Think About It."

Muskie was asked to prepare remarks reminiscing about his start in politics and his climb to success, presumably as an encouragement to new talent and especially to women. Obediently, Muskie does the reminiscing, but without underlining any special lesson for women. He's seldom as strong with such generalities as he is with his own issues. His talk goes over mildly. As we walk out a side door of the hotel toward Delehanty's car, suddenly, in full vigor and cream blazer and blue-eyed splendor, appear Billy Cohen and a short, young, earnest, headed-for-important-things aide. Cohen offers a friendly hand and a guileless, almost sheepish smile. Muskie, in a mock growl, informs him, "I tore you to shreds up there." Cohen pshaws, "I doubt that you did."

Through the dusk, we begin a two-hour drive to Rumford, the paper-mill town of Muskie's birth, childhood, and young manhood, and on the way we're to stop at a restaurant in Skowhegan, the Candlelight, that serves a good vodka martini and steak. Muskie rides silently, grimly, as he often does after a speech or glad-hand gathering. I don't know whether it's John or I who makes some idle remark that includes the word "schedule." But whoever or whatever, it releases a thunderous flooding, like a huge cracked dam, just waiting, straining to split under the urging of one extra ripple.

"Do you think they have any conception of the miles they're making us do today?" he begins, with a tremble of voice, an anguish, a promise of rage to come that is out of proportion to his question. "They ought to go out on the road themselves. They don't know what it's like. These people are working me day and night. Don't they think I'm human? Don't they think I need a little rest? I've hardly had a day's vacation this whole recess. Do you think they stop for a moment to consider that I'm *sixty-one years old?*" He falls into silence, smoldering. John absorbs it in silence. I wait for more, which will come. Just who is the "they" in Washington who is the target of this rage? Then I realize it is no one "down there." It is that trim, athletic figure of his anticipated opponent, of Billy Cohen; those brilliantly blue eyes, that perfectly fitting, perfectly pressed cream blazer so creamy you could spoon it, the terrifying vigor and youth of a comer. All the legislative achievements in the world can't match that for pleasing the crowd. "They won't be satisfied that they've gotten everything out of me until they exhaust me, and I tell you it's going to make me emotionally and physically exhausted, and that can only lead to some kind of boner, some kind of slip-up, some kind of disaster of the kind that happened in Manchester." This is the only time I've heard him mention, unprompted, that day in New Hampshire in 1972 when tears supposedly welled up and, according to the political press, was the beginning of the end of what had seemed an easy drive for a sure presidential nomination.

The good martini and steak are settling, and eventually we arrive at the Madison Motor Inn, west of Rumford. It looks closed, but a woman and a young girl come running out of the darkened office. The elder one exclaims, "Mr. Muskie, I just wanted to say hello to you and to introduce you to my daughter. You remember me? You flunked me in history." Muskie laughs, asks her name, and says, "Oh yes. Sure enough."

It turns out that, while studying for his bar exam after graduation from law school, Muskie took work in Rumford as a substitute teacher for half a semester. After the woman gives us our keys I ask furtively if he was a good teacher. She whispers, "A good teacher, but *very* shy."

Rumford, Maine
Wednesday, August 27

The streets of Rumford's compact business district this summer morning are eerily empty and chilled by a crisp wind. As directed by the schedule, at eight-thirty we stroll into Razzano's, a lunch counter and restaurant on Congress Street, "for coffee and handshaking." A few old-timers in work clothes are at the counter, half a dozen men and women breakfasting at tables in their private early morning worlds. The apparition of their United States Senator ignites a wakefulness in a few faces; some, with steadfast Maine reserve, refuse to be stirred. The old-timers at the counter accept Muskie's big hand, a couple of the men deigning to banter with the public servant. One comments, "Good to see you back in the state again." A greeting or a dig? Muskie lets it pass. A waitress in blue with a short, pasta plumpness and the personality zing of hot peppers shrieks from behind the counter, "Mister Muskieeeeeeeee!" and dashes out, leaping up at him with a flying tackle, barely reaching his waist. He sort of hugs her back, patting her shoulder, pleased but confused by the high-spirited greeting. She breaks into an Italianesque dance. Muskie sits down for coffee with three men who bottle and sell the pure water of a nearby "moontide spring," so called because its water seems to gush best at full moon. Unhurriedly they talk about business—theirs, the town's—and Muskie is in his element, far more so than with the glad-handing and banter.

When we emerge into the sun a little after nine, the breeze has relaxed, and the nose is dramatically informed that the town's big industry is a paper mill. The air is thick and syrupy with the gluey breath of pulpwood cooking, the pungency of prosperity, the taste of jobs, as pleasing a waft to the paper worker as the rusty smoke of Gary, Indiana, is to the wage earner in steel. Only the stranger in town misses the beauty of it.

We cross the empty street, go down a block or so, and climb a rickety flight to the radio studio of WRUM where news director Ken Ellis, escorting the Senator to his cramped interview booth, remarks, "Well, I see what you fellows mainly seem to be doing is raising your own pay and taking vacations." I'm ready to appreciate his low-key smile, the poke of elbow in the Senator's rib. Neither is there. His comment is just Maine matter-of-fact.

We proceed to the sprawling plant of the Oxford Paper Company. What the Hershey Company is to Hershey, Pennsylvania, what gambling is to Las Vegas, what the Mississippi is to New Orleans, the Oxford Paper Company is to Rumford, Maine. For the people of Rumford, "the Oxford" is the source of cash flow and beef stew and warm mackinaws and gas for the car and Christmas for the kids and hope for the future. It is the fount of the sweet stink, of the filth flowing down the once pristine Androscoggin River. The Oxford *is* Rumford.

We are here ostensibly to see the company's expensive new

clarifiers, whatever they are, but we are also here for Muskie to be seen by the hundreds of papermakers he passes, nods at, shakes hands with, as we climb ladders, tread catwalks, circle down spiral back stairs from department to department, past the ear-crushing chipper that gnashes huge logs into splinters in three seconds; past the heat of five-story-high vats that boil the natural glues out of the huge stew of chips; past elephantine tubs that soak the remains into pulp; past machine after machine that presses the goop of pulp progressively into paper, then into fine paper, then into glossy enamel paper. At the enameling machine, a worker proudly informs me that these rolls form the entire paper supply of the *National Geographic* and of the centerfolds of *Playboy*. "This paper is what makes those *Playboy* pictures look so good." I look for his wink, his wry grin. Not there. Just matter-of-fact Maine.

Finally, outside, the clarifiers. They are not, as I assumed, devices for improving the paper. They are for improving the Androscoggin River: tremendous round, concrete pools with awesome machinery for cleansing the glues and slimes from the factory's water before it is returned to the river. One price of doing this, a company official tells us, is that some gunk that previously flowed down the river in one form is now flung into the air in another but far less of it. The other price, of course, is that the clarifiers for this one plant cost millions. Those millions multiplied by the dozens upon dozens of paper plants across America total up to the cost of reducing—not eliminating—pollution in only one filth-producing industry out of many.

The officials escort us out of town, back to the Madison Motor Inn, not to our rooms but to theirs. The company keeps an apartment of rooms plus a conference room and large living room, bar, and kitchen. We have cocktails and a catered lunch of fried chicken, shrimp, scallops, hearts of palm and marinated artichokes, and a choice of four desserts. An immense picture window grandly displays the Androscoggin flowing virtually beneath our luncheon table. The paper officials say pridefully how good it is to see the tranquil river almost clean again, that before long even the fish may be back.

"So it can be done," Muskie comments.

"Sure it can," says an Oxford man. "It's just that nobody can do it voluntarily or alone. When a law requires us *and* our competitors to do it, too, sure it can be done."

Which, of course, means the cost turns up in another form, as higher prices. If every paper plant—times millions of dollars—has to do it, no wonder the cost of newspapers, of books, of the operation of every business that consumes quantities of paper, is up. Same for autos with catalytic converters. Same for power plants with scrubbers. Et cetera, et cetera. All is not pure inflation that goes by that name. Some rising costs (about which we complain) are the costs of reducing civilization's garbage (about which we also complain). Put another way, we can avoid the cost, indeed avoid pollution, by getting rid of civilization.

The Oxford man remarks that, while cleaning of water seems to be moving along nicely, the Clean Air Act has industries in Maine worried, and even more so, the building trades unions, "because of some of the threats contained in that working paper of the House committee."

"What House committee? What working paper?" Muskie asks, puzzled.

"I'm not sure, but I gather that's what'll be coming up at your meeting with labor people tomorrow."

That's even more puzzling, because a "meeting" tomorrow afternoon with building trades union officials is just to be an informal handshaking and general chat session. Muskie shrugs away his puzzlement.

His sister, Lucy Paradis, with facial features like Muskie's, who can't prevent a gentle warmth from slipping through her armor of shyness, has been a silent guest at our luncheon. And now John Delehanty drives brother and sister, accompanied by me, on a ritual visit up a great hill north of the city to the cemetery where their mother two years ago was buried next to their long-dead father. Inspecting the relatively fresh grave's details in the manner of an absentee owner of property, Muskie, satisfied, suddenly says to his sister, "Well—" They both kneel on the grass, Muskie's hands folded tightly before him, head bowed reverently, privately. After a time he and Lucy cross themselves, rise, and are ready to go.

As we descend the hill through back roads, Muskie says, "Oh, I've got to stop by to see Charlie Fontaine. Saw his brother this morning at Razzano's and he said I ought to drop by Charlie's, and I said I would." In Maine, if you say you will, you do. Muskie directs John to a big old house where Charlie Fontaine runs a country eating place at a crossroads that appears barely able to sustain one, and the restaurant appears barely sustained. Muskie goes in. Soon he emerges, his promise kept. Looking buoyant, he says earnestly, "Charlie says not to worry, that I have no problem next year." He adds significantly to Lucy, "He's a Republican, you know."

The reference to Republicans reminds Lucy to tell of her run-in with city hall. At each end of town on U.S. 2 is a sign saying, "Welcome to Rumford, Hometown of Senator Edmund S. Muskie." The sign on the east end had grown shabby and Lucy called the selectman, who doubles as city manager, to urge that the sign be either repainted or removed. "He's a Republican, too," says Lucy, "and he said, 'We'll bring it up at the next selectmen's meeting.'" Soon after the next meeting she ran into the man who does the town's sign painting and he said, "They told me to paint the sign, so I'm doing it, but they said they didn't know where the money was going to come from, whether it was going to be local or federal."

Muskie wants to see the sign, so we head for the east end of town. He directs John to swing the car around so he can photograph it. Lucy asks, "Why not get out and take it right?" "No, I'm not going to be seen taking a picture of the damned thing. I'll take it from the car." I suggest that no one driving by would believe it's he taking it, but the town would earn ecstatic compliments for having put up such a lifelike statue of its most prominent citizen. Unbudging, Muskie photographs the sign from inside the protective cover of the automobile.

Dropping Lucy at her home, we head for Livermore Falls, a forty-five-minute drive south, for what the schedule lists as "Labor Reception—Gary Cook Residence." The residence, fronting on the main highway, is a plain house next to an auto body shop and its parking lot of hopeless wrecks. An addition to the rear of the dwelling is wrapped in uncovered tarpaper. The back yard, where the party is gathered, contains a prefab swimming pool, beach chairs, and a table laden with spiked punch, six-packs of beer, and bowls of Fritos. As we enter, a half dozen men in sport shirts and T-shirts introduce us to their wives, small children shyly watching. "I've always wanted to meet you," one wife fawns. "I've seen you on television." The men are carefully unimpressed. Introductions completed, the women retreat with their children to a picnic table, leaving the men to gather in a semicircle of beach chairs around the Senator. Jim Case, who has arrived from Washington to take the baton from John Delehanty, joins us. Talk, at first aimless, heats up upon drifting to the subject of Farmers Home Administration (rural land-and-building) loans, the way some people get them, and others, equally qualified, don't. Muskie directs Jim, "We've been hearing this before and we've *got* to look into this." Then a fellow named George in a yellow polo shirt leans intently toward the Senator and, getting down to business, says:

"We know that among labor people there's a lot of controversy about pollution, and we want you to know that we're your friends. We may not agree on everything but we're your friends, and we don't want that meeting on pollution tomorrow to spring any surprises on you."

That's the second reference to it today. Muskie quickly asks, "What meeting on pollution tomorrow?"

Surprised, George says, "The meeting tomorrow at the building trades headquarters at Augusta."

"That's not about pollution," Muskie snaps.

Puzzled, George says, "Well, that's where they're going to bring in the doctor and his report, and we didn't want you to be surprised. A letter went out to several unions and they're going to bring out the doctor to jump on your ninety-page staff report."

"*What* staff report?"

"Your staff report."

"I heard something this morning about some House staff report."

"No, your staff report."

"*My* staff report?"

"I have all that," Jim Case says quietly, handing Muskie a sheaf of photocopies covered by a photocopied letter on a law firm's stationery.

Muskie riffles through it, annoyed, and declares, "I never heard of any of this."

A fellow in a red baseball cap demands, "It's your staff, isn't it?"

"This thing says it's a summary of Staff Working Print No. 3, August 8. Whose summary? What working print? I haven't seen any such working print. I haven't been in Washington or been in touch with my committee staff since August 1. I don't know anything about this."

The fellow in the red baseball cap, not as reassuring of friendship with Muskie as the fellow in the yellow polo shirt, repeats insistently, "It's your staff, isn't it?"

"I can't be responsible for anything I haven't seen or approved. Part of what a staff does—if this was done by my staff—is to present alternatives, present options. Until I look at it, I don't know what this is about."

Red Baseball Cap looks Muskie hard in the eye. "How can you say you're not responsible for it? It's your staff, isn't it?"

Agitated, Muskie rises to go, saying he'll have to find out about this. Yellow Polo Shirt assures him, "We're your friends and we didn't want them to spring any surprises on you tomorrow."

In the car returning to Rumford, Muskie looks again at the lawyer's letter and "summary." It is addressed to Harold G. Loring, mayor of Portland, a former bricklayer and mason who rose in politics from the construction trades unions. The letter indicates that identical ones were sent to seven labor leaders. The signer is Daniel E. Boxer. A labor lawyer? Not exactly. The firm of Pierce, Atwood, Scribner, Allen & McKusick, in which Boxer is the environmental specialist, is Maine's largest law office, representing virtually every paper manufacturer and power company in the state. Boxer's letter says:

Dear Harold:

As promised, I enclose a summary of portions of the latest draft of the proposed amendments to the Clean Air Act. The summary contains some editorializing by me in places where I think comment is worthwhile. . . . Dr. Mahoney is busily preparing his report covering the effects of the amendments on the State. I know he is running into some time problems because of the computer modeling necessary to make his predictions, and probably the report will be made available to everybody on the 28th.

Very truly yours,

Dan

Why is Maine's largest corporation law firm lavishing expensive computer studies and high-priced legal analyses on a collection of rough, tough, gruff labor leaders—for free?

On the drive back to Rumford Muskie scorches Jim Case with

angry conjecture over what the staff of his subcommittee is trying to do to him. Did someone leak a printed copy of the working paper that the subcommittee would not see until after Labor Day? Is it conceivable that it was officially released? His anxiety explodes in a stream of accusatory questions:

"Do they realize what they're dealing with? Do they realize we're going into an election year, that I'm fighting for survival down here? Do they realize that powerful forces, the most powerful forces in the country, are lined up to destroy this bill, and destroy me if they can?"

After a smoldering pause, he instructs Jim: "Get Leon on the phone the minute we get back. Wherever he is. Find out what's going on."

What's going on, we learn minutes after settling into our rooms, is that Leon simply gave a copy of the printed working paper to an industry lobbyist because he was asked for one. He asserts this to Jim with no apology. Muskie's subcommittee led the Public Works Committee, indeed the entire Senate, in a policy of open markups, open information, open documents. The staff has observed a policy—as it did in this case—of not going out of its way to release and circulate documents in the working stage, but furnishing them upon specific request.

Muskie clamps his jaw glumly on getting this word from Jim. Leon is not at fault. The discomfiture Muskie is sure to feel tomorrow is a price he'll have to pay for open government, and he'll have to defend himself the best he can.

We head for dinner at the home of his sister, Irene Chaisson, the oldest of six in the Muskie family, Edmund being the second-born. We met Irene briefly this morning at Oxford Paper, where she works in the research lab. A widow and mother of grown children, she is a vigorous, trim, light-haired woman who looks younger than her Senator brother. She lives alone next door to the house where she and all her brothers and sisters grew up.

I mix vodka martinis for Muskie and me, and Lucy Paradis arrives with her son of twenty-two who is about to start teaching school in a nearby town. Lucy's husband Henry, a contractor of small construction projects, is in a hospital for surgery. The six of us, including Jim Case, encircle the kitchen table for a dinner of pot roast, a family favorite, and vegetables all grown in Irene's garden. The family talk is lively, yet somehow not relaxed. The sisters ask their renowned brother no questions about the election, politics, national affairs, Washington, or the Washington personalities who are the daily routine of his life, and he volunteers nothing touching on his public life. The conversation conveys the impression that the two sisters do not think a great deal beyond their private lives and cannot cope with the worldliness and fame of their brother. That impression, however, is wrong. Before the evening is out I am to learn that Lucy, for example, was an outstandingly bright student, the salutatorian of her graduating class, later became moderately involved in politics and was elected to the city's school board.

It seems a family trait, perhaps an aspect of Maine reticence, to carry Edmund's accomplishments lightly, almost to the point of ignoring them. When Muskie was Humphrey's vice-presidential candidate in 1968, Muskie's mother, then almost eighty, was out sweeping her porch when a reporter asked patronizingly if she planned to vote for her son. She shrugged and snapped, "I guess, unless someone better comes along." But it's not just diffidence that suppresses dinner talk about Muskie the celebrity. There's some feeling in the family, even as there is among some of his constituents, that he's grown out of their reach. Lucy mentions some occupational accomplishment of one of their nephews. Muskie says, "Nobody told me that." Lucy replies, "I didn't think you were interested." But he is already saying something else, and Lucy, fearing her comment has been lost, repeats it a mite more forcibly: "I didn't think you were *interested.*"

After dinner, when talk turns to the house next door (which is unoccupied; it's been purchased by a foundation formed by a group of civic leaders as a possible historical site) and to early family history, Irene goes upstairs and brings down an armload of scrapbooks and envelopes. Muskie becomes absorbed in newspaper clippings of his election as president of his high school student council, being named valedictorian, winning debating prizes, earning a law degree at Cornell, his election as state representative, and finally, proclaimed in page-one headlines, his stunning victory as governor. We look at photographs of his immigrant father and his mother. I search the photos for character traits, but old photographs posed in old neighborhood photo studios don't show character traits; they show men in mustaches holding derby hats, and ladies seated demurely, wearing their Sunday best. From an envelope Irene draws a bill of sale, amounting to something like $254.17, that Father Muskie plunked down the week before his wedding day in a single store for a houseful of furniture. In another store—and all listed on another single bill of sale—he bought all their dishes and utensils. Every one of those articles, Irene tells me, is still in the house next door and was used until the day their mother died.

I ask Muskie how all these early bits and pieces look to him now. Without lifting his absorbed eyes from the scrapbook, he responds, "Very fascinating, and just a bit depressing." He does not amplify.

After a while he asks matter-of-factly, as though part of a ritual, "Well, shall we go next door?" Irene fetches a key and, through a dark porch, we make our way into what is a near twin of Irene's house. A small front parlor and dining room are sedate with turn-of-the-century furniture, the best to be found on the main street of turn-of-the-century Rumford. A gaudy pillow on the stuffed couch is embroidered, "Muskie," celebrating the politician in the family, not the patriarch. Upstairs the master bedroom was not the parents' room but the Muskie girls'. Three sisters sharing it needed the largest. A smaller room with a double bed was for the parents. The smallest—with a double bed—was occupied, during all their childhood and adolescence, by Ed and his younger brother Eugene, now a steelworker in California. Ed and Eugene were as dissimilar as brothers can be; Eugene a funster and good chum, Ed shy, solemn, studious. Mother Muskie basked in Eugene's sunniness, often admitting she really didn't understand Ed, who would sometimes sit silently for hours on a window sill, looking out, as today he mutely gazes from cars and airplanes. But Father Muskie, impatient with time-wasting tomfoolery, would lecture Eugene, "Be like Ed! Be like Ed!" And Eugene would retort rebelliously, "I don't want to be like Ed. I want to drink beer."

Muskie is not the tour guide through all this but more the tourist, almost wordless, peering at this and that. Not with nostalgia but with curiosity. A kind of puzzlement.

Rumford, Maine
Thursday, August 28

It's a sunny morning and I am first to arrive in the motor inn dining room, soon followed by Muskie. Jim is delayed, raising Leon Billings on the phone again with added questions. The visit last night to a United States Senator's beginnings in the cramped home of an immigrant tailor is still on my mind. Muskie's easy acceptance of my first question is a clue that he's not finished with it either.

Did his parents stir ambition in their son in some unusual way? Did they communicate something special?

"Well, certainly my father— My mother was too busy with all the things women had to do in those days, the cooking and sewing and housekeeping. My father would talk *to* us, and it was very good talk. But he didn't have the knack for reaching inside us, or even asking."

Was he an intellectual man, or perhaps a moralist?

"He'd talk a lot about his boyhood and his parents, and in that way communicate values that he considered important. We'd get involved with other kids throwing baseballs or trespassing on a neighbor's property, and he would talk to us a lot—about Mr. Hemingway, oh, Mr. Hemingway, that we've got to respect Mr. Hemingway's rights. And when we did those things my father wouldn't defend us. He'd identify with and defend some of those ogres, those mean old men. He'd take their side. He was very good at that, but he didn't have a way of really digging inside of us."

"Any way of accounting for your life coming out so differently than the others in your family?"

"I think—I was the only one sent to college, and I think that's part of it. I think college made an awful difference for me. Of course, Lucy's the only one who sought to achieve excellence in high school

as I did. That was important to her as it was to me. I think Lucy
could have done a great deal with an education. And the others
could have."

"Do you think your father envisioned you as a public man?"

"He didn't push me in this direction at all. He'd talk about politics
at home, and a lot in his shop with his customers. I worked in his
shop."

That direction lights no fires. Muskie falls into silence, gnawing
over something, then says:

"You see, my big drive was to overcome shyness. I can remember
going back—I can remember the first time I was given a birthday
party. I wasn't more than four years old. I was so shy I—I wouldn't
stay in the same room with the guests. I took my ice cream and went
into another room to eat it. At four years old. I felt somewhat dominated, I think, by others who were outgoing. Defensive toward them,
very sensitive. I remember being sensitive about being called a
'Polack.' Sure, in those days French kids were called 'Frogs' and Italian kids 'Wops,' but when you're called something yourself, it hurts.
Something stays. It's there. So there was that. And there was the fact
that so many of the boys, all my friends in a sense, were outgoing
and extrovertish. I wasn't. I was withdrawn."

"Were you a big kid?"

"No, I was not tall and I was very skinny. So I wasn't strong physically. And then I did like books and studies, and that sort of set me
apart. I just got things very quickly. In the first Latin class I ever
went to we were given a reading assignment. I read it immediately.
So I could pick up things very quickly, and I suspect that sort of set
me apart from the others. I could memorize a poem, or a bunch of
facts, in no time at all.

"You know, I used to answer these ads of how to become a public
speaker. I'd write and they'd send me literature. Of course I never
did anything about it because I didn't have money to enroll and I
never talked to my father about it. But the desire was there. Because
I didn't like being shy. I wanted to be—I wanted to have the capacity of projecting myself, being myself, holding up my head, holding
up my end of things. I knew I had it in me. I wanted to be one of
these outgoing guys. They accepted the world so much more easily.
Or so it appeared. I wanted to be recognized, to let people know,
you know, what I could do. That I was someone who had thoughts,

someone of substance. Yet I never dared follow those ads through. It was my junior year in high school, I think, when the debating coach began to pursue me to try out debating. I just kept away from her for weeks. And she finally caught up with me, and I went through real agony, forcing myself to get up and make a speech. But I was determined to do it, just determined to master it now that I'd started. I just wanted to beat shyness to death.

"I just had this drive for achievement, you know, never satisfied. I'd break one barrier and I had to go to the next one. I don't know when I decided that I was, by God, going to be valedictorian of my class. I think it must have been when I was ten, eleven years old. I wanted, by God, to be class president, which I never communicated to anybody. I never made class president, but I made president of the Student Council. I tried out for athletics but was too weak physically. All just to defeat shyness. I just had to keep proving and proving."

"And I suppose the Hollywood movie image of lawyers pleading histrionically before juries led you into law?"

"Oh no. That was accidental, law. When I graduated from Bates, I was offered a scholarship to go to Cornell Law School, and so I went. It wasn't because I had had law as a goal. I didn't find law the kind of fulfillment I was really looking for, although I thought I did at the time, and I think I had a potential for being a very good lawyer. But I suppose the same thing that made me want to become class president eventually drew me into politics."

"At what point did you discover that your speaking. ability, your debating ability, had something special?"

"I guess in the legislature. Of course the law had helped and school debating experience, too. In the legislature I did my homework and I was beginning to learn that I had a capacity to influence others that people thought was unusual at that time, even when I was a freshman legislator. The other side recognized it. The third house —the lobbyists—recognized it and the press recognized it. So I began to notice that I had that effect on people. Apparently I'm good at getting to the heart of a question in simple terms. Fritz Hollings, who sits just a couple of seats from me, said to me the other day, 'Goddamnit, Ed, you've got the best goddamned way of wrapping up an argument I ever heard.' He's a little awed by it. And so I know I have it. But in social ways I'm as shy as I ever was. In politics, in my work, I'm sure of myself. And in social ways I'm not.

"So that quality worked in the legislature. Then in the first campaign for governor I began to catch fire. The first time was up in Rangeley, Maine. I've forgotten why, or what I was talking about. But that night in Rangeley, Maine, the campaign lifted off the ground. And I began to practice at it and do it more and more. By the end of the campaign it wasn't any longer that 'He's got intelligence' or 'He's a nice guy' but there was an emotional quality about it. So I can make a speech either way now."

"Before you walk into a room, do you know much beyond your opening remarks?"

"No. Just the subject. As a matter of fact, I can do it better that way than sitting down to write a speech. It used to be the reverse, but now I find I have an awful hard time writing a speech. If you really want to achieve the ultimate—the fellow who can stand out there in front of a crowd and be sure of himself—it's got to come extemporaneously. That means you've got to have a damned good connection between this and this." He jabs his forehead and his mouth.

"Now that you have that confidence, do personal relationships go more easily? Let's say, with Phil Hart, or Tom Eagleton, or Gene McCarthy who used to sit next to you? Does the boyhood shyness still hold you back?"

"Well, Phil Hart and I, you know, we can communicate without ever talking. And I'm more comfortable that way. When we do talk, we might talk about the Senate or about a piece of legislation. But the kind of intimate talk that—well, there the shyness still comes in. I can't dig into, for instance, his personal life or his feelings. He's dying of cancer, you know. It would be wrong to do it, anyway. But I couldn't do it. In large part, because I'm—I find it very hard to talk the language of love and affection. I feel it. And I can demonstrate it. But I can't talk about it. I just can't."

"The life of a Senator certainly takes a man away from his family. What has been the impact on yours?"

"Well, I don't know. To answer your question, you'd have to be able to say how things would be different if things were different. That's all speculative. I have a feeling that maybe we've overprotected our kids, which you would think would be the reverse. You would think that maybe they'd have been neglected, allowed to run loose and so on. But I get an idea they've been overprotected. In Washington, my wife finds herself constantly driving kids, including Ned, our youngest son, to a dance somewhere, and no other parents of kids involved will do it. Then they call up and ask her to come after them, and she's the only one who will do it. So in a sense, maybe because of some sensitivity that maybe we're neglecting the kids, she'll go overboard to mother them, to give them, well, services, when they'd really be better off using public transportation and insisting that their friends occasionally get someone to do the driving. But no, she'll fill in the breach. Hell, last year she had the most miserable year, on the road all day long taking those pimply kids here, taking them there. It's a terrible kind of thing to do to a woman. She had no life of her own at all.

"So I don't think we've neglected the kids. But I think that what we've not had, that we should have had a lot more of, was a kind of communication and talk, companionship within the family. I think that's been sacrificed. Whether it's been sacrificed to a greater extent than it is in families that are busy for other business or professional reasons I don't know. But I feel the lack of that. And I feel my kids would have benefited from it. All of them, in one way or another, reveal problems or concerns that might not be there if we'd had more of that. And of course if you haven't had it, it becomes more difficult to communicate as they grow older. Because you haven't established a common ground or common interests, and it gets more and more difficult to communicate in an intimate kind of sense. Sure, there are a lot of things you can talk about, but I'm talking about revealing those inner forces that create frustration for kids, or problems that give them hangups. It's hard to get people to talk about those things to each other. And if you haven't established a habit of doing so with your parents when you're young, it's awfully hard to do it later."

At 27 Randall Street, Augusta, in a neighborhood of blue-collar family homes and ma and pa stores, the headquarters of the Building Trades Council is a functional box of a building, a big meeting hall with no visible offices. For today's gathering of union officials with their Senator, tables and chairs are arranged in a huge, square-cornered U, so huge that the most innocent exchange invites long-distance shouting. Muskie, wary, unsmiling, is given the folding chair of honor, at the head of the U, equidistant from the wings. Jim Case always the invisible man, sits in the last chair of the head table, as distant from attention as he can get, yet close enough to the Senator to furnish a piece of paper at the flick of his boss's eye. Conversation starts informally, about the job situation in Maine, hassles with employers over the Occupational Safety and Health Act, Farmers Home Administration loan inequities ("Yes, we talked about that yesterday with some of your people and we're going to look into it"), the status of the common-site picketing bill.

Then Muskie decides to crack the egg: "I understand that some of you are concerned about the Clean Air Act, and I want to discuss any aspect of it that you want, and as extensively as you want. Last night for the first time I saw a copy of a letter—"

Mayor Loring interrupts to suggest that "this is probably as good a time as any to bring in the doctor and Dan Boxer, who we locked in a room somewhere around here until we finished our other business. You want to go get them, fellas?"

The "doctor," presumably a holder of a Ph.D., is James R. Mahoney of an independent firm in Concord, Maine, called Environmental Research & Technology, Inc. As Boxer and a pair of Mahoney's staff people take seats along the side, Mahoney distributes copies of a bound report, about fifty pages, much of it inscrutable mathematics, and eight two-page maps, entitled "ERT Document No. P-1992, Proposed Clean Air Act Amendments: Implications of Nondeterioration Rules on Maine." The cover is dated August 28, 1975—today! It must be still quivering from the presses.

"At this point, no law has been written," Muskie goes on, ignoring the newcomers. When Mahoney works his way around the table to Muskie, handing him a copy, Muskie accepts it absent-mindedly and keeps talking. "No proposed law has been introduced. The committee hasn't adopted any positions." (That statement startles me.) "What we've been doing since the first of the year is discussing the problem: what, if anything, can we do to protect the relatively clean air areas of the country, like Maine, from becoming as dirty as Chicago or New York or Los Angeles? One option open to us is not to write a new law at all. We can leave it to the courts to decide what, if anything, should be done. That idea doesn't seem to please anybody. Everyone concerned would like to have a little more in the way of guidelines, standards, targets, rather than leave it to the courts. That's the only reason we're bothering with it at all. Otherwise we wouldn't even think of writing a law to cover that difficult subject.

"Since we are in the middle of it, we suggested to the staff before we left Washington on August 1 that they put together a working paper for discussion purposes, so that when the committee comes back we can begin to go through the issues, discuss them, debate them, try to resolve them. That's where the process is at this moment.

"Last night I got a copy of a letter from Daniel Boxer enclosing a summary of portions of the Clean Air Act of 1975. There is *no such act!* Throughout, the summary refers to *the Act*—'the *Act* specifies,' and so on. I have no way of knowing if it's an accurate summary of the staff working paper, because I haven't seen the staff working paper. The summary refers to a *fait accompli*—something that's been passed, that's now a law, that now imposes certain obligations. In that sense, the summary is *misleading*." Hurling that charged courtroom word, he glares directly at Boxer. "And I think it's a little unfortunate that you should be conducting your testimony, your discussion, on that kind of assumption. Because what we tried to do in Washington is open up the process of writing legislation, and let the public and the press sit in on every session we've had. For eight weeks. Open discussion of all the issues. To have that working paper dealt with as though it were the law of the land for the purpose of shooting holes in it I think is a very bad start for discussing the issues. If you understand that, the discussion can be useful."

Boxer is surprised—and alerted—by the ferocity of this assault from an adversary who far outweighs him, a corporation mouthpiece, in trust and good standing with this jury of labor men. Switching on the tone of a confident young prosecutor against Clarence Darrow, Boxer declares, "We're talking about something that *could* happen. I was in Washington attending one of your work sessions. I saw your committee take a vote on some important issues in this draft."

Muskie and Boxer are dueling, not over the evironment but over one another's credibility. Perfectly true, "the *committee* hasn't adopted any positions," as Muskie says. But the Environmental Pollution Subcommittee has. What Boxer saw on his visit to Washington was the *sub*committee "take a vote on some important issues." Boxer, busy defending the honesty of his summary, has missed that technicality slipped across by Muskie. The subcommittee *has* approved, although tentatively and only in broad outline, an approach to the difficult issue of non-degradation (or non-deterioration) of ambient air, restricting expansion of industry that would threaten air quality, even in regions where air quality is higher than the minima set by law. Upon taking votes just before recess, the subcommittee instructed Billings and the staff to translate those broad principles into working detail, a first stab at getting reaction to the approach from lobbyists and the "public." That instruction was what led to Staff Working Print No. 3. But by exaggerating the significance of the working paper, Boxer has brought down on himself the full force of the Senator's attack to combat his audacity in organizing these labor union leaders, Muskie's natural constituency, for this surprise confrontation. Furthermore, Muskie, a relative expert on the environment, needs time, staff assistance, and a computer analysis of his own to evaluate the complex study just handed him by Mahoney. Distribution of the imposing book to these union officials, who have neither the training nor the computers to evaluate it, is pure grandstanding that Muskie further resents. So he relies for the moment on indignant denials that the "committee" has done what the subcommittee indeed largely has done, and on going for Boxer's credibility.

"Mr. Boxer," repeats Muskie, leaning forward, lips stretching at one side, voice turning gravelly, his tromping-on-Montoya tone, "you say here 'the Act specified.' However, there *is no act*. You're lawyer enough, and experienced enough in legislation by your own statement, to know that. You should have said clearly what you have just said—that is, anything is possible. Of course this *could* happen. The world could end tomorrow. But I don't expect it to. You people on the outside who are impacted by legislation have complained for years that these markup sessions are closed, that what goes on is something you don't know until we finally report a bill, and that then you have to react to it. Now because we've let you in on the process you abuse it in my judgment based wholly on my reading of your summary. That is not constructive. Right here, your title says, 'Summary of Portions of the Clean Air Act Amendment of 1975.'"

"But right underneath that title," protests Boxer, "I say, 'Staff Working Print No. 3.' I was asked to put together a summary and—"

"Why didn't you say, 'Summary of Portions of Staff Working Print'? There are no Clean Air Act amendments that had the endorsement of a single member of that committee. And I think you know that. You could have made that clear in all the rest of the rhetoric in these pages that follow. Now we've been trying to be candid and direct and open with industry, with environmentalists, and with the public. And I consider this an abuse of that openness."

"I'm sorry if that is the impression that you got. I did say that it was a summary of the staff working print and anybody who—"

"You did *not* clearly indicate that what we're talking about is a working paper that no member of the committee has seen. You couldn't convince any reasonable person that that's the case."

"I disagree. I will finally say that—"

"You *disagree?* You think that that does clearly indicate what this is?"

"Yes."

"What is it?"

"It is a working print from which you—"

"A working print of *what?* A working print of *what?*"

"Of proposed language for you to look at."

"Does this say that?"

"Everybody who got this knew that this wasn't—Anybody who got this heard us talk a few weeks ago."

"Well, I got it, and I didn't hear you talk two weeks ago."

"It wasn't addressed to you or a copy sent to you. It was addressed to people who know the context it was written in."

"In other words, you wanted a few people to get an understanding of that working paper that I didn't have."

"I didn't give it to you. The whole purpose—"

"Oh, you mean that this should have been kept secret from me? Was it classified? Was it classified? Were they told not to distribute it?"

"I'm sure that they weren't."

"Are you offended that this got into my hands?"

"I'm not offended by that. But I am offended by the implication that I have been dishonest when the people that I was asked to give the summary to knew that we were talking about legislation that was not yet enacted but that was being heavily considered in Washington."

Mayor Loring, apparently not distracted by the diversionary attack on his lawyer guest, interjects, "Dan, let me ask you this right now. Is Professor Mahoney's presentation, that he's going to give us this afternoon, in reference to the same working paper?"

"Yes."

"A working paper that I haven't seen yet," growls Muskie.

"We're here," calls out one of the labor leaders, impatient with Muskie's continued focus on Boxer's letter and summary, "because we're concerned that this kind of thing is going on, being planned, being considered and well could be proposed. It may not be accepted. We don't know that. But we are concerned with certain things that are being done in Washington. Isn't that why we're here?"

"Of course that's why we're here," Muskie concedes. "But are you suggesting—"

"Well then, what's so wrong about the whole setup? Let's forget that summary thing as far as I'm concerned."

"That's fine with me. I'm perfectly willing to do that, perfectly willing to do that. But I'm not going to come in here under a misunderstanding and have a snow job done on me. You and I have been friends for a long time, and we're going to continue to be as we have been, because we've been frank with one another. The first time I heard that this subject was coming up today was yesterday in a luncheon with company representatives—with *company* representatives." His eyes swiftly scan the group to see if that sank in. "I said, 'That can't possibly be so. I'm meeting with the building trades about common-site picketing, about OSHA, and some other issues. I don't know anything about the Clean Air Act being brought up.'"

"I think these people would agree," re-enters Boxer, "that I never pulled anything on anybody. And I don't think we ought to go on with this. And I think you're the judge of what's been said here and it's not anybody's intention to require you to defend yourself or to debate anything, but to make a presentation which was not allowed to be made in Washington."

Boxer's inopportune re-entry provides the perfect moment for Muskie to drop the cleaver, an attempt to split the company lawyer from his labor "clients":

"You're trying to alarm these people, because what's involved here is employment. Jobs. Construction, development, growth. And that's what they're concerned about." Muskie has neatly divided his audience into *you* and *they*. "You've made your interpretations on behalf of your client, the International Paper Company, and you've come

here with that interpretation. They've got a right to get the other side
of it. Now you go ahead, Dr. Mahoney, and I'll stay here as long as
anybody wants to talk."

Mahoney unveils charts and labors through a long, dry, technical
exposition of how, according to his firm's interpretation of the working paper, Maine would be restricted against new construction of
plants, shopping centers, the kinds of developments that are direct
bread and butter for construction union members, long-term providers of new jobs for labor in general.

For the first time Muskie deigns to open the cover of Mahoney's
report, glancing at the pages cursorily. A notation acknowledges that
the report was prepared "under the sponsorship of the American
Paper Institute," the trade association of large paper companies.
That helps explain why Oxford Paper officials were so up to date
yesterday on what was to take place at a "labor" meeting today. The
episode is notably consistent with a feature article of a few days ago,
August 5, on page one of the *Wall Street Journal,* headed

Business Blitz—Aided By Lobbyists, Corporations Avert "Disaster" In Congress

Limousines and Grass Roots

The article describes an unexpectedly successful year that major
corporation lobbyists have had in influencing a labor-minded Democratic Congress. Their newly discovered formula is to de-emphasize
lobbying in Washington and to step up pressure at home. A local
banker or plant manager, laying out a case to a Congressman who is
visiting his home district, is more effective than a Capitol Hill lobbyist who can seldom get past a member's staff. But it is even more
effective for big business to *launder its lobbying* through the grass-
roots pressure of labor unions. And the way to enlist organized labor
to lobby for big business is to frame every business issue as an issue
of saving jobs or creating new jobs.

"Jobs, that's the No. 1 issue on the Hill today," the article
bluntly quotes William G. Whyte,[1] Washington vice-president and

---

[1] Whyte is soon to be on page one again, making the embarrassing admission
during the presidential election campaign of 1976 that he was host "several
times" to former House Minority Leader Gerald R. Ford for expense-paid
golfing weekends.

chief lobbyist of U. S. Steel. "The more we can relate our needs to providing jobs, the more we can have some success."

Mahoney's disquisition is long enough and dry enough to permit Mayor Loring to gather a few fence-mending thoughts, and for Muskie to mentally rehearse a statement on the real issue of the meeting: the impact of the Clean Air Act on jobs. Small as this meeting may be, it is of critical importance to his re-election that Muskie leave here with the confidence of these labor leaders. If the Clean Air Act is to be an albatross rather than an asset, Muskie could easily lose the election to Billy Cohen.

"It wasn't our intention to sandbag you on this," Loring begins as Mahoney sits down. "I look at this picture of you in the *Labor News* here, and it says more jobs will occur. Well, that's what we're concerned about. We're concerned about work. Development in the state of Maine is what really affects us very closely. In the last year we've been down the line defending the additions and expansions of paper mills, and we've had our own EPA problem here in the state. None of us are against environmental protection. We don't want to weaken the laws. But we don't want them so damned restricted that we won't be able to *do* anything. We don't care about the people who come down from Massachusetts to farm and fish and what have you in the state of Maine. We're concerned with making a living. And if we don't have some input as to what is going on, then we might as well forget it. That's the reason we're sitting down and asking you to be here. And believe me, when I asked Jim Case to set up this meeting it was with the clear understanding that we were going to talk about the Clean Air Act."

"I'm sure it wasn't your intention to sandbag me," Muskie assures him, adding with a twist: "I won't talk about other people's intentions. But the implication that I want to destroy jobs for Maine people—if there's any question about that, you know, you just ought to tell me to get out of public life now. What the hell have I been working for for twenty-five years? You just made the speech that I've been making for twenty-five years.

"I went through the Oxford yesterday and stopped at the computer room. This is the place where two guys keep matched up against production in Richmond, Virginia. They put in a question, and within seconds they had an answer back. The operator said to me, 'Senator, the information that comes back from that computer is only as good as the information we put into it.' Now the good doctor puts certain information into his computer, including certain *assumptions* about what the committee is talking about doing. And these are the answers he got back. If the information that goes in is wrong, the answer you get back is wrong. As long as you understand that point, I don't care if you listen to this stuff for the next twenty-four hours. It may have nothing to do with what the committee does. I listen to that kind of stuff hours on end, day after day, as people come before hearings. They have a right to say what's on their minds, so I listen. But I just want to be sure that you put this into the proper perspective.

"So let me tell you what we are trying to do with this Clean Air Act, and you can tell me in terms of our objectives whether we are off base or not. First of all, our objective is not to eliminate jobs from the state of Maine, it is not to eliminate development, it is not to eliminate growth. Let's make that clear. We've got a problem of dirty air.

"I fly into Maine and see smog all the time. But it's much cleaner than what we see flying into Boston or New York. Now the question is—and this is the problem we've been struggling with that raises all these fears and doubts—how can we provide reasonable protection for our present air quality and avoid slipping into the problem of the New Yorks and Chicagos?

"When we fight for decent working conditions, aren't we told over and over again that industry in Maine, or the economy in Maine, can't afford it? Does working in Maine mean that we can't have a decent environment? Employers complain to us constantly about how terrible and costly a thing we did when we passed the Occupational Safety and Health Act. I've been going through paper mills here looking at what OSHA prescribed. The Oxford yesterday had a closed, soundproofed place in the wood room, right near the chipper, so people could get a break from the noise. Is that bad? It's costing them money. I went through another mill and they showed me an air-cooled room right near the paper machines where guys could escape the heat. Is that bad? It's costing somebody money. If you're entitled to clean air beside a paper machine in a paper mill, aren't you entitled to clean air outside the walls?

"I still think that working in Maine doesn't mean you have to sacrifice safety or decent pay for the work you do, or a decent environment in which to live and work. Now if I'm wrong on that, just tell me. I remember fighting with employers who said, 'Senator, you're fighting for wage scales in our Navy yards comparable to those in Boston, and we can't compete up here if our people are paid the same as them for the same work.' And I said, 'Am I going to put a sign at the border saying "Second-class Citizens Only"?' That's what we're talking about. I'm not going to put you guys out of work. I'm going to try to help insure that your kids will be able to work in Maine. As for what the good doctor has said, an awful lot of pretty solid work has gone into this, and I don't want to do it the injustice of acting too casually or irresponsibly. We will take it home and look at it."

Tuesday, September 9

The Senate reconvened six days ago, but efforts to scratch up a quorum late last week for clean air markups were fruitless. Yesterday's call failed and so did another for this morning. Other committees are demanding attention—the CIA investigation, Armed Services where military appropriations rouse strong feelings; every committee's work swelling to its annual post-Labor Day climax—and members have pushed clean air down to a low priority. Why shouldn't they? As its problems get thornier, the temptation rises to let someone else solve them. Moreover, while the vague desire for clean air remains universal, the cost of cleaning it is impinging on more and more economic groups in increasingly painful ways. It's no longer an issue that makes a Senator tingle to get home so he can take bows. Politically, it's getting to be a no-win bill. So why come?

Meanwhile, that confrontation in Maine caused Muskie to return to Washington somewhat shaken. Without a blink he has withstood pressure from Detroit, pressure from power companies, from all sorts of interests pinched by the environmental imperative. But now his impenetrable armor has been cracked by the sharpest pressure of all, the wrath of his own constituents.

Muskie has summoned his subcommittee staff for an unusual meeting in his office this morning. Unusual because I cannot recall a previous instance when he wanted to talk with an entire staff.

The clean air situation in subcommittee and the clean air conflict in Maine are combining into a single huge glob of frustration, stalemate, uncertainty—and a threat to Muskie's re-election. A TV interview on a Portland station by Billy Cohen has provided a feast for politics-hungry Maine newspapers. Cohen, clearly running furiously, said he'll make a "final decision" on whether to run sometime in January. Is he really undecided, or is he merely putting off the official announcement for certain legal advantages gained thereby, such as remaining immune to FCC restrictions on candidate appearances on radio and TV? Muskie, Maynard, Charlie honestly don't know, but they're going to extreme lengths to help Cohen make up his mind. Their plan, hatched early this year, of Muskie romping all over Maine, weekend after weekend after weekend, they have freely admitted to me, is purely and simply a plan to scare Cohen out of the race.

Cohen's pollster seems to have confirmed the findings of Muskie's pollster. Drawing a bow melodiously across the strings of Muskie's vulnerabilities, Cohen reported to his TV audience with blue-eyed sincerity that, because Muskie has been "pursuing the presidency for the past seven years, he's lost touch with the people. They resent that fact. They'd prefer to have the type of Senator who's kept much closer contact with his constituents and serviced them better." Drawing a caricature of Muskie as aged and barnacled with power, Cohen confirms he's running, yet gives reasons for not running: "The Senator will have eighteen years as Senator and four years as governor. That's twenty-two years of state-wide office, which gives him great advantages in terms of notoriety and visibility." Asked to compare his philosophy against Muskie's, Cohen's response was rehearsed and ready: Muskie recently received a hundred per cent rating from the liberal ADA. He, Cohen, got a middle-of-the-road fifty-six per cent. He explained that he sometimes displeases liberals by supporting programs "that would return as much power and money to the localities as possible." An agile and formidable fellow, this rising young man of Bangor.

At 10 A.M. sharp into Muskie's office file Leon, Karl Braithwaite, mustached Haven Whiteside, and Charlene Sturbitts, the clean air staff's youngest professional, an evening law student.

"What is this, a hearing?" demands Muskie in mock surprise.

"A listening," corrects Leon, in mock subservience. Leon reveals the purpose of the meeting. "You asked us to give thought to what would be the essentials to keep if this were trimmed down to a minimum bill." Muskie nods. "We came down to five points. Auto emissions with deadlines, which now seem resolved. Civil penalties for non-compliance, not now provided, but which shouldn't be too difficult. Non-degradation, on which there seems to have been agreement, subject to how they react to our working paper. Then there's the simple matter of enforcement provisions relative to deadlines for stationary sources, and finally, what could become the insoluble matter of transportation controls."

Muskie gnaws silently on Leon's points. He can't fault them. But a tension is on him heavily, generated chiefly by the still echoing confrontation in the Augusta union hall.

"This damned thing is ninety-eight pages," he says, lifting and distastefully dropping the working paper on his desk. "Does this bill need anything that can't be said in ten? Who can swallow all this? Who can understand it? Do we need to have laws that people can't understand? People are fed up with bureaucrats coming into their lives and smelling around. Every provision of these ninety-eight pages gives some bureaucrat an additional authority to become a little Hitler, to drive people nuts." He's not angry. He's troubled. "I sense that the Senate is getting impatient with us. We can't get Senators to a markup, and when we do, so many red flags go up, it looks like the Supreme Council of Soviets. I don't think that most of these ninety-eight pages could pass ten per cent of either house. People are fed up with these goddamned regulations around their necks, and the members know it."

Leon and Karl, experienced Senate operatives, are fine-tuning their receptors. Muskie is down-shifting so forcibly, you can hear the gears grinding, and they need to get his message right. How much of it is instruction and how much to blow off steam?

He resumes, more gently, less steam: "We have to give them as little as possible to deal with in a bill, without opening gaping holes in what we're trying to achieve. We have to be pragmatic, not purist."

Waiting alertly to make sure the Senator is through, Leon responds, "I think there are enough areas for compromise in these pages so you can give up plenty without giving anything important away."

"What happened," says Braithwaite, slipping behind his report-laden desk minutes later, "was a perceptive legislator looking ahead and preparing options. What he did was have us start Alternative Plan B in motion so that we're ready if things start going badly in committee. That's why, as we got up to go, he said this was just for this group to be thinking about. If we have a quorum tomorrow, and if Muskie finds that members are willing to do things he didn't think they would, then the stuff we discussed today won't ever see the light of day. It's much more likely that part of each will occur. He's just setting in motion the development of a different tailoring, an altered approach, so that he'll have it ready if he needs it. His radar is telling him things. Partly it's Maine, and partly that members won't show up. He knows he can't do this bill alone, and he knows he's not going to cram it down people's throats."

Suppose, I suggest, the strong bill as originally contemplated were to start moving again at a reasonable pace through committee. That would not relieve his problems in Maine. And isn't he looking at Maine as a microcosm of the nation, something that helps explain to him why other Senators are balking?

"On non-degradation, yes, exactly. Cars don't especially matter up there, nor do transportation controls. I don't think the Senator would want to make the first move to reopen non-degradation after the subcommittee more or less charted its direction through having us float that working paper. Now I don't think he'd be unhappy if somebody *else* were to call for taking a second look at it. If nobody calls for reopening it, I don't know what'll happen. If Muskie feels that what he learned in Maine forces him to call for a second look, maybe later in the game he'll be the one."

Wednesday, September 10

Today could be a big day and I arrive at the Muskie office with a charge of anticipation. There's to be a two-thirty meeting with Henry Ford II and Leonard Woodcock (together!) and Pehr Gyllenhammar, president of Volvo, who is visiting from Sweden. I knew of this meeting before leaving for Maine in Auguest and, on the assumption that he did too, I mentioned it to Muskie. "When?" he demanded. "Who the hell scheduled them? What do I want to see *them* for? You think I want to reopen *that* again?" Having futilely blown his steam off to me about the obligation, I doubt that he raised a word about it to his staff upon returning to Washington. There was no reasonable way he could turn away that trinity of power, and I doubt that he seriously wanted to. In any case, if he wasn't looking forward to it, I was.

The slightly overripe, *bon vivant* grandson and namesake of the skinny genius who did not invent the automobile but invented the mass production of it is loitering in the central corridor of the Capitol, pushed and shoved by intent tourists looking for important sights to tell relatives about. Waiting with Henry Ford for Senator Muskie's appearance is the equally unnoticeable Woodcock, accompanied by Dick Warden, a UAW lobbyist with thinning red hair. The only suggestion of glamor in the group is the athletic, sauna-glow, crew-cut vitality of Gyllenhammar of Volvo. I arrive with Leon, who admits us to S-199. Ford looks around, impressed.

Muskie arrives. Woodcock begins by explaining that Gyllenhammar requested this meeting because Volvo plans to open an American manufacturing plant next spring, thus becoming an American producer, that he has some thoughts on the Clean Air Act, and that he requested Henry Ford's presence.

Quite possible. It's also possible that Ford wanted the meeting, also wanted Woodcock's presence for the special lobbying influence he may have on Muskie, and suggested Gyllenhammar come as a pretext for reopening an old conversation. It's also possible that Gyllenhammar asked for the meeting, suggested Woodcock's presence, and that Woodcock suggested Ford's presence, because Gyllenhammar might not be taken seriously as an American manufacturer.

In accented but otherwise flawless English, Gyllenhammar, who scarcely looks forty and exudes great sincerity and, well, I've got to say it, *credibility,* sings an old song but with fresh chords in a new key: "If the suggested legislation goes through, it might rule out interesting alternatives, like the stratified charge, the diesel, the Stirling engine. It could result in our being stuck with the very thing that it would be best to do away with, the piston engine. Perhaps we could go farther in perfecting these alternative ways if we had, say, five years. Perhaps there could be some modification, so that instead of requiring 2.0 on NOx, the legislation might say something about going to 1.0 in the laboratory."

Leon asks for clarification. No specified date for requiring 1.0 for cars on the road?

In the laboratory only, for the five-year period.

Leon asks what Volvo proposes as standards for HC, CO, and NOx.

Gyllenhammar replies, obviously immersed in the engineering and alchemy of turning auto soot into spring air, .9, 9.0, 2.0.

The same as the present special standards for California, says Leon.

"Indeed," says the handsome Swede. (Volvo is meeting California standards comfortably. American cars are having trouble. Ford fidgets.) "California standards for all cars would provide the guarantee that manufacturers would be hard pressed." Gyllenhammar further urges that the two national goals—emission control and fuel economy—be tied together into a unified formula, a single policy, "so we don't shoot for emission control first, then have to start all over on next year's fuel economy requirement, as prescribed by another law."

Muskie, suppressing weariness at the interminable haggling over seemingly insoluble technical conflicts, rubs taut fingers back and forth across his forehead and says:

"A few days ago, in my home town in Maine, I visited the Oxford Paper Company. They've put in these huge clarifiers, a kind of scrubber arrangement, at huge cost, but it's cleaned up our beautiful river. 'Wonderful,' I said. 'Now, what are you doing about the odor?' They said, 'Well, the law doesn't require anything. You can't expect people to focus on what they're not required to do.' Well, that's a realistic response. The job of industry is to look after the interests of stockholders, to protect and improve its profit position. It's our job to require industry to conform to standards of health and safety, and so forth, to protect the public welfare."

The Swede puckers his lips, granting Muskie's precept as a given.

"But our deadlines have not been met," Muskie pleads. "Not by auto manufacturers or stationary sources. Deadlines are slipping all through the water pollution program, the subject of another law. If these laws are to mean anything, they *have* to have credibility."

All the participants assent by silence. They sense the Senator isn't done.

"If you don't have pressure, you don't investigate options," Muskie singsongs a paradox, "and if there's too much pressure you abandon options. You're right, and we're trying honestly to find a useful compromise. We'll listen to any suggestion, to anybody. Industry has asked for five years more. They've asked it repeatedly. But they've given no clue as to what they might *do* with the five years. What risks are they willing to take? We know you can't predict results, but you'll find us willing to listen, willing to evaluate any suggestion that shows reasonable promise of producing results."

Ford, who's been scribbling left-handed with an embossed gold pencil, muses aloud the admission of the day. "It's very difficult to get the research people to say, 'We're through,' and put something into production. So there's no question, you have to set standards and dates. You'd like to legislate an end to cancer, but if you don't know how to do it and have to depend on the researchers, at what point do you say the research is finished?"

Leon's gaze snaps to Ford. Is Ford saying that an alternative engine is virtually ready to go but the researchers are afraid to let go of it, and that's why the harping on a five-year moratorium?

"I feel it is possible," says Gyllenhammar, "to combine restrictions with incentives. Perhaps there should be a tax incentive."

"Even in the industry," says Ford, shaking his head, "there's no agreement. You know, I've been told by good friends that if I came down here with Pehr the rest of the industry might cut my throat."

"And I promised I'd protect you," says Woodcock, with a faint big-brother grin.

"Right, Leonard will protect me," says young Ford with a wisp of condescension. He addresses Muskie earnestly. "Do you know that, to meet the 1977 California standards, in our company we have to spend between forty and sixty million dollars?" Muskie nods sympathetically. "We have a terrible capital formation problem in this country. I'm seriously perturbed about whether we can maintain the kind of employment we've had in the industry, with the possible exception of GM. If—if we could have a pause"—this is supposed to be Gyllenhammar's show, but now Ford has taken over the hard sell —"we would see what's feasible, what's politically feasible, what's feasible in design."

"Well, we have to stay in touch and work this out," says Muskie. "But meanwhile you fellows in the industry have got to look into your own hearts and ask yourselves what you can really do and how we can devise something that will really give assurance that you'll do it. With specific goals and deadlines and guarantees. I don't mean through handshakes and good will and promises, but something that can be written into law. Your people have got to stop saying no, and if you don't like the way *we're* doing it, look into your hearts and ask, What do we propose as the better way to do it?"

Ford seems to be swallowing it down, as untasty but the right medicine.

Muskie continues, "The other thing we've got to put an end to—or at least account for—is the National Academy of Sciences telling us one thing about what's possible, and your people and the EPA people, as though they live in a different world under a different set of physical rules, telling us another. Somehow this has all got to be reconciled. If we're to make a decision based on what the NAS has told us, your people and the EPA people and our people have *got* to be brought together and agree on one set of facts."

Leon has an idea. "Do you mean literally together?"

An indecisive but acquiescent shrug runs through the principals.

"Suppose I call them all in next week," Leon suggests, looking at Ford inquiringly. Wordlessly, Ford assents.

After the visitors and Leon file out, Muskie says to me, half in weariness, half in relief, "I certainly wasn't in a mood for *this* today. I'm so goddamned tired after being up all night I just couldn't bear the thought of a confrontation. So I thought a little molasses might sweeten things up and accomplish something. Who knows, maybe it did." Sighing uncertainly, Muskie sinks into his big chair. "At least I wanted to convey to them that I'm not all beast. That if they won't be so adamant, just loosen their stone wall, they'll find us willing to listen and be flexible. Maybe this time that got through."

An expected long, single buzz buzzes. Muskie, like a fighter staggering punchily into the thirteenth round, goes to the floor to cast a vote to override President Ford's veto of a bill to hold a lid on oil prices.

Wednesday, September 17

After an early rising (which brings the news that yesterday's election runoff in New Hampshire produced a victory for the Democrat, John Durkin) I scurry to the Public Works hearing room to get in before eight-thirty when Leon Billings locks the door. Only the small subcommittee staff including Hal Brayman, the minority's man, and five obviously tense men from General Motors are admitted for the first of the company-by-company meetings that Leon suggested at the Muskie-Ford-Woodcock-Gyllenhammar huddle last week.

Only one face is familiar to me, that of Bill Chapman, GM's lobbyist on the Clean Air Act. Of the other four, all technical men who flew in last night from Detroit, all seem to defer to one, a chunky, gray-haired, husky-voiced fellow named Ernest Starkman, who turns out to be GM's vice-president in charge of environmental affairs. During pre-meeting chatter, clearly annoyed at interrupting his life for this summons by the government—an organization he seems to regard irreverently as having somewhat lesser rank than his own—he sticks the toe of a well-shined shoe into a crevice of a round utility cover on the floor, demonstrating that he can make it spin around, then cracks, "I told you there's a screw loose in the Senate. There it is." I soon learn that Starkman's history has not been as a GM man. Before joining the corporation four years ago he was an engineering professor at the University of California at Berkeley, and a leading researcher in thermodynamics, combustion, and air pollution. He is president-elect of the Society of Automotive Engineers.

We seat ourselves around a square of tables and, in answer to a question from Leon, Starkman reports that the "decrement"—first time I've heard that substitute for the word "loss"—of fuel resulting from catalytic converters remains about the same, ten per cent, for 1976 cars as for 1975.

Maddening, the contradictory implications of public statements by auto companies on that subject, with no attempt to qualify or clarify or reconcile the seeming contradictions. In *Harper's* magazine GM has just run a full-page ad headed, "A breath of fresh air in automotive technology." It displays a catalytic converter, looking something like a hot water bag, festooned with a congratulatory flower at its top. "The catalytic converter," the ad sings, "is a device for people and flowers and trees, for every living thing . . . . The converter is also a device for pocketbooks and for energy conservation. According to EPA figures, it helped GM engineers to increase gas mileage in city driving by 28% on a sales-weighted average." Talk about working both sides of the street! Just a few days ago, General Motors joined the other three American auto makers in full-page newspaper ads across the country urging citizens to write their Senators and Representatives to freeze this year's emission standards for five years on the ground that *"your gas mileage could be reduced by 5%* to as much as 30%" (italics mine).

Commenting on the subcommittee's newly relaxed emission proposal, Starkman reports flatly, "The goals of 4.1/3.4/1.0 are out of the question for the kinds of systems we're using now. There's no way to get there without going to the next step, three-way catalysts or at least two-way catalysts."

"With the three-way, what's to stop you from going all the way to .4 NOx?" asks Braithwaite.

"We're not aiming for 1.0 NOx but for .4," says Starkman with a mix of mischief and virtue. "The present law says .4. Our experience with the three-way is that after five thousand miles we get a fast deterioration and it blows the standard for both HC and NOx. The CO remains okay."

That's news. Important news. If true. The environmentalists and the catalytic converter lobby, not to mention Gary Hart and his staff adviser, are basing their commitment to the .4 goal entirely on the three-way catalyst. The big unknown element has been its durability.

Leon tries to clear the air of numbers haggling and poses the basic question of these meetings: "Suppose Congress gave, say, a one-year moratorium—five years being totally impractical—what assurance could you give as to how the time would be used? How would you demonstrate to Congress, thus to the public, that the time is being used to greatest advantage?"

"Off the record," Starkman begins with a hoarse whisper of extreme confidentiality, "off the record—and I mean if this gets out through any of you, it's the last time I'll tell you anything—we're going to offer the diesel as an option for 1978 passenger cars and pickup trucks. It'll be a gasoline-style engine but a diesel head. We can now get 2.0 NOx without trouble. That's .9/9.0/2.0. We're still having a little trouble on NOx and HC but we're getting there."

Remarkable coincidence. Those numbers are the present requirements for California cars which conventional engines have been straining to achieve, and they are Russell Train's recommendation for national requirements starting with 1980 models. So apparently GM is bargaining for interim California standards to become a longer-term national goal. They are giving way a bit on what is "impossible."

As the meeting ends about two hours after it began, I compare notes with Haven Whiteside on what took place. His summary: "They came here to say they can't do it, yet in two different ways they said they could. They can do it with a conventional car, but with a fuel penalty. They can do it with a three-way catalyst, probably without fuel penalty, but it wears out after five thousand miles. They said nothing about what they're doing to overcome that five-thousand-mile-problem. Also, they're going to offer the diesel. But the main question—what plan you offer for demonstrating good faith?—went entirely unanswered."

Asked his estimate, Leon intones sonorously, "On a still sea, even the faintest hint of breeze is enough to stir hope."

For the meeting of Ford's people in the afternoon, I show up early and chat in the hall with another early arriver, who turns out to be Dave Hogan, chief engineer for advanced projects, who flew out of Detroit at 11:15 A.M. after "doing a day's work." That closing phrase is added suddenly, emphatically, as though to convey that this trip is crammed into the throwaway part of the day. The other three Ford representatives who arrive are Washington men, including the company's two clean air lobbyists, Wayne Smithey and Bob Smith. Fishing, I try to say something sympathetic to Hogan about the difficulties of providing information that is not yet buttoned down, and he makes a revealing reply: "These things get caught between the company's policy types"—he casts a quick glance at the three Washington men—"and the technical types, each restricted by what the others are willing to say."

Answering a question from Leon soon after the meeting begins, Hogan says, "If the great breakthrough were reported tonight, it would take a year for internal confirmation, then two years to go through the hoop, to final stage of pinning down sources of supply, their delivery schedules and so forth. So you'd be talking about 1979 or 1980 cars for the next stage of emission standards."

Leon and fellow staff members spring, trying to pin Hogan down to 1979 as a target if the "breakthrough" were at hand. Hogan digs in his heels at 1980, finally protesting: "You talk about *our* credibility. If I said '79, I can sense you'd assume that in '79 it would all be there. But *I* know that in one of those steps I'd *have* to have one slip-up."

This meeting stirs not even a faint breeze of hope. Nothing new at all.

Afterward I run into Karl in the basement corridor. Why, I ask him, must there be so much dependence on auto company research? Why not introduce a bill to authorize a large-scale, crash-program research contract in the same way—I bite my tongue as I recite the cliché—the same way we put a man on the moon? Why not just go ahead and design the desired engine, if there's so much confidence it's designable, and make it available to the auto companies?

"That debate," says Karl, leaning against a cigarette vending machine, "has been going on since 1970. Leon, for one, has always been against that approach, and his resistance has proven sound. First of all, it's almost impossible to get the money out of Congress. You get this peculiar combination of conservative economizers and anti-business liberals who oppose the idea on the grounds that why the hell should the government subsidize the auto companies this way? Representative Bob Casey of Texas, a conservative, led that fight. Someone always will, so that the money never gets through, and that's exactly what the auto companies want—for it not to get through.

"Another problem is that, if it did get through, two years would go by just to get the agency started, and a couple of more years to get the research started, and a few more years for proving out and certifying whatever they developed, and so forth. It would be just *years*. Senator Domenici has been in favor of this approach rather strongly, and still is."

How important was this morning's revelation that GM is going to offer the diesel?

"The diesel is *a* way to go but not *the* way to go. It still has the disadvantage of smelliness, which probably can't be eliminated totally, and people still confuse the odor with pollution. Another problem is that you'd never get people to buy diesels in Cadillacs and other heavy cars, because those people don't care about the cost of gasoline or how many miles they'll get on a gallon.

"Funny thing about that 'revelation' this morning," Karl muses. "A couple of years ago Ernie Starkman shoved a warning finger into Leon, after seeing a set of projected standards, and said, *'Don't legislate the diesel.'* I guess what he meant is, don't force the industry to go in the direction of a car that consumers will resist. It'll hurt the American auto industry and employment and so forth. Now here comes GM first with the diesel."

Isn't the fact that California requires cleaner cars—and that auto companies are making special cars for California—proof that they can do better than they're doing nationally?

"That cuts another way. California is also a place where auto companies can afford to fail—in fact, may find advantage in failing. They've already lost approximately forty per cent of the California market to foreign cars, their biggest loss in the country. Any additional loss of ten per cent just represents one per cent of the national market. Therefore, they can fail there and use it as an effective excuse: 'See? We really can't do this.' So they can afford to use California as a kind of fooling-around laboratory, to improve emission control systems, yes, but also to prove that systems can't be improved."

Today's Congressional Record carries—a pure coincidence with the foregoing conversation—a multipage insertion by Senator Domenici of a report recently issued by the Jet Propulsion Laboratory, builders of unmanned space vehicles, entitled "Should We Have a New Engine?" The study was financed by a $500,000 grant from the Ford Motor Company but was conducted entirely independently of influence by the grantor, says JPL. It concludes that either of two engine types could be perfected by 1985 and bring a thirty to forty-five per cent increase in fuel mileage while virtually eliminating pollution. The cost of developing the engines would be a billion dollars. "The reduction in gasoline usage would yield a saving . . . worth about eight billion *a year* at current prices," says the report (italics mine). "This might be a good place for public funds or incentives."

The two engine types that JPL believes could be perfected over the next ten years are the turbine, a version of which is almost universally used on modern airliners, and the Stirling, which achieves great efficiency and destruction of pollutants through ingenious methods of alternately cooling and heating its fuels, constantly recycling the unburned residue of gasoline to drive its pistons.

Muskie and a party of other members of Congress and their wives cruise the Potomac aboard the presidential yacht *Sequoia* tonight. Their hosts, President and Mrs. Ford, turn out to be absentees, but Donald Rumsfeld of the White House staff is there to convey the affection of the White House toward members of Congress. In midcruise, Muskie is paged to the ship's phone, to which he responds with a look of pro forma annoyance. The call is not from an intrusive staff member this time, but Spencer Rich of the Washington *Post*.

House-Senate conferees have chopped $250 million from the military procurement bill, including the entire start-up fund for the nuclear strike cruiser. Armed Services Chairman Stennis told Rich that he hasn't yet talked to Muskie about whether the cut is acceptable to the Budget Committee—a new tone of accommodation—but said, "We're going to try to pass it," adding he thought it could be passed even if the Budget Committee is still unhappy. Does Muskie, Rich wants to know, have anything to say?

Muskie says he hasn't decided what to do about this new figure, which is still somewhat higher than the budget guideline, but adds, "John did some good things—elimination of the strike cruiser. I give him high marks for that."

Another $85 million is saved by reducing from ten to nine the plans for the number of patrol frigates. These frigates are slated to be built in Maine, but Stennis assured the reporter that this cut "is not any kind of retribution" against Muskie for his audacity in beating back a military bill. Rich does not ask for Muskie's comment on that, and Muskie volunteers none.

Thursday, September 18

This morning it's Chrysler's turn, a team led by Vice-President Sid Terry, a forceful man:

"Fifty thousand miles? Anybody who says what's going to happen to an emission control system over a fifty-thousand-mile history of a car is pure guessing. We have absolutely no information. Look, we're telling you all we know. Don't ask us to tell you stuff we don't know.

". . . On the turbine engine, there's no use talking about it till we know what *you* fellows are going to do. It'll cost about a billion dollars to tool up for that engine. It has to be good for ten years of production, so the tooling will cost us one hundred dollars an engine. If you guys change the ground rules on us after five years, the tooling cost goes up to two hundred dollars an engine.

". . . On a lab basis the turbine"—Terry looks around warily, re-thinking whether to say it—"looks pretty good. It can meet the stat-

utory standards. The NOx looks pretty good. But it needs more lead
time on research, several more years of development work before
getting to the stage of testing its durability.

". . . They're all—all the companies including us are trying to tell
you we're making progress. But we're afraid to say it. We're all
worried that if we sound hopeful, what will the damned standards be
tomorrow?

". . . Suppose research gives us a go-ahead on something today.
That's only the beginning. Then we go into testing, product design,
tool drawings, tooling, looking for purchasing sources, and that's all
before finding the bugs. You're talking about seven years."

Leon poses once again the question that underlies these meetings:
"How can you *demonstrate* progress?"

"The good faith question," Terry rewords it, nodding. "Look, a
man is innocent until he's proven guilty. That ought to go for industry too. You know, our best guys are all tied up writing reports instead of innovating and inventing. . . ."

On Muskie's behalf, Billings has now asked each of America's Big
Three what *they* can suggest for providing evidence of progress
under pressure if the present subcommittee proposal is further
relaxed and, as they have done without letup since 1963, they have
offered zero.

At a few minutes after twelve Senate attendance is unusually high
although no major roll call is scheduled, and the galleries, including
those for staffs and special visitors, are packed to the last seat.

"Mr. President," says Mike Mansfield, addressing the acting president pro tempore. Who is *that* in the chair? The presiding officer is
Norris Cotton, the man who retired from the New Hampshire seat
last year, making way for the Durkin-Wyman race, and who was
recently appointed to fill the temporary vacancy. "Mr. President, I
ask the chair to lay before the Senate the credentials of the Senator-
elect from New Hampshire, the Honorable John A. Durkin."

A clerk reads the short certification from Governor Meldrim
Thomson, Jr., of New Hampshire, "that on the sixteenth day of September, 1975, John A. Durkin was duly chosen by the qualified electors of the State of New Hampshire a Senator. . . ."

"If the Senator-elect will present himself at the desk," commands Cotton, "the oath of office will be administered to him."

Unaccustomed to sharing his state's representation with a fellow Democrat, a beaming Senator McIntyre escorts black-haired, florid, stocky, thirty-eight-year-old Durkin down the center aisle from the rear of the chamber where for nine months he was permitted to sit behind a flimsy table, watching the Senate refuse to decide his political fate.

Upon completion of the oath, the entire Senate stands and applauds warmly and extensively. Including Lowell Weicker. Including Jim Allen.

Senator Durkin leaves the chamber to meet a throng of photographers on the Capitol steps. Senator Cranston quietly slips out the Capitol door and waits for a moment to pull Durkin aside. His long tally sheet in hand, Cranston whispers intently to Durkin. The next vote is to be a close one on whether the federal pay rise is to be mandated at 8.6 per cent or be limited to President Ford's preference— and the budget resolution's allowance—of 5 per cent. John Durkin is being lobbied for the first time by a fellow Senator.

Friday, September 19

This morning's Volvo meeting, contrasting sharply with the previous ones, is direct, friendly, and productive. Its "witnesses" are three Swedes, two of them tall and blond, one short and dark, who all seem to be under thirty-five. They report that they are meeting present California standards (.9/9/2.0) with a system that costs the customer only sixteen dollars. With adjustments, that system can meet 1977 national standards (.4/3.4/2.0), but with a fuel penalty. Down the pike, report the Swedes in American corporatese, they see a breakthrough with either the diesel, the stratified charge, or the turbine. Unlike Detroit's men, who either stonewalled or hedged their predictions into invisibility, the Volvo team guilelessly announces that it is shooting for—and "we plan to achieve"—10,000 cars in 1977 with a new three-way catalyst that will meet the law's requirements on NOx without intensifying the hydrocarbon problem. True, that's only one sixth of the number of cars Volvo sells in America, and there will be a fuel loss. But it's a beginning. And the Volvo men are talking about what they *are* doing, what they hope to achieve later, not what they can't or won't do.

"I hate to break this up," says Leon, mindful that a markup is scheduled for 10 A.M. "It's the most encouraging thing that's happened around here in some time."

"It made the whole week of meetings worth while," adds Karl.

As Leon unlocks the hearing room door to let the visitors out of the secret meeting, and lobbyists into the open one, I ask Karl for his present estimate of having a new law.

"Right now," he says, "I think the most optimistic schedule is for us to be out of conference with a bill and having it signed by Christmas. We can still do that as of now, including non-degradation, everything."

Today's *Wall Street Journal* has a two-column headline proclaiming, "GM Plans to Manufacture Diesel Engines for Some Models Possibly by Mid-1977." Just forty-eight hours ago the subcommittee staff was pledged to protect that explosive morsel of intelligence.

Unimportant, perhaps, but one more instance of bamboozling, of GM's playing children's games with members of the United States Senate.

For the markup, only Senator Stafford shows up to join Muskie. After a long head-to-head with Leon, Muskie announces for the benefit of the stenotypist—for the revered "record"—that time is getting close if the legislation is to be approved this year, and that therefore he is instructing his staff—Stafford nods assent to each phrase—to draw up a "minimum" bill for the subcommittee to approve and send quickly to the full committee. So he has decided to

go to what Karl has called "Alternative Plan B." Muskie concludes
with the hope that the bill can be ready for the floor in two weeks because his Budget Committee must soon start hearings, which will
make a major claim on his time.

On the way back to the office Muskie tells me he decided overnight to go along with Stennis—his conference report of a $250 mil-
lion increase for military procurement, drastically less than the conference figure the Senate previously turned down. I ask whether he
consulted other Budget Committee members or was the decision his.
"I just don't have time to consult with everybody," he says. Not even
Bellmon, the ranking Republican? "I probably would have consulted
if I decided *not* to go along," he explains.

In this day of waning power of the all-powerful chairman, the
chairman's power—by common consent and acquiescence—remains
awesome.

During my first week here Maynard Toll told me he had decided
he never wants to run for public office, having observed first hand
how the lives of Muskie and other Senators must be managed by
others if they're to work effectively. Having lost interest in the dream
of becoming a Senator, Maynard, not surprisingly, has reconsidered
staying around on a Senator's staff. As frequently happens to young,
personable, able members of higher rank on Senate staffs, Maynard
has received an offer he can't refuse, from First Boston Company,
international investment bankers.

Tonight Maynard and his spirited wife Kay are giving a party for
the office at their home in the fashionable district west of Wisconsin
Avenue and north of Georgetown, not far, in fact, from Rockefeller's
Foxhall Road. I accompany the Senator there. Driving over, he's in a
growly mood and it takes no prodding to find out why. The Budget
Boys, Bennet and McEvoy, came late in the day for approval of a
press release announcing that Budget Committee economists predict
that government revenues for the year would run three billion dollars
higher than previously anticipated. Wonderful news, no? No.

"Why the hell didn't you tell me this earlier?" demands Muskie of
the Budget Boys. "We didn't know earlier." "But this information
had to be somewhere. *Somebody* must have seen it coming. Why did

they wait till now?" The Budget Boys shrug. "We just learned it today and that's why we're here."

Just twenty-four hours ago Muskie had to endure a pain that appears to be a recurring discomfort of his Budget Committee chairmanship. Again he had to get up and plead for the Senate to reject something he personally favored, in this instance the federal pay raise amendment to permit an 8.6 per cent increase for the civil service, keeping apace with the rise in the cost of living, instead of the 5 per cent lid recommended by President Ford. Of the various bulges in expenditure tromped down by the Budget Committee, this is the one that Muskie believes is most deserving of reconsideration under a changed revenue picture. The ironic thing is that the difference between the approved 5 per cent and the 8.6 per cent that he helped defeat comes to just about three billion dollars. "If only I'd had these figures yesterday—just *yesterday*—I could have stood up and justified that break in the budget through this rise in revenue." I ask, "Doesn't this, on the positive side, give you a chance to play Santa Claus?" "Well, there's really no undoing that so rapidly. But I sure as hell don't want to announce to the press tomorrow that we just found three billion dollars. We're going to have to find some way of holding back that information, say, for ten days or two weeks, until it's no longer associated with the pay raise."

We're the first to arrive, which I'm sure is not the way the Senator would have planned it. As staff members, their spouses and dates slowly gather, I mention to Muskie the week's meetings with auto companies and how pessimistic they were. Muskie says, "All they have to offer is their difficulties. Negativism. You'd think they'd be inspired by their own history. Early in World War II, F.D.R. announced one day that we had to build sixty thousand airplanes a year. It was just a figure he pulled out of the air. We were just not equipped to do it. Nobody knew how to do it. But we *did* it. And mostly right around their own city of Detroit. You remember Willow Run Airport near Detroit? That enormous barn of a passenger terminal was built by the automobile people to be the factory where they turned out a lot of those sixty thousand planes a year. Where is the old American spirit that enabled us to do that? God, can these guys raise resistance."

There's a hubbub of greeting near the door, and Gayle Cory breaks away from a conversation to join it. Mrs. Muskie—Jane—has arrived. Compared to the dimensions of her husband, she is a short woman, with a heart-shaped face that radiates with impending laughter. Gayle takes her over, introducing the Senator's wife to spouses and dates and new staff members who haven't previously met her. Mrs. Muskie clearly enjoys being first lady of this domain. I remark to one of the staff women that I can perceive none of the shyness I have heard belongs to the Senator's wife. "She loves meeting people," says the staff person. "The shyness comes out in other ways. It comes out in being able to deal only with *her* people, not the Senator's people." "What do you mean, her people and the Senator's people?" "This is something that happens in a lot of Senators' offices, probably all of them after they're around long enough. Part of the staff gets all involved with the family, and vice versa, and pretty soon the Senator can't tell where the staff ends and the family begins. This probably comes from all the Senator's travel arrangements, then all the arrangements for the family to travel, and all the time that a Senator can't tend to home details because he's so busy, so he asks staff to do them."

How does the staff-family mix-up show?

"What kids normally ask fathers to do, Senators' kids learn to ask staff to do. I've seen Gayle have to drop everything to call Maine because one of the kids needs his driver's license renewed. When the washing machine breaks down, you don't call the plumber, you call Gayle and Gayle calls the plumber. When this really sets in, especially the 'his' and 'hers' thing, you can't imagine how far it goes. One day I was relieving on the reception desk, and Jane called, asking for Gayle. Gayle was out. She asked if Susie was there. Susie was out too. Then, Is so-and-so there, or so-and-so, going down a descending list of 'her' people. Finally she said, kind of desperately, 'But I've got to get a message to Fran Miller.' I was puzzled, but then told her, 'Fran is here. Would you like to talk to her?' There was a long pause, and then she said, 'Well, I guess that would be a good idea.' You see, Fran, as office manager, is one of *his* people."

Soon it is my turn to meet Jane, and she tells me warmly— although with a hint of duty clouding her eyes—that she hopes I'll come home later "with Ed," that is, if I don't mind having a Friday dinner of just scrambled eggs and bacon. I assure her I love scrambled eggs and bacon. Jane leaves early to prepare for her unexpected guest. After Muskie offers remarks of obvious fondness for Maynard and appropriate appreciation of his work, we depart.

The Muskie house is a brick colonial, painted beige, lively with roof angles and corners and windows nosing busily in every direction, erected proudly on a rise of earth high above the sidewalk. Inside, walls are hung generously with paintings, mostly by young Maine artists; shelves and end tables display a panorama of art objects and mementos collected on political travels around the world. One end of the house used to be a sunporch, but in Washington when it's warm enough to sit out on a screened porch it's too humid to enjoy it, so the porch has been closed in as an inviting, cream-toned second living room. Bedrooms, all upstairs, include two for the last of the five Muskie children who are still at home, Martha and Edmund, Jr. (Ned), both in high school. The children are out for the evening and, during our family-mood, kitchen-table supper, the senior Senator from Maine, whom captains of industry have trouble reaching, answers the constantly ringing telephone to say, "No, Ned's out, Martha's out, can I take a message?"

After a tour of the paintings on two floors—Muskie takes paintings seriously, replacing works on his office walls every couple of months with loans from Maine's famous Farnsworth Museum—he opens a chest in his den of additional mementos and gifts. With an absence of fuss, he sets up a slide projector and screen in the den and tells me I would love Campobello. Slowly, inviting savor of each, he clicks off his slides of and around the enormous barn-red house that F.D.R.'s mother ludicrously called a "cottage" where F.D.R. walked his last unaided steps before polio crippled him. One shot of night reflections on a swimming pool is stunning, and all are thoughtfully, some artfully, composed. I have yet to see him do anything carelessly, as a throwaway.

About midnight, after a pleasant evening, I suggest a call for a cab.

Thursday, October 2

No more dallying and dawdling if he can help it. Muskie is calling—virtually commanding—the subcommittee members to a markup that will finally push the clean air bill up into full committee. A letter to all members, signed "Ed" and "Jim," goes out today:

Honorable Pete Domenici
United States Senate
Washington, D.C.

Dear Pete:

At our last markup, the staff was instructed to prepare a "minimum" bill that encompasses essential issues with which we must deal.

We have scheduled a markup for 2:30 P.M. Wednesday, October 8, to try to vote on those issues which have not yet been resolved. They are summarized in the attached list. A staff print of legislative language will be delivered to you tomorrow.

The Subcommittee has held 19 markups and 14 days of hearings. We know what the issues are.

We have generally agreed that these are areas in which we must act. However, in order not to preclude any consideration of alternatives, we would hope you could suggest any additions to this list of issues as possible amendments by Monday in order that we can move immediately to votes on Wednesday.

We know how busy you are but these issues are too important to be delayed. We hope you can clear your schedule for Wednesday afternoon.

Sincerely,

EDMUND S. MUSKIE, U.S.S   JAMES L. BUCKLEY, U.S.S.
Chairman, Subcommittee on   Ranking Minority Member
Environment Pollution

Leon today passes a memo to Muskie entitled "Senator Baker's Staff Proposal." Howard Baker and Jennings Randolph, ex officio members of the subcommittee while serving as the two party leaders of the full committee, have carefully maintained a distance from subcommittee deliberations on clean air. Their purpose derives mostly from the unusual composition of the Environmental Pollution Subcommittee—of the full committee's fourteen members, eleven belong to the subcommittee. If the idea of moving a bill from subcommittee to full committee is to give it a hard-nosed review, the only way to accomplish that is for the three non-members of the subcommittee—Democrats Randolph and Burdick, Republican Baker—to avert their eyes, then look at the bill freshly. In reality, that comes down to Baker. Burdick is not too interested in this intricate subject that scarcely affects North Dakota. And except for looking after the bill's implications for coal and steel, Randolph is terrified of getting involved. In Randolph's style of leadership of the Public Works Committee, the important thing is not so much what the parade is about but that you're leading it grandly. So in the full committee's review of the most difficult provisions of the Clean Air Act, particularly those on auto emissions, Randolph is not likely to contribute any Newtonian breakthroughs. But Baker, an avid motorcyclist who might have become a crackerjack car mechanic in his Tennessee village if he had not been sidetracked into law and fame, has been itching to get his creative hands greasy on this biggest engine-overhaul job ever undertaken by government.

Baker's active entry into the auto emission picture is indeed important, considering the rumors that McClure has been huddling with Baker; that Buckley, whose initially strong stand on tough standards is rapidly buckling; and Baker's apparent desire to ram through a bill quickly. Last night Charlie Micoleau, now Muskie's new a.a., told me that "something is going on" with Baker, that Leon is being "tight-lipped" about it, but also that Baker is to meet Muskie as soon as possible—he hopes today—for a "real talk" about getting a minimal bill through committee on auto emissions.

I soon learn that the idea out of the Baker office is a nifty way to threaten the auto industry with choking itself on the very thing it says it wants most. If Detroit wants to freeze auto emissions for five years, give them just that—and more. Freeze everything. The companies would be forbidden to introduce new models unless the new models comply with the next stage of emission standards. Do they want to keep polluting at 1975 levels? Let them—as long as they're willing to keep making and selling 1975-model cars. Then let the market, not Congress, force Detroit to shape up.

Leon's memo reads:

> Senator Baker's staff has come up with an auto emission proposal to which Senator Baker's initial reaction is good. . . . Senator Baker is concerned with the potential impact of this proposal on the work force. If it is not expected to have negative impact, Senator Baker would surface it. At the same time he does not want to make the proposal public so that it can be shot down by the White House or the auto industry before he has had an opportunity to fairly test its validity.

> I suggested to Senator Baker's staff that you might be willing directly or indirectly to try to get a reaction from Leonard Woodcock. If Leonard thinks the idea has value he could surface it with the industry through Henry Ford. Senator Baker may wish to meet with you on this today as Charlie has indicated on your schedule.

> For the past several weeks the staff has attempted to find a mechanism which would cause the industry to *want* to meet the standards. It has been my view that it is more important to phase in percentages of new production in compliance with statutory standards than to change the standards every couple of years on all models produced. This was the basic intent of the Muskie-Buckley proposal and this is the intent of the Baker proposal.

> Senator Baker has discussed this idea with Senator Buckley.

> I am concerned that the labor impact could be dramatic if the sales of the industry are based on styling changes and the intro-

duction of new models and engine combinations. In any event I
think the idea is worth discussing with Leonard. . . .

Even if this clever idea drops dead under Leonard Woodcock's
scowl—I suspect it will, and clearly Leon suspects it may—it has another ominous meaning: that the auto emissions controversy which
was supposedly "resolved" long ago in subcommittee is scratching
annoyingly at members' nerves and is far from resolved.

Before going to see Senator Baker, I arrange a couple of short-no-
tice appointments for catch-up talks with two minority members
most likely to influence and be influenced by him, Senators Buckley
and McClure.

A CONVERSATION WITH SENATOR BUCKLEY

*On auto emissions, which have been tentatively set, are you taking
a second look?*

—Yes, very definitely. In fact, I can't think of anybody who wants
to stick with what we have. You were there. It was obviously a decision to get on to other business, to put the auto issue on a side
burner. Now people have had enough chance to think through the
practical implications.

*Do you see the "second look" coming before the subcommittee
lets go of the bill, or in full committee?*

—I suspect it might happen in the full committee.

Has Senator Baker been in touch with you?

—We've been in touch—yes.

How does that form of "being in touch" take place?

—It's extremely sort of haphazard, I'll say that. From time to time
I have, in passing him on the floor, said to Howard Baker, "Let's not
try to do everything that needs to be done in terms of updating the
Clean Air Act this year, or we'll get nothing done. Let's focus on
two, three, four areas that have to be changed, the urgent decisions
that are awaited out in the country." Obviously, auto emissions is of
prime importance. So he said, "Fine, let's do that." I've privately had
a few ideas that I've tested out and mentioned to him, and that my
staff has brought to his staff's attention. He, very recently, has been

working on another kind of theory, something by a member of his staff, which Hal Brayman and Bailey Guard ventilated with me. So we've had this—not direct communication—but indirect communication in this way.

A CONVERSATION WITH SENATOR McCLURE

Have you gone to Senator Baker, or to Senator Randolph, or anyone, and said, "What I think is happening in the subcommittee is such and such, and in the full committee we have a chance for a new cut at it, so let's . . ."?

—I talked to Baker about it. I haven't talked to Randolph, but I understand that Randolph has been talked to about it by other people. And I think there's a feeling now that, while the subcommittee's been unable to resolve it, we'll move it to full committee and resolve it there. The make-up of the full committee's slightly different. You get quite different forces. For instance, Bentsen is obviously going to look at it differently than Randolph.

You think Bentsen will become active at the full committee level?

—Yes.

I hear that Senator Baker is confident there'll be a second look.

—I think there will be, and of necessity in this case. And there's a suggestion I made to Muskie some time ago that I think is probably going to be the result. We'll try to split out of this bill what has to be done now. Then if we can't put the entire package together readily in the full committee, we'll be prepared to split out the portions that have to be passed this year. And very frankly, about the only one that really *has* to be passed is the auto section.

Then you're hopeful that a breakoff will be accomplished?

—Yes.

To what degree does staff control this process?

—Staff controls it to a very great extent. Partly because there's not sufficient diversity in the staff. I think they're not inclined to give Senators as broad a range of options as they might. But when you talk about what it is that's changing and moving things now, I sense that the real catalytic change here is that organized labor has become concerned for jobs and is putting pressure on individual members. I

think Senator Muskie has moved quite a bit, and I sense that it's
pressure of organized labor that's done it. That's occurring in many,
many places.

Tennessee's senior Senator, Howard Baker, has enough status so
that he could easily arrange for space in the Russell Office Building,
the older one that most old-timers prefer. But how could he forsake
the Dirksen Building, being married to the daughter of Everett Dirksen? Besides, having virtually his pick of Dirksen offices, Baker has
located himself across the hall from his favorite room other than the
Senate chamber itself, the hearing room of his beloved Public Works
Committee.

His office has no desk but an elegant table and leather-backed
armchair behind it, no swivel. Scattered before him are four chairs
for visitors, covered with a rose-patterned tapestry. A carefully har-
monized carpet and delicate lamps and small tables leave the tracks
of a decorator of notably feminine taste. They also suggest that the
occupant is a self-conscious fusspot, which Howard Baker certainly
is not. He is the only Senator I have seen in the line of the employees' basement cafeteria, and I hear that he's been seen having
coffee in its less reputable quickie offshoot down the hall, the Plastic
Palace. Effortlessly, he achieves a democratic air that Senators Jim
Abourezk and Gary Hart don't quite manage despite their staffs first-
naming them. One Senate employee I know (who has never met
Baker) calls him "the Johnny Carson of the Senate" because he
seems a bundle of easy quips and surface sugar, not to be taken
seriously. Senators and senior staffers who have dealt with him are
under no such illusion.

A CONVERSATION WITH SENATOR
HOWARD BAKER

*The subcommittee is almost done with the Clean Air Act, yet
there's the feeling that it's still all up for grabs.*

—In most committees, whatever the subcommittee sends up, the
full committee generally stamps and sends to the floor. In Public

Works, whatever the subcommittee sends up, likely as not, will be changed in full committee.

What is the advantage of your keeping hands off the bill until the arduous subcommittee markups are all done?

—We've noticed in the past—I'll presume to speak for Randolph a little—that when the full committee meets, even if the personnel is substantially the same, the full committee tends to want to rethink the thing some. So Randolph and I decided that, beginning this session, we'd just drop off all subcommittees. We'd just sit there, the two of us, and see what all subcommittees bring into the full committee and give a fresh look, at least from our standpoint. That's not meant to say that Randolph and I are going to have a superior or even a different viewpoint.

Is there less partisanship in the real decision making of the Senate than most outsiders think?

—I think Public Works is a unique committee. For two or three decades it's been the most underrated committee in Congress. I stay on it in preference to any number of other committees I could have gotten on. Where else can you deal with the biggest utility company in the world, the Tennessee Valley Authority; the interstate highway program, the most expensive civil works program we have; with air pollution, water pollution, economic development, the waterways, urban mass transit? The only trouble with the Public Works Committee is its name. It ought to have another name. And for the life of me I can't convince Jennings Randolph of that.[1]

—There's been a tradition of bipartisanship. You know, the Public Works Committee has the most favorable ratio for the minority in its division of staff of any committee in the Senate, which not only instills a sense of fair play, but it also means that the minority is fully up to speed. It can compete with the majority in what goes on. Contrary to some people's belief, I happen to think that being well staffed and well prepared probably avoids controversy instead of creating it. It increases opportunities for alternatives, for good compromises.

What lesson would you draw from this about the legislative process that you might wish you could spread through other—

—If it says anything in general terms, it says that committees lend

[1] The name is soon to be changed by the 1977 reorganization of the Senate to the Environment and Public Works Committee.

themselves far better than the floor of the Senate to being the place where you knock the rough edges off controversy. On the floor of the Senate people usually don't know what's going on. With deference and respect to my colleagues, they don't know that much about the Clean Air Act of 1970 or the Water Quality Act. Maybe we ought to do even more of the working out in committee. I think in other committees there's a greater tendency to just agree to disagree, often on a partisan basis, and just send to the Senate floor a majority report. In Public Works we don't always get unanimity, but we do try to find what most of the committee can feel comfortable with, what most of us can go down there and support. And in Public Works parlance, "most" most often doesn't translate into just the Democrats, just the majority party. It usually means most Democrats and most Republicans.

On a major bill like clean air, do you keep up with what's happening in the subcommittee?

—You better believe it. I get briefed almost every day. Plus the fact that, in all modesty, I know a lot about this thing, an accumulation of a lot of years.

I amble up to Leon's office, two floors above, and learn that the meeting with Muskie requested urgently by Baker was held earlier today but that Baker didn't show up. Instead Bailey Guard, the committee's minority counsel, presented Baker's model-freeze proposal. Senator Buckley, however, was there. Even Leon was surprised at Muskie's reaction.

"Muskie's immediate concern, interestingly enough," says Leon, "was not the impact on the work force, but purely the clean air concern. How long do we let them off the hook? How long would those old cars be permitted to not comply? The Baker proposal deals with means without insuring the result. Muskie's first reaction was: If we're giving them an option for not complying, no matter how much it may seem to encourage compliance, we're changing the purpose of the law, which is to clean the air, to compel them to control emissions. After that, we talked about the jobs thing.

"Also Buckley came up with a proposal—the financial incentive, an increasingly heavy penalty on dirty cars, and an offsetting reward for clean cars. So in 1978 you might penalize them $100 per car if they're dirty but you give them a $250 reward if they sell a clean car. In 1979 the penalty would go up to $250 for a dirty car, and the reward down to $200 for a clean one. In other words, the consumer, who's going to wind up paying the penalty or getting the rebate, pays more for a dirty car. It's a self-financing penalty-reward system, the collected penalties theoretically paying for the rewards. The trouble with it, of course, is that if a penalty is high enough to encourage good emission control systems, won't it be so high as to be confiscatory? And if it's not fairly close to being confiscatory, it isn't going to work.

"So what we agreed in the end is that I'm to take these proposals and bounce them off Leonard Woodcock. Why Leonard Woodcock? He may crap all over the proposals, but if he does it'll be because of their negative impact on the work force. Industry would crap on them even if they were workable. Industry doesn't want to do them simply because it would make them uncomfortable. The other thing about going to Woodcock, as Muskie said to me later, is that this is a way of indicating to Leonard that we care about what he's saying and that we're trying to work something out. If any of these proposals have any appeal for him, he'll probably take them to Henry Ford.

"The problem that Baker quite frankly has—nobody knows about his proposal outside of the people in that meeting, and if it doesn't go anywhere nobody *will* know about it—is finding a way to surface this without having the White House crap all over it. Bear in mind the White House is still committed to nothing less than a five-year moratorium, and here are Buckley and Baker who, with Muskie, want to keep the pressure on to get to the statutory standards as soon as possible."

A lot of people, I comment, would be astonished that the Republican White House is powerless to get the Senate's leading Republicans on the issue to go along.

"You have to remember that Baker considers the environmental issue to be his issue. During the Nixon years he flat out told the White House to leave him alone on the environmental issue. He's quite undoctrinaire about it. And Buckley, an old-values conservative who believes in the market place and so on, also believes that the economic system can't correct environmental problems. Now that Baker's in it, Baker will be the catalyst."

And Howard Baker, of all people, will catalyze a solution that will appeal to liberals, too?

Leon suddenly adopts a puzzled, troubled, faraway tone. "I've been trying to figure out what it is about my liberal friends. They oversimplify and mount a big charge and massively overwhelm a problem. Then, after finding out it's complicated, they walk away from it."

"Have you noticed something else?" I ask gingerly. "Have you noticed that the individuals on this committee most inviting to know personally, who show something personal of themselves, can be ranked in about the same order as their political conservatism? With Buckley, you make personal contact. He talks to *you*. About equally so with McClure, and then Baker; to a lesser extent, but still pleasantly, Domenici. Gary Hart sits there and delivers an address. He's a nice guy; he tells people to call him by his first name, but no personal contact whatsoever. Culver doesn't look at you. I had lunch with him the other day, wanting to talk about his favorite subject, Senate reform, and he pontificated interminably, never making eye contact, impossible to bring down from lofty abstraction to a single specific example or anecdote to illustrate what he wants to correct or how he'd correct it. Even Muskie, whose whole tendency is to be open, rarely makes personal contact."

Leon, luminescent with a mischievous secret, says, "So *you've* found that out too. That's true about liberals, absolutely true with one exception, Tom Eagleton. Look at Ralph Nader—a misanthrope if you ever saw one. Here he is, supposedly a protector of the people, and he's a fascist. He's a corporate statist, and I believe corporate statists are fascists. He advocates federally chartered corporations, a supergovernment regulating big business, and he believes *that* will be good for the quality of life in America. Do you know, Ralph Nader once called me up and asked me to change a provision of a bill? The House-Senate conference had just agreed upon their conference report of the Clean Air Act of 1970, and Nader asked me to change something in the report. I told him to go to hell. Can you imagine what he'd say if General Motors asked for the same thing?

"A thing to remember is that most Senate liberals are introspective and shy. What I've had to learn over the years as a staff person is how to deal with the shyness syndrome. You know, Gary Hart is very shy. Put this in the back of your mind as you wander around this place: watch the wives of the introspective members. Democrats have more aggressive wives than Republicans. More ballsy, more political wives. Make sure you meet—well, never mind."

Years ago I edited a magazine that published a long, saucy poem by Ellen Borden Stevenson, the estranged wife of presidential candidate Adlai Stevenson. I had not yet met many leading politicians, and therefore thought she was inflicting a mean and personal dig at Adlai (rather then setting forth a keen and *general* observation) in this fragment:

> When a man is unable to govern
> His wife, his mother, his nurse,
> He takes a particular pleasure
> In running the Universe!

Monday, October 13

Muskie got quite a weekend press over a speech he "delivered" last Thursday night to the annual dinner of the Liberal Party of New York State. I use "delivered" in quotation marks because neither he nor Senator Jackson, his fellow guest speaker, could get there to speak. The Senate had to stay late Thursday to ratify the Sinai agreement, so at the last minute Muskie asked his lawyer friend, Lester Hyman, to fly up and read it.

To be invited as a headline speaker at the Liberal Party dinner in a year approaching a presidential election means you're being looked over as a possible everyone-knows-what, and to try to get the Democratic everyone-knows-what without support of the Liberal Party is to risk trying to get it without New York State, which is one good way not to get it.

Thursday's pronouncement by Muskie—even if he wasn't there—was high-risk and from the gut. Before today goes by I plan to trace how a major policy speech such as this comes about, through a talk with its ghost writer. But first, here are some fragments of the speech itself:

"We failed in 1972 . . . and on the eve of 1976, we face the grim possibility of failing again. . . . How can that happen? After seven years of a Republican administration distinguished only by its failures, how could the American electorate fail to vote for a new liberal administration? When we *know* what's right, how can so many Americans not follow our leadership? How can so many Americans miss the point?

"The answer, I submit, is that *we* have missed the point.

"For in the past decade liberals have developed an ideology and state of mind that is narrow, unimaginative, and often irrelevant. . . . Four decades ago we discovered the possibilities of government action to better the lives of Americans. People . . . prospered as a result. But something has happened since then—and it's basically happened through us. People are still discontented. They still want change. . . . Yet when the average citizen turns to us for help, what does he find?

"Consider, for example, the 1972 national platform of the Democratic Party. It runs about fifty pages, nearly fifteen thousand words, and reads like the catalogue of virtually every problem that we liberals think bothers the American people. . . . Wonderfully comprehensive and esoteric. . . . It showed that we knew all about government, and knew just what government programs needed change.

"In promising so much for so many, it was meaningless. Nowhere in there was there any statement of what those hundreds of changes would cost. How much, for example, would the new towns program cost? Would we need higher taxes to pay for it? How many people really would be helped?

". . . The Democratic Platform of 1972 represents to me the culmination of years of liberal neglect—of allowing a broad-based coalition to narrow—of progressively ignoring the *real* fears and aspirations of people—and of assuming we know best what the people need. . . .

"I read my mail. I talk with voters in the towns of Maine, and I listen. . . . Most important, they don't believe that government really cares about them. All they need is one encounter with some government bureaucrat to confirm that. In Maine, for example, it now takes a full year to process a Social Security disability claim. . . .

"My basic question is this: Why can't liberals start raising hell about a government so big, so complex, so expensive, and so unresponsive that it's dragging down every good program we've worked for?

"Yet we stay away from that question as if it was the plague. We're in a rut. We've accepted the status quo. We know that government can do much to improve the lives of every American. But that conviction has also led us to become the defenders of government, no matter its mistakes. Our emotional stake in government is so much that we regard common-sense criticism of government almost as a personal attack. We resist questioning the basic assumptions of the structure and role of government, fearing the unknown, fearing that somehow we have more to lose than gain through change.

"Budget reform *could* mean cutting back spending on health programs, but it could also mean fewer gold-plated weapons systems. Productivity standards *could* cost union support, but they could help restore public confidence in the many government workers who work hard. Or regulatory reform *could* jeopardize health and safety regulation, but it could also loosen the grip of special interests on agencies. Plainly, we cannot move forward without questioning such basic assumptions—and running certain dangers. . . .

"We must adopt government reform as our first priority—as an end in itself. We must recognize that an efficient government—well managed, cost-effective, equitable, and responsible—is in itself a social good.

"We must do this secure in the conviction that first priority on efficient government is *not* a retreat from social goals but simply a realization that without it those goals are meaningless."

Bob Rackleff, in his early thirties, is tall with an unruly shock of curly brown hair that lofts at an angle from his head. He meets the world with a mild, easy smile. His crowded workplace, at which no writer can imagine another writer writing, is in one of the lower-price

Carroll Arms rooms of Al From's Intergovernmental Relations Sub-committee. Like Jane Fenderson, with whom he shares the room (and a secretary, crowding it further), he is on the payroll of the subcommittee.

A CONVERSATION WITH BOB RACKLEFF

You've known for some time that this speech was scheduled?

—I've known since June it was coming up and knew it was important. Unlike normal speeches, interest in this one spread wider than IGR. For example, Doug Bennet of the Budget Committee asked his staff people to take a shot at a draft. Lester Hyman, who'd worked in the '68 and '72 campaigns, was interested in it and sent in some thoughts, similar to a draft. An academic friend of Maynard Toll's sent in three or four pages of thoughts, which you might call a draft.

Were these solicited?

—These people knew something was coming up. Perhaps Muskie, seeing some of these people, mentioned it was an important speech and "if you've got some ideas to contribute, why don't you send them in." I assume that happened, but I don't know. Over the summer I did a great deal of reading and thinking and research, and we talked within the IGR staff right here, particularly with Al From, about what kind of theme we wanted. That was continuous. Then a couple of weeks ago he was scheduled for a speech at Canisius College at Buffalo, which seemed like a good opportunity to try out the theme and some rhetoric.

He wasn't too crazy about the Canisius speech, was he? He just laid aside the script and spoke extemporaneously.

—Right. I don't even remember the speech I gave him. But I knew that there was a theme buried in there somewhere that was useful, one that he'd like and one that we needed. It was just a matter of articulating it the right way. The problem was how you express a liberal's concern for the plight of government today. How you take what has been in the past an orgy of breast beating about the failure of liberalism, the junking of the ideals of the New Deal, and turn them positive and affirmative: let's make liberalism work, let's be proud that we're liberals, et cetera, et cetera.

—In terms of that final speech draft, it was just a matter of coming in the Sunday before the speaking date and just sitting down at the typewriter. Time was getting tight and I didn't have anything. That was five days before the speech.

Are you terrified when you get that close and have no speech?

—Sure I am. It's a pressure situation that every writer gets himself into. So I just came in determined to have a speech drafted. Did the first draft that day, in about four or five hours—ten pages. Next day I reworked some of it and Al looked at it. Jane looked at it. Other people on the IGR staff looked at it and made some suggestions. All that day.

Nobody in Muskie's office saw it?

—Right. Nobody.

—So by about six o'clock Monday night we had a typed speech. It looked good. Reaction from people around here was pretty positive. So I felt pretty good, and I walked over to Muskie's office knowing he was getting ready to leave for home. I ran into him in the hall. He was on his way to his car. I handed him the envelope and said, "Here's the draft of the Liberal Party speech." He gives me that look and says, "Oh, another one?" By this time he's already rejected all the other drafts. Not only a rewrite of my Canisius draft but the Budget Committee draft and that outside stuff.

Suppose he rejected this too. Would he have spoken extemporaneously?

—Apparently he didn't want to, but I'm sure he could have. As far as I'm concerned, for ninety-five per cent of his speeches he doesn't need a speechwriter. He's been doing this long enough. He's articulate enough. He can sit down and, on the back of an envelope, write a stirring speech, then deliver it well. He's really a pro.

—So I handed him the draft and he said, "Oh, another one?" And I said, "Well, I think you'll like this one," which is out of character for me, but I felt good about it. And then he said, "Thanks," and kept on walking.

—The next day I flew up to Boston with him. On the way back— he hadn't read my Liberal Party draft the night before—he took it out and started to read it. He didn't say anything, read through it kind of leisurely. My hands were filling up with pools of sweat. Then he finishes it and opens his briefcase and puts it in there and closes his briefcase and says, "Pretty good speech. I'll read it a second time." That's when I went back and checked out the bar on the plane.

—I guess it was next day I got word from Charlie to just run the speech as it was. He didn't have any changes. None. So we just mimeographed it and began distributing it widely. This is now Wednesday. Bob Rose had his press release done. The first mailing was five or six hundred pieces at least, and then there've been a couple more printings after that.

So that before the press reaction he knew he liked it?

—Right.

Then on Thursday the Sinai thing came up on the floor. When did you find out that he wasn't going to New York to deliver it?

—I guess Thursday afternoon, but it remained unsure till the last minute.

Were you crushed?

—No, not especially, because having done this kind of thing for a while, I knew there are a lot of functions for a speech. One of the least important is the entertainment—delivering it in order to entertain and perhaps inform people. I also knew it was a fresh theme and that it was going to sell. Attract attention in the press. So yesterday we met with Muskie—Al and I and Charlie—on how to follow up on the theme, maybe develop it toward more concrete proposals, maybe developing legislation. It's very rare to talk like that with him and actually get some pretty good feedback from him that may help on the next speech. Toward the end of the meeting he gave me a terrific lift. I mean, it was just a classic Muskie reaction, but it was terrific praise. He looks at me and says, "Well, you had a best seller last time, but just remember that Margaret Mitchell had only one *Gone With the Wind*." So I answered somewhat ruefully, "Yeah, and she got run over by an automobile, so I'd better watch out."

Tuesday, November 18

Today is the big day when the full Public Works Committee addresses itself to the Clean Air Act. The subcommittee, at its October 8 meeting six weeks ago, just managed to cram through the unresolved portions of the bill.

All seems the same as in subcommittee markups—same room, same audience of lobbyists—except for a subtle heightening of tension and the occupancy of the presiding chair by florid, dainty-mannered Jennings Randolph. Whimsey-faced Howard Baker is beside him. Promptly at nine-thirty Randolph coos, "A pleasant good morning to you, ladies and gentlemen, and our guests, members of the committee. . . ." Only three Senators are absent of fourteen committee members: Senator Montoya, who has dutifully delivered his proxy to Chairman Randolph and will have no truck with this incomprehensible business of environmental pollution; Morgan, who is both intrigued and terrified by the intricacies of the subject, and wishes he had time for it, but has so far made sure he doesn't; and Culver, deep into Armed Services business, who has often dropped in at subcommittee markups just long enough to be assured that Gary Hart has the situation well in hand.

With the exception of Hart and possibly Culver, every committee member now seems convinced that if the Clean Air Act is to be enforceable the requirement of .4 NOx must be expunged. But whoever proposes this change will be accused of leading a retreat from clean air and virtue. Who will be first? And what euphemism will he employ to make it easier for others to join him?

After two hours of eleven men pirouetting and toeing toward and leaping around the subject, several members edgy about neglected obligations elsewhere, Senator Muskie offers, "I'd be glad to make a proposition you could vote on today if you'd like."

"Sure, let's do it," Baker eagerly responds.

"I'd like to propose that, as a modification of the subcommittee proposal, we establish .4 NOx as a research objective."

"I second the motion," Baker snaps.

"If it were proper, Mr. Chairman," Senator Stafford thirds, "I would second it too—"

"It is proper," Randolph assures him.

"—even though," continues Stafford, "it modifies what Senator Hart and I proposed."

So even the proud co-author of the "compromise" that enabled .4 to stay in the bill now abandons the decimal-point figure that has become a symbol to the environmentalist lobby of purity of soul as well as of air.

"I think what you're reaching toward," clucks Senator McClure, "is the same thing I tried to reach toward in a somewhat different way when I offered the amendment in subcommittee to set the .4 as the ultimate goal, but set it in a time frame that would indicate to the industry that we didn't expect them to attain it under the present technology, and giving sufficient time for Congress to look at this again. . . . I'll support this amendment because I think it's better than what we're now doing."

"At the appropriate time," says Baker, reinforcing Muskie's suggestion, "I intend to offer an amendment for the creation of a National Air Quality Commission. Frankly, Jim, I would hope that the National Air Quality Commission would be mandated to examine not only the technical feasibility of attaining .4 NOx or some other level in the future, but the necessity for it, its health effect and its co-relationship to other pollutants."

"I would like to ask a question and then make a statement," says Senator Hart warily, blinking tensely at Muskie through his pink-tinted glasses. "What is the incentive? What is the goal? I don't understand the concept of a research goal."

Muskie reviews the collapse of .4 as a defensible goal, adding, "If we still want to keep it on the back burner, either in a research way, or in the sense that Senator Baker suggests, *that* I can support. That is, frankly, my position."

"I think the technology presently exists to meet the .4 standard,"

Hart asserts. "I think that rush-hour levels of nitrogens of oxide in the air in certain parts of this country are presently unacceptable. The automobile is responsible for that. There is one way to solve that problem. That is to mandate the industry to meet a standard which the National Academy of Sciences, among others, has said is the standard that human beings can live with. I think if we don't have that standard in there, the research will never be done."

"Senator Baker," chimes in Senator Domenici, predictably mounting a seesaw, "I tend to agree with Senator Hart in this respect. I think there has to be some substantial motivation to do the best we possibly can. I don't know that .4 fits in terms of feasibility, doability. It appears to me that once we take it out—and I will support taking it out—there will be no focal point for a real effort to get there—if, in fact, your commission were to find it is needed."

And so it goes until the buzzer for a floor vote late in the morning halts the meeting, and members agree to convene again at 3 P.M.

The break gives Muskie and Leon a speck of time to work out a specific new proposal they judge to be supportable by the present mood of the full committee. At the afternoon meeting Muskie puts forward a formula (including the "research objective" of .4 NOx) that lays out, following a series of interim standards for 1977 through 1979, a final statutory standard for 1980 of .41 HC, 3.4 CO, and 1.0 NOx. The committee agrees to vote tomorrow.

Upon adjournment, as Muskie picks his way through the buzzing crowd, he hesitates and looks blankly back at me, a look I have learned means he's too shy to say, "Join me." I catch up with him. As we shove through the door he comments, "Well, I don't know if the iron is hot, but at least we've struck."

Wednesday, November 19

In the familiar ambience of the Public Works chamber, the full committee again gathers. An hour of colloquy brews down to an intense exchange between Hart and Muskie.

"The automobile industry," asserts the younger Senator in his final, now-or-never plea to retain .4 NOx, "has put enormous resources—dollars and talent—into design. I would ask each member of this committee to ask himself: If even a fraction of those resources had been put into making an engine both efficient and non-pollutive, couldn't that great industry have solved those problems by 1979? I have great confidence in that industry. I have more confidence in that industry than those who speak for it. With all respect to Senator Baker, we are talking about creating another bureaucracy at a time when people are fed up with bureaucracies. We are going to create an Air Quality Commission perhaps to do the job the EPA is already mandated to do. I see more delays and more studies. I think we already have plenty of facts. I have heard a lot more talk in the last two days about what is good for the industry than I have about what is good for the health of the people of this country. I would have preferred that a lot more people were speaking up about lung cancer and the effects of air pollutants on health, and not only our health but our children's health and their children's. As I said yesterday and say again this morning, I think the issue is what motivates new technology. Is it voluntarism on the part of industry—or a congressional mandate?"

"The passage of the 1970 act," responds Muskie quietly, with a faint air of paternal patience, "disposed of voluntarism versus mandates. I don't think anybody is more closely identified with the notion that you have to *force* technology by statutory mandates than I am. But there is also the question of credibility of the statutory requirement. . . . If you ask for the impossible, I doubt that you really get the kind of motivation you need."

For all the near unanimity, and for all the sighs of relief at Muskie's escape hatch of a "research objective," still nobody's happy with it. Stafford, the canny upper New England compromiser, tries a new compromise: an amendment to the Muskie proposal, retaining .4 NOx as a standard, but delaying its deadline until 1985. It gets only three votes: Stafford's, Hart's, and Culver's through a proxy voted by Hart.

"The vote," counsel Barry Meyer announces immediately, "is now on the Muskie amendment to establish .4 NOx as a research objective." Only two votes against it: Hart's, and Culver's cast by Hart. It is adopted 12–2.

The committee is now to vote on Muskie's proposal for "ultimate" standards of .41/3.4/1.0—but not on deadlines for those standards. Much confusion finally compels Muskie to clarify that the vote is to adopt those standards "for some part of production at some point in time" to be determined by a subsequent vote. The standards are approved 11 to 2—the two negative votes cast by Hart for himself and Culver.

Next enters the question of time. "I haven't heard much support for it," Muskie says dolefully, "but I would like to have a vote on achieving those standards by 1980 for all production."

"How strongly, Ed," solicits Randolph, "would you oppose 1982?"

"I would like to vote on 1980."

"For all production?" Buckley asks glumly.

"Yes."

McClure moves to substitute 1982, "to give us the opportunity for Congress to take another look at this between now and the time they must go into production."

"I would further modify the McClure amendment," says Buckley, offering a substitute to the substitute, "to say we set no standard for NOx for 1982 so as to guarantee that we have the input from this [Air Quality] Commission."

"I don't know how we are going to get through this morass," moans Howard Baker. "What I'm going to aim for finally is that by 1979 we get ten per cent production at 1.0 NOx. That's what I'm reaching for. For the life of me, I don't know how I'm going to reach it."

Domenici is sure that Baker's tongue has slipped: "You said 1979?"

"That is right."

"Senator Buckley," asks Chairman Randolph helplessly, "are you going to pursue this no-final-date?"

"Yes, I am," Buckley gently says firmly.

"Will you call the roll," Randolph wearily instructs Meyer. Buckley's no-time-for-NOx loses 11 to 2, only its author and Senator Baker supporting it.

Immediately Meyer calls the roll on the McClure substitute to delay final targets until 1982. This could pass, and the difference to the auto industry is incalculable. Not only two years for continued research, and two years free of the burden of new technology to recoup profits lost in the recent recession but, perhaps most important, two more years to lobby for a new five-year moratorium.

The vote is closer than any today, its composition curious. The McClure delay loses 8 to 5. McClure, of course, casts his vote for it, and, not too surprisingly, so does Buckley, whose position has drifted far from Muskie's since the days of the Muskie-Buckley "deal." The other three, however, are all cast by Senator Randolph, two of them the proxies of Gravel and Montoya. That is a foreboding crack in the solid core of votes Muskie normally counts on. For forthcoming votes Muskie will have to reassess his support carefully, taking nobody for granted. And narrow victories won't do. Just as Randolph does not relish Muskie opposing him on the floor, Muskie would certainly not wish to take a politically explosive anti-pollution bill to the floor, where the country's most powerful industries would like to gun it down, and find himself opposed by his own committee chairman.

Finally, counsel Meyer calls for the vote on Senator Muskie's target of 1980 for the final statutory standards of .41/3.4/1.0.

Of thirteen votes cast—Bentsen, absent, has left no proxy on this issue—ten Senators vote for Muskie's date, and three, Buckley, McClure, and Baker, vote against it. Randolph, whose three votes a few moments ago gave McClure's 1982 deadline respectable support, has now switched to Muskie's 1980.

Suddenly there is hubbub. Meyer has not yet announced the tally.

Senator Burdick is whispering to Meyer, to Randolph. Apparently he wants to change his vote to no. That would make the tally 9–4. A twitch of realization on Randolph's face is flicked at Meyer. The chairman gets up and trundles to the conference room. Meyer follows. His three votes, if switched, would now defeat Muskie, 7–6. Randolph is in there calculating with his counsel on how best to employ the power of decision suddenly thrust upon him. Should he defeat the tough 1980 deadline? In favor of what? McClure's 1982 has already been put down lopsidedly. Whatever new alternative he can think up, does he want to take on Muskie's ire—not only in this committee but possibly on the floor—shielded only flimsily by a one-vote edge?

Returning to the chair, Randolph purrs, "You will understand that we are asking for the call of the roll again, not for any delaying tactic."

Except for Burdick's change, the roll call proceeds identically. That apparently is what Randolph wanted to know—whether anyone else would switch to no, generating a tide he would be happy to swell. Holding his two proxies until the roll is completed, he now casts three votes aye—for Muskie's deadline. The revised final vote, however, is far from the solid victory that its 9–4 makes it appear. At the whim of an inscrutable man it could have gone the other way.

Collecting his folders upon the meeting's adjournment until Friday morning, Karl Braithwaite says that so far it's coming out about the way he originally thought it would and that he and the staff are reasonably satisfied. I tell Karl that I perceive consternation among the lobbyists for environmental organizations.

"The environmentalists," Karl says in his scholarly way, "forget the effectiveness of Muskie's legislative technique in putting through the original Clean Air Act, and in many battles since—his way of searching out the secure middle and pushing through the best bill he can get that will be carried by a substantial, secure majority. Their legislative philosophy is different. The environmentalists are very proud of their tremendous victory on strip mining. They fought to retain every provision, giving away as little as they could, and scratched around for every vote they could get till they had their bare majority. And of course it was vetoed, and there weren't enough votes to override. So they enjoyed their victory, but today there's no strip-mining law. On this thing—on clean air—the White House has

made it perfectly clear it's in direct opposition to what this committee
is doing. Courting a veto on this bill is just *not* what all these people
have put in a year of work for."

I catch the attention of Barbara Alexander of the Sierra Club,
draw her aside, and ask her reaction. Her eyes are swollen with fury.

"It was a big sellout."

By whom?

"By Big Ed Muskie."

Why?

"Because he didn't fight for the .4 on NOx."

Isn't it evident that the Clean Air Act will be destroyed if Muskie
presses for the maximum on every point?

"Pressing for the whole thing," she asserts, "is the only way you
get anything done in this town. I'd rather lose the whole thing than
get these incremental bits. Have you ever seen any real change take
place incrementally?"

Her group heads for the cafeteria. I stroll with them to the elevator. A moment before the automatic elevator doors slide shut, Art
Mackwell, a short young man with straight sandy hair, and with a
certainty matching Barbara's, declares, "You never know what votes
you could have had until you fight."

I ask around as to who this Art Mackwell is, and the answer di-
verts me for the rest of the day, piecing together its intriguing background. He's here daily to represent not an underbudgeted environmental organization but a multinational corporation that grosses
more than five billion dollars a year. His client—Mackwell is not
directly in its employ but belongs to a small Washington law firm it
retains—is the Engelhard Minerals and Chemicals Corporation that
mines and sells rare metals and minerals, fuels and fertilizers. As
leading miners and marketers of platinum, the catalytic agent used in
mitigating the bad breath of automobiles, Engelhard obviously has a
major interest in catalytic converters. In fact they have become manufacturers of catalytic converters on their own, and have led the development of the three-way catalyst. The environmentalist lobby
bases its commitment to the .4 NOx goal on the existence of the
three-way catalyst and the hope its performance will improve. So the
multinational Engelhard Corporation and the public-interest environmentalists have a perfect coincidence of lobbying goals.

To harvest the full irony of the strange alliance requires going

deeper into personal relationships—and back in time. Last spring, at
about the time the auto company presidents and Leonard Woodcock
found themselves on the same side of this bill in hearings, Muskie realized that the auto emission standards were about to encounter opposition in both dimension and kind unlike any that previous ver-
sions of the Clean Air Act had to survive. Unless an equally
compelling pressure could be applied from an opposite source, Senator Muskie feared, his subcommittee might cave in under the combined industry-labor assault, based on the unsubstantiated argument
that auto emission control could only be accomplished at the cost of
jobs and precious fuel. Or the Senate itself might back off from the
law.

One day Muskie plumbed these apprehensions with a close Washington friend, a lawyer. This particular lawyer-friend, named Berl
Bernhard, served as manager of Muskie's 1972 campaign for the
presidential nomination—and more recently has become a Washington lawyer for the Engelhard Corporation. Although time and again
Muskie has deplored Detroit's "taking the wrong road" to clean air
compliance through makeshift add-on devices instead of developing
a totally redesigned, cleaner, more fuel-efficient automobile engine,
at this moment he and his friend had one interest in common. Something *had* to be done to generate nationwide, grass-roots opposition
to the auto lobby, whose freshened campaign might devastate any
chance of cleaning the air.

A few days after that conversation a public-spirited contribution of
$10,000 was sent from the New York headquarters of the Engelhard
Corporation to the headquarters of the Sierra Club in San Francisco,
the sum earmarked specifically for plane tickets and hotel rooms to
enable hinterland, amateur lobbyists to enliven Washington with
home-grown, spontaneous demands for cleaner air—and, incidentally, more catalytic converters. (Muskie asserts he never suggested
that donation, nor did he have any advance knowledge of it.)

Contributions in the nature of that $10,000—from the very rich to
the deserving poor who happen to have coincidental lobbying interests—are made every year. In the ethics of lobbying, there's nothing shady about the practice. It derives from the same new technique
of big-time lobbyists that inspired the American Paper Institute when
it armed labor union leaders with computer-derived "research" and
maneuvered their confrontation with Muskie in his own state.

Weeks ago, in a casual conversation about lobbying techniques, Richard Lahn, the gentle-mannered former buttonholer for the Sierra Club who sits through markups wearing a railroad cap, remarked to me: "There are a couple of rules for good lobbyists, and an important one is never make enemies. You have to agree to disagree. No matter who you are and who your adversary is, if you work around here long enough, today's adversary will someday be on your side of some issue."

Early in the evening I drop by Muskie's office to close out the day, and Bob Rose tosses me a two-page, single-space press release with occasional whole sentences underlined and phrases in capital letters. "For further information," it says, contact Barbara Reid Alexander, who is identified not as Sierra Club lobbyist but as Environmental Quality Chairperson, League of Women Voters of Maine. (A denunciation by the League of Women Voters will hurt Muskie in Maine far more than one by the Sierra Club.)

"She stormed into the Senate press gallery," Bob reports acidly, "to deliver it by hand to Don Larrabee."

Larrabee, the gallery's only Maine correspondent, covers for the Portland *Press Herald* and the Bangor *Daily News*. Bob tells me he's already learned that both papers will be running it prominently tomorrow. The release begins:

The League of Women Voters of Maine today strongly criticized Senator Edmund Muskie for leading [sic] the Senate Public Works Committee's efforts to substantially weaken the 1970 Clean Air Act's strong controls on auto emissions. . . . "For the Senator known as 'Mr. Clean' in the nation, Senator Muskie has performed miserably," stated Ms. Alexander.

Thursday, November 20

All committee meetings are banned this morning because the Senate is meeting in executive session—closed to the public and virtually all staff, with tight security at all doors—to discuss the CIA investigation.

Dropping in on Leon, I find him defensive about yesterday, but in an admirable way for a staff man: going out of his way to take heat off his boss. I ask just when Muskie decided not to support .4 NOx for any year in the near future, and what factor settled it.

"I'm the bad guy in this," Leon is quick to say. "The night before last I'd written him a memo with a paragraph saying that if he felt .4 was a political necessity, maybe the thing to do would be to support it for 1985. But I crossed that out. As we started our meeting I said to him, 'In good conscience, Senator, there is no basis for supporting .4 as a statutory mandate. There is no way that in good conscience I can recommend it to you.' So I'm the bad guy in this."

"Yet Gary Hart feels, in good conscience, he has to go the other way."

"I don't understand it at all."

"You don't understand what?"

"I just don't understand people who like pyrrhic victories. Either technologically or politically, that number isn't defensible, it isn't credible. Power is credibility, remember? Muskie has to defend this bill—not Jennings Randolph, not Joe Montoya, not Mike Gravel, not Gary Hart. *They* don't want the job of defending this bill on the floor. Therefore, they know that what goes out of this committee must be something that Muskie is willing to defend. Now Muskie knows *he* has to have a couple of things. He needs to have some reasonable certainty, for example, of the support of Howard Baker."

"Which he didn't have yesterday with reasonable certainty."

"He has it now, and some other bipartisan support. When this issue comes to debate, Baker is going to be the linchpin. Muskie knows the auto industry will line up some very shrewd people on the floor to attack this bill. If it were just auto emissions, that would be fairly easy. But we're going to the floor with transportation controls, with non-degradation, with enforcement, a package that's sufficient to cause a majority of the Senate—a *majority* of the Senate—to oppose it constitutionally. I don't mean that with a big *c,* I mean oppose it viscerally. They're going to feel that this clean air business has gone too far, and they're going to be picking at it. So it's got to be credible not only as a total bill, but credible in each of its parts."

Leon's voice turns quiet, far away, speculative. "Speaking of Burdick supporting Muskie yesterday, the whole auto lobby is descending on Burdick today. They're up there right now. They're after Morgan, too."

"What can they do at this late hour?"

"I don't know. Don't have the slightest idea. I just know they're sure as hell up there."

Friday, November 21

"Let's get this straight," demands Quentin Burdick minutes after the start of today's climactic meeting. The months of subcommittee wrangling and indecision and anguish, and the automobile standards it finally decided to propose, will either be confirmed or countermanded by today's votes. What the full committee approves today for auto standards is what will eventually be *the bill,* to be defended by floor manager Muskie before the full Senate (unless he refuses to support what comes out), and probably what will eventually go to a House-Senate conference. "I'm a bit handicapped," explains Burdick, "because I'm not a member of the subcommittee. You mean to say that at 1.0 NOx you get as much fuel efficiency as you do at 2.0 NOx? Is there testimony in the record to this effect?"

"Yes," Billings asserts flatly.

When Quentin Burdick demands to "get this straight," you know there's trouble coming. He is a blunt country lawyer, nothing slick or courtroom phony about him. His leathery face, unruly brows, and stubborn jaw, his dark brown suit of Sears Roebuck mail-order cut with pants cuffs, bespeak a lifestyle of no nonsense. Hours after most Senators head home to their apartments at Watergate and the Sheraton Park, or to manors in Bethesda and McLean, Burdick, a widower during most of his fifteen years in the Senate who commutes to North Dakota to see his new bride on weekends, works in his office late and alone, then walks to a small basement flat on C Street, N.E., blocks from the Dirksen Building, in a low-rent, racially mixed area of congressional staffers, young families, students, and dropouts.

"Could I add one thing to that?" says Hal Brayman to Leon's flat affirmative. "That depends on whether you go to new technology, which the industry says does not exist at this point. If you go to existing technology, as the industry probably would on smaller cars, you would have a fuel penalty." (As ranking Republican, Buckley has drifted from Muskie's position; in parallel, Brayman's comments at markups have dutifully separated from Leon's.)

Diminutive Senator Morgan, like a pony raring to race, taps his toes nervously on the floor, which they barely reach. "*Is* the technology available? You say the industry says it isn't. What do *you* say?"

"The best technical people outside the industry—" Billings begins.

"Why did Russell Train recommend 2.0 NOx?" Senator Burdick breaks in.

"Russell Train recommended 2.0 NOx because he was concerned with the sulphate issue. Number two, because he estimated that at that time it would be adequate to meet the problems of the cities."

"How early," Morgan asks Senator Baker, "do you anticipate the Air Quality Commission would be able to be of help to this committee if it comes about?"

"I would think that by February of 1977, or at the latest the first of March, the Air Quality Commission could report at least on the NOx standard."

"I find myself in a doubtful position," Morgan confesses. "I've been trying to study this problem since I started sitting in with Senator Muskie. I find the information I get from varying sources so conflicting that I'm just not in a position really to resolve the issues in my own mind at the present time. The Air Quality Commission looks good to me."

"I guess I've been around this about as long as anybody," Muskie cautions him. "EPA was established to provide us information. Once the industry didn't like EPA's point of view, EPA became labeled as biased. Then the industry urged us to use the National Academy of Sciences. At the recommendation of this committee—Senator Domenici was the author of that proposal—Congress funded a half-million-dollar study to review this thing again. So now the National Academy of Sciences releases its advice and we are told that, well, they are not for real, that they are a bunch of ivory-tower scientists, because their findings are contrary to the position that the industry would like the Congress to take. So now *they* are biased. I would expect that if this commission—which I think would be a rational and sensible kind of tool—if this commission is created, and comes up in 1977 with recommendations that the industry doesn't like, the industry will find a way to establish a bias in *those* findings. You are never going to get a report from any source, from this commission or any other, that is going to be accepted by everybody who is affected by it. In the last analysis *we* are going to have to make the decisions."

"That is exactly right, Mr. Chairman," chimes Chairman Randolph.

"I like the commission argument," Muskie continues, "but if we do it as a way of further delay, then I would oppose it. I think we've got to make some decisions today. I think the decisions ought to be at the cutting edge of technological potential. If we leave the industry comfortable, technologically, we are going to be here in 1980 talking about a 1985 deadline. I just hope that we keep that in mind as we make these decisions."

"Let me assure you," says Domenici to Morgan, "that you're under no handicap having started fresh. Some of us have heard all the conflicting testimony. If I were to look back at it all, I might just have spent the last two weeks reading up, forgetting about all the rest, and I'd know just as much as I know now. Secondly, I believe

Senator Muskie has put it in its proper context when he spoke of the cutting edge of new technology. But I regret to say to my distinguished friend it doesn't help me to come up with an answer because I don't know where the cutting edge is."

McClure states his agreement.

"Mr. Chairman," says Baker remorsefully, "I have to leave in five minutes to go to an executive session of the Intelligence Committee to hear testimony from Dr. Kissinger."

"Do you have some spare intelligence?" Muskie pleads. "Would you bring some back?"

"So far we've found none."

Baker, Hart, and Morgan agree to stay long enough to vote on a Culver amendment to penalize service stations as well as factory-franchised auto dealers for tampering with emission control devices. It passes 13 to 1, only McClure opposing it.

"Incidentally," beams Chairman Randolph, "that is the largest attendance that we have had."

Baker quips back, "I will accommodate the committee by leaving." He departs with Hart and Morgan.

"How far are we going on this bill today?" asks Burdick. "There are a couple of areas we have already acted on and I'm not satisfied with what we did."

"How long do we need a discussion on your matter?" Randolph asks Stafford regarding a pending amendment.

"Not on *his,*" says Burdick. "I'm ready to vote on his. I have questions on what we *have* done."

The audience laughs nervously.

"You're always going to have them, too," adds Muskie.

Stafford's amendment provides that the 1980 standards (including 1.0 NOx) would be required in 1978 and '79 of ten per cent of all cars over 4,500 pounds, not including California cars, which would already have to meet tough standards. The amendment, a gracious retreat from the fifty per cent requirement of the original Stafford-Hart compromise in subcommittee, is a device for keeping immediate pressure on the industry.

Senator Buckley serves notice that he prefers going to the ten per cent in 1979 instead of 1978.

"Why don't we vote on Stafford's first?" presses Muskie.

"Fine," Buckley defers.

The Stafford amendment is supported only by Stafford, Culver, and Muskie, losing 8–3.

Next, Buckley wins, 8–4. So the pilot ten per cent of cars don't have to meet 1.0 NOx until 1979, still another year of grace for Detroit. Two newcomers to the issue, Burdick and Morgan, whose questions this morning reveal only last-minute cramming, have loosed a rockslide. Two days ago Muskie put together one majority after another. Today the reversal began with Burdick's "Let's get this straight." Then Morgan, joining the opposition, hands his proxy not to Muskie (as he has done through most of the summer) but to Randolph. Randolph, uneasily penned in the Muskie corral, takes strength from the two loose-running newcomers and makes his break —with the proxies of Montoya and Bentsen. And so, in a single morning, the subcommittee's deadlines crumble, so fragile were the political props that supported them.

"Due to the information I received today," Senator Burdick at last gets his chance to announce, "I would have voted no on 1.0 NOx in 1980. Can we have that on the record?"

With elaborate generosity, Randolph grants putting on the record what Burdick, by saying so, has already put on the record.

On second thought, Burdick is not satisfied: "Mr. Chairman, I think I would make a motion to put the 1980 NOx to 2.0. Not until 1981 have the 1.0. I move it."

Smarting from the votes on Stafford and Buckley, Muskie sits glumly through the roll call. The vote comes down to four in favor— Burdick and Randolph, as well as Morgan's and Bentsen's proxies cast by Randolph—and six against. Before the committee recesses at 11:25 A.M. counsel Meyer reports that two more members, returning to the proceedings, have recorded their votes on the Burdick motion, one in favor, one opposed, "so that under any circumstances it would fail for want of a majority."

The auto lobbyists who visited Burdick and Morgan yesterday earned their keep.

Considering Billings' beet-red anger at Barbara Alexander's public attack on Muskie (especially painful because Barbara's husband,

Don, his former staff member, remains a close friend of Leon's), his comment after today's markup can only be termed restrained: "If the so-called environmentalists, instead of attacking their friend Ed Muskie, had done what they should have been doing—working on strengthening the positions of Burdick and Morgan—we wouldn't have had this loss. That's the tragedy of people like that and the things they do."

It is astonishing that General Motors didn't even have a lobbying office in Washington until 1969, when a sudden assault by auto safety laws and early anti-pollution legislation forced the previously unregulated automobile empire to open diplomatic relations with the United States. Even today, GM's vice-president for governmental relations bases in Detroit rather than at the seat of government. GM's war against the Clean Air Act is fought by one man in Washington, William C. Chapman, an automotive engineer, retired Navy officer, former U. S. Embassy attaché, and Ph.D. candidate in Russian studies, as well as a soccer buff. There is, somewhere, a local boss over Chapman and his small band of colleagues who lobby on other issues, but, says Billings airily, "In my ten years here I've never met his boss."

A Michigan Congressman close to GM explains (as long as his name is unmentioned) the corporation's reticence: "They've always been highly fearful of anti-trust action. As a result, they've traditionally preferred to let legislation go against them rather than attract attention through lobbying."

In one of Washington's new downtown office buildings off Connecticut Avenue, Bill Chapman receives me in his spacious layout. His conversation is pungent, rambling, and uninhibited. "Oh no, I can't complain about the Senate understanding the problem," he admits with surprising candor. "They've done their homework. The Senate committee knows three times as much about this as the House committee knows." That remarkable statement is his reply to my question as to why he expects to do better in the House. Inadvertently, it also answers my unasked question as to why his activity has been low-key for months among Senate committee members until yesterday afternoon.

A CONVERSATION WITH WILLIAM C. CHAPMAN

*You and your colleagues from other auto companies, as I under-
stand it, spent time yesterday with Senators Burdick and Morgan.
The visits were apparently very successful. What happened?*

—Burdick's from a farm area out there where they don't have a
pollution problem, and at this point he'd had nothing to do with the
bill at all. I guess the others—the environmentalists and maybe the
committee members themselves—assumed that Burdick was part of
Muskie's little group on the environment. Same for Morgan.

—I didn't make that assumption. So yesterday I went to Burdick's
staff man and told him our point of view. He seemed receptive and
reasonable, so I said, "Can we talk to Burdick?" I had one of our
technical guys from Detroit with me. We got in to see him and I
started to explain the bill. Burdick just couldn't believe some of the
things we were telling him about what this bill would cost in fuel
economy. He was aghast at the deadlines, at the whole bill as we
went through it point by point. He'd say, "God, how could they expect you to do this kind of thing?"

—Morgan is hard as hell to see. We kept making appointments
and he kept breaking them. I can go in any time and talk with his
staff man, Bill Smith, but I don't know if it goes any further. This
time all four lobbyists of the four auto companies went together and
said, "We've got to talk with him." As I recall, we got an eleven
o'clock appointment for which we waited until one, then it got put off
until two. So we went to lunch, came back at two, and waited for another hour. At five o'clock we're back there, and we ended up finally
seeing him at six-thirty, and it was eight before we got out. By the
time we finished pouring those figures on him he was as aghast as
Burdick.

*Over the years in dealing with Congress, what has been hardest
about selling your point of view?*

—We talk health and we talk costs and all that sort of thing. The
thing we don't talk, don't do a good job on at all, is business risk.
I'm trying to figure out an effective way to articulate it. Ernie Stark-

man got all sorts of criticism up there for stating in testimony that we are running a risk of business calamity. Suppose we hadn't done our work right on the physical properties of those damned catalysts, and at the end of 15,000 miles suddenly those little pellets in there turned to dust. Then we've got to go out and change every damned catalyst on four million cars. [Suppose] we then discover that we don't know how to fix them, discover there is no fix. If you had to recall a million cars and put new engines in them, just forget it. If you're American Motors, you're done. If you're Chrysler, you're probably done.

—If it turned out that the South African Bantus got into a nasty rebellion over there and we've got no source of platinum, or if EPA should decide that the unleaded gasoline program is unworkable, and they stop in midstream and leave us hanging there with catalysts that get ruined by leaded gasoline, or if the courts decide that the EPA and unleaded gasoline regulations are illegal or unconstitutional or something, where are you?

What do you want more time for? To develop a better catalytic converter?

—We normally like to phase in new things. The automatic transmission took us seven years to spread across the lines of all cars. The catalytic converters—we had one year. Also we want better data to make business decisions on, and that gets back to the risk thing. To get platinum, you have to negotiate with either the Soviet Union or South Africa. We have to have a guaranteed supply. We can't be dependent on some outfit up in Jersey, Engelhard, that could go out of business and leave us hanging. Well, the Soviet Union's offer wasn't so hot, and the South Africans' was, so we made a commitment with Impala, Ltd., down there for, I think, a ten-year supply, and underwrote the building of company towns. We got a lot of claptrap from the anti-South African groups and so forth. It's not a comfortable place for doing business. Well, all that took lead time.

—Now another argument comes in: what we're learning. Platinum and palladium will do part of the job but won't get all the way there. So you've got to go to the next thing, which is rhodium and ruthenium, which are by-products of the same ore that you get platinum and palladium from. I think you've got to dig something like

750 tons of ore to get a pound of platinum. For every twenty or thirty ounces of platinum, you get one ounce of rhodium and ruthenium. Well, we can't get enough. There isn't enough in the world by our calculations.

Now that the committee has decided what auto standards it's ready to propose to the whole Senate, will you now start working other Senators to get them on your side for the floor vote?

—The Senate, we're playing hands off. There's no way you're going to convince fifty-one Senators to go against those fifteen guys on the Public Works Committee.

So your hope is in the House, and then in conference.

—Yes.

Will you handle the whole House alone?

—On this one, we're going to enlist the whole Washington crew. And we've got other avenues. We've got Congressmen from our plant cities and the greatest letter-writing program going. And then we've got all our dealers.

What can you accomplish at the conference stage?

—In conference you're down to a little less posturing and a little more of the real world. For example, I don't expect the ten per cent thing—the cars that are supposed to hit 1.0 NOx in 1979—to survive the conference. I don't know any way you're going to get the Senate to throw it out, the committee having voted for it. But I don't expect it'll be in the House bill—and that makes it negotiable in conference.

What does lobbying look like from the other side, not from an office like Muskie's, but from that of a newcomer to Washington, to whom the issues are too many and confusing, his channels of information not yet sorted out? I head for the office of Robert Morgan of North Carolina and, as Bill Chapman did time and again, settle for Bill Smith, his legislative assistant on environmental pollution, among other issues. Morgan has a corner suite in the Dirksen Building. Smith, a North Carolinian, about twenty-four, with long brown mane and connecting mustache, carries on his considerable responsibilities in a room jammed by five people and two mailing machines. He calls it the bull pen.

A CONVERSATION WITH BILL SMITH

On what aspects of the Clean Air Act have you been lobbied most? And by whom?

—The signficant deterioration provisions, or non-degradation. By the environmentalists especially. They want it. They're hard-line on it. Especially the idea of designating secondary areas to be protected —Class Two—in addition to your regular Class One, national forests and so forth. When the air is better than the minimum required in a certain area, they want to forbid letting it deteriorate down to minimum requirements. They want a nationwide policy, whereas industry would want it for the states to decide. That's the biggest area of concern in the bill, I think, because it's one of the hardest to define. Even the people who know the most about it have a hard time defining exactly what they're trying to do.

What does that mean for North Carolina, for your Senator?

—Industry in the state, like the paper company, the textile industry, utilities, and so forth, say that if we use Class One and Class Two designations we basically wouldn't be able to build anything. It would be a totally no-land-use policy, no growth—no future growth is how they put it. Mountainous states are at a disadvantage. We have these hills and valleys, and if you locate a plant in a valley, the bad air is trapped in there. And if you locate on a hill, you might spread it to someone else.

Have you decided how you'll vote on it?

—No, we really haven't. There have been a lot of times when he's not been able to go to subcommittee, especially being on the CIA. He gave his proxy to Muskie almost across the board when we had subcommittee votes on auto emissions. So he voted in the record as Muskie voted.

Because he sees eye to eye with Muskie and because Maine and North Carolina are somewhat similar topographically?

—Because he feels that Muskie's been with this thing longer than anyone else, and he trusts his judgment. At least, that's the way he felt when he gave his proxy then. His thinking may have changed now from the input he's gotten from the lobbyists, the utility lobbyists. They say, "If you give us this significant deterioration statute, you're not going to see any more growth in North Carolina." And then they start talking about jobs. And these are touchy areas.

How about autos?

—He's gotten a lot of lobbying on that. He made a two-week travel across the state during the August recess and met with some auto dealers. They basically said, "If you put these harsher restrictions on cars, the price of the car is going to go up and we're not going to be able to sell as many." They're worried that there's a great potential for loss of jobs, for shutdowns of lots of plants that feed the auto industry, and that has to hurt car sales. I think the Senator came back from there feeling like some of their points were good, and because he hadn't had enough chance in the subcommittee to really learn in depth the different angles of the problem, he felt like he was not able to completely defend some of the votes that Muskie made for him by proxy in the subcommittee.

Or even evaluate whether he's put his proxy in the right hands.

—Exactly. At least in the beginning stages of being a Senator, he's got himself having to depend a great deal on his colleagues. It's all right, but it's kind of a scary thing. He wants to know what's happened, he wants to have a full idea of what's going on, but he's been spread out so far in his different duties—there just aren't enough hours in the day.

When Chapman or Bob Smith came to see you from the auto companies—before they met with the Senator personally yesterday—how would they try to persuade you?

—Plenty of reports. Before we were going into the auto votes in subcommittee, Chapman came day after day. I think he felt that Morgan was not sure which way he was going. Naturally, they're going to go after the guy they think has doubts. But mostly it's the talks with our own dealers, who may not be qualified, but they are our own constituents. They know what makes a car salable.

Along the way, I have been collecting observations about lobbying. To the outsider who sees Capitol Hill only as a movie set, it may come as a surprise that more than ninety-nine per cent of lobbying effort is spent not on parties, weekend hosting, and passing plain white envelopes, but trying to persuade minds through facts and reason; some of it performed extremely well, some with comic incompetence. I have heard suspicious and disgusted whispers about one Senator on the Environmental Pollution Subcommittee who "may be on the take." If there's anything to the whispers, it must be in regard to some other issue. On the Clean Air Act, he has been notably inactive, uninfluential, and apparently uninterested, although he makes much in his home state of his devotion to the environment and opposition to virtually any form of nuclear experimentation. Most of the time he has let one colleague or another vote his proxy and has busied himself elsewhere. The point is that bribery or more elegantly wrapped forms of vote buying occur in the Senate, but probably with no more (and perhaps no less) prevalence than buying the decisions of federal judges or newspaper editors or corporate purchasing agents. Some Senators forever cater to the TV-cultivated caricature of the moneybags lobbyist by introducing bills to "regulate" lobbying. But no one has yet devised a way to curtail the perceived "evils" of lobbying (bribery aside) without also crippling underfunded lobbying as practiced by "good guys"—and, moreover, without colliding head on with the First Amendment.

Wednesday, December 3

The confusions and pressures around a single bill can distract the onlooker from the confusions and pressures that absorb the life of the whole Senate. This institution of one hundred, by constitutional design the more politically independent of the two bodies of Congress, the more serene as well as more august of the two, on some days resembles a madhouse.

Today's clean air markup is stillborn with the unusual absence of Muskie as well as seven other Senators. In a half-hour chat among committee members present—Randolph being hopeful that Muskie and a quorum might yet show—Senator Morgan, ever amazed by the demands on Senators, wonders aloud how the Clean Air Act can be expected to make progress in the next few weeks.

"This morning we're debating the Railway Act," Morgan protests. "Senator Hart and I were just talking about that. The committee report only came out two days ago, several hundred pages long. No member of the Senate can read it in that period of time. It involves something like nine or ten billion dollars, an awful lot of money. The truth is, all of us ought to be over there listening to the debate. The New York [financial emergency] situation is coming up next week and, unless I change my mind, I intend to object to any committee meeting during that debate because I think the public deserves our attention on that. While we've got this markup session this morning, there's a markup session in Banking on mandatory fuel requirements for federally financed homes. What can we do to get this clean air bill out?"

"Senator Morgan," commiserates Senator Randolph, "of course you raise a problem that is recurring, and the intensity increases in the final days of the session. Yesterday on the floor we were voting on amendments that had not been printed, that were just sent to the desk, in some instances ten minutes of debate and ten-minute roll calls. We were engaged in the Appalachian Conference, and we hurried to the floor, barely reaching it. We voted on the amendment and didn't know what the amendment contained or the implication of it. What you raise here today indicates the chaos the Senate is in. I use the word advisedly. What can we do? I have no solution at this moment because nothing can be put into effect that I know of."

"I don't think," says Morgan, "that I've ever felt this frustration more than trying to think about this Railway Act and New York Act and Clean Air Act all at one time. In addition, the Intelligence Committee is conducting public hearings."

"Someday," predicts Randolph, "perhaps the public will rebel against the way we operate."

A long buzz sounds—roll call. Helplessly, Morgan says, "If they knew what we know, they probably would. This Railway Act, nine or ten billion dollars, and we're here in a markup session while it's being debated."

"You don't know until you get to the floor what is being voted on in that roll call we're facing now," says Randolph, "and the Senator from Tennessee doesn't know, nor the Senator from New York, nor the Senator from North Dakota. We will recess for a roll-call vote."

Wednesday, December 10

Minutes after this morning's eight-thirty markup begins, Senator Baker offers an unusual comment: "This is the first time, really, that we've had a full-blown experience with open markups in the full committee. Two or three things are beginning to emerge from it. The first is that a significant number of people do attend from the public. I think that's excellent. The second is it's producing a different sort of reaction. I'm not complaining, just observing. Heretofore when the committee acted in executive session—privately—there was a hue and cry of those who agreed or disagreed with what we'd done after we had done it. Now, we're seeing people who sit here all day long and hear these conversations and debates. And they're intent on talking to us individually after the meetings to express their opinions. It creates some ruffled feathers. I think the open markup sessions are working well, Mr. Chairman, and I'm pleased even though I've probably made everybody in the room mad at me at one time or another."

Baker's gentlemanly comment provides Muskie with a cue for a sermon he's apparently been storing up to lay on unnamed lobbyists: "I would hope that something develops among those who watch and listen and afterwards accost. I hope they're getting a chance to observe that no interest has all its own way in the development of legislation like this. There are conflicting interests. Yet someone representing a particular interest sometimes is disposed to think he can have his own way all through the legislation, that there's no need to give anything, just insist upon taking. I wish that those who have an interest in legislation would address themselves just occasionally, just occasionally, to trying to figure out what they can *give* in order to help achieve a balance. I've found"—he leans forward, staring directly into the audience, not just commenting but scolding now— "I've found more intransigence outside this committee than I've found within it. That does nothing but slow down the legislative process. I address that to anybody who would like to take it to heart."

The entire audience erupts in laughter. Clearly, he must mean someone *else*.

Friday, December 19

The Senate is shooting for a recess at 6 P.M. today until January 5. I'm to meet Muskie in S-199 for a year-end chat. I ride to the Capitol in the subway trundle car with Jim Case, who has been assigned to sit vigil for Santa Claus; that is to say, the annual end-of-session "Christmas tree" bill will be making its way through the floor this afternoon, a mass of last-minute goodies tossed into a pile from every direction, and Jim has to watch out that it contains nothing obnoxious either to the Senator from Maine or to the chairman of the Budget Committee.

In the headlong rush of roll calls that characterizes every closing day, Muskie can purr with one satisfaction. After weeks of tie-up in a House committee, then in conference committee, then back to both floors, Senate passage on Wednesday constituted final congressional approval of the public works bill, including $1.5 billion to launch countercyclical assistance. President Ford's decision to sign or vee-toe the bill will be an unmistakable flash of the stance Ford will take on economic issues during his re-election campaign.[1]

A CONVERSATION WITH SENATOR MUSKIE

Let's look back for a moment at Black Friday, November 21. Quentin Burdick, a Democrat, a liberal, from a small, mainly rural state of progressive tradition, should be your kind of fellow. What really happened? First of all, after GM lobbied him did Burdick check with you to ask for your side of the story?

—No. In fact, he said in the markup he didn't check with me.

Isn't that unusual?

—Well, as someone said to me yesterday on the floor about Burdick, he has a different senatorial lifestyle than anyone here. He's very independent and does a lot of his own staff work—personally—very reluctant to rely on staff. Call it the prudence of a rural man. Quentin likes to reach his own conclusions, and once he's reached them he can be quite stubborn. I think he may have concluded—remember he's never been a member of our subcommittee and didn't join the Public Works Committee until long after he came to the Senate—that those of us responsible for the subcommittee decisions weren't as practical as we should have been and that maybe he was in a better position to be fresh and objective. This is all speculation. He hasn't said these things to me. But I'll tell you, I regard Quentin Burdick as one of the most honest men, intellectually, in the Senate. So I just put it down to Burdick's style. When a question bothers him personally and he decides he needs to make a personal judgment, that he ought not lean on Muskie or staff or those who've been associated with the bill all along—that maybe people on the outside have a legitimate grievance—he goes ahead and makes that personal judgment.

Doesn't he come from a political tradition that would cause him to view the auto lobby with suspicion, if not with outright hostility?

[1] From the ski slopes of Vail, Colorado, during Christmas week. Ford announces that he doesn't like the bill, that it costs too much, that it will help too little—and signs it.

—Well, there's—you know, a lot of this business of the Clean Air Act, a lot of what we've written into it, is designed to put pressure on people to do things that may not now be technologically doable. And that may strike peculiarly on a fellow from a small state who talks to farmers and people who have to deal with the hard, practical realities of life. It may strike him as a little idealistic. And so a fellow comes to him saying, "Look, we're doing our best. There's no way we can accomplish those numbers now." That kind of simple argument would conceivably make a deep impression on a fellow coming from that background. It influences all of us, in fact. But we made a calculated decision in 1970 to challenge the industry to produce things that were not then in existence as essential to cleaning up the environment. It took us quite a while to come around to the conclusion that that's the only way—the forced technology concept—the only way you're going to prod this technology. We understood the risks fully. And I suppose, coming fresh to it, someone like Burdick finds —hearing people say there's only so much you can do and it's going to cost so much and it'll carry an energy penalty—it's not surprising he accepts those arguments as credible.

—What he doesn't understand—I don't know what he does or doesn't understand—what he *may* not understand is that the energy penalty associated with clean air standards has nothing to do with the standards. It has everything to do with the technology that the industry *chooses* to meet the standards. That's hard for people to grasp.

But when you see a potential ally drifting away, you don't like—as some chairmen do—to lobby members of your own committee. Or seeing to it that your staff lobbies his staff.

—Well, if I'd had a clue, which I didn't, that he was having trouble with the question, I'd have no reluctance to ask staff people—I wouldn't twist his arm. I wouldn't ask him to vote against what he thought was right simply because I was chairman or his friend or anything like that. I rely heavily, of course, on full and free discussion at the subcommittee level—which is no good if he's not there.

And GM got to him first.

—Yes. That was a very unpleasant surprise. And Morgan too. Morgan came to the subcommittee, you know, almost delegating his proxy to me early in the game.

I remember one time you declined to vote his proxy because you said you didn't know how he would vote on that item. There are chairmen here who wouldn't have hesitated to use the proxy. [Muskie chuckles.]

—You never win by doing it that way, you know. Not really, in the long run. I think you've got to build credibility and confidence here just as you do with the public. I'd rather lose a vote than misuse the proxy. Especially with these open meetings, you know. If I cast a fellow's wrong—wrong for him, although perhaps right for me—and the press comes across that vote, that's playing very dangerous games with a colleague's political career.

After that Friday markup I asked Barbara Alexander for her reaction to your losses on three or four votes, and she hurled what I suppose she intended as the ultimate charge against a chairman: "He's lost control of his committee!" [Muskie nods sadly.]

—On this notion that somehow I control, or that anyone can control, I think she and her kind overlook that if you're going to control a committee you've got to establish some common ground the committee can stand on. One of the reasons that I had to go back on .4 NOx was that there was no goddamned way of holding the committee together on .4. And if I wanted to hold them together on 1.0, which was in serious question at the time, one thing I clearly had to do was give up .4 and give up a little time on the deadlines. But she wouldn't be able to comprehend that. How do you keep control except by finding where you can keep it? And she's totally incapable of understanding that. From her point of view, as long as I am pure—by her definition of purity—that purity in and of itself ought to—

[He decides to leave that thought in mid-sentence.]

Do you think that Gary Hart understands and accepts your approach?

—It's his disposition to support me. I think Hart sees it better now than he did when he fought me on .4. But fighting me on that was fine with me. You know, another way of establishing what she calls control is to have people on both ends of the issue, at each extreme, so that you can then position yourself in the center. It's a very effective way, so I don't object if Hart feels better about asserting the pure position, and if McClure wants to assert the pure position on the other end. That's fine. That then gives us a lot of territory in the middle to work in, maneuver in, to establish sound policy in.

Has Hart ever given you any indication that he was establishing his position to help influence where your center would be?

—No, he never told me, but I told *him* that. One day I told him, "That was great, Gary, great for you to bring that up. That gives me a chance to work out something."

Did he seem to appreciate your comment?

—He *understood* it. I don't know [*an ironic laugh*] how much he welcomed that analysis. But I wanted him to understand.

In a letter you sent on Black Friday to the president of the Maine League of Women Voters to answer Barbara Alexander's press release, you pointed out in a P.S. that the losses of that morning were evidence of the extremely tender situation on the committee, and added that you hadn't yet decided whether you would be able to support the weakened bill. You then deleted that last comment from the letter actually sent. Leon later told me you felt you could make that threat in public only once and that wasn't yet the right time or place to make it. Are you still, at least privately, thinking—

—I still want Randolph and the others to think of that possibility. And from what I observe and from what Leon tells me, they understand that clearly, and that's why I continue to get a measure of co-operation from them. I'm still trying to buy all I can for this bill by leaving my own support in doubt.

And it's a threat to industry, too.

—In fact, that was one of my little lectures this week. I pointed out that all these subjects are covered by existing law, that one of the options available to this committee is *not* to pass a new law. If people, I mean these various interests, are just going to sit back and object and criticize and not try to move toward an accommodation, one of our options is to leave the law as it is. The courts are still there. The enforcement agencies are still there. All these things can just be worked out by rulings from the courts and regulating agencies, if that's the way they want it. You understand, of course, that the reason we're now considering these changes in the law is because these industries asked us, begged us, demanded of us, that we revise the law. The interpretations of the existing law by the courts and the EPA, they said, were killing them.

—Take the steel industry. They have 150 out of 200 plants that are in violation of standards and, because of the areas they're in, can't possibly be in compliance for years to come. And they're under terrific economic pressure to expand in these areas where they're not now in compliance. What in the world are we to do for them? Well, the staff put together an amendment that I thought was pretty ingenious. McClure began to raise questions about it, implying this was anti-industry, an anti-growth amendment. Actually, industry, except for U. S. Steel, was sitting in back of the room chewing their fingernails. They *wanted* it. After about a half hour of McClure's questions I said to Randolph, "Mr. Chairman, this isn't my amendment. I haven't offered it. If an amendment designed to help industry is going to be contorted into an anti-industry position, I don't have any particular enthusiasm for it. So why don't we put it on the bottom of the agenda and return to it later if we have time." The steel boys just went through the roof. They didn't want McClure's pure principle and it appears since then that they've gone to work on McClure. A couple of times that item has crept up from the bottom of the agenda. Each time I'd say, "How'd this thing get up here? It's supposed to be at the bottom." Twice I've done that.

Who was McClure representing in his opposition?

—Oh, it's just his natural way. He just instinctively responds with the industry point of view. And he just assumed this was another one of those goddamned liberal amendments and he started picking holes in it. That's all. He hadn't been sicked on it by anybody. But I thought I'd teach him a little lesson.

—But keeping my own support of the final bill in doubt [*that mischievous chuckle again*]—it's done wonders for some of the attitudes on the committee. And you'll notice that I've not tried to push or hurry. I'm very careful to be there every morning that Randolph wants us there. Nobody can say Ed Muskie is dragging his feet on this.

Just yesterday Henry Ford said in this clipping here, "We wish they would make up their minds down there."

—We could return the compliment.

—I'm ready to go to votes. But for one reason or another, often stimulated by industry, my colleagues insist on raising more questions and debating. Let them talk. I'm not going to try to force votes, especially votes that are likely to go a way that I don't like. So I just let the process continue. You saw this morning that we could get only one vote in two hours. I'm not accusing anybody of deliberately delaying, but they just find it very difficult to resolve these damned issues where people, who claim they're in a hurry, insist on standing at polar extremes. I can't blame committee members who follow an instinct to delay votes.

Sunday, December 28

Muskie is in Maine, the legislative machine in the Capitol is shut down except for a few staff members keeping it at slow idle, and I'm at home in Connecticut. Today, NBC's "Meet the Press" does an imaginative and decent thing. Its guest—actually, guests—are Muskie's 1958 "classmate" and closest friend in the Senate, Senator Phil Hart of Michigan, and his remarkable wife, Janey Briggs Hart, who, besides being a Briggs of the Chrysler Briggses, is an anthropologist, pilot, and Democratic county vice-chairperson. Everyone on the panel knows, and Janey Hart knows and the Senator himself knows, why he was asked to come in this week of political calm, of Christmas, of the New Year, a good week for contemplation of human values. Phil Hart is dying. Without mentioning his health or his cancer, he has already announced he will not seek re-election in 1976, and indeed he is not expected to survive that year. Knowing that, and having been a most admired man in the Senate by both ally and adversary, he has things to tell us.

He's thin. His hollowed cheeks make his chin whiskers appear a little more dominant. But his eyes twinkle with life and he speaks directly and simply:

Martha Angle of the Washington Star: Senator Hart, do the people get the politicians they deserve, or do they get better or worse?

Senator Hart: I think they get better.

Ms. Angle: In what sense?

Senator Hart: Darned few people pay much attention to politics. Those who do generally have a special interest they want served. If that's taken care of, that is enough. I think we do better at trying to determine the right answer to complex questions than the constituency does in its degree of patience with us while we try to find it. My hunch is politicians have never been held in too high regard. We revere our Founding Fathers, but they got chopped up pretty badly by their contemporaries. I think the level of integrity among politicians is at least as high as among lawyers—I am free to speak of lawyers, I was one—if for no other reason than that we are under the gun. We are observed, and that exercises its own discipline.

George F. Will of the National Review (to Mrs. Hart): What, in your judgment, is the biggest mistake he has made as a legislator?

Mrs. Hart: I haven't really thought about any particular mistakes he's made. Impatient I have been with what seems to be a failure to make things happen, and that is perhaps because I refuse to understand that the legislative process is terribly, terribly slow. When I read the paper in the morning, I find out that 500,000 gallons of oil have just been spilled in Alaska. I am furious, you know, that they went ahead with the pipeline . . . and I yell at him about it. But as far as specific mistakes, I can't think of any.

Bill Monroe, moderator: Senator, are you discouraged?

Senator Hart: Sure, on a day-by-day basis I'm discouraged. If I was more absolutely certain that I was right on all the positions I take, I'd be dismayed at the slowness with which people respond to my ideas. But again, if you stand back, we began to learn to read symbols on the wall six thousand years ago, and illiteracy is still rampant. If it takes that long to make progress in that kind of social problem, which is relatively simple, we should not be dismayed that when we try to develop the concept of justice—much more complex —that it is slower still. So, when you get up in the morning and feel very depressed, think of the time clock of civilization and understand we are still in evolution, and hope that we will stagger through.

Mr. Will: Senator, you were elected in 1958 as part of a great Democratic landslide. You have been here through the New Frontier and the Great Society. There are those who say that there's an aroma of disappointment about liberals today, about many of their achievements, and basically their ability to control social change with federal programs. Do you share that disappointment?

Senator Hart: Yes. I think you describe accurately the mood of the movement. And I think it's correct to say that the optimism we brought in 1958—that whatever the problem was, we could get a handle on it and fix it—we don't have that kind of optimism any more. Yet with this dismay, we must not forget that some programs have worked, and maybe if Congress spent more time in oversight of programs we would have less waste and more success. I suppose things are in cycle. I'm sure there will be a day sometime long after all of us are gone when liberalism will be in fuller bloom than it was in '58. But certainly it is less impressive now than it was then.

Ms. Angle: Why is it so difficult to get rid of programs that don't work?

Senator Hart: Multiple reasons. They build up a constituency once they are on the road. Also, certain members of Congress who sponsor them hate to deny parenthood and always seek to buy a little more time because they are convinced that it will work out in the end.

Hugh Sidey of Time *magazine:* Mrs. Hart, the recent literature suggests that men who pursue power in the national government lose a great deal of their sensitivity, their feelings about their families, their wives, about other people, that they are on a stage and they go through this act rather relentlessly. Do you agree with that? Did that happen to your husband?

Mrs. Hart: It did not happen to us. Perhaps he was not questing for great power. His motives are quite different. But I think it also happens to the executives of large corporations. Their quest for power is just as potent, just as strong, and I think their family lives are just as disrupted in exactly the same way. They are just as absent. I think it all comes out pretty much the same.

1976

Friday, January 2

Next Wednesday in Maine Muskie will officially announce his candidacy for re-election. In preparation for it, he is at home in Washington this morning with his wife and most of the members of his family, posing for campaign pictures. Besides the family shots, the photographer, with a trunkload of lights and cameras, poses the Senator in a procession of Senator-hard-at-work tableaux in the den: in shirt sleeves thinking deeply over papers, on the telephone, reading a newspaper. Muskie strikes the poses obediently. What the photographer can't think of for an imaginative next shot, Charlie Micoleau suggests.

At 10:55 A.M. the phone rings. Word is brought to Charlie that it's for the Senator. When told whom the caller is, Charlie doesn't go to the phone to screen it but says immediately to Muskie, "It's from Bangor—Billy Cohen." Without the faintest hint of bracing himself, not even acknowledging for a split second Charlie's significant gaze, Muskie lifts his desk telephone and greets his caller. He listens. The message must seem interminable to Charlie, judging by his face, catatonic with attention and adrenalin-pink. At last the Senator says gravely, "You know, Bill, you're going to be under a lot of pressure to change your mind." Cohen responds and Muskie closes the conversation, "You're very thoughtful to call, Bill."

Cradling the phone, Muskie reports, with only the most shadowy tip-off of relief, "He's not going to run." He adds that Cohen will be making the announcement on Maine television at eleven o'clock—three, four minutes from now—and this was his last call before going into the press conference.

The conversation that follows between Muskie and Charlie is almost as surprising as Cohen's call. Not a word of glee, of what-a-load-off-our-minds, but purely of how to "handle" the news if reporters call—chiefly what a fine fellow Cohen is and what a fine race it would have been. Then Muskie comments that the news is not pure blessing, that with Cohen out of the race the job of steaming up interest in the campaign may be difficult. Especially, it will pour cold water on fund raising. Charlie suggests that fund raising will depend on a continued show of running very strenuously—even during the next three months when the Senator may be running against literally nobody. They agree that the "presidential thing" is what can cause them the most trouble. Obviously, there is no talk of slamming the door against the "presidential thing," but speculation on it will have to be discouraged as much as possible because nothing would suck Cohen back into the race faster than widespread talk that Muskie may not be running for Senator after all, because Muskie can't resist running for what Hubert has already run for and lost, what Kennedy hasn't run for but can't—and for what there appears to be no other "viable" Democratic candidate.

Sure enough, in a few minutes Don Larrabee, the Maine papers' Capitol correspondent, calls. Muskie repeats that Cohen's notification was thoughtful, that it would have been a tough and constructive campaign, that he (Muskie) knows only one way to run and that's to run hard, and that his goal in spending every day he can in Maine is to re-establish confidence and trust between elected officials and people they serve. Then he listens to a question, smiles, and allows, "Well, of course it does lessen the pressure."

Later, in the sun porch of Charlie's home on Porter Street, N.W., about halfway between the National Cathedral and the National Zoo, I chat with Muskie's "political man" about events that led up to Cohen's decision that the House is a good enough home:

"I went to Bowdoin College with the Congressman and with his principal campaign adviser, this guy Chris Potholm who's now a professor of political science at Bowdoin, and officially is staff man for Cohen's district office in Maine. Unofficially he's his political man. We don't play at false secrets. We took polls the same week, each of us knowing about the other one, and we kidded each other about how they came out—not that we ever revealed the numbers. For example, we made no secret of our objective, which was to increase

Cohen's risk to the point where he wouldn't run. And his strategy was waiting us out, just seeing whether we could do it. Potholm and I talked just a couple of weeks ago, ostensibly to wish each other a Merry Christmas, to kid each other about the polls and see what each of us could learn."

"How do you manage to ask questions of the 'enemy' about his polls, his campaign plans, without his feeling invaded?"

"You don't ask questions. You just goad the other guy. Here's an example of how we deal with each other that I think is hilarious, and which you'll appreciate since you're one of only three or four people who've read our poll. He wrote a long article for the Bangor *Daily News* on how the press lets itself be misused by candidates who self-servingly leak poll results. Apparently their poll, with a sample designed differently than ours, showed him doing better than ours did. Anyhow, to support his point that candidates leak results when it serves their purposes, he makes the claim that we leaked ours—and he goes ahead and prints *our* poll results." Charlie laughs joyously.

"How did they get them?"

"I don't know. I've never talked to Muskie about this, and I don't think I will, but I suspect they came from Muskie. Here's my guess, although I have no way of knowing. There are only three staff people who knew those numbers—Maynard, Doug Bennet, and myself. Then the Senator, Clark Clifford, Pat Caddell, and you. No one in Maine. Those seven only. My guess is that the Senator told someone in Maine, and I think I know who it might be, who would then tell somebody who is associated with Bowdoin, who would then tell Potholm. If I had to take my pick of who the Senator told it to, it was Shep Lee, a car dealer in Lewiston, one of the Senator's old friends. I may be wrong. It's sheer guesswork on my part."

"And do you have their poll results?"

"I have some figures. I don't think they really know for sure that what they have are our figures. And of course I'm not sure about theirs. Anyhow, when they screw up something, or when they think we have, each of us is quick to call the other to kid about it. Because, in kidding, we might pick up something. You never get a straight answer but you do get some indication of where they think they're at. There's this constant game of you assessing their problems and them assessing your problems.

"I'd see these guys socially and at one point—I guess that was last

May—Chris Potholm and I had one of these all-night sessions, and we wound up agreeing that there was nothing magical about this whole process. Cohen, you know, is as cautious as Muskie about making decisions of this nature. He knows he's extremely popular; on the other hand, also vulnerable. He's got a safe seat that pays forty-two five and a rosy future, and being asked to give that up to run for the Senate and maybe lose—On the other hand, if he's successful he'd be immediately catapulted into the national limelight. My guess was that he wouldn't really have to decide until after October 1, and as it turned out it was December 19, when he got the information on which he made his decision. That's when Congress recessed, and Mohammed went up to the mountain with his tablets, which were carved in Detroit by Market Opinion Research, and contemplated his fate. But there was nothing magical or secretive about his decision. He decided months ago not to really do anything but to watch us. And I always felt that we had at least until October to demonstrate that we could beat him, that we could increase his personal risk to the point where he'd have to decide not to run. He's a very methodical, bright, rational guy.

"About the only time I got really nervous was in late October or early November when there was a Republican Issues Conference. There's nothing more dangerous than a group of politicians of either party getting together and stirring up rumors. I began getting reports saying that Cohen was pissed off because people were saying he was scared. Everyone was throwing an arm around his shoulder saying, 'You're not going to chicken out.' So I said, 'My God, the guy's going to run.' Like everybody else, he's got to prove himself a man.

"The other thing that bothered me was that Cohen was coming up with silly reasons for possibly not running. It's important to have a plausible reason for getting out, and if you don't lay one down for yourself you can find yourself locked into running even if you don't want to. He was saying, 'I'm going to take a poll and look at it.' That's silly, getting people to write stories that he's going to read those numbers and decide. To my mind, that makes a guy sound like he's running for public office for the crassest reasons. Then there was the pension speculation. You've got to serve six years. If he leaves the House after four and loses for the Senate, no pension. So Cohen goes into a big press conference and denies the pension is a factor, thereby calling more attention to it. A whole bunch of people who had never heard about it started saying, 'Gee, he's got pension problems if he runs.' So I finally started kidding Potholm, saying 'For chrissake, you've got to come up with a better reason than that. You know you're going to have to back out because we're going to clobber you so badly. You've got to have a reason.' I laid out two or three scenarios for them, one of which, not particularly original, was that, with two great candidates opposing each other in one campaign, the big loser would be Maine. If we now have two effective representatives in Washington, why should one of them be sacrificed?"

While Charlie is talking to me, at Muskie's office in the Russell S.O.B. the news ignites an office party. Even Leon comes down to join it from his lookout office atop the Dirksen S.O.B. To say that these people are celebrating a heightened probability of their job security is to oversimplify. It's a great emotional victory for their team, for their identity. As any staff member who has done so can attest, losing your Senator can be a terrible trauma that goes beyond mere bereavement. It means having to withdraw your loyalty and kinship, and repledging that loyalty to, assuming that kinship with, a total stranger.

"While the polls showed that it would be possible to win a Senate race, it was clear that the contest would be very close," says Cohen at his news conference in Bangor. He adds high-mindedly, "A Senate campaign might very well become a bitter and divisive one, thereby dissolving the cohesiveness and effectiveness of the entire Maine delegation that has for the past three years worked in a non-partisan manner for the benefit of all Maine citizens." Having thus invoked one of two standard reasons for withdrawal—the good of the citizens —he makes sure to use the other: "Our sons are at an age where they need a father and friend on something more than a part-time basis."

Translation: Wait till next time.

Thursday, January 22

Last night Muskie addressed the nation on live television on all three networks simultaneously—what broadcast people call a "roadblock"—in the Democratic Party's "equal time" reply to President Ford's State of the Union Address. The assignment, a couple of weeks ago thought to be a magnificent opportunity, turned out to be an ordeal, and probably an end to Muskie's faint presidential hope.

Mike Mansfield picked him. Only Mansfield knows his reasons, but the probable ones were (1) Muskie's spectacular success in a similar assignment five years ago when, immediately following a Republican film of a tense and bitter harangue of a California street crowd by President Nixon, Muskie, in behalf of his party's congressional candidates, spoke intimately, eloquently, reassuringly from a seaside living room in Maine, instantly implanting himself in the nation's consciousness as a first-rank statesman, and (2) that in the absence of any leading—even probable—Democratic presidential candidate next year, Mansfield may have been advancing "non-candidate" Muskie as his favorite. Whether the latter was part of Mansfield's thinking or not, Hubert Humphrey smarted and openly grumbled at the display given his possible rival. Frank Church and Birch Bayh were miffed, and Henry Jackson, who regards most of his colleagues as undeserving minority stockholders, sizzled for two solid weeks.

Muskie had to strain through almost a month of balancing on a high wire. On the one side, he and his people had to summon up a fresh look of shock at any mention that this speech could have anything to do with a possible run for President. Not only did Humphrey, Jackson, et al., have to be mollified but, more urgently, Billy Cohen must not be drawn back into a Senate challenge. On the other side, since any hope for a Muskie candidacy would rise entirely from the success of this speech, it had to be scaled as a presidential address. So Richard Goodwin, the celebrated lyricist for Presidents Kennedy and Johnson, candidate Eugene McCarthy and, in fact, composer of Muskie's famous seaside speech, was spirited into Washington from Kingfield, Maine and instructed to type quietly and stay out of sight. And Muskie's presidential campaign TV adviser (who had staged the seaside spectacular), Robert D. Squier, was hired to produce last night's appearance. The opportunity overwhelmed Squier, who ran elatedly out into the streets and blew the cover. "It's the most bully pulpit any opposition figure has ever been offered," Squier blabbed to Chris Lydon of the New York *Times,* "at a moment when the vacuum among Democratic presidential candidates out there is so great you can practically hear it. . . . I'm taking the position that I'm Dr. Frankenstein. We invented Muskie in 1970 and we can invent him again in 1976."

After much dyspeptic conferring, Muskie and Charlie concluded that firing Squier would only spread a grass fire of his bright sayings across all of the American press. Better to let the words die with the *Times.*

Muskie spoke from Mansfield's sumptuous digs across the hall from the Chamber. One of two teleprompters broke down, forcing overuse of an unfortunately distant camera shot of Muskie in a straight-back chair, as personable as a stone likeness in a memorial monument. The visual stiffness accentuated Richard Goodwin's failure to overcome a problem that perhaps was impossible to overcome: the man he was composing for, Edmund Muskie of Maine, was not free to take flight in a solo aria. He was speaking for the Democratic Party. And in this difficult year of no-easy-answer energy problems and recession problems and ever spreading disgust with big government, congressional Democrats have not worked out an arrangement of what they can sing together.

So the speech was organ-toned—and flat.

Late this afternoon a reporter asks Muskie if he feels that the senatorial response to the President's State of the Union has stirred the nation. Muskie's succinct reply: "No."

Thursday, February 5

The Public Works Committee gathers at eight-twenty this morning with the weary hope of final approval today of the Clean Air Act.

Yesterday was a day of bloodletting. Senator Morgan, who has emerged as the dependable instrument of virtually any put-upon business lobby, introduced an amendment that trashed the land-use section of the bill. It passed over Muskie's strong objection, and before the debate was over, Morgan knew of Muskie's disgust. Muskie significantly chose Domenici, who supported the Morgan amendment, as the target for his favorite scolding: that everyone "supports the objectives" of the present Clean Air Act but too few want to make the "tough choices" of making it workable. Domenici, whose face is permanently set in an attitude of troubled sincerity, cringed under the blast. Later he called Leon to his office and said, "First, I want to apologize to you for voting the way I did." Leon, taken aback by the overshow of courtesy, replied, "You don't have to apologize to *me*, Senator. Apparently the committee has decided to establish a higher standard for protecting deterioration of the air than for protecting public health." If his track record is any clue, a remorseful reversal by Domenici can be expected today.

This morning Burdick becomes the compromiser, coming in with an alternative to the Morgan amendment. Leon thinks it's a very favorable alternative and whispers that opinion to Muskie. But Muskie is determined to soak the committee in its own juice. He tells the committee that he won't be rushed into a hasty assessment of the Burdick proposal, refusing to declare his support for it. Pleading another meeting—which he might on any other day have ignored—Muskie leaves. During the committee's lunch break Leon finds Muskie and they converse for twenty minutes, a long exchange for them. Muskie asserts—this time for real—that he now seriously doubts whether he should vote to report out the bill. The downslide ever since Black Friday has been too long and too steep. Leon urges that the Senator vote to approve it "because, if you don't, I lose control of what the committee report will say. If we don't have that leverage we'll lose even more of what we have in the bill." Muskie says nothing, which means he'll think about it.

Actually Leon is not as dejected by the deterioration of the bill as Muskie—who, Leon feels, may temporarily be reacting more to the sting of setbacks than to the bill itself. "It's a modest bill," Leon assesses it for me. "It's not as bad as it might have been, and not as good as we'd have liked it to be."

I wonder aloud whether the environmentalist lobby will withhold its support from the bill in its present state. Leon shrugs. Suddenly he brightens and says, "Got a fantastic letter from Barbara Alexander the other day, three pages, very, very critical of the Senator."

"Have you replied?"

"Besides the message being pretty bad, the typing was very messy. So my reply was to send her a litmus-cloth typewriter cleaner."

At 3 P.M. Muskie deigns to return. Morgan is carping combatively at Burdick's alternative. Morgan's zeal to do in Burdick's amendment results in doing in his own—because it goads Muskie into supporting Burdick. Burdick's wins, which, as a side accomplishment, seems to quiet the mutiny, restoring Muskie to some measure of command.

As members realize they are about to take their final vote—on a motion to report the bill out—Senator McClure says, "On a matter as complex and protracted as this, I'd ordinarily ask that we see the actual text of the final bill before voting to report it. However, because we know there'll be several attempts to make changes on the floor, I'll not make that request."

Muskie leaps in to play gander to McClure's goose: "I have reservations about several provisions in this bill. I have not formed a final judgment on the whole of it. So I'll support reporting the bill to the floor, reserving my position on the bill as a whole, on whether or not I'll seek to modify it on the floor, and on whether or not I'll include a separate statement of my views in the report. May I add, Mr. Chairman, that I'll want to see what the report looks like before I form final judgments."

"Before we call the roll," McClure responds with curious emphasis, "I'd just say that I would second the sentiments by the Senator from Maine almost exactly, and the stenographer could repeat them all after my name."

"You could put a ditto there for me," chimes in Senator Buckley.

Behind this gush of courteous concord lie implied threats—first by Muskie, then by McClure and Buckley. Even after the final roll call, about to come, and even after sixty rolls calls on individual issues, the committee battle may still go on—over the committee report. The report is a straight-prose analysis, written by staff, of what the final bill, composed by lawyers, really says and means. The report, not the bill, is what the rest of the Senate will read in deciding how to vote on the floor. Years hence, courts may interpret the "intent of Congress" from the plain language of the report should the legal language of the bill lead to dispute. McClure and Buckley are warning Billings that each paragraph, each sentence, every word of the report is now subject to the challenge: "That's not what we meant when we voted for that provision."

Dryly acknowledging McClure's and Buckley's unwelcome "dittos," Muskie sighs, "If this keeps up, I may have a rare chance to get a majority vote."

"We are going to have a unanimous vote," cracks Johnny Carson Baker, "to report the bill—with fourteen separate statements of views."

Unamused, Senator Hart announces, "Unfortunately, I cannot go along with the unanimity. I subscribe to what the Senator from Maine has said, but I reach a different conclusion. I cannot vote to report the bill."

To allay the suspicions of McClure and Buckley and any others adjusting their microscopes to scrutinize the report, Billings says: "After we pull together all the bits and pieces of language for the bill that we have, we will get those into galleys, and then we'll sit down, the committee staff and the staff of members, and go through this line by line. Where there's dispute, we will come back to the members involved and resolve that dispute. We'll do the same thing on the report. That's the way we've done it for ten years on this committee, and it's worked very well."

"Thank you very much, Leon," Domenici says sincerely. "I appreciate that."

Baker moves to report the bill. Domenici seconds. Meyer starts calling the roll. Except for Hart's negative, the roll call produces a procession of ayes. Senators Bentsen, Culver, Gravel, and Morgan are absent. Muskie votes Culver's aye by proxy; Randolph, those of Gravel and Morgan. The vote of Bentsen, who has been absent almost consistently throughout these months of markups—a combination of running for the presidential nomination and an apparent eagerness to escape the demands of this thankless issue—is the only one to go unrecorded. And as a maraschino cherry atop the whipped cream, there beams Senator Montoya, who has entered the room moments before the final vote to unburden Chairman Randolph of the Montoya proxy, to cast his own aye.

As if the final vote has suddenly released the audience from the discipline of silence, the lobbyists burst into an excited buzz. Pressing further on his earlier warning, McClure says, trying to surmount the din, "I'm certain that individual members of the committee—"

"May we have order, please, in the room?" demands Senator Randolph, gaveling gently.

"Thank you, Mr. Chairman—individual members of the committee are going to want perhaps a little more time than normally to look over both the galleys of the bill and the report, with sufficient time *after* the report is finalized to write whatever individual views we may feel compelled to write."

We have not seen the last of delay.

At 4:40 P.M. the Public Works Committee recesses, to reconvene subject to the call of the chair.

I ask Leon the earliest date the bill might go to the floor.

"March 1. Randolph always likes three weeks for interested parties to react. It could come up March 1 or could wait till the next week. When we file the report in two or three weeks, we'll begin to negotiate our floor schedule with Charlie Ferris and his people. I'm not sure I want it to lie around until the second week in March. I'd like to get to the floor with as little notice as possible, just to avoid a lobbying campaign."

Friday, March 5

On the floor of the Senate yesterday the news fell. Mike Mansfield of Montana announced to his colleagues that he will not run for re-election this year, thus automatically retiring as one of the more revered Majority Leaders in the history of the Senate. "There is a time to stay and a time to go," the gentle man of seventy-two said. "Thirty-four years is not a long time but it is time enough."

Much of the day's session was taken up with expressions of professed surprise, genuine sorrow, unrestrained tribute and affection, and predictions that the Senate will never again be graced by the like of Mike Mansfield.

And only a day later—today—three of his colleagues are racing to fill his boots. As expected, Majority Whip Robert Byrd of West Virginia is a candidate and considered front runner. Senator Ernest Hollings of South Carolina is in it; not a front-line Senate power, Hollings, it's assumed, hopes to slip in between stalemated heavy-weights. And surprisingly, Muskie of Maine. The surprise, at least to me, is not that he's in, but that he leaped in so fast. His natural reticence has created in him a style of waiting till power comes to him of its own locomotion, the only style in past years he has carried off comfortably and effectively.

Oh yes, there's Hubert Humphrey, too. His staff is telling reporters today that the former Vice-President has "a very serious interest" in becoming Leader, but that he doesn't plan an active campaign for support "at present." They seem to have taken that from his stock script about running for President. Since the Majority Leader won't be chosen until next January, clearly Humphrey hopes he can maneuver to hold this race open while he sees what's to become of his "not running" for President. A shy violet he is not. There's not a glory worth having that he doesn't hunger for, even lusting for high offices two at a time, elbowing his dearest colleagues out of the way, holding them at bay while history decides whether Hubert is chosen for the higher post or must settle for the lower. He carries it off with such gusto, such bear hugs, such "politics of joy," that no one dares admit anything but deepest affection for Hubert in this institution where throbbing rivalries and animosities are controlled by calling everyone "my good friend."

Bobby Byrd can count on two votes at the very least. Two colleagues, Alan Cranston of California and Frank Moss of Utah, have announced they'll run for Majority Whip, a race that becomes a far better bet if Byrd is promoted out of it.

Tonight Muskie and Dolores stay late at the office, Dolores tracking down every Democratic Senator and switching him to Muskie's phone. She is ready to give up on Sam Nunn when she finally locates him at James Schlesinger's home, having dinner. In Dick Clark's case, Dolores fails. Mrs. Clark says resignedly, "I haven't seen him for an evening at home in six weeks. I don't know where the hell he is." At the Eagleton's, one of the Senator's children asks Dolores, "Is there a big vote in the Senate tonight?" "No, dear," Dolores says, "Senator Muskie just wants to talk to your father." "Oh, I thought there must be a big vote going on," the child explains, "because Senator Byrd and Senator Hollings just called too."

Some Senators thought to be likely supporters surprise Muskie with sorries, already committed. Others, presumed allies of Byrd or Hollings, turn out to be up for grabs. Ostensibly this three-way race to be first on the phone is for the purpose of the candidate making a personal "survey," nothing more. But there's no doubt a few long-standing pay-on-demand notes have been called.

Thursday, April 29

Twelve weeks ago today, when the Clean Air Act cleared the Public Works Committee, Leon stated with some assurance that floor debate on it would open during the first week of March. Delay until the second week of March, he said, might drown the bill in lobbying.

It didn't come to the floor the first week of March or the second. One major setback in that schedule was that Senator McClure, as he served notice he might, took issue with some of the wording of the report. (Perhaps Leon saw that as a delaying tactic and a nuisance, but Hal Brayman didn't. "Everybody felt it was a healthy thing," Hal told me later. "They had two committee meetings at which members went over controversial points in the report. I've never heard of a committee doing that in the six or seven years I've been up here. Baker kept talking about it for days afterward. 'Boy, we really got into that, we really went through it. We can stand behind that report.' I think it was a good thing to do.")

Then Senator Allen created backups and jams in the parade of bills to the floor by trying to kill this or that with prolonged gusts of wind. Finally it was scheduled "absolutely sure," Leon informed me, for the week of March 29. But Jake Garn of Utah, the former Republican mayor of Salt Lake City, wanted the bill delayed until after the Easter recess—scheduled for April 14–26—so Senators not benefited by the months of committee meetings could "study it properly." The leadership customarily honors such a request. What Garn actually meant, of course, was that he—and some people he listens to with great attention—had studied the bill very closely indeed and dreaded it. One obvious dread was that the non-degradation provisions would put an end to plans for building the mammoth Kaiparowits power plant thirty miles north of magnificently scenic Glen Canyon on the Colorado River in southern Utah. It would be the largest coal-fired plant in the nation, providing electricity for southern California and booming Arizona, and cost $3.5 billion, a stimulant to jobs and industrial activity in Utah.

Utah environmentalists, led by actor Robert Redford, bitterly opposed the scheme, but giant power companies are not accustomed to giving up easily. Yet to almost everyone's surprise, including Garn's and Utah Governor Calvin Rampton's, on April 14, the first day of the recess, the powerful sponsors of Kaiparowits did give up. Whether this collapse will reduce blockage of the clean air bill or inflame new fears of its anti-industrial potential is anybody's guess.

The third-floor Caucus Room—historic scene of the McCarthy hearings, the Watergate hearings, even the memorable "hearing" in the film *Advise and Consent,* to confirm Henry Fonda as Allen Drury's Secretary of State—is the center of attention of Capitol Hill and the nation today. The cameras, the lights, the reporters, the eager crowd of Senate staffers, and the few outs· ·rs who can fit in are all there. Hubert Humphrey is going to announce *whether* he'll run for President. He has successfully wafted a fetching fragrance of doubt, and nothing grabs this place more than the suspense of impending decision.

For weeks, wise and knowledgeable seers have been foreseeing that non-candidate Humphrey is a shoo-in for the nomination after the sorry band of Democratic hopefuls knock one another off in the primaries. Even the Republican White House keeps leaking President Ford's expectations that his opponent will be either Humphrey or Muskie.

The word today from Humphrey is surprising, tear-choked, and short. It is "No." The ominous prospect of possible defeat in the coming primaries in New Jersey, or Ohio, or California, or *two* of them, is too much for the stomach and pride of a warrior whose battle scars are healed yet still tender. "But I'll be around," he says at the end, wanly.

Well, there's always Majority Leader.

The day before yesterday, a day made memorable by Jimmy Carter's stunning victory in Pennsylvania, Muskie awoke with a severe, almost paralyzing pain in the neck, an inflamed nerve that has been bothering him on and off since last fall. That evening he checked into Bethesda Naval Hospital.

Today, by advance arrangement, Hubert Humphrey checks into Bethesda, shortly after his news announcement. He's had treatment for a nasty condition—not malignant, but not safe from becoming one—that needs periodic watching. He's given a room down the hall from Muskie's and, buoyant after throwing off the weight of this morning, he spins up and down the hall in his wheel chair having a high old time. He's in Muskie's room giving a monologue when a nurse brings word of a get-well call for Muskie from his Maine colleague, Senator Hathaway. Humphrey grabs for the phone. Affecting an almost convincing Maine flatness of vowel, the Muskie impersonator says, "Hi, Bill. I'm sitting here with Hubert, and don't believe a word he said this morning. We're cooking up the old ticket of Humphrey and Muskie and we're going to take it all. How do you think you'll like being senior Senator?"

What will Muskie's pain in the neck do to the short-term prospects of a floor vote on the Clean Air Act? Nobody knows. The bill that seemed fairly sure to clear the floor last August, then quite certain to make it in September, then *had* to get through in October, will now surely dally until deep May.

Friday, May 21

Muskie is out and much better, although the same cannot be said for the prospects of the Clean Air Act. It was scheduled for an absolutely sure opening of floor debate on May 4, but one thing and another put it off. The positively-without-question date, Leon assures me, is now June 2.

Last fall's Liberal Party speech was not just perfume in a heavy wind. Bob Rackleff told me at that time that he and Al From were conversing with Muskie as to where to take the theme from there. It has since acquired critical mass in the form of a more prominent pronouncement yesterday and, in fact, the fashioning of what appears to be a formidable bill.

Yesterday Muskie appeared before the pre-convention meeting in Washington of the 1976 Democratic Party Platform Committee. With TV cameras grinding, he reprised some of the phrases of the Liberal Party speech to chide the product of the 1972 platform committee:

"In those 15,000 words, we catalogued virtually every problem that we thought bothers Americans. . . . Yet the election results showed that our platform was irrelevant. . . . For every new program we promised, Americans wondered about the ones we already have—and felt cheated that we ignored the waste and inefficiency of existing programs. . . .

"They see today over one thousand federal programs—that touch virtually every aspect of daily life—with nobody in Washington who knows how well most of those programs work. They see a government grown needlessly complex, expensive, and ineffective—suffocating too many of the programs we worked for. And they see too many political leaders who either ignore or pay lip service to government reform. We have reached the point where government reform—using each tax dollar more effectively—is a social good in itself. For every dollar that is wasted—whether for health care or fighter-bombers—that much less is there to meet human needs.

"We have also reached the point where government reform will be accomplished. Americans demand it. They will get it. The only question is, *who will carry it out? . . .*"

Now Muskie leads into his new bill:

"The Democratic Congress has already begun this reform, [having] taken control of the budget. . . . Congress is now considering spending reforms to pinpoint wasteful programs. . . . Some people call it the 'sunset bill.' It would mean just that—sunset for federal programs that overlap better ones, or that have outlived their usefulness, or just don't work any more. It would make virtually all federal programs and agencies rejustify themselves every five years. If they don't make a strong enough case they go out of business. . . .

"Some Democrats seem to accept waste and inefficiency as a cost of helping people—a commission we pay for a Faustian bargain to protect what little we have gained—and that attacking waste somehow amounts to a repudiation of the New Deal.

"Well, all I can say is, what's so damned liberal about wasting money?

"What do waste and inefficiency have to do with the New Deal? I never heard Franklin Roosevelt say that waste and inefficiency are unavoidable if we want to help poor people. And I never heard Franklin Roosevelt say we had to reject reform ideas because we had more to lose than to gain. Instead, I heard him call for 'bold, persistent experimentation,' and say in 1936 that 'government without good management is a house built on sand.'"

Then reaching wide to assure reflexive liberals that, really, it's not blasphemous to be listening to all this, Muskie carefully added, "That is the kind of government my good friend Hubert Humphrey described when he said recently that 'we do not need to defend blindly everything that government has done in the last forty years. There have been mistakes, and there is a special obligation on those who believe in positive and strong government to understand and correct these shortcomings.'"

Muskie's testimony yesterday earned a TV editorial last night from CBS's Eric Sevareid: "The Muskie bill can be the real litmus test of the sincerity of liberals. . . . If Democrats are to go for the Humphrey-Hawkins [job creation] bill, national health insurance, and other massive concepts, it would appear the part of electoral wisdom this year to support the sunset concept, too, and with equal vigor." In what amounts to a personal campaign to support Muskie's sunset bill, Sevareid began praising it last February 10. That evening, however, he concluded with the jab: "But no mention is made of the Congress itself. It is breeding committees and subcommittees like rabbits or wire coat hangers, to an overlapping, duplicating total now reaching around the 400 mark."

The other day I was leafing through a play-by-play narrative history of the Budget Act. The report, in the *National Journal,* asserted that perhaps more than any other major piece of legislation in recent memory the Budget Act was a product of hard work, resourceful innovation, and intelligent negotiation by *staff*. It quoted Senators saying so. And the narrative singled out Alvin From as one of two staff individuals most responsible for helping create the Budget Act. The Budget Act is what has brought on the reshaping of Senator Muskie as liberalism's new fiscal manager, leading him into the countercyclical assistance approach of turning off the money faucet when a target has been reached, of the sunset bill, and the manifestos that bind these laws and bills together: the Liberal Party speech and yesterday's Platform Committee testimony. Little Al From's hand is not only visible on the Budget Act but on each of these elements of the new national posture of Edmund Muskie. That compels the question: how many of the wonderful and terrible public acts that we praise and damn our Senators for are really the brain children of our elected Senators, and how many are attributable to their staff members, of whom we hear little and know less?

Anyhow, I want to find out more about this sunset bill, so it's back again to Al From's corner office with bath at what is no longer the Carroll Arms.

A CONVERSATION WITH ALVIN FROM

—Muskie calls it the "spending reform" bill. The "sunset bill" is a name Common Cause gave it. We introduced it in February, and it would require every program to come up for reauthorization every five years. The authorization would just expire unless it was positively re-enacted. It would also look at what could be done for less than the current spending level. You'd ask: "What happens if you eliminate this thing entirely? Then what happens if you spend seventy-five per cent of the current amount? Fifty per cent? Twenty-five per cent?" That changes the basic assumption of the way we budget now, which is just starting where we were last year and then deciding whether to increase.

—The bill has been remarkable in that we now have over fifty co-sponsors. Actually, fifty-one, a majority of the Senate. The co-sponsors range from Humphrey, McGovern, Kennedy, and Mondale on the left to Goldwater and Bill Roth and Laxalt and Helms and Eastland on the right.

Take McGovern. Why would he want to co-sponsor this?

—One thing that's probably encouraged liberals like McGovern to support it is that it includes a review of the Defense Department. Defense authorizations get terminated too. The only exceptions across the board are Social Security, Medicare, and programs to which people actually contribute their own dollars with an expectation of some later return. I think the feeling in the country is so pervasive—that there's a lot about government that doesn't work—that almost everybody's ready to agree that you've got to evaluate everything fairly regularly.

—One of the other aspects of this bill that has made it attractive is that programs come up every five years according to the functional categories established by the Budget Act. What that means is that 150 to 160 separate health programs all come up at the same time. Actually, there are 228 separate health programs, but some straddle the functional categories and are not categorized as health. The appropriating committees—say, Labor and Public Welfare, that authorizes most health bills—are going to have to face this in a way they've never done before. The budget resolution is going to say, "Look, you're going to have a fourteen-billion-dollar line, so if you want three billion for some new thing, where do you want to take the three billion off?" Bringing up all health programs together makes it practical to face the question of how you divide the pot. A lot of small programs that aren't really very significant, that just got on the books and then got forgotten about, will be consolidated into major programs. Or dropped. When overlap becomes visible you can begin to remove it. I think that even the interest groups are starting to feel that you need some cleansing of low-priority things to free up resources for new initiatives.

You think that liberal Senators are ready to risk going on record to consolidate—or even kill—social programs?

—No, I'm not at all sure they are. But I know *one* liberal is, and that's Ed Muskie. Muskie was one of the first people, and I'm sure the first liberal, to realize the importance of budget reform. It took two years to hammer out the budget bill. Now, after the school lunch thing, and the military procurement conference report, almost everybody accepts it as essential.

You seem to have had a hand in every step along this way. Who's following whom?

—Oh, Muskie first introduced something like the sunset bill in 1965 when I was still in college. So he's not new to it. That first idea was part of the original Intergovernmental Cooperation Act. Just before the act's passage, the "sunset" part got knocked out. Then Muskie and Brock tried again, pushing for a provision in the budget bill to limit major program authorizations to three years. That got knocked out. What we've done since then is take a raw idea and develop it, refine it into a very sophisticated process.

—After the success of the Liberal Party speech we started kicking around the idea for a sunset bill. Muskie agreed to it, thought it would be a great idea but probably wouldn't get very far because we'd tried it before. But I had a gut instinct that this year's politics was ready for it. In January when he did the Democratic answer to the State of the Union, we mentioned it, but without detail. In retrospect, that was probably a great mistake. This was probably the one idea that could have made that speech catch fire. But the bill wasn't quite ready to go at that point.

—In early February the bill was ready, and Muskie decided that on the day it was introduced he wanted to read a speech about it on the floor. Meanwhile, John Glenn and Bill Roth were all over me to let them be the only advance co-sponsors printed on the bill. In fact, neither of them wanted the other one on it. So the three of them, Muskie, Glenn, and Roth, paraded on the floor and read their goddamned speeches—and everybody who was on the floor jumped on it immediately like it was a bandwagon. Muskie's speech was right after a vote, so members were there. Bellmon wanted to be listed as an additional co-sponsor and Nunn and Huddleston and Hugh Scott, the Minority Leader. Mansfield was one of the first liberals to get on. We did a "Dear Colleague" letter soon after, signed by Muskie, Glenn, Roth, and Bellmon, and with no follow-up we wound up with twenty-six or twenty-seven co-sponsors, an enormous amount for not really pushing. After lots of press and three pieces by Sevareid, we did another "Dear Colleague," figuring if we added ten more it would be terrific. We're now up to fifty-one and they're still trickling in. In that second round we started getting committee chairmen, even though I think chairmen will still linger back as our likely opposition.

—The day Muskie introduced it in the Senate, the Washington *Star* had a big story on it, and that night I got a call from Representative Jim Blanchard, a freshman from Michigan, and he says, "Look, I want to put your bill in. Do you have any objection?" I said, "No, go ahead." You know, there are seventy-five freshman Democrats in the House, and they really have some clout, a lot more than freshmen ordinarily have. I talked to Blanchard this morning and he said, "You know, if you went to the seventy-five freshman and asked if they would rather run for re-election on the Humphrey-Hawkins bill or 'sunset,' seventy of them would say 'sunset.'" If the Democratic presidential nominee turns out to be Jimmy Carter— what he's saying and what this bill says are very much the same thing. Carter's aware of this bill. He wants to get together with Muskie and talk about this and budget reform.

Do you see any problem for the bill in the Government Operations Committee?

—Ribicoff likes it and announced publicly that he'll mark it up before the end of June. We've got every Republican on the committee as a co-sponsor except Javits.

What's his problem?

—I'm not sure. I suspect it's that Javits is an appropriating committee guy, basically. He's ranking member on the Labor Committee, and Labor appropriates for most of the social programs. As for committee Democrats, we don't have McClellan, whom we haven't even tried for, or Jackson. I guess we'll get Jackson eventually. Belatedly, Humphrey and a lot of others have jumped on the sunset bill. It doesn't ring true. Basically, they're still thinking politics as usual. Muskie is the only guy in this town who has constantly been looking at this kind of government reform. A couple of weeks ago the *National Journal* called him "the emerging theoretician of Democratic liberalism."

How much of the "emerging theoretician" is attributable to staff?

—It's both. We like to kick that around here a lot, too. The Liberal Party speech, Muskie's great philosophical statement, or at least the first major one on this theme, to be sure, was written by Rackleff.

But after several drafts by different people were rejected, I had conversations with Muskie. Then Bob Merriam, the head of the Advisory Commission in Intergovernmental Relations, came in about something else, and Muskie pumped him on government reform. Then we had some more conversations and I absorbed what Muskie wanted to say, which Rackleff then put into words. Sure, I presented the Senator the idea of this bill, but he took it and ran with it. And it wasn't an original idea on my part. I don't think there are many original ideas around this town. I think the way you make something go in Washington is through timing, having a sense of the right moment to run with an idea, when to avoid sticking your chin out and getting a good idea clipped before it's ready.

—Muskie once said—it was either his sixtieth or sixty-first birthday party in his office—that there are three stages in a political life. One is when you're young and you're brimming with new ideas. The second is when you have fewer, but you're better at recognizing good ideas when they come to you, and you're in a position to run with them. The third is when you reject out of hand any idea that's new. And he said, "I'm in the second stage." It was his roundabout way of expressing his appreciation to his staff. And as you know from being around Muskie, he's not the kind of guy who says things he doesn't want to say. He tried that at one point in his life, the '72 campaign, and he's not about to do it again.

Tuesday, June 1

When I double-check with Leon from my home by long-distance phone this morning, he says, "Absolutely." The Clean Air Act debate will open tomorrow. We make a date for dinner tonight in Washington.

Meeting me at my hotel at about six, Leon blithely informs me that an Allen-of-Alabama filibuster on an anti-trust bill has put off the clean air debate. Yes, he knew it this morning. "But," he says, "you've been away too long. There's a lot to catch up on." Postponed till when? Most likely June 10, certainly no earlier. That is a very troubling disappointment. On June 8 I have an unbreakable commitment to lecture aboard the *Queen Elizabeth 2* and won't return until July 2. How in the world will I reconstruct the debate and possibly the House-Senate conference? From other people's accounts? Very vexing.

Learning that this trip I'm on an expense account of the *New York Times Magazine,* Leon suggests the newest and most overpriced place-to-be-seen near Capitol Hill, Hugo's restaurant atop the still unfinished Hyatt Regency Hotel, where the wine list is a work of splendor and our check comes to $58.92.

To start my fill-in, Leon hands me a sheaf of pages from recent Congressional Records, each an artillery shell before the real battle erupts over clean air. First, on April 13, a notice by Senator Bentsen —what *ever* came of his consuming quest for the presidency that kept him out of markup after markup?—that he would introduce an amendment reducing the bill's requirement of a 50,000-mile warranty for pollution-control devices to 18,000. Also, same date, a long statement by Senator Moss of Utah on his amendment, of far broader significance, to suspend the entire non-degradation portion of the bill for one year until completion of a "study." On April 27 another insertion by Moss, lamenting the "noticeable dearth of information" on the potential disasters to be brought on by the non-degradation policy. Moss lists co-sponsors of his amendment, and the list signals a difficult battle over this crucial portion of the clean air bill. It includes Democrats Metcalf of Montana, Eastland of Mississippi, Johnston of Louisiana, Stone of Florida, McClellan of Arkansas, McGee of Wyoming, Cannon of Nevada, Hollings of South Carolina, and Symington of Missouri.

On April 29, Muskie began the counteroffensive with a long insertion headed "Nondegradation Is Necessary." Perhaps more effective in reaching doubters, on the same day Senator Buckley, under a heading "The Myths of Significant Deterioration," defended the committee's bill and attacked lobbyists and their "analyses" of the bill's impact on industrial growth. On May 2 a powerful missile is launched in defense of the committee's non-degradation stance: a

"Dear Colleague" letter signed by all Republican members of Public Works—Buckley, Baker, Stafford, Domenici, and McClure. (The cooperation of Leon Billings and Hal Brayman is showing.) On May 4, Senator Moss takes a blow to the cheekbone. His—as well as Muskie's—1958 classmate, Gale McGee of Wyoming, retreats from his co-sponsorship of the Moss amendment. He supports a "study," all right, but not one that "would delete or delay the implementation of nondegradation. . . . I believe that any changes that result from such a study can be implemented by Congress at a later date."

On May 19, Muskie adorns the Record with a two-pronged insertion, a curious and puzzling statement. First it says, "There is apparently some doubt in some quarters as to my views on the pending Clean Air legislation. I introduced the committee bill. My name appears on the committee report. I support this legislation. I am prepared to take this bill to conference. . . . I consider this a responsibility and an obligation." Then comes the other prong: "What apparently has not been understood, however, is that I think the Clean Air Act as it was enacted in 1970 is basically a sound law. . . . I am convinced that a modification of the NOx standard is the only necessary change in the Clean Air Act. . . . I think the courts and the Administrator can resolve the nondegradation issue. I think the EPA and the courts are capable, through the use of injunctions and criminal penalties, to enforce the deadlines in the Clean Air Act for stationary sources. . . . Therefore . . . I am today submitting an amendment . . . to strike the committee bill in its entirety [and] substitute a 1.0 gram per mile NOx standard. I have not finally concluded as to whether or not I will [actually move the adoption of] this amendment. But we have an obligation to the auto industry to finalize the question of emission standards. The committee tried to discharge its responsibilities. . . . Should the Senate deem that response inadequate, I will propose my amendament as a means of resolving the issue."

"It's Muskie's way of saying," explains Leon over escargots, "that if all these people want to rewrite the Act on the Senate floor, then this is his advice on how best to rewrite it. If everyone wants to play games, this is how he'd like to play. It was sending up a signal. This is the ultimate fulfillment of the basic Muskie strategy which goes back almost a year: Give me a minimal bill.

"Weeks and weeks ago, before the big show of unity you see in those Congressional Record inserts, the question came up, would he be the one to file the committee report or not? Obviously, the Chamber of Commerce wanted to put off a vote until after the Easter recess."

If the committee has voted out a bill, how can Muskie refuse to file the report?

"Let someone else do it. Let Chairman Randolph do it. Just stand back, stay out of it. But Muskie's sponsorship was needed on that final bill to make it an environmentally acceptable bill—perhaps not an environmentally progressive bill, but at least acceptable. Muskie and I met down at S-199 and I said, 'You don't have to file this report. You just ought to tell people that you're prepared to not file it if all their friends are going to start tearing the bill apart on the floor.' He said, 'I'm not going to tell people that. I'm going to tell people I don't care when the bill comes to the floor. When my colleagues are ready to agree on a report, I'm ready to file the report. I don't care if the bill doesn't come up till after August.'

"This finally reduced to the ultimate simplicity. After he got back from his pain in the neck he put in that amendment: Except for 1.0 NOx, the Clean Air Act doesn't need any amendments. Sort of like the ugly girl who's sitting over against the wall waiting for someone to ask her to dance. She really wants to dance but doesn't want to look so anxious that everyone knows she wants to dance. And he played it beautifully. Just beautifully. You've got some of the results in those statements here."

Over brandy, Leon concludes my catch-up with the news that Senator Baker has accepted the ranking-member status of the new committee overseeing intelligence affairs (a permanent committee to replace the Church investigating committee), and since a Senator may hold only one chairmanship or "rankingship" of a full committee, Baker is no longer ranking on Public Works. Buckley has replaced him, and Baker has replaced Buckley as ranking member of the Environmental Pollution Subcommittee. Leon crystal-balls: "If Buckley gets beaten this fall, that would make Stafford the ranking member, and that would be no less comfortable than Buckley was. Of course, Stafford's got a tough race too."

Who's next after him? Domenici?

"No, McClure." I'm not supposed to see Leon's rolling of the eyes. Abruptly he says:

"Oh, let me tell you about McClure. Randolph had an anniversary party, his tenth as chairman of the committee. It was at the University Club. Senator McClure and I were tablemates and we had a great talk about political philosophy. He finally said, 'Jesus Christ, you and I are very close philosophically.' And I said, 'Yes—except on gun control.' And he said, 'Why in the world are you for gun control?' And I said, 'Because you're *against* gun control.' "

Friday, June 4

Dolores is emitting an overweening glint this morning, dying for me to probe into why. I probe. Whirling histrionically toward me in her swivel chair, her high-arched, deigning brows carefully in place, she recites, "My friend, Elsie Vance, secretary to Gary Hart—well-known, glamorous, *young* Senator—just called, on her Senator's instructions, to find out *who* does Senator Muskie's *hair*. And don't think that George McGovern didn't ask the same question the other day. I told Elsie, Joe Q. Yes, that's all he calls himself, Joe Q. And Elsie says, 'Didn't I read in a column that Joe Q has gone to visit Italy? What does the Senator do when Joe Q is in Italy?' And *I* said, 'Oh, we just fly the Senator *there*.'

An hour later Dolores bursts out of the Senator's office, stenographic book in hand, her eyes glazed with recent tears. This time I don't ask. She tells me: "I'll show you later."

Later I find on my desk a couple of sheets of typing. It has to do with a dinner the Muskies held last night at their home to honor Senator Phil Hart. Muskie, searching diligently during his last trip through Maine for an appropriate gift, came upon and chose a pair of hand-carved gulls of surpassing grace. Guests at the dinner were people especially dear to Hart or Muskie or both, among them Senators Ted Kennedy and Quentin Burdick; Abigail McCarthy, estranged wife of former Senator Eugene, who has remained close to Jane Muskie; Senator Tom Eagleton and Barbara as well as Senator Howard Cannon and Dorothy.

After the dinner, Hart, moved by Muskie's tribute, asked for a memento copy of it. Muskie's word memory being excellent, this morning he dictated his extemporaneous remarks to Dolores. That's why she went to pieces. What prose! The sheets she left me say:

"I have known Phil for more than twenty years. He is my dearest friend in the Senate. I love him more than anyone outside my family. . . . I have tried to find some way to symbolize what Phil means to me and to others of us. What I selected, finally, are these sea gulls.

"The sea gull is not the noblest of birds. The species identified with Maine is often called the 'laughing gull' because of its strident call. It is a symbol of the oceans to us in Maine, and the tempestuous forces which lie under the surface and the distant lands beyond the farthest horizon, which we can see on a clear day. It is not confined to the sea, but follows our rivers and streams and lakes into the lonely wilderness forests. It does not fear the unknown or the elements with which it lives. In flying, it is a thing of grace and beauty.

"It is not a perfect symbol, or the complete symbol of the decency, integrity, courage, and compassion which we all identify with Phil. But in its grace, beauty, and willingness to dare the unknown, it is the kind of free spirit we see in Phil Hart. . . ."

Joining him a couple of hours later for a luncheon chat in S-199, I find Muskie in a good mood, unmarred by the continuing delay in resolving clean air.

A CONVERSATION WITH SENATOR MUSKIE

Will the time demands of Budget, and now of "sunset" and government reform, permit you to continue the leadership on the environment?

—It's time-consuming. I really think I should give way to someone else. I think it's important that someone else, someone younger, assume leadership, because the issue is going to be around long after I'm gone. The subject's no longer fresh to me. I've got some scars from all the battles I've had to fight.

—You know, I happen to believe that somewhere down the way the Senate ought to change the committee system so that Senators somehow rotate committee assignments. I've served on two committees of which I'm not now a member and that's been valuable to me. I started on Banking and Currency and, years later, left it to take a vacancy on Foreign Relations. Then I left Foreign Relations for Budget. I think Senators ought to become generalists, besides making their contributions in special fields. To be stuck for a whole Senate career specializing on one subcommittee can be a little deadening.

—But that reform will take some time, I'm afraid. For now, I'm inclined to narrow the range of my responsibilities to become better at them, especially the budget process that has such great potential for changing this institution, our country, our directions. It's a full-time job, not something that ought to be done with one hand.

Budget has become the generalist committee.

—That's right. I've got to be knowledgeable in every subject that goes before the Congress, and debate issues with committee specialists. It's going to take more and more time.

Would being Majority Leader really be that much more desirable than being Budget Chairman? Does history really remember Majority Leaders?

—Well, there's nothing that says they're mutually exclusive. A Majority Leader may be a chairman of a committee. There are precedents. But if I had to choose, I think your point is legitimate that people don't remember great Majority Leaders over the long haul. Fifty years from now, who's going to remember who the Majority Leader was fifty years ago? Who's even going to remember that Lyndon Johnson was a Majority Leader?

—The environmental issue could well be my place in Senatorial history. And the budget thing could well be.

What would you say was Mike Mansfield's major contribution?

—There's a thing that some people call the Mansfield Principle: He doesn't run the Senate. The Senate runs the Senate. The Senate is a body of equals. That means a hundred equals, not even divided into two parties. Every Senator has equal rights. Only when the Senate as a whole works its will has the Senate spoken. And no committee rules the roost. All Senators, all committees, have duties and responsibilities, and if you're going to get things done you've got to work together. You've got to accommodate.

—On this constant curiosity of how Senators deal with each other individually, on a personal basis, the principles are no different in the Senate than in life as a whole. Yet in the Senate it's more difficult than that, because you've got people with vested power. So you have not only the personal relationship to accommodate, but you have their power prerogatives to accommodate. People don't give up power easily or casually. So, one, you have to assert your own rights. But, two, you have to respect the other fellow's. You accommodate on little things, giving up your back seat or your front seat to someone else, but not on the essentials. And around here there's only one essential thing—and that's power. I don't mean that in an invidious way. I mean that the Senate and House together are the power to legislate policy for a great world power. The United States of America is a great power. I'm not saying that in the sense of selfish power. I'm talking about very real, practical power.

—The thing that draws people to this level of political office is the power to influence great events, great issues. We are deciding issues. There's a personal satisfaction in that—but also a heavy responsibility to do it right, the accountability for which is very real. Once you've put in your years here and your colleagues have given you power with respect to particular policies—you guard it. Not only for your own ego satisfaction but because you have the responsibility of guarding it, making sure that it's not undermined, making sure it's handled well.

—And that's *the* great satisfaction out of a political life. I don't know what else there is that even begins to match that. So if you've got that kind of power, and then a new institution comes along, like the Committee on the Budget, and you're not entirely sure about this new guy who is chairman, and he seems a little ambitious, a little aggressive—you start guarding.

Monday, July 26

While aboard ship during June, almost a week each way, and for two weeks between crossings, keeping up with American news was hit or miss. Plenty about the Democratic Party's collapse at the feet of Jimmy Carter after June 8, but I couldn't find a word about the Senate's disposition of the Clean Air Act.

I couldn't wait to get off the pier on July 2 before calling Washington. To my astonishment, Leon told me the bill did not come up June 10—in fact, had not yet come up at all.

Today, finally, the Clean Air Act of 1976 will make its debut on the Senate floor. Maybe. In long, all-day sessions, the Senate is operating on a "two track" system, one major bill in the morning, another in the afternoon, so some progress can be made even if one of the bills is being talked to death.

To help make profitable an otherwise impatient morning, I suggest to Charlie Micoleau, now in his tenth month as administrative assistant, that we have a long-overdue talk. Muskie being off somewhere, Charlie and I settle into the Senator's big leather couch.

A CONVERSATION WITH CHARLIE MICOLEAU

How has the Senator taken a series of disappointments this year— the non-materializing of the "President thing," almost becoming Carter's vice-presidential candidate, and the bid to be Majority Leader, which doesn't seem to be in the cards?

—The Majority Leader one, I'm not sure how much hope he ever had. Also it's not over. He had long ago given up the presidential race, before some of his staff did. As Carter took over in New

Hampshire, I think he just faced facts and never allowed his hopes to get up. Besides, he knew you couldn't run for President and be Budget chairman, at least not the way he was operating the Budget Committee. There were maybe a couple of times when people seriously tried to tell him, "The thing's wide open," or "You're the only one who can stop Carter." But by then that certainly wasn't his perception. So that was not a real disappointment, except maybe in the most global sense.

Did you sense any letdown after the close brush with the vice presidency?

—Oh, no question about it, a totally different thing. But first, he's very good at protecting himself psychologically. It's a natural trait. We all have it if we're smart. At first, even though his name appeared on speculative lists fairly early, he didn't think that amounted to a hill of beans. And I have some evidence—some personal evidence—that he never was seriously considered by Carter personally until he was asked down to Plains. When Carter's scout, Charles Kirbo, was making his rounds, he put the question to Muskie and also asked Muskie to make recommendations. We couldn't tell which question he really came here to ask. Muskie said no for himself, then mentioned three people to Kirbo: Stevenson, Mondale, and I'm not sure if the third was Glenn or Church. What I know he did say is that Carter should have someone younger, from his own political generation, and someone who's been tested, who has a constituency, preferably someone who has gone through the primary route and has developed the skill of being sensitive to public opinion and mood. Then there was that question of filling out that questionnaire for Kirbo. Some newspaper story, I don't know where the hell it came from, kept getting repeated that Muskie told Kirbo that he doesn't fill out questionnaires and that Kirbo could take it and shove it. It's absolutely not true. He was never given a questionnaire. And Kirbo later told me that that was his understanding of Carter's instructions to him, not to give him a questionnaire because he wasn't under consideration at that time. My best guess is that, as you approach that famous trip to Plains on July 4, Muskie was seen as a fallback. People have told me that Carter used precisely those words to George Meany—that he's considering Mondale and Glenn, but if they don't work out, Muskie or someone like him will be the fallback. I got that through a source. This gets a little fuzzy, depending on whom you believe, but my guess is that Kirbo went back and told Carter he really ought to consider Muskie. It's fuzzy because there's another version that had Kirbo plugging Jackson right to the very end, the very, very end. But some of this comes from the Jackson people and they tell weird stories. The other thing that was happening, Pat Caddell was one of the few people in the inner circle who's not from Georgia. Caddell was pushing Muskie. I know that from several sources. I'm sure Pat was motivated by Muskie being a Catholic—Carter was having problems with the Catholic vote—but I think Pat's prime motivation was that he thinks Muskie would have been the best vice-presidential candidate.

—Well, Muskie got the call Saturday night, July 2. Carter said simply, "I'd like you to come down sometime next week," to which Muskie replied, "The only time I can come down is Monday, the fourth." He went down thinking this was not serious, that the whole thing was sort of a media event. But he came back obviously aware he was being seriously considered. Also, he came back impressed with Carter. But I think he was still convinced that Carter would choose a younger man. The rest of us, if you want the truth, were convinced that Carter would choose a *shorter* man. No, I'm not kidding. Carter's much too interested in the visual, how he looks. Anyhow, the Senator came back saying he was going to stick to his plan for a fishing trip during the convention, and that became a great debate here. He was not a delegate and didn't plan to go to the convention at all. In a lot of ways, the smartest thing he did was to go fishing. Worse than just fishing, actually. He was off at some lake in Canada—one side of the lake was in Maine but the camp was in Canada—and we couldn't call in except for one hour a day. He could call out if somebody cranked up the generator. Maybe he had a radio with him for keeping up with the news, but knowing him, I doubt it. But he'd planned this fishing trip long before the convention and he has this great sense of knowing when he can't do anything. That was his whole approach to the question: What's going to be will be, and we're just not going to do anything about it.

—At the staff level, we had a great debate among ourselves and with him: Should we try some aggressive activity? But nothing came of that. I don't think he knew how intense it had become until he arrived in New York late Tuesday afternoon during the convention and found those headlines, that it was either Muskie or Glenn, or

Glenn or Muskie, or Muskie or Mondale. By Tuesday he was frankly damned nervous.

With all the dissatisfaction every Vice-President's had with the job, the powerlessness, being picked up and dropped by the President like a toy, why would he want it?

—Come on, what are you talking about? What a great way to crown off his career, Vice-President of the United States. He doesn't need any more challenges. You've heard him say that.

—Sure, it's a real crummy job, a real dead-end street. There are a lot of arguments against it for a guy like Muskie, that he's very powerful, that he's in a position of great independence vis-à-vis any President, he has a bigger staff than he'd have as Vice-President and probably a better staff. To give all that up to hang around and wait for someone to die, why, you saw Rockefeller's remarks yesterday where he said that he just tuned out of the vice-presidency, about this great jealousy from the White House staff, and he finally said screw it. Apparently he gave the finger to the White House staff privately before he did it publicly. Those are the counterarguments for all the things I said a minute ago.

—We prepared quite a book for Muskie on a variety of matters relating to the vice-presidential possibility. I made sure to include some very strong arguments as to why the office of Vice-President is a lousy thing even to consider. I did that for a couple of reasons. One, I felt an obligation to have a balanced point of view. The other was, I hoped, to give him something to fall back on if he didn't get it. Part of that was for our staff protection. I wanted to make sure that if he did go into a blue funk after not getting it he could never say that we oversold him. But if you want to know where his head was at on this thing, he read that stuff pretty carefully, and about those negative parts he made the remark, "If you think I want to be the bookkeeper of the United States Senate for the rest of my career, you're crazy."

—But I think he kept his options under control and handled it pretty well, given the tension. The tension was just incredible. He's said publicly that he woke up that morning and knew he didn't have it. I think he sensed it the night before. I certainly did. Let me make one concluding observation about the way he handled the disappointment. Having watched him after other disappointments, including the presidential one, I was really proud of him. I don't think it lasted more than four days. Moreover, I don't think the acute disappointment lasted more than thirty minutes. We'd agreed not to say anything to the press until Carter had his press conference [announcing Mondale as the choice], which was at ten. We got the call about eight-thirty, with the Senator and Jane and me and Charlie Lander, a very old friend, sort of an aide-de-camp during political campaigns, locked in the room. I mean literally locked, because there were eight million press out there. So after he called his kids, within thirty minutes—this was spontaneous, not a calculated thing—he said, "Get me the people involved in the Maine campaign," and we pulled together a meeting and discussed what we've got to do in Maine. It was great. And next day he went back to Maine and was campaigning—I remember, it was the Yarmouth Clamfest. His head was all together.

Maynard Toll once said that he assumes Muskie's next six-year term will be his last. What do you think?

—Clearly, he's approaching it that way, as the culmination of his career. We forget the guy's a human being who's had a long, productive life, who has spent from 1968 until this year running for office— eight years of almost constant campaigning. That's a hell of a long time, and he's now sixty-two, and he thinks more and more of what it would be like to be out of it. He sees old friends dying, or retiring and enjoying life, while he's still running around putting in fifteen-hour days. Sure, he worries about his place in history, but the young visionaries around here, Al From and Doug Bennet, are far more anxious for him to carve out his place in history than he is to do the carving. He wants to be there in history, but there's this tugging on this other side that says, "What would it be like if I weren't here having to do all this?"

At about one o'clock Majority Leader Mansfield calls up S. 3219, "a bill to amend the Clean Air Act, as amended." Chairman Randolph makes an opening presentation, which runs long, partly to kill time because Muskie is not on the floor. Then Senator Buckley, as ranking member, makes his. Two Senators, William Scott of Virginia and John Tower of Texas, serve notice that they plan to fight the bill, opposing its non-degradation provision.

And that is it for the opening act of the Great Clean Air Debate. The Senate spends the rest of the afternoon on tax reform.

Wednesday, July 28

The full Senate, which normally meets at noon after a morning of committee meetings, convenes today at 8 A.M. to try to slosh its way through the third day of the clean air debate that stagnated yesterday. The sticking point is the Moss amendment to knock non-degradation out of the bill until completion of a one-year study. Moss has insisted that debate on his amendment not begin until today, and he is now upset over an amendment offered by Chairman Randolph—for a one-year study *without* suspending non-degradation. If Randolph's passes, it will deaden the wind driving the Moss amendment. So Moss doesn't want the Randolph amendment considered before the Moss amendment is considered.

In short, the mode of this debate has shifted, as it often does in the Senate, from the weaponry of facts and persuasion to the weaponry of time and maneuver.

A few minutes after eight, taking advantage of the almost empty floor—including the absence of Moss himself—Muskie presses for a vote on the Randolph amendment.

"Mr. President," comes the instant call from Dick Stone of Florida, whose desk-microphone voice has the soothing resonance of an all-night disc jockey. Senator Stone is one of Moss's floor lieutenants. "The Senator from Utah has requested that we not take action on the pending amendment until he arrives, and he had a previously scheduled commitment that he could not avoid, until about nine o'clock."

Serene Mike Mansfield rises gravely and surrenders to annoyance: "I talked with the Senator from Utah yesterday. He said he would be here about eight-fifteen. It places the Senate in a most difficult position in view of the schedule we have. I would hope some word could be gotten to the Senator from Utah to get over here as soon as possible. It was to meet *his* convenience that the Senate met at eight o'clock this morning."

"The Senator from Utah," explains freshman Stone, trying to prevent an embarrassment that could be far more damaging than loss of a debating point, "was called as a witness on the House side, their first scheduled witness, and did plan to come as quickly as he could. We can call over there and urge them to hurry up."

A more experienced Senator would not have pricked that raw nerve. Using the House as an excuse to delay the Senate?

"This is more important, I think," Mansfield snaps indignantly, "than appearing as a witness before a House committee. He could certainly put a statement in the record there. We came in at eight o'clock to give him a chance for a free-wheeling swing, which would take him four or five hours, he indicated, to present his amendment."

"The Senator from Utah," further apologizes Stone, "is willing for the extra forty-five minutes to be deducted from the time he indicated to the leadership he needed."

"Well, he used up that time yesterday," scolds Mansfield, "when he took up an hour and a half of the Senate's time on his amendment. We have a tight schedule. On August 11 we go out until August 23. *The business of the Senate must always come first.*"

Moss's gaucherie gives Muskie the upper hand, and Muskie tries hard to press it only lightly, but can't resist: "I appreciate the right of the Senator from Utah to present his amendment any way he wishes. Frankly, the pending Randolph amendment is for a very simple study. I mean it could have been disposed of yesterday very quickly. Or we could have disposed of other amendments. But the Senator from Utah decided that consideration of the Randolph amendment yesterday might prejudice his rights. So he proceeded to debate his amendment. Last evening we had a Public Works Committee hearing on the Clean Water Act until nine-thirty. It was not very easy for me to get home last night and then get up early enough to arrive here at eight o'clock this morning. Frankly, I can see no reason why we should not vote on the Randolph amendment. It does not prejudice the case of the Senator from Utah in any way whatsoever."

It is 8:21 A.M. "In view of the circumstances," says Mansfield, "I suggest that Senator Moss be contacted and asked if he can, if possible, be here at eight-thirty. I ask unanimous consent that the Senate stand in recess until eight-thirty." That is as close as the Senate will ever get to a principal ordering an unruly school boy to the front office as fast as his feet will carry him. Presiding Officer John Durkin of New Hampshire gavels the recess.

The morning is haggled away by Moss supporters, eventually joined by Moss, opposing a vote on the Randolph amendment prior to a vote on the Moss amendment, yet resisting a vote on the Moss amendment. Finally Muskie gets consent to bring up the Bentsen amendment, which is defeated, 51 to 45, a major psychological as well as practical victory for the committee bill.

Thursday, July 29

It gets nastier today.

"I deplore the delay we have gotten ourselves into," deplores Moss, borrowing the floor from Allen of Alabama. "I was assured that my amendment would be considered first."

"The Senator received no assurance from me," asserts Muskie, the bill's floor manager. "I have been—"

"I don't have the floor and cannot yield," dodges Moss.

"Will the Senator from Alabama yield so I can correct the record?" asks Muskie of Allen.

The condescending reply comes not from Allen but from Moss, "All right."

"The Senator received no such assurance from me," repeats Muskie. "I have agreed to postpone bringing up the Clean Air Act time and time again since last April, several times out of deference to the Senator from Utah. I have tried to reach an agreement to deal with the Moss amendment first. On Monday there was nothing but talk. Then Tuesday came, and the leadership—not the Senator from Utah—pressed me to get amendments disposed of in order to get the bill moving. The Senator from Utah made it quite clear to me he didn't want his amendment brought up until Wednesday, so I scurried around looking for other amendments, non-controversial amendments, to fill the time on Tuesday. We proceeded in due course to the Randolph amendment which, as far as we knew, was non-controversial—a mere study. The Senator from Utah chose to interpret that move as an assault on his position, which was not the intention whatsoever."

"May I now proceed?" asks Moss indulgently.

"The Senator from Alabama has yielded to me."

"*May I now proceed?*" needles Moss.

"The Senator from Alabama has the floor," rules Durkin.

"I have yielded to the distinguished Senator from Utah," drawls the high-register croak of Allen, "and I shall not yield to anyone else without the permission of the Senator from Utah."

"I asked to have that said," scolds Moss, "because the manager of the bill jumps up and constantly interrupts that he wants to correct the record. If we do not get to the Moss amendment, then we will probably have no bill, and I would regret that. . . . I would expect to have some rather extensive remarks following the Senator from Alabama, and I understand he has very extensive remarks to make, and many others have come to me and said they, too, have some rather extensive remarks to make."

And so Moss defends the economic interests of the state of Utah —its right to promote industry despite its purple mountain majesties —through the most powerful weapon offered by this moment of the Senate work cycle: time. The threat of "extensive remarks" is a threat against every Senator with a strong proprietary interest in some *other* bill packed away in that suffocating backlog of bills. Any pending bill not passed before the mid-August recess faces an even tougher battle for attention in September, the final month of the Ninety-fourth Congress. For many bills (and many Senator-sponsors), it's the next few days or die.

Next to me in the gallery, a tourist family of three, parents and a high-school-age girl, are given seats by the usher. They are awed, hushed, adjusting to the realization that the great chamber below them is not television but the place itself. After a while the daughter asks, "What are they talking about?" Dad says nothing. He's been trying to pick up the drift of debate and can't get a handle on it. Soon he starts to shake his head in wonder. These grown men, famous men who he hoped would stir faith and patriotism in his daughter, these windy men don't seem to be making any sense. Obviously Muskie and that Moss fellow are annoyed with each other, but about what? All they seem to talk about is how long each one is going to talk. Is *that* what they think their electors hired them to do at high salaries? Just jab each other's overfed egos while outside the doors human problems—unemployment and energy shortage—go neglected? Is *this* how they run their government? *Our* government?

That *is* what it looks like. There's no way for the citizen walking in cold to perceive that those men are not time-squanderers and idiots; that they are keenly aware of the high stakes of the game played on that floor; that what often seems idiocy may be virtuosity, deliberate and highly intelligent use of the most effective means at a given moment for protecting or advancing an interest. At stake behind all that niggling, as Muskie measures it, is two years of committee labor and, moreover, the national commitment to make the air breathable again and forever. Moss is for clean air too. But as the Senator elected by Utah, he insists upon a limit to what any one state can be asked to do. Because his state is blessed—or cursed—with border-to-border splendor, is Utah to accept a relative prohibition (as he sees it) of wealth-producing industry, staying a permanently underdeveloped land for the amusement of tourists from other states? If that condemnation of Utah can be forestalled by delaying a vote on the palliative Randolph amendment, Moss will go to any reasonable length to stall it—including looking the villain and the fool to the gallery (knowing his Senate colleagues are not similarly deluded).

The purpose of the debate, at least for now, is not debate but diversion. And behind the diversion lies further diversion. While Moss and Muskie grapple on the floor, diverting from the substance of non-degradation with Moss's threats of "extensive remarks" and Muskie's wide-eyed innocence over the harmlessness of the Randolph amendment, these bitterly antagonistic camps are in intense and hopeful communication through the leadership. Over there is Bobby Byrd jawboning with Moss; Mansfield, laconically, scholarly eyes directed thoughtfully at the ceiling, working something out with Muskie; Charlie Ferris, their majority secretary, is desk-hopping around the chamber, pinning down details.

In midafternoon Mansfield breaks into the "track two" debate on the Tax Reform Act to offer a unanimous consent agreement to limit debate on the Clean Air Act, to which he knows there will be no objection because all the interested parties have already agreed to it: Debate on S. 3219, the Clean Air Act, shall resume next Tuesday at 8:30 A.M. Any amendment or motion shall be limited to one hour of floor time, equally divided by each side, except for an amendment by Gary Hart and another by Robert Packwood, which shall each have two hours, and another by William Scott of Virginia, one and a half hours. Immediately after those amendments are disposed of, and no later than 1:30 P.M. Tuesday, the Senate shall vote on the Moss amendment. Muskie shall be allocated one hour each opposing the Scott and Moss amendments. A vote on final passage of S. 3219 shall occur no later than 1:45 P.M. next Thursday. The total time of debate on the bill between Tuesday morning and voting time on Thursday shall be no less than fifteen hours, with two hours reserved for Jim Allen of Alabama. (Allen, a relatively junior Senator, not even on the sponsoring committee, snatches more than one eighth of the debating time by the simple power of demanding it; if he doesn't get it there is no unanimous consent. And people wonder why the word "accommodation" is so prominent in the vocabulary of Senators.)

"The manager of the bill," points out manager Muskie, in support of Mansfield's effort, "is limited to less time than the proponents of the Scott and Moss amendments, which is something that I have agreed to. But I want it clearly understood that with respect to all other amendments the time is to be equally divided—the manager of the bill having half the time."

"The Senator is correct," says the Majority Leader.

"Mr. President," joins in Moss, his badgering tone of this morning now mellowed, "I appreciate the efforts of the Majority Leader, and especially the efforts of the Senator from West Virginia [Randolph], in working this out. It was a difficult parliamentary situation. I appreciate what has been done, and I think I can live with the proposal."

Tuesday, August 3

When the stakes are high, as they are in this debate, members of this "club" reach for any gentlemanly sword or, when necessary, the nearest switchblade knife. Rivals become allies and friends become enemies.

A weapon that fell in Muskie's lap yesterday to use today against Frank Moss, his classmate and fellow Democrat, was a decision by the U. S. Court of Appeals. It upholds EPA's right to have decreed its tough regulations on non-deterioration—tough administrative directives that helped force Congress into considering the present legislative substitute. Muskie now points out that the committee's bill somewhat relaxes those EPA edicts, and wonders with righteous innocence how anyone in his right mind could question the wisdom of the committee's bill:

"When we have Senator McClure on one end of the political spectrum of this committee—and I will not pick anybody but myself at the other end, lest I hurt somebody politically—and they supported this *unanimously,* and the more conservative members have been among the most ardent and vigorous and most enthusiastic proponents of the committee provisions, there must be a *reason.* The only reason I can suggest is the reason well reflected in the language of the court's opinion yesterday. We did not all agree in committee. Some of us wanted stricter standards. I cannot recall anybody who wanted anything that would have deliberately weakened the bill."

Muskie is playing his strongest card—committee unanimity—one that will trump almost any opposition play. It is too strong a maneuver to go unchallenged by Moss:

"I find in the committee report many statements of separate, individual views—by Senators Randolph, Muskie, Montoya, Gravel,

Bentsen, Morgan. . . . Then Senator McClure, Senator Domenici, and Senator Hart—"

"Will the Senator yield?" roars Muskie indignantly.

"—each had individual views."

"Individual views are not necessarily dissenting views."

"I did not say they were dissenting views."

"The vote was 13–1 to report the bill."

"I am not challenging that. I was just saying that the Senator—"

"For what purpose," thunders Muskie, changing weapons, "is the Senator wasting valuable time?"

"I will not yield for that. The Senator kept saying the committee was unanimous, the committee was unanimous."

"I mean on this provision."

"Will the Senator please not interrupt me? I will yield if I am asked to yield, but I do not like this constant interruption, interruption, interruption. The committee may have voted finally to report the bill, but if we are talking about great unanimity, why in the world did every Senator on that committee feel he had to register his individual views? That is the point I am trying to make. The Senator himself pointed out—I quote him from last Tuesday's record: 'The whole area of environmental pollution is replete with *uncertainty* because of our dynamic, ongoing industrial society, so that we can never have a status quo.' *That's* what we who favor the Moss amendment are talking about. We are playing with uncertainties. This is replete with uncertainties. *That's* why we see all these individual views, because of those uncertainties. Does that not argue for having a full, complete study of this matter before we go forward?"

And finally, a couple of hours later, the reckoning. The Moss amendment crashes badly—and, to Muskie and Billings, somewhat surprisingly. It collects only 31 votes against 63 for the committee position.

At last we know that there were purpose and cunning to the buffoonery and time-wasting quibbling that puzzled gallery visitors. The lopsided vote helps explain it. Moss and his supporters had to make the Senate take the Moss amendment seriously, and the only way to do it was to create the illusion that Moss was backed by votes. Muskie, Billings, the committee took the threat seriously, giving Moss time to go out and try, unsuccessfully, to scavenge those votes.

Thursday, August 5

Today the Senate *works its will* (a favorite phrase around here), voting up or down the Clean Air Act of 1976.

It's a big story. More reporters than usual are in the press gallery for the roll call. In a group of gallery seats beside them, TV reporters observe solemnly and make notations. The puffy leather couches around the wall of the chamber are stuffed with grave-visaged staff assistants of Public Works Committee members. In the third-floor corridor the long queue of summer tourists waiting for gallery seats makes little progress. The gallery is full of lobbyists—the same audience that filled those folding chairs in the committee room for month after month—and none of them will give up a precious seat. Tonight the vote will be reported in the big time—the evening news shows of the three television networks, as though something important and startling has happened. But, of course, the story's all over. It's been grinding itself out day by day, month by month, through the markups of the Environmental Pollution Subcommittee, then of the full Public Works Committee, and the news media reported scarcely a word about it. If they had, hardly anyone would have paid attention. We read news for climaxes. And today is the "climax"—even though the story is over.

The Senate today approves the Clean Air Act. It mandates revolutionary restrictions on America's favorite love objects, automobiles, as well as on pollution-producing industry. Judging by the overwhelming vote in favor of it, 78–13, the casual observer would conclude that the bill was a simple subject of relatively little controversy and overwhelming national craving.

Wednesday, September 15

Yes, there *is* a House of Representatives, a fact forgotten around the Senate with surprising ease, and what the Other Body does counts too, and today is the day they're going to do it. For all the months the Senate Environmental Pollution Subcommittee has been wrangling over the revisions of the Clean Air Act, the House Health and Environment Subcommittee (of the Interstate and Foreign Commerce Committee) has been doing the same thing.

No, not the same thing. Working toward the same goal, yes. For substantially the same reasons, yes. But writing a bill of its own, starting from its own scratch, with little communication between the staffs of the two subcommittees (except what they have been hearing through lobbyists who actively commute across Capitol Hill, and such communication is not inconsiderable).

If anyone is seriously holding his breath over the outcome of the House vote today, it's not over the up-or-down vote on the bill itself but over one amendment on auto emission standards, the Dingell amendment. John D. Dingell, Jr., a Michigan Democrat, for twenty years has represented southwest Detroit and its smoky "downriver suburbs" that include River Rouge and Ecorse and their vast colonies of auto-worker dwellings as well as Ford Motor Company's colossal car-building site, the Rouge plant.

The Dingell amendment would "resolve" the excruciating question of a NOx standard by having Congress walk away from it, surrendering it to the individual who, five years hence, will occupy the office of EPA administrator, a person whose identity, views, and party are at present unknown. More specifically, the amendment would maintain a 2.0 NOx standard through 1981. After that, the administrator would be authorized to tighten the NOx figure to any level he considers "reasonable"—or he may leave it at 2.0. Thus Dingell would have Congress specify no long-term NOx standard at all. The White House has mass-mailed a "personal" letter to every Representative, personally signed by President Ford's signing machine, urging adoption of the amendment by this liberal Democrat. The combined lobby of auto manufacturers has focused its force on it.

"I think we'll win on that amendment," Bill Chapman of GM told me confidently in June. "Then the conference committee would have to come down somewhere between the Senate numbers and the Dingell numbers."

I wrote off his prophecy as lobbyist smoke.

Today the Dingell amendment arrives on the floor of the House and virtually everybody is surprised at the dimensions of the outcome. The amendment passes with elbow and knee room to spare, 224 to 169.

Outside the House gallery I ask dismayed Rafe Pomerance of Friends of the Earth what he thinks put it across. His analysis is crunched into a single word: "Dealers." It would not have worked in the Senate where members, according to Chapman, "know three times as much about this" as House members. But in a campaign by "local, independent" businessmen, quietly inspired by Detroit, the corridors of House office buildings have been so alive with local-franchise auto dealers, you'd think the new models were being shown there. In a congressional district an auto dealer is often a community leader and quite likely to be among a Congressman's leading campaign contributors. That is clout. It's hard to find concrete support for the popular, naïve notion that mammoth corporations, by virtue of controlling billions, *directly* influence—or control—large blocs of votes in Congress. A Congressman from, say, Kentucky couldn't care less about the concerns of the Detroit Economic Club since neither Detroit nor its billions can do much to affect directly his political survival. But the Congressman does heed the song of his local Dodge Boys.

So the Clean Air Act now goes to the critical legislative stage of conference. Two co-equal houses of Congress, each having struggled almost two years, have come up with two different bills, different in language and content, each house jealously defending its own.

Is it possible, even thinkable, that these disparate works can be reconciled by two suspicious teams of prima donna authors—in just a few days? Two weeks from this Friday the Ninety-fourth Congress is scheduled to go out of business. In that suffocating pressure of time, not only must the conference committee in effect write a wholly new clean air law, but the two full houses of Congress—beneath a crushing pile-up of other unfinished business—must approve the conference's compromise bill.

Thursday morning, September 23

"Serious students of Congress," recently wrote David E. Rosenbaum, a serious student himself as congressional correspondent of the New York *Times,* "have had a rare experience in the last month —the opportunity to watch a conference committee at work. . . . A conference committee is the essence of the Congressional process. It is where . . . the laws of the land are finally written."

If anyone ought to understand the powers of a conference and ways to manipulate that power, it is President Gerald Ford, veteran of more than a quarter century in the House and a party leader there. And it appears that Ford would like to manipulate this conference into failing to come up with any bill at all. Either signing or vetoing any conceivable clean air bill in the next few weeks has to hurt him in November when he runs the grave risk of becoming an ex-President before ever having been elected President.

True, if no bill survives, his native Michigan cannot begin building next year's automobiles. But that potential disaster, Ford apparently reasons, would press so hard on the incoming Ninety-fifth Congress that surely within a few weeks of its opening session in January the Ninety-fifth would be forced to rush out a soft bill that would decriminalize the sale and possession of a new motorcar.

The White House plan, so simple and unusual it might almost be called imaginative, was to persuade enough conferees, particularly from the House, to be busy elsewhere. The conference, lacking a quorum, could not legally function, and the bill would die, leaving not a trace of blood or a fingerprint. The plan failed. In a confidential memo that later slipped into unauthorized hands, chief White House lobbyist Max Friedersdorf was informed by his deputy William Gorog that a senior conferee, Representative James Broyhill, a North Carolina Republican, ardently devoted to blocking the bill, "advised that preventing a quorum would be extremely difficult." He therefore suggested White House pressure on thirteen conferees: seven from the Senate—Baker, Buckley, Domenici, McClure, Morgan, Randolph, and Stafford—and six from the House. The pitch, Gorog suggested in his memo, should go as follows: "As you know, the President sought 18 months ago to have the questions of significant deterioration and auto emission standards dealt with by the Congress. However, it does not appear to us that an acceptable bill can come out of this conference. I hope you would act to keep an unacceptable bill off the President's desk." Oh no, that doesn't mean kill the bill, an embarrassed Gorog assured an inquirer about the leaked letter. What it meant, he said, is that the President would like a bill that is "more acceptable."

For two days the conference has been meeting between floor roll calls, off and on, in fits and starts, dawdling, stumbling, bogging down, agreeing on cats-and-dogs details, leaving the big issues for later. Later is today. If they don't get down to the sticky business of auto emissions today, with non-degradation still ahead, there's just no hope of a bill. They're to meet early this afternoon on the Senate side of the Capitol (with meticulous protocol, yesterday's was on the House side). This morning at ten the Senate conferees gather in unofficial caucus in the Public Works conference room to work out strategy.

"If you're here, this must be air," says Gary Hart, spotting his aide, Kevin Cornell, and pitter-pattering on his slippery-soled boots to a junior seat at the table. The meeting collects Senators Culver, Morgan, McClure, Gravel, Domenici, and Public Works Chairman Randolph before Muskie gavels it to order at ten-twenty.

"We met with the House staff early yesterday morning," Leon Billings begins, "and agreed that reconciliation of all issues from both bills is impossible. I suggested we try a trade-off approach. We put together packages from both bills side by side that seemed to lend themselves to trade-off from a viewpoint of neatness in bartering, if not from a viewpoint of policy."

"Leon," breaks in Senator McClure with a non sequitur that is actually supremely relevant to the main question at hand—whether the Senate conferees will hang together, "I want you to know I fully appreciate your difficulty and that I'm going to listen with a thoroughly open mind."

"The staff did a brilliant job," head-pats Gary Hart from the opposite political corner. "I want you to know that I can compromise on everything except non-degredation. On autos, I can't go any further than the committee position. If the conference report goes further, I couldn't sign it. I say that now because I must go to something else."

"I agree with that," says Muskie.

That is not a casual remark, and McClure and other members take notice. It's more than a thank you to Hart for abandoning his fealty to .4 NOx, more than an assurance that Muskie will stand firm on 1.0 and deadlines. It means, in effect, that he will oppose any compromise with the Dingell amendment. If the House does not swallow whole the Senate emission standards—which will go down hard—there will be no bill. So by standing with Hart, Muskie solidifies the support of all the Senators behind the Senate bill.

"I will not vote for anything blind," McClure serves notice. "If it's not in both bills, or at least in the Senate bill, I won't vote for it without knowing what it says, what it means, without the detailed discussion we've given our bill. We've spent more than a year—you, Mr. Chairman, more than that. What we do will have a profound impact on life and the economy. If we can't take the proper time, I'd rather do nothing."

Thursday afternoon, September 23

"Do you realize," sandy-haired Ted Maeder, a lobbyist, says in the finely lathed vowels of downstate Virginia, "that the American industrial and finance establishment is all here in this line?"

And it is. We are queued outside S-146 in the Capitol, a committee room that cannot possibly accommodate as audience the whole crowd of lobbyists and observers, easily 150. With Maeder—who represents the makers of Gould catalytic converters—are lobbyists and observers for the Mortgage Bankers Association, National Realty Committee, the nation's mightiest electric power interests, the National Association of Manufacturers and the U. S. Chamber of Commerce, and the oil industry. In all, it's a chatty, lighthearted assemblage, with much banter across the fences of opposing interests. Like rival teams traveling together for an exhibition series, these people have become closely acquainted and, to a degree, mutually respectful. The doors open, and George Hanna, the coffee gofer, backed by the authority of a capitol policeman and instructions from Barry Meyer, admits staff first, then newsfolk (not many here), and finally about a third of the lobbyists to fill the remaining "public" seats. No standees are permitted.

"Not having had a chance to study your legislative language," says Muskie across the center-of-room table to his opposite number, Representative Paul Rogers of Florida, "the Senate side is reluctant to do any blind voting. One option for cutting this Gordian knot is to eliminate any provision that is not in both bills in some form. Of course, that will mean eliminating provisions that some people are interested in."

The suggestion touches off hassling on both sides over procedures.

The wrangling brings out that the House is not in session tomorrow (Friday) or Monday, to permit weekend campaign trips home. Muskie points out that he must be in Maine on Tuesday (all know he has difficult campaign problems of his own, facing Bob Monks, who is spending much of his personal fortune on TV assaults against Muskie). More hassling. Eying the wall clock, Muskie warns: "We're not going to have a bill."

"Would you rather have a bill or the present act?" inquires Congressman Broyhill, the White House adviser on how to arrange no bill, no embarrassment for President Ford.

"In more respects than not," says Muskie, "I'd rather have the present act."

"Maybe that's the solution," says Broyhill just a split second too soon, disclosing a shade more eagerness than he wants to show.

"I purposely worded that ambiguously," needles Muskie. The audience chuckles. Broyhill grins, one-upped. Muskie continues: "I don't like staying with the present law because all the pressures lean the other way. But our side needs to be educated on the House bill. It's been produced by a knowledgeable and thoughtful committee. And we don't have time for that education. So I'm reluctant."

"I'd be agreeable," says Rogers, chairman of the House Subcommittee on Health and the Environment, "to not changing the law at all now, but I'd like to point out that we've already agreed on twenty-two of seventy-five items. I'd urge that we see how many more we can do by two o'clock." Rogers does not point out that none of the twenty-two were of the group called "controversial." And it's now one-fifty.

"Let's try," shrugs Muskie. "Jim Allen's going to kill the afternoon, anyway. We may as well go ahead."

Harley Staggers of West Virginia, chairman of the full House Commerce Committee, cautions that "three or four" bills are coming to the House floor in the next two hours. Broyhill gladly adds: "I have to be involved with my bill in committee in the next hour."

Muskie has slipped out of the room, gone.

Rogers brings up a provision to impose a fine on garages that tamper with emission controls. The House bill provides a fine of $10,000, the Senate's one of $2,500. The House side of the table readily accepts the lower figure.

"The only trouble with that is—" McClure starts to complain. Rogers breaks in, "I said, we *accept* the Senate provision." "Oh, I see, I'm sorry." McClure blushes.

Gary Hart leaves. Domenici bustles in, inquires glintily of the blonde stenotypist, "May I steal your cigarettes?" He extracts one from her pack. Morgan enters, sits worriedly for a minute, then speaks up:

"On procedure. We're supposed to have a sunshine law, but a lot of my constituents are out there and can't get into this room. Couldn't we do better than this? There are more people out there than in here."

"I concur," concurs Domenici. "We're working out a law for the whole country. And there's more real knowledge of this bill out there than in here."

"As far as our side is concerned," continues Paul Rogers, ignoring Domenici's point, but testing whether Muskie's "no bill" scare can be turned around to scare the Senate into accepting the House bill, "there is no sentiment for changing our bill. So maybe we ought to stay with the present auto standards including .4. Maybe a conscious effort is being made to produce *no* bill. As for me, I'm ready to continue work until we have a bill. I don't want the President calling us back into session because we have no bill."

"One good question," says Congressman James Florio, a New Jersey freshman, working toward his merit badge for team spirit in this, his first conference, "is whether there's a quorum on the Senate side. You don't see us taking part in these filibustering tactics."

"We're dealing with provisions," says Morgan, reverting to conversational topic B, "for which we haven't seen language. Cases have gone to court for months over the meaning of a single word in this act. Yet we have those people out there, standing in the hall, who don't know what's going on here."

"We came here with a tougher bill than you did," taunts Domenici, getting back to topic A. "Doesn't that say we want a bill? I've been working on this for two years. I've attended no less than a hundred and twenty markups. If you say we don't want *any* old bill, so be it. But it's impossible to balance the issues of clean air for this country in the remainder of this day."

"I'm willing to work all day Friday," volunteers House Committee Chairman Staggers.

"I don't see," says Rogers righteously, "why members can't be here Friday, even Saturday, Sunday, to work on this."

"Ahem!" comments Representative Tim Lee Carter of Kentucky, a medical doctor and ranking Republican on the Health and Environment Subcommittee. Everybody laughs. Carter adds, "This *is* an election year, and there *are* other problems, such as family."

"Let's not cast aspersions within this room," implores Senator McClure. "I agree with Senator Domenici. No one here can be said not to want a bill." Then McClure thrusts in a direction he has been hinting at for months: "I move to my Senate colleagues that we act only on auto standards."

"My only problem with that," says Senator Gravel, chairing in Muskie's absence, "is that I would like to defer to my chairman on that one. Could we adjourn for fifteen minutes—until two forty-five?"

"The auto industry is in my district," says Representative Charles Carney, a Democrat of Youngstown, Ohio, and former organizer of steel and rubber workers. "The industry needs to know where it's going." McClure nods. The meeting breaks up.

At three o'clock Muskie is back, a few Senators collect, and while House members are still out floor-voting I learn where Muskie disappeared to, and that even under the pressures and confusions of this day he's got his priorities on straight. He walked out on the go or no-go of a national clean air law to attend to friendship.

Three weeks ago the Senate did an extraordinary thing, for which Muskie is not without responsibility. Senate office space is soon to be doubled with the completion of an "annex" to the Dirksen Building that will have as much space as the present Dirksen and Russell Buildings combined. On August 30, by voice vote, the Senate decided to name the new structure the Philip A. Hart Senate Office Building, an unprecedented tribute to a living and currently sitting member. No one expects Phil Hart still to be alive when the building is opened in 1979.

"Phil was brought to the Capitol this afternoon for a cloture vote," Muskie tells me as he waits for a quorum to accrete. "Well, after we named the new building for him, I got the idea of giving Phil the water color of the architect's sketch, signed by every Senator. We mounted it in the cloakrooms and got the signatures of every one of the hundred, except his. Today, when I heard he was coming in for the vote, I figured we better do it, so we got hurry-up word around, and we got a pretty good core of Senators to meet way up on the gallery floor in the sergeant at arms' office, and I presented it to him, saying, 'We've got all the hundred names except yours and we want you to sign it.' And I said, 'There's a lot of things we'd all like to say but we're not going to try. We've named this building for you not because we think a block of marble represents you, but because we would like it to symbolize our hope that your standards become the heart of what goes on in that building.' That's all. And the Senators kept coming in, leaning against the walls, a few sat on the floor. Must have been twenty-five or thirty there. And you had old-timers, some hard-bitten types. Scott and Griffin, the Republican leaders, and Bob Byrd came for Phil. And then Phil, just sitting there, began to talk, and as he talked he became more alive, visibly stronger, you know. Just a very moving thing. He talked for five or ten minutes, about what this meant to him, how he enjoyed the Senate, some of his hopes for the Senate, you know, what it ought to be. Then he looked at the sketches of the inside, just had a marvelous time."

"How does he look?"

"Oh, emaciated. Thank God for that beard. But he can walk."

A pudgy man with straight brown hair is dealing intently with House conferees one by one, sometimes in twos. He is Bob Howard, a staff assistant of John Dingell. I'm now sitting on a side table, sharing it with Roberta Hornig of the Washington *Star,* who asks Howard whether he can save his boss's amendment. Howard shakes his head in frank negative. "We had the votes on the floor, but not in this committee. Maybe three. So I'm telling them that the numbers reported out by the committee—which weren't anywhere near as bad as the Senate numbers—would be an acceptable compromise."

"They're lined up outside for the second show," announces Leon, passing by, faintly flushed over the box-office appeal of his bill. "And the ones who'll never make it in because the line's too long"—he prompts himself from a scribbled slip of paper—"represent paper, public utilities, steel, oil, shopping centers, construction, autos, mining, and the environment."

Muskie opens with a proposal that the conference proceed by accepting the Senate bill as a basis for amendment, pointing out that the Senate bill has thirteen basic provisions that remain to be acted upon, while the House bill, constructed far differently, would require action on thirty-six basic provisions.

Rogers proposes that the House bill be the basis of further discussion and amendment.

"So we're back where we started," says Muskie, abandoning that tack.

The meeting soon breaks again for votes, scheduling resumption for six-thirty. At seven twenty-three it resumes.

"I said I couldn't get back here next week," says Muskie, obviously newly armed by either a skull session with Leon or a private agreement with Rogers, or both. "And I don't intend to, unless there's some *real indication* that we can accomplish this. I'd like to propose now that we proceed by taking up the Senate bill—the Senate bill—beyond the provisions we've already agreed to." (Rogers is nodding!) "And that we meet again on Tuesday."

"I think this is helpful," assents Rogers, with the look of someone who's just won something, while covering up a cave-in of the House position. His problem is that it's harder to amend the other side's bill than to push acceptance of your own. Also any House proposal not in the Senate bill is virtually barred.

"But in exchange for this," I say to Muskie, trying to sound sympathetic on the subway ride back to the office after a long day, "your campaign in Maine has to suffer by a day or two."

He looks at me, smiling mischievously. "Not really."

I laugh. And, chestily, he laughs. And I laugh at his laughing, and he laughs at mine. He is immensely enjoying his ploy, gloating over its dramatic effect in turning the conference into exactly the direction he wanted.

Thursday, September 30

Last night at 11 P.M. the conferees agreed on a bill. In this morning's late hours the staffs of the two committees finished an overnight ordeal of assembling a report that reflects what the Senate-House conference committee resolved.

The bill is a compromise, as it must be, but it leans heavily to the Senate side. Its auto standards are the "Senate numbers," but set back another year—to 1981. Environmentalists, needless to say, are disappointed by the additional slippage but are supporting the compromise bill. The UAW is for it. Flatly opposing the bill are electric utilities, the oil industry, paper, and chemicals. The stunning overnight surprise, however, is that each of the major auto companies has put out a press statement *against* the bill. In a stupendous gamble, they are swallowing the poison of the present law's .4 NOx requirement—which means accepting the illegality of next year's cars—on faith that the incoming Congress will hasten to the rescue with an antidote by early spring.

"Remember the generals in Vietnam," blinks Leon, dumfounded, "who said they had to destroy a city because it was the only way to save it? I'm not sure this isn't exactly the same kind of intellect. It's totally irrational."

Muskie's tactical plan is to press Bobby Byrd to get the bill to the floor at the earliest possible moment. Jake Garn, Utah's Republican junior senator, appears to have taken over from his senior Democrat, Frank Moss, the baton of the opposition and has made his intentions perfectly clear, notifying Muskie last Friday that he will object to floor consideration of the conference report "unless the bill is available far enough in advance that it can be studied. . . . The best thing would be to adopt Mike Gravel's suggestion that we drop the contro-

versial sections and pass a simple extension for the automobile industry." This week Garn emerged from the White House with the
announcement that he would filibuster the bill—promptly adding
that the filibuster was his own idea, not the White House's. Against
these threats, Muskie's planned counterpressure is the pile-up of
other bills that are imperative to other Senators. Every unpassed bill
is a crowbar to help break Garn's filibuster.

Muskie obtains Byrd's estimate—a promise? a mere hope?—that
clean air may be called by 3 P.M. He does not stray farther from the
floor than S-199, a minute away. At five-thirty comes word from
Byrd, "Be on the floor." After seven, Muskie, smoldering, leaves the
floor with Leon and they mix a drink in S-199. In another hour, tension mounting, Muskie says, "Let's get something to eat." In the Senators' dining room, they join Howard Baker and his family. "If I
order dinner," fidgets Billings, "sure as hell the bill will be brought
up." Leon orders. Before the food arrives comes the message, "Get
to the floor, here comes the bill."

"Mr. President," announces battle-fatigued Byrd, "I hope to proceed with two other matters this evening. One is payments in lieu of
taxes"—Muskie's head snaps Byrdward—"and the other is the conference report on the Clean Air Act. I have already stated to Senators that, so far as I am concerned, we can be here all night to get
our work done."

Muskie has had it. "Will the Senator yield?"

"With the understanding that I keep my right to the floor."

"It's now almost ten o'clock. It is no secret in this body that every
effort is going to be made to defeat the Clean Air Act by extended
debate. If we're to have any chance at all to act on this vital piece of
legislation we must get to it and get to it immediately. I have lost my
patience with these other matters. I will object to any unanimous-
consent requests to consider other matters. We are going to decide
this one, one way or another, if I can get it before the Senate. So I
would like to know what the Assistant Majority Leader's intentions
are."

"Will the Senator yield?" calls Garn.

"If the chair will protect my right to the floor, yes," responds
Byrd.

"So that there is no doubt in the Senate," says baldpated, sun-
browned, black-browed Garn, "we know what is going to go on if

the Clean Air Act is brought up tonight. I guarantee that we *will* be here all night, and we will talk for a long time. And it doesn't make any difference to the junior Senator from Utah whether that is all night tonight or tomorrow or Friday night or next week. So that everybody understands what is going on—and the Assistant Majority Leader does—we do intend to be here as long as necessary to kill the bill."

"And I am prepared to stay here all night, I say to the Acting Majority Leader," Muskie roars back. "I am not about to let two years' hard work go down the drain because one Senator thinks his will must prevail over that of two houses. The record will be very clear as to whose responsibility it is, sabotaging the careful work that has gone into this. All I want at the moment is the starting gun, and I am prepared to go. I am prepared to go tonight, tomorrow, tomorrow night."

"If I may respond to the distinguished Senator from Maine," soothes Byrd, "I fully understand his feelings. He has waited patiently all afternoon. He canceled a trip to his native state."

"Precisely, and that affair in Maine, involving a visit by our party's presidential candidate, is now over."

"Exactly," allows Byrd. "Now, I am between the rock and the hard place. So I am going to do this. I am going to payments in lieu for no longer than twenty minutes. If this matter is not disposed of in that time, I will yield to the Senator from Maine so he can call up the clean air conference report."

"A lot of those Senators who are going to filibuster the Clean Air Act," protests Muskie, "are interested in that payments in lieu. I see no reason why I should just roll over and play dead so they can get their goodies. I know where the payments-in-lieu-of-taxes legislation comes from, what states are interested in it. I am not going to give these Senators their goodies in advance so they can torpedo the Clean Air Act, filibuster indefinitely without price. I refuse. Have I made it clear enough?"

"Oh, the Senator has made it clear," allows Byrd. When the Acting Leader moves to call up the payments-in-lieu bill, objection is heard from Senators Helms, Tower, and Griffin, for reasons other than Muskie's. Byrd surrenders to Muskie, who introduces the conference report on S. 3219, asking for its immediate consideration.

"Mr. President," calls Garn, "I ask that the conference report be read in its entirety."

Read the report in its entirety? It is 200 pages of deadly legalese, at least five hours of reading. So Garn does not plan to filibuster. He'll have the Senate clerk filibuster.

"The Senate will be in order," commands Presiding Officer Dick Stone of Florida, trying to gavel the chamber—including the gallery —out of its amused uproar.

At 1:14 A.M., having made the point of his determination, Garn consents to a recess until 9 A.M.

Friday, October 1

What Garn extracted from Byrd in their post-midnight deal was that, as further delay, the Senate this morning would have to endure a one-hour "live" quorum call, followed by a roll-call vote on whether the clean air conference report shall indeed become the order of business. Like passage of the bill itself weeks ago, the lop-sided vote does not indicate the intensity of the controversy. Muskie's side wins it, 54 to 10, probably an exact test of how the report itself would fare if Garn and his opposition colleagues permitted it to come to an up-or-down vote.

"Mr. President," thunders Muskie, turning to the substance of the bill, "it's clear to me, from every evidence of the reaction of the automobile industry to this bill, that they are doing their best to kill it, notwithstanding the fact that if they kill it they will be manufacturing automobiles illegally before another law is likely to be passed. And what is the industry attitude? Their attitude is, 'Well, Congress wouldn't *dare* hold us accountable for failing to meet the law. We're too *important*. There are too many jobs involved. We're *above* the law. We'll break the present law and *dare* Congress to do anything about it.' "[1] Summoning and siphoning all the nervous energy called up by a short, sleep-robbed night, Muskie wags a menacing finger directly at the early morning crowd of lobbyists packing the public gallery and warns slowly, emphatically: "If they think they can come back in the early months of next year and get a quick fix from the Senate to make them legal, they better take a lot of long careful thoughts about it."

Hours later, at 4:15 P.M., the bombshell hits, resolving the issue of clean air for the Ninety-fourth Congress. It sounds so routine and dry that a sleepy, inattentive head in the gallery of lobbyists might not catch what is happening.

"Mr. President," states Bobby Byrd, "I am shortly going to send to the desk the concurrent resolution providing that the two houses of Congress shall adjourn on today, Friday, October 1, 1976, and that when they adjourn on said day they stand adjourned sine die. . . . Mr. President, may we have order in the Senate? . . . I am in a difficult and painful position. Before the Majority Leader left to go to China, he and I made an announcement which was taken at face value by the leadership in the other body, taken at full value by the members of this body: that it was the intention to adjourn sine die today or tomorrow. . . . I convened the Policy Committee only a few days ago, got unanimous consent to take up certain measures with the understanding that if we could not dispose of them in a reasonable length of time, and reasonable length has to depend on a narrowing time frame, then I was to take steps to set those measures aside and go on to something else.

"The conference report now before us was brought up late last night. There is a filibuster in progress. I support the legislation. But I feel I have a duty to implement the announcements, the commitments, that have been made by the leadership. . . . Now we only have seven hours and forty-five minutes remaining before midnight. I have attempted to delay setting aside this conference report as long as I felt I possibly could. I know the distinguished Senator from Maine feels strongly about this measure. . . . We have before the Senate also the black lung bill. No measure means more to me personally than the black lung bill, because of my own circumstances in

[1] Before day's end Muskie's characterization is borne out by E. M. (Pete) Estes, president of General Motors, who asserts defiantly to a wire-service reporter: "They can close the plants. They can get someone in jail—maybe me. But we're going to make [1978] cars to 1977 standards."

representing a coal-mining state, and waiting behind that is the mine safety bill. Other members want to see action on other measures. I hope the Senate will pass the black lung bill, but every passing minute diminishes that chance.

"So what I am about to do is certainly not meant to offend any Senator. It is not taken because of my personal animus to any Senator."

"May we have order, Mr. President?" cries Dale Bumpers over the hubbub.

Byrd yields to Muskie, without giving up his possession of the floor.

"I appreciate the courtesy," Muskie begins throatily, gravely, beyond resentment. "It must be obvious that we have discussed this off the floor, and I indicated my strong opposition to the action that the distinguished Assistant Majority Leader is about to take. It leaves me virtually defenseless, since it is a privileged, non-debatable motion. So I'll have no opportunity except these few minutes—on which the Senator has proposed no limitations, may I say—to give my reasons for opposing it." (So that is why Byrd has served notice he will *soon* introduce the adjournment resolution, rather than simply introducing it. The resolution being non-debatable, if he introduced it straightaway he could not extend to Muskie the courtesy of rebutting the move—and the added special courtesy of not imposing a time limit to the rebuttal.) "My point, Mr. President," Muskie continues, "is this: when a major Senate priority such as the Clean Air Act, which has consumed two years of intensive work, reaches the last two or three days of a session, it should not be possible for a handful of Senators to frustrate the will of the Senate, and to block even a *vote* on that major measure. I told the distinguished Senator from West Virginia in our private conversation that I thought this step was unwise, against the public interest, and I still think it is. This is not to denigrate his intention or his integrity. I have watched his performance on the Senate floor and it has been superb. It is not easy to manage the business of the Senate and to manage its floor.

"What are we asking for? We are asking for nothing more than a vote—a *vote*—the last step of many agonizing steps, occupying hundreds of hours of effort. The last step is all we ask."

Muskie is through with his plea. But he does not sit down. He blesses Byrd with another spray of niceties until his feelings break through:

"I certainly don't want the Senator from West Virginia to think I take any personal offense at his action. He is doing his duty as he sees it. But even another twenty-four hours could have made a difference. Thirty-six or forty-eight hours could have meant the Senate could have had that vote, in the interests of the people of the nation. The Senator from West Virginia, by proposing this action, has effectively torpedoed any chance we have to break this filibuster.

"I am deeply regretful. No personal bitterness, but I'll tell you, if January rolls around and somebody says to me, 'Senator Muskie, don't you think it's time to begin working on another Clean Air Act?' I'll say to them, 'Gentlemen, obviously, I'm not the man to do it. I presided over a two-year effort that you killed. The prospect of another two years to find out what we should do differently next time is so forbidding—just so forbidding—that I can't see any point to making the effort.' "

Again a complete halt. Then suddenly:

"How do you please these people"—a wide-open hand reaches with beseechment and disgust to somewhere vaguely across the chamber—"when you write a bill, take hours to explain it—with the help of a committee that will always rank as high as any group of men I have ever worked with; whose members gave their intelligence, their understanding, their legislative expertise, to bring about sound balance and judgment. To see all that wasted, so utterly wasted, gentlemen, is what prompts me to say what I have had to say. I thank my good friend from West Virginia for his usual courtesy. Again, I understand he is doing his duty as he sees it."

Byrd yields to Gary Hart.

"The effect of this resolution is to kill it," Hart declares. "What this suggests to me is that a few companies in a handful of industries still can control the great Senate of the United States. It's as simple as that."

Muskie, who has a visceral distaste for any complex conflict being made "as simple as that," thanks Hart dutifully for stating the case "precisely as I see it." But Garn cannot let Hart escape unchallenged:

"I must say to my colleague from Colorado, our neighboring state, I resent the continuing implications that somehow big business lobbies are running this Senate. Nobody has talked to me from industry." Then, slapping back of hand into palm, syllable by syllable, with palpable indignation, Garn asserts what every Senator is prepared to understand. "*I* am *try*ing to pro*tect* my *state!*"

"Mr. President," Byrd announces, to end it at last, "I send to the desk a concurrent resolution and ask for its immediate consideration."

The clerk reads: "Resolved by the Senate (the House of Representatives concurring), that the two houses of Congress shall adjourn on Friday, October 1, 1976, and that when they adjourn on said day they stand adjourned sine die."

Muskie is on his feet. "Mr. President, I send an amendment to the desk and ask for its immediate consideration."

The clerk reads: "The Senator from Maine proposes unprinted amendment numbered 521, to amend the resolution by striking 'Friday' and inserting 'Saturday.'"

Byrd moves to table the Muskie amendment. And the roll call begins. It is going to be close, but if Muskie is dangling in suspense, he doesn't show it. He swivels his chair so that his back is to the chamber.

Muskie's motion goes down, 36–33.

The 1976 amendments to the Clean Air Act are dead.

The Senate has worked its will.

Or, in this case, its absence of will.

More than being a measure of sentiment for or against a new clean air law, the vote is, in a manner of speaking, a precise measure of the Senate's will or lack thereof—indeed the nation's—to commit itself to a high price for improved quality of air. In that sense, the Senate as a system has worked remarkably well.

Several healing weeks after this debacle, I risk stirring Muskie's bitterness by commenting that perhaps the unhappy ending of the 1976 clean air bill bespeaks the character of the Senate; that the Senate, while seldom accurately reflecting the pro and con balance of national opinion, more often reflects the intensity of national will.

He replies, with not the faintest trace of bitter residue, "The bill died, but the Senate is a continuing institution. It was not a happy ending. But there can't ever be a happy ending here—because there's never an ending."

On November 2, 1976, the people of Maine returned Edmund Muskie to the Senate for a fourth six-year term. The dimensions of his victory surprised Muskie as well as Robert Monks, his opponent. Muskie swept most Republican towns as well as his traditional base in the cities.

The ranking Republican member of the Environmental Pollution Subcommittee, James Buckley of New York, was defeated by Daniel Patrick Moynihan.

Senator Bill Brock of Tennessee lost his seat to a forty-year-old Democrat, James R. Sasser, 1972 staff member of the Muskie for President drive. Brock soon was elected chairman of the Republican National Committee.

Senator Joseph Montoya of New Mexico was retired by a "stranger who came down from the moon," Dr. Harrison H. Schmitt, a forty-one-year-old geologist and former astronaut.

Frank Moss, the liberal Democrat from conservative Utah, was removed from the Senate by the victory of Orrin Hatch, a forty-two-year-old lawyer and Mormon bishop.

Robert Stafford, the Vermont Republican and quiet compromise designer of the Environmental Pollution Subcommittee, was reelected, as was Quentin Burdick of North Dakota.

Among new, young faces arriving in the Senate was that of Don Riegle, Jr., thirty-eight, Republican turned Democrat, to take the seat vacated by the retirement of Senator Philip A. Hart.

Jimmy Carter was elected President of the United States.

On the day after Christmas, 1976, scarcely a week before the expiration of his term, Muskie's dearest friend in the Senate, Phil Hart, died at home.

Epilogue
1977

Friday, August 5

When first I lunched with Senator Muskie in S-199 to talk about this book there was little reason to doubt that the Clean Air Act would be wrapped up by August. August of 1975.

Today, two years later than that target date, the Senate and House at long last approve a conference report and pass a new Clean Air Act. It is to be signed into law Monday by President Jimmy Carter in the study of his home at Plains, Georgia.

The labor of two-and-a-half years has brought forth a strong law. Strong, not because environmentalists won most of their points. Strong, not because the new law is as tough as its 1970 predecessor, the very "toughness" of which made it unenforceable and weak. The law passed today is more lenient than the subcommittee bill of 1975, than the committee bill which "weakened" it, more lenient even than the compromise conference report snuffed out in 1976 by the gavel of Senate adjournment. The new law extends the current emission standards for two more years—through 1979 models. In addition, it permits waiving federal restrictions on building a power plant if the waiver is approved by the Interior Department and the appropriate state governor or, if they disagree, by the President. Although never mentioned in the debate, that provision is aimed at permitting development of the huge Intermountain Power Project next to Capitol Reef National Park in central Utah. That concession removed a threat that Jake Garn might again employ the tools available to any determined Senator to maneuver a bill into oblivion.

The environmentalists are not gleeful over the new law, but find it acceptable. The United Auto Workers are not ecstatic, but find it acceptable. The auto makers, while not happy about it, have decided to live with it. (Pete Estes, president of General Motors, after threatening an industry shutdown with layoffs of thousands if the conference did not reach an acceptable decision by the end of this week, now says he's "relieved . . . that we can now get on with the job of building our 1978 cars.") Muskie himself is satisfied that the law has located itself at that magical point of political balance: the boldest feasible act in the public interest that takes into account the relative political strengths and conflicting demands for justice by all contenders.

The politics of the strong vanquishing the weak—which sometimes masquerades as the "right" doing in the "wrong"—gives rise to decisions that are vulnerable, therefore weak. The purpose of politics is to advance the public interest through mediation among conflicting contenders.

That is the essence of life in the Senate. What gallery observers sometimes disdain in what they see in the chamber below is that what happens in the Senate is a fairly pure distillation of real life, and they wish it didn't have to be. What the observer witnesses is compromise—which Senators call by a more elegant name, "accommodation." Every Senator has power, just as every political group, every citizen, indeed every family member within a family, has power. The most common purpose of accommodation—in the Senate as in real life—is to cool someone else's passion for using it.

INDEX